Sex and Privacy in American Law

Henry F. Fradella

W. B. Sheridan Law Books

Sex and Privacy in American Law

Henry F. Fradella

W. B. Sheridan Law Books

Academica Press
Washington~London

Library of Congress Cataloging-in-Publication Data

Names: Fradella, Henry F. (author)
Title: Sex and privacy in american law | Fradella, Henry F.
Description: Washington : Academica Press, 2023. | Includes references.
Identifiers: LCCN 2023940848 | ISBN 9781680538335 (hardcover) |
9781680538342 (e-book) | 9781680538359 (paperback)

To Ryan, with Love

Acknowledgements

I thank Gerald Eastwood for his excellent research assistance helping to code the nearly 500 cases in the sampling frame for this study. I also thank Dr. Aili Malm, Dr. Weston Morrow, and Dr. Danielle Wallace for their assistance helping to run and interpret the logistic regressions reported in this study. I acknowledge, with appreciation, Arizona State University for granting me a sabbatical leave to work on this project. I am especially grateful to Dr. Jon B. Gould for his support.

I am grateful to Academica Press for publishing this monograph. And, finally, I wish to thank the editors and staff of the *Tulane Journal of Law and Sexuality* for their insights and assistance on the articles that they published using the data and analyses contained in this book.

Contents

List of Tables

Chapter 1:

Introduction

In June 2003, the U.S. Supreme Court issued its landmark decision in *Lawrence v. Texas*.[1] Writing on behalf of himself and four other members of the Court, Justice Anthony Kennedy invalidated all of the remaining sodomy laws in the United States as applied to acts between consenting adults in private, reasoning that these laws impinged on liberty interests protected by the Due Process Clause of the Fourteenth Amendment to the U.S. Constitution.[2] Justice Sandra Day O'Connor concurred in the result, but would have decided the case on equal protection grounds.[3]

Shortly after the release of the decision in *Lawrence*, scholars began to critique the reasoning in the majority opinion.[4] Some questioned whether *Lawrence* represented genuine or illusory progress for LGBTQ+ rights,[5] largely because the language the Supreme Court used in *Lawrence*

---

1 539 U.S. 558, 578–79 (2003).

2 *Id.* at 564–79; *see also infra* at Chapter 2, Section. For an exploration of the Supreme Court's "chaotic" liberty jurisprudence and a proposal to stabilize it, see Deana Pollard Sacks, *Elements of Liberty*, 61 SMU L. REV. 1557, 1558 (2008).

3 *Lawrence*, 539 U.S. at 579–85 (O'Connor, J., concurring in the result)

4 *E.g.*, Henry F. Fradella, Lawrence v. Texas: *Genuine or Illusory Progress for Gay Rights in America*, 39 CRIM. L. BULL. 597 (2003); Bernard E. Harcourt, *Foreword: "You are Entering a Gay and Lesbian Free Zone": On the Radical Dissents of Justice Scalia and Other (Post-) Queers [Raising Questions About* Lawrence*, Sex Wars, and the Criminal Law]*, 94 J. CRIM. L. & CRIMINOLOGY 503 (2004).

5 At that time, some of us writing about *Lawrence* used the term "gay rights." *See, e.g.*, Fradella, *supra* note 4, at 597. At that time, it was not uncommon to use the word "gay" as "an umbrella term for people who identity as lesbian, gay, or bisexual." Jerome Hunt, *A History of the Employment Non-Discrimination Act*, CTR. FOR AM. PROGRESS (July 19, 2011), https://www.americanprogress.org/article/a-history-of-the-employment-non-discrimination-act/ [https://perma.cc/HWE9-GVQW], at n.1. In recognition of how such usage contributes to the erasure of other nonnormative sexual orientations and gender identities, the preferred umbrella term today is "LGBTQ+," the letters of which refer to lesbian, gay, bisexual, transgender, and queer people. The plus sign (+)

presented a substantive due process conundrum for the advancement of equality.[6]

On one hand, the Court in *Lawrence* used sweeping rhetoric to situate privacy and autonomy rights within substantive due process vis-à-vis the Fourteenth Amendment's protection of liberty:

> Liberty protects the person from unwarranted government intrusions into a dwelling or other private places. In our tradition the State is not omnipresent in the home. And there are other spheres of our lives and existence, outside the home, where the State should not be a dominant presence. Freedom extends beyond spatial bounds. Liberty presumes an autonomy of self that includes freedom of thought, belief, expression, and certain intimate conduct. The instant case involves liberty of the person both in its spatial and in its more transcendent dimensions.[7]

The majority opinion went so far as to reject the notion that the constitution

---

acknowledges there are sexual and gender identities beyond those in the five-letter version of the acronym, including intersex, questioning, and asexual persons. This study therefore uses the more inclusive term to recognize people who have a range of sexual orientations or gender identities—those who identify as something other than being both cisgender and heterosexual. *Acronyms Explained*, OUTRIGHT (Sept 20, 2021), https://outrightinternational.org/content/acronyms-explained [https://perma.cc/W5TN-4TUB]; *see also* Patrick Englert & Elizabeth G. Dinkins, *An Overview of Sex, Gender, and Sexuality*, *in* SEX, SEXUALITY, LAW & (IN)JUSTICE 7 (Henry F. Fradella & Jennifer Sumner eds., 2016).

6 Fradella, *supra* note 4, at 602–03.

> [T]he result in *Lawrence* is not unambiguously pro-gay. . . . [It] does not so simply or unambiguously advance the interests of all self-identified gay men, lesbian women, queers, liberal (pro-gay) heterosexuals, or others who are gay-friendly yet reject sexual labels. The problem is not just the potential backlash against gay men and lesbian women that may follow the *Lawrence* decision. The rub is that the proliferation of sexual projects makes it far too simplistic today to think about a decision such as *Lawrence* in dichotomous terms—as either "good" or "bad" for "homosexuals." Who wins and who loses depends on a much closer parsing of sexual projects. Justice Scalia is only partly right: the decision does favor the liberal pro-gay-rights position and in this sense is gay-friendly. But it may, possibly, ill-serve the interests of many others who oppose the dominance of what Judith Butler refers to as "the defining institutions of phallogocentrism and compulsory heterosexuality."

Harcourt, *supra* note 4, at 511–12 (quoting JUDITH BUTLER, GENDER TROUBLE: FEMINISM AND THE SUBVERSION OF IDENTITY, at ix (1990)).

7 Fradella, *supra* note 4, at 602 (quoting *Lawrence*, 539 U.S. at 562).

permits criminal law to be used to enforce morality "absent injury to a person or abuse of an institution the law protects."[8] In doing so, the Court arguably embraced the "harm principle" which, consistent with its roots in utilitarian philosophy,[9] maintains that criminal law should only prohibit acts or omissions which cause harm to others.[10] Indeed, the seeming repudiation of legal moralism coupled with the broad scope of appeals to "personal dignity and autonomy" led Justice Antonin Scalia to argue in his dissent that the case represented "the end of all morals legislation."[11]

On the other hand, despite the numerous passages in *Lawrence* referencing liberty, autonomy, and human dignity, the Court did not declare any specific right to be "fundamental," which, in turn, would have subjected laws intruding into the personal and private sex lives of

---

8 *Lawrence*, 539 U.S. at 567.

9 *See, e.g.*, JOHN STUART MILL, ON LIBERTY 80, 139 (David Bromwich & George Kateb eds., 2003) (1859).

10 Fradella, *supra* note 4, at 602–03; *see also, e.g.*, Sonu Bedi, *Repudiating Morals Legislation: Rendering the Constitutional Right to Privacy Obsolete*, 53 CLEV. ST. L. REV. 447, 454–55 (2005) (interpreting *Lawrence* as a rejection of morals legislation); Harcourt, *supra* note 4, at 503–04 ("The Court's ruling is the *coup de grâce* to legal moralism administered after a prolonged, brutish, tedious, and debilitating struggle against liberal legalism in its various criminal law representations."); J. Kelly Strader, Lawrence*s Criminal Law*, 16 BERKELEY J. CRIM. L. 41, 43 (2011) (arguing *Lawrence* embraced the harm principle over legal moralism); Eric Tennen, *Is the Constitution in Harm's Way? Substantive Due Process and Criminal Law*, 8 BOALT J. CRIM. L. 3, 4–5 (2004) (arguing that *Lawrence* represents a culmination of precedents that incorporated the harm principle into contemporary criminal law jurisprudence). *But see* Miranda Oshige McGowan, *From Outlaws to Ingroup:* Romer, Lawrence, *and the Inevitable Normativity of Group Recognition*, 88 MINN. L. REV. 1312, 1313 (2004) ("*Lawrence* does not hold that the Constitution incorporates the harm principle. In fact, *Lawrence* is more of an equal protection case than a substantive due process case. Justice Kennedy's opinion does not talk about the rights of persons generally as against the state. Rather, the opinion constantly refers to the rights of 'homosexual persons' and the right of gays to make 'choices central to personal dignity and autonomy."' (internal citations omitted)).

11 *Lawrence*, 539 U.S. at 599 (Scalia, J., dissenting). Law professor Cass Sunstein argued that despite the sweeping language in *Lawrence*, it is actually a narrow opinion. Cass R. Sunstein, *What Did* Lawrence *Hold? Of Autonomy, Desuetude, Sexuality, and Marriage*, 2003 SUP. CT. REV. 27, 48–49. Sunstein maintained that rather than announcing a broad constitutional right, rooted in autonomy, which protects consensual sex that does not harm others, *Lawrence* is limited to recognizing that, on the whole, social values have changed such that society no longer views acts of oral or anal sex—even between members of the same biological sex—as warranting criminal punishment. *Id.*

consenting adults to strict scrutiny.[12] Nor did the Court recognize LGBTQ+ people to be either a suspect or quasi-suspect class for equal protection purposes.[13] Rather, the Court seemingly applied the rational basis test—the lowest standard of review—which, in turn, could result in defeats for those seeking LGBTQ+ civil rights in post-*Lawrence* litigation.[14] The decision also heralded the very real possibility of serious backlash against LGBTQ+ people and their quest for equality because the logic of the decision rested, in part, on changing public views regarding sexual orientation, both domestically and abroad.[15]

Some of these apprehensions about the logic of the *Lawrence* decision appear to be well-founded. *Lawrence*'s reliance on liberty as the basis for a majority opinion unquestionably represented a major departure in a

---

12 Fradella, *supra* note 4, at 603. Some scholars insisted that *Lawrence* recognized something akin to a fundamental right without using that nomenclature. *E.g.*, Laurence H. Tribe, Lawrence v. Texas: *The "Fundamental Right" That Dare Not Speak Its Name*, 117 HARV. L. REV. 1893, 1898 (2004) (arguing that *Lawrence* recognized a right that should be treated as fundamental—one that implicates the interaction of liberty, human dignity, and equality). Others apparently viewed the lack of a fundamental right declaration as a positive shift in the jurisprudence of constitutional rights. Law professor Randy Barnett, for instance, maintained that *Lawrence*'s silence on any fundamental right represented a potential rejection of the outdated fundamental rights framework in favor of one that embraced the more comprehensive notion that governmental interference with "liberty" is presumptively unconstitutional. Randy E. Barnett, *Justice Kennedy's Libertarian Revolution:* Lawrence v. Texas, 2003 CATO SUP. CT. REV. 21, 35–36.

13 Fradella, *supra* note 4, at 606.

14 *Id.* (criticizing the Court's "continued refusal . . . to put discrimination on the basis of sexual orientation on the same level as gender or racial discrimination"); *see also* Francisco Valdes, *Anomalies, Warts and All: Four Score of Liberty, Privacy and Equality*, 65 OHIO ST. L.J. 1341, 1342 (2004) ("*Lawrence* thereby moves sexual minorities into an interstitial place in constitutional law—from the status of formal outlaws but shy of the status of formal recognition; a traditionally subordinated social group now to be tolerated, but not necessarily accepted.").

15 Fradella, *supra* note 4, at 606.Professor Harcourt similarly expressed concern about the potential backlash against LGBTQ+ people in the wake of *Lawrence*. Harcourt, *supra* note 4, at 511. For an illuminating discussion of backlash against *Lawrence* and other key judicial decisions criticized as taking sides in the so-called "culture war," see Francisco Valdes, *Culture by Law: Backlash as Jurisprudence*, 50 VILL. L. REV. 1135, 1170 (2005) (exploring the "tactics and techniques of backlash jurisprudence" as a means curtailing the evolution of law and policy in ways that benefit "neocolonial elites").

substantive due process case decided after the New Deal.[16] Indeed, some scholars hailed the focus on liberty as a watershed moment for the expansion of privacy rights in a libertarian tradition.[17] Other scholars, however, argued that the Court signaled it did not mean for *Lawrence* to be a broad libertarian decision, but rather deliberately intended for it to be narrow.[18] *Lawrence*'s exclusion of sex acts between minors, public sexual conduct, acts of prostitution, marriage between persons of the same biological sex, and sex between persons "who might be injured or coerced or who are situated in relationships where consent might not easily be refused,"[19] caused some commentators to criticize *Lawrence* as an inherently conservative opinion that offers only freedom from criminal prosecution to "respectable" LGBTQ+ people—assimilationists who

---

16 *See, e.g.*, Barnett, *supra* note 12, at 33–37. Professor Barnett noted that in the co-authored plurality opinion in *Planned Parenthood of Southeastern Pennsylvania v. Casey*, 505 U.S. 833, 843–902 (1992), Justice Kennedy did not situate abortion rights within a privacy framework, but rather as liberty interest protected by both the Ninth and Fourteenth Amendments. Barnett, *supra*, at 33 (quoting *Casey*, 505 U.S. at 848). Barnett referred to Justice Kennedy's logic in *Casey* as "newsworthy, but little noticed." *Id.*; *see also* Nan D. Hunter, *Living with* Lawrence, 88 MINN. L. REV. 1103, 1104 (2004) (hailing *Lawrence* "as marking the emergence of a new approach to substantive due process analysis, one that has been simmering in the concurring opinions of Justices Souter, Stevens, and Kennedy for the last decade [but now enjoys] a majority for extending meaningful constitutional protection to liberty interests without denominating them as fundamental rights").

17 *See, e.g.*, Barnett, *supra* note 12, at 21 ("[W]e have in *Lawrence* nothing short of a constitutional revolution, with implications reaching far beyond the "personal liberty" at issue [in the case]."); *see also* Hunter, *supra* note 16, at 1109 ("[T]he logic of *Lawrence* will reverberate in future substantive due process cases touching on marriage and morality."); Sonia K. Katyal, *Sexuality and Sovereignty: The Global Limits and Possibilities of* Lawrence, 14 WM. & MARY BILL RTS. J. 1429, 1435 (2006) (asserting that *Lawrence* presents "a vision of sexual self-determination . . . that represents the intersectional convergence of three separate prisms: spatial privacy, expressive liberty, and deliberative autonomy").

18 *See, e.g.*, Dale Carpenter, *Is* Lawrence *Libertarian?*, 88 MINN. L. REV. 1140, 1141, 1162–69 (2004) (arguing that *Lawrence* is most properly understood not as broad libertarian decision, but one "within a conservative tradition favoring incremental change over sudden and wholesale ruptures with the past"); *cf.* Libby Adler, *The Future of Sodomy*, 32 FORDHAM URB. L.J. 197, 218 (2005) (criticizing *Lawrence* for not going far enough when stating that it "could have done more good by regarding sex as dignified in its tautological and paradoxical sense").

19 Lawrence v. Texas, 539 U.S. 558, 578 (2003).

embrace traditional values like romance, monogamy, and geographical privacy.[20]

The decisions of some lower federal courts grappling with applying *Lawrence* shortly after it was decided suggest that the latter group of scholars correctly predicted that the case would be narrowly construed. Consider the oft-cited example of the Eleventh Circuit's decision upholding Florida's ban on same-sex couples adopting children.[21] The court rejected the notion that *Lawrence* recognized any fundamental right to private sexual intimacy and refused to infer any new fundamental rights from *Lawrence* because its "language and reasoning are inconsistent with standard fundamental rights analysis."[22] The court also went on to reject an equal protection challenge to Florida's adoption law under the rational basis test because the case did not involve either a fundamental right or a

---

20 *See, e.g.*, Elizabeth J. Baia, Note, *Akin to Madmen: A Queer Critique of the Gay Rights Cases*, 104 VA. L. REV. 1021, 1062 (2018) (arguing that reliance on assimilationist values "to justify extending rights to LGBTQ[+] people runs the risk of making it more difficult to extend protection in areas where these values are absent"); Katherine M. Franke, *The Domesticated Liberty of* Lawrence v. Texas, 104 COLUM. L. REV. 1399, 1401 (2004) ("[T]he liberty principle upon which the opinion rests is less expansive, rather geographized, and, in the end, domesticated. It is not the synonym of a robust liberal concept of freedom."); *cf.* Margo Kaplan, *Sex-Positive Law*, 89 N.Y.U. L. REV. 89, 145 (2014) ("[*Lawrence*] is oddly, almost obsessively, focused on the role of sex in reinforcing emotional bonds. In seeking to demonstrate that sex (and the right to engage in it) is not always about sexual pleasure, the *Lawrence* Court seemed to forget that it can ever be about sexual pleasure."); Laura A. Rosenbury & Jennifer E. Rothman, *Sex in and Out of Intimacy*, 59 EMORY L.J. 809, 824 (2010) (stating that *Lawrence* "can be read as protecting sex only when it promotes emotional intimacy and the potential for a long-term bond between two people"); Teemu Ruskola, *Gay Rights Versus Queer Theory: What is Left of Sodomy After* Lawrence v. Texas?, 23 SOC. TEXT 235, 239 (2005) ("In the end, the crucial rhetorical limitation of *Lawrence* is precisely its inability, or refusal, to imagine (legitimate) homosexual sex that does not take place in a relationship and does not connote intimacy."); Mark Strasser, *Monogamy, Licentiousness, Desuetude and Mere Tolerance: The Multiple Misinterpretations of* Lawrence v. Texas, 15 S. CAL. REV. L. & WOMEN'S STUD. 95, 98 (2005) ("Much of the Court's focus in *Lawrence* was on same-sex relationships rather than on same-sex relations."). For a brief and easily digestible summary of the often heady philosophical and political positions of "radical" queer theorists and activists who reject assimilationist values, see Harcourt, *supra* note 4, at 517–23.

21 Lofton v. Sec'y of Dep't of Child. & Fam. Servs., 358 F.3d 804, 815–16 (11th Cir. 2004).

22 *Id.* at 816.

suspect or quasi-suspect class that would trigger heightened levels of scrutiny.[23]

The narrow interpretation of *Lawrence* in the Eleventh Circuit's decision upholding Florida's adoption law is not unique.[24] As Justin Reinheimer and others pointed out, for several years, *Lawrence* "had remarkably little impact on subsequent lesbian and gay rights litigation."[25] Marriage equality serves as an example. Courts in at least nine U.S. jurisdictions upheld states' refusal to recognize the rights of same-sex couples from marrying without so much as finding "that *Lawrence* suggest[ed], let alone require[d], a different outcome."[26] Several of these

---

23 *Id.* at 818.

24 *E.g.*, Seegmiller v. LaVerkin City, 528 F.3d 762, 764, 771 (10th Cir. 2008) (upholding the discipline of a police officer for having an affair, reasoning that *Lawrence* did not recognize any fundamental right to engage in private, consensual sexual conduct and, therefore, the case does not protect "all important, intimate, and personal decisions").

25 Justin Reinheimer, Note, *What* Lawrence *Should Have Said: Reconstructing an Equality Approach*, 96 CAL. L. REV. 505, 505 (2008); *see also* Jonathan M. Black, *Sexual Privacy After* Lawrence v. Texas, 10 GEO. J. GENDER & L. 297, 330 (2009) (noting that *Lawrence*'s impact "has been limited"); Kim Shayo Buchanan, Lawrence v. Geduldig: *Regulating Women's Sexuality*, 56 EMORY L.J. 1235, 1237 (2007) (stating that lower courts had construed the scope of the right to sexual liberty announced in *Lawrence* "quite narrowly"); Tobin Sparling, *A Path Unfollowed: The Disregard of Dignity Precedent in Justice Kennedy's Gay Rights Decisions*, 26 TUL. J.L. & SEXUALITY 53, 82 (2017) ("[N]otwithstanding the significance of the outcomes in *Romer* and *Lawrence*, these opinions have had only a marginal effect on subsequent jurisprudence in the lower courts.").

26 Reinheimer, *supra* note 25, at 520 (citing, *inter alia*, Standhardt v. Superior Court, 77 P.3d 451 (Ariz. Ct. App. 2003) (upholding Arizona's ban on same-sex marriage), *abrogated by* Obergefell v. Hodges, 576 U.S. 644 (2015); *In re* Marriage Cases, 49 Cal. Rptr. 3d 675 (Cal. Ct. App. 2006) (upholding California's ban on same-sex marriage), *rev'd*, 183 P.3d 384 (Cal. 2008); Kerrigan v. State, 909 A.2d 89 (Conn. Super. Ct. 2006) (upholding Connecticut's ban on same-sex marriage), *rev'd*, 957 A.2d 407 (Conn. 2008); Morrison v. Sadler, 821 N.E.2d 15 (Ind. Ct. App. 2005) (upholding Indiana's ban on same-sex marriage), *abrogated by* Obergefell v. Hodges, 576 U.S. 644 (2015); Varnum v. Brien, No. CV5965, 2007 WL 2468667 (Iowa Dist. Ct. Aug. 30, 2007) (invalidating Iowa's ban on same-sex marriage on both due process and equal protection bases), *rev'd*, 763 N.W.2d 862 (Iowa. 2009), *abrogated by* Obergefell v. Hodges, 576 U.S. 644 (2015); Conaway v. Deane, 932 A.2d 571 (Md. 2007) (upholding Maryland's ban on same-sex marriage), *abrogated by* Obergefell v. Hodges, 576 U.S. 644 (2015); Hernandez v. Robles, 855 N.E.2d 1 (N.Y. 2006) (upholding New York's ban on same-sex marriage), *abrogated by* Obergefell v. Hodges, 576 U.S. 644 (2015); Li v. Oregon, 110 P.3d 91 (Or. 2005) (upholding Oregon's ban on same-sex marriage), *abrogated by* Obergefell v. Hodges, 576 U.S. 644 (2015); Andersen v. King Cnty., 138

courts ruled in such a manner for the very reasons some commentators predicted shortly after *Lawrence* was decided—namely the lack of any recognition of a fundamental right in the case and its failure to establish a framework for any heightened standard of review for the evaluation of constitutional challenges to laws burdening LGBTQ+ people.[27] Of course, *Lawrence* eventually played a role in advancing marriage equality in the United States as evidenced by the U.S. Supreme Court's reliance on *Lawrence* in both *United States v. Windsor*, which invalidated the federal Defense of Marriage Act (DOMA),[28] and *Obergefell v. Hodges*, which made marriage equality the law of the land.[29]

P.3d 963 (Wash. 2006) (upholding Washington's ban on same-sex marriage), *abrogated by* Obergefell v. Hodges, 576 U.S. 644 (2015).

[27] *Id.* ("In rejecting claims for same-sex marriage, courts have held that *Lawrence* did not recognize a fundamental right and that *Lawrence* did not itself apply or require any type of heightened review that would be appropriate in a marriage context." (internal citations omitted)).

[28] United States v. Windsor, 570 U.S. 744, 775 (2013) (invalidating DOMA as an unconstitutional deprivation of the liberty protected by the Fifth Amendment). The majority in *Windsor* relied, in part, on *Lawrence*:

> DOMA undermines both the public and private significance of state-sanctioned same-sex marriages; for it tells those couples, and all the world, that their otherwise valid marriages are unworthy of federal recognition. This places same-sex couples in an unstable position of being in a second-tier marriage. The differentiation demeans the couple, whose moral and sexual choices the Constitution protects, see *Lawrence* . . . .

Id. at 772.

[29] Obergefell v. Hodges, 576 U.S. 644, 661–62 (2015) (recognizing that the legal question of marriage equality arose "[a]gainst the background" of *Lawrence* and *Romer v. Evans*, 517 U.S. 620, 635 (1996), which "invalidated an amendment to Colorado's Constitution that sought to foreclose any branch or political subdivision of the State from protecting persons against discrimination based on sexual orientation"); *see also, e.g.*, Kenji Yoshino, *A New Birth of Freedom?:* Obergefell v. Hodges, 129 HARV. L. REV. 147, 163 (2015). Yoshino claimed that the "*Obergefell* majority unmistakably echoed the *Lawrence* passage in its discussion of tradition":

> The nature of injustice is that we may not always see it in our own times. The generations that wrote and ratified the Bill of Rights and the Fourteenth Amendment did not presume to know the extent of freedom in all of its dimensions, and so they entrusted to future generations a charter protecting the right of all persons to enjoy liberty as we learn its meaning.

Id. (quoting Lawrence v. Texas, 539 U.S. 558, 578–79 (2003)); *Id.* at 173 (noting that *Obergefell*'s analyses drew on *Lawrence*'s situation of the issue "as a substantive due process case inflected with equality concerns"); Steve Sanders, *Dignity and Social Meaning:* Obergefell, Windsor, *and* Lawrence *as Constitutional Dialogue*, 87

Still, one can hardly argue that the decriminalization of sodomy and the legal recognition of same-sex marriages somehow transformed LGBTQ+ people's lives such that they enjoy full equality and social acceptance.[30] Gays and lesbians experience violent victimization at a rate twice that of heterosexuals, while bisexuals experience such victimization at a rate more than 6.5 times that experienced by heterosexuals.[31] Additionally, the rate of violent victimization against transgender people is 2.5 that of cisgender people.[32] And even in the absence of criminal victimization, LGBTQ+ people routinely face adversities that negatively impact their "financial, mental, and physical well-being" because they experience "discrimination in their personal lives, in the workplace and the public sphere, and in their access to critical health care."[33]

FORDHAM L. REV. 2069, 2106 (2019) (arguing that *Obergefell* and *Windsor* drew on the principle announced in *Lawrence* that gays and lesbians are entitled to "personal dignity and autonomy").

30 *See* SHARITA GRUBERG, LINDSAY MAHOWALD & JOHN HALPIN, CTR. AM. PROGRESS, THE STATE OF THE LGBTQ COMMUNITY IN 2020: A NATIONAL PUBLIC OPINION STUDY (2020), https://americanprogress.org/wp-content/uploads/2020/10/LGBTQpoll-report.pdf [https://perma.cc/KL8B-AK42]; Paula M. Neira & An Na Lee, *Under Attack: Transgender Health in 2020*, 24 J. HEALTH CARE L. & POL'Y 109, 122 (2021) (detailing the obstacles LGBTQ+ people face in the face of discriminatory laws and policies).

31 JENNIFER L. TRUMAN & RACHEL E. MORGAN, BUREAU OF JUST. STAT., VIOLENT VICTIMIZATION BY SEXUAL ORIENTATION AND GENDER IDENTITY, 2017–2020, at 1–2, 3 tbl.1 (2022), https://bjs.ojp.gov/content/pub/pdf/vvsogi1720.pdf [https://perma.cc/F7VC-SGC3]. *See generally* Grace Hauck, *Anti-LGBT Hate Crimes Are Rising, the FBI Says. But It Gets Worse*, USA TODAY (June 28, 2019), https://www.usatoday.com/story/news/2019/06/28/anti-gay-hate-crimes-rise-fbi-says-and-they-likely-undercount/1582614001/ [https://perma.cc/D8SM-2BRK]; Mark Potok & Janet Smith, S. POVERTY L. CTR., *Anti-Gay Hate Crimes: Doing the Math*, INTELLIGENCE REP. (Feb. 27, 2011), https://www.splcenter.org/fighting-hate/intelligence-report/2011/anti-gay-hate-crimes-doing-math [https://perma.cc/TB3N-2NWQ]; Jo Yurcaba, *Anti-Gay Hate Crimes Fell Slightly in 2020, While Anti-Trans Crimes Rose, FBI Says*, NBC NEWS (Sept. 1, 2021, 11:44 AM), https://www.nbcnews.com/nbc-out/out-news/anti-gay-hate-crimes-fell-slightly-2020-anti-trans-crimes-rose-fbi-say-rcna1846 [https://perma.cc/B9A4-THCK].

32 TRUMAN & MORGAN, *supra* note 31, at 1–2, 3 tbl.1.

33 GRUBERG ET AL., *supra* note 30, at 1; *see also, e.g.*, Alex Reed, *Beyond* Bostock: *Employment Protections for LGBTQ Workers Not Covered by Title VII*, 23 N.Y.U. J. LEGIS. & PUB. POL'Y 537 (2021) (highlighting that fewer than half the states prohibit discrimination on the basis of sexual orientation and gender identity and explaining how that impacts workers not covered by Title VII and the decision *Bostock v. Clayton Cnty.*, 140 S. Ct. 1731 (2020)); Kyle C. Velte, *The Precarity of Justice Kennedy's*

Additionally, although *Lawrence* "marked a dramatic milestone in efforts to limit state power to control homosexuality,"[34] there can also be little doubt that there has been strong backlash in the wake of judicial rulings recognizing select constitutional protections for LGBTQ+ people. To be sure, empirical research suggests that although there have been documented decreases in public support for LGBTQ+ civil rights in the wake of key court cases expanding such rights, the effects have been largely short-lived.[35] But post-*Lawrence* apprehensions about backlash were not necessarily rooted in negative public opinions to the decision.[36] Rather, those concerns were (and largely continue to be) about legal backlash—changes in law and policy as a result of counter-mobilization by powerful elites who expend money and political capital to stymie LGBTQ+ equality by enacting legislation and harnessing the judicial role.[37] Such legal backlash unquestionably transpired as evidenced not

---

Queer Canon, 13 CONLAWNOW 75, 89–90 (2022) (explaining how religious exemptions to antidiscrimination law protecting LGBTQ+ people remaining an open question).

34 Nan D. Hunter, *Sexual Orientation and the Paradox of Heightened Scrutiny*, 102 MICH. L. REV. 1528, 1554 (2004).

35 *See, e.g.*, Benjamin G. Bishin, Thomas J. Hayes, Matthew B. Incantalupo & Charles Anthony Smith, *Opinion Backlash and Public Attitudes: Are Political Advances in Gay Rights Counterproductive?*, 60 AM. J. POL. SCI. 625, 626 (2016); Andrew R. Flores & Scott Barclay, *Backlash, Consensus, Legitimacy, or Polarization: The Effect of Same-Sex Marriage Policy on Mass Attitudes*, 69 POL. RES. Q. 43, 46 (2016).

36 Scholars who study backlash refer to this as "mass opinion backlash." Benjamin G. Bishin, Thomas J. Hayes, Matthew B. Incantalupo & Charles Anthony Smith, *Elite Mobilization: A Theory Explaining Opposition to Gay Rights*, 54 LAW & SOC'Y REV. 233, 234 (2020). They explaining the concept at follows:

> Of particular concern for minority rights advocates is the possibility . . . that pressing for policy gains will boomerang by mobilizing the public against them and make it more difficult for the group to achieve its objectives. If pushing for policy angers the masses, then the public might not just oppose the policy in question, or increase dislike or distrust of the group, but also help create lasting barriers to achieving policy gain.

Id.

37 *Id.* at 233 (defining elite-led mobilization as "a reaction by elites seeking to prevent gays and lesbians from achieving full incorporation in the polity"); Robert Post & Reva Siegel, Roe *Rage: Democratic Constitutionalism and Backlash*, 42 HARV. C.R.-C.L. L. REV. 373, 389 (2007) ("Legal scholars who now discuss the "Backlash Thesis" in connection with *Brown v. Board of Education*, or who now lament "the disastrous backlash that occurred in the wake of *Roe v. Wade*," use the term "backlash" to focus on questions of judicial role and judicial authority. These contemporary accounts of

only by inaction—such as the failure of Congress to adopt any federal antidiscrimination protections for LGBTQ+ people,[38] but also by discriminatory actions. Examples of the latter include, but are not limited

---

resistance to *Brown* or to *Roe* often implicitly adopt the perspective of courts, worrying that judicial decisions have unleashed "the kind of backlash that undermines both the Court and its holdings." (internal citations omitted)).

[38] Bella Abzug, a democratic U.S. Representative from New York, introduced the first federal bill to combat discrimination against LGBTQ+ people in 1974. Equality Act of 1974, H.R. 14752, 93rd Congress (1974). It "never earned enough support to make it out of committee in the House, and it was never introduced in the Senate." Hunt, *supra* note 5. After twenty years of revisions and advocacy, during which time efforts to address the AIDS epidemic were given priority by activists, Hunt, *supra* note 5, a narrower bill aimed at employment discrimination on the basis of sexual orientation (but not gender identity) was introduced in 1994. Employment Non-Discrimination Act of 1994, H.R. 4636, 103rd Cong. (1994); Employment Non-Discrimination Act of 1994, S. 2238, 103rd Cong. (1994). The bill never made it out of committee, a situation "that would be repeated for the next several years (though in 1996, ENDA received a floor vote in the Senate but failed by a one-vote margin). After 1996 a version of ENDA was introduced in every session of Congress except the 109th. Hunt, *supra* note 5. It took until 2013 before versions of ENDA that included gender identity protections were introduced in both chambers of Congress. *See* The Employment Non-Discrimination Act (ENDA) of 2013, S. 815, 113th Cong. (as passed by Senate, Nov. 7, 2013); Employment Non-Discrimination Act of 1994, H.R. 1755, 113rd Cong. (2013). It was never enacted into law. The same is true for its successor bill, the U.S. Equality Act, first introduced in 2015. U.S. Equality Act of 2015, H.R. 3185, 114th Cong. (2015). The Equality Act would provide far more protections than ENDA because it not only prohibits employment discrimination, but also extends to discrimination and segregation in public accommodations, education, federal funding, housing, banking, and jury selection. *See, e.g.*, Victoria D. Manuel, *The Future of LGBTQ+ Equality After* Obergefell *and* Bostock, 49 RUTGERS L. REC. 60 (2021) (urging the enactment of the Equality Act and explaining its terms and effects); Jace Valcore, Henry F. Fradella, Xavier Guadalupe-Diaz, Matthew J. Ball, Angela Dwyer, Christina DeJong, Allyn Walker, Aimee Wodda & Meredith G. F. Worthen, *Building an Intersectional and Trans-Inclusive Criminology: Responding to the Emergence of "Gender Critical" Perspectives in Feminist Criminology*, 29 CRITICAL CRIMINOLOGY 687, 690 n.4 (2021) (explaining the reach of the U.S. Equality Act, H.R. 5, 116th Cong. (as passed by the House of Representatives, May 17, 2019)). For a discussion of failed attempts to enact federal laws targeting anti-LGBTQ+ discrimination, see Jeremy W. Brinster, Note, *Taking Congruence and Proportionality Seriously*, 95 N.Y.U. L. REV. 580 (2020) (advocating for enactment of the Equality Act and analyzing its constitutionality in the affirmative).

to, legislation[39] and judicial decisions[40] sanctioning religious exemptions from antidiscrimination laws; state high courts refusing to honor the full scope of *Obergefell*'s mandate by extending to same-sex spouses the same public employee spousal benefits offered to opposite-sex spouses;[41] states

---

[39] For instance, at the time of this writing, two states (Kansas and Mississippi) have laws permitting private businesses to deny services to same-sex couples who seek to marry; nine states (Alabama, Arkansas, Florida, Illinois, Mississippi, Montana, Ohio, South Carolina, and Tennessee) have laws that permit medical professionals to refuse to serve LGBTQ+ patients; and thirteen states (Alabama, Arizona, Kansas, Michigan, North Dakota, Oklahoma, Mississippi, South Carolina, South Dakota, Tennessee, Texas, Utah, and Virginia) enacted legislation permitting "state-licensed child welfare agencies to refuse to place and provide services to children and families, including LGBTQ people and same-sex couples, if doing so conflicts with their religious beliefs." *Religious Exemption Laws*, MOVEMENT ADVANCEMENT PROJECT (June 13, 2023), https://www.lgbtmap.org/equality-maps/religious_exemption_laws [https://perma.cc/6JUD-NN85].

[40] *E.g.*, Chelsey Nelson Photography LLC v. Louisville/Jefferson Cnty. Metro Gov't, No. 3:19-CV-851-JRW, 2020 WL 4745771 (W.D. Ky. Aug. 14, 2020) (holding that the governmental interest in protecting LGBTQ+ people from discrimination was not compelling as applied to a photographer who refused to photograph same-sex weddings due to her purported religious beliefs because "in the absence of some further, legitimate end, this object is merely to allow exactly what the general rule of speaker's autonomy forbids"); Brush & Nib Studio, LC v. City of Phoenix, 448 P.3d 890, 914 (Ariz. 2019) (holding that a nondiscrimination ordinance could not be constitutionally applied to printers who refused to create custom wedding invitations for same-sex couples). As Stacey Sobel explained,

> When a baker refuses to bake a cake, a photographer declines to take photos, or a florist denies a request to create flower arrangements, they send a larger message: the government may recognize your marital status, but I do not need to do the same. These rejections are subordination activities to limit marriages of same-sex couples to a contractual status recognized by the government that does not relate to other parties or non-governmental benefits. This is an effort to consciously separate legal marriage from individual recognition and if successful, anti-discrimination laws would create formal equality, but not actual equality of treatment. People who want to limit or subordinate LGBTQ[+] rights are now using the courts in an attempt to legitimize their claimed primacy of rights.

Stacey L. Sobel, The Backlash Boomerang: Using Reverse Animus and Hostility to Limit LGBTQ Equality, 22 U. PA. J. CONST. L. 1155, 1182–83 (2020).

[41] Pidgeon v. Turner, 538 S.W.3d 73, 86 (Tex.), *cert. denied*, 138 S. Ct. 505 (2017) ("*Obergefell* may have recognized a 'fundamental right' to same-sex marriage and may 'require States to license and recognize same-sex marriages,' but, [the plaintiffs seeking an injunction against providing equal benefits should be able to litigate that *Obergefell*] did not recognize a fundamental right 'to spousal employee benefits' or 'require States to give taxpayer subsidies to same-sex couples.'"). For more details about *Pidgeon*, see *infra* notes 994–1004 and accompanying text.

with laws allowing officials to refuse to officiate marriages for any couples of whose unions they disapprove;[42] the on-again, off-again ban on transgender people serving in the military;[43] laws limiting transgender people from accessing bathrooms or playing sports consistent with their identities;[44] laws outlawing gender-affirming health care for trans youth;[45] and "don't say gay" laws of questionable First Amendment validity which

---

42 Mississippi and North Carolina both have such laws. *Religious Exemption Laws*, *supra* note 39.

43 *See* Rose Gilroy, Meredith Johnson, Rachel Keirstead, Kelley Kling, Elizabeth McGuire, Shea O'Meara, Fulton Wald, Katie Wiese, Ricky Yeager & Melissa Zubizarreta, *Transgender Rights and Issues*, 22 GEO. J. GENDER & L. 417, 426–32 (2021) (documenting the long-standing ban, its reversal during the Obama administration, its reinstatement during the Trump administration, and the relifting of the ban during the first month of the Biden administration); Victoria D. Manuel, *Trump's Transgender Military Ban: Policy, Law, and Litigation*, 29 TUL. J.L. & SEXUALITY 75 (2020) (advocating for passage of the USA Equality Act to address anti-LGBTQ+ laws and policies, including the military ban in effect when the article was published).

44 Gilroy et al., *supra* note 43, at 466 (discussing the enactment and release of HB2 (codified at N.C. GEN. STAT. ANN. § 143-760(b), (d) (West) (repealed 2017) and legislative attempts elsewhere to enact so-called "bathroom bills"); *Bans on Transgender Youth Participation in Sport*, MOVEMENT ADVANCEMENT PROJECT (June 14, 2023), https://www.lgbtmap.org/equality-maps/sports_participation_bans [https://perma.cc/VF5J-W6W5] (reporting that twenty-two states ban trans youth from participating in school sports, including Alabama, Arizona, Arkansas, Florida, Idaho, Indiana, Iowa, Kansas, Kentucky, Louisiana, Mississippi, Missouri, Montana, North Dakota, Oklahoma, South Carolina, South Dakota, Tennessee, Texas, Utah, West Virginia, and Wyoming); *see also* Henry F. Fradella & Alexis Rowland, *Baseless Anti-Trans Claims Fuel Adoption of Harmful Laws – Two Criminologists Explain*, THE CONVERSATION (June 5, 2023), https://theconversation.com/baseless-anti-trans-claims-fuel-adoption-of-harmful-laws-two-criminologists-explain-206570 [https://perma.cc/P9RX-HWFA]; Alexis Rowland & Henry F. Fradella, *A Surge in Anti-Trans Laws Ignore Criminology*, CRIME REP. (May 16, 2023), https://thecrimereport.org/2023/05/16/a-surge-of-anti-trans-laws-ignore-criminology/ [https://perma.cc/BKF4-N5KS].

45 Gilroy et al., *supra* note 43, at 435–49; Alexa Sussmane, *The Far-Right Push to Outlaw Gender-Affirming Treatment for Minors*, 30 TUL. J.L. & SEXUALITY 91 (2021) (documenting such laws and discussing their implications for the health, safety, and welfare of transgender and gender nonconforming teenagers). Some states have gone so far as to include penalties for parents seeking to provide for their children's gender-affirming health care. KERITH J. CONRON, KATHRYN K. O'NEILL, LUIS A. VASQUEZ & CHRISTY MALLORY, WILLIAMS INST. PROHIBITING GENDER-AFFIRMING MEDICAL CARE FOR YOUTH (2022), https://williamsinstitute.law.ucla.edu/wp-content/uploads/Trans-Youth-Health-Bans-Mar-2022.pdf [https://perma.cc/KTF2-95JB].

censor the ability to speak about LGBTQ+ people or issues in schools.[46]

The anti-LGBTQ+ legal backlash continued unabated after *Obergefell* and even increased after the U.S. Supreme Court's decision in *Bostock v. Clayton County*,[47] which ruled the employment discrimination protections on the basis of sex contained in Title VII of the Civil Rights Act of 1964[48] extended to sexual orientation and gender identity.[49] Consider that legislatures proposed a record number of bills targeting the LGBTQ+ community—more than 500 just in the five months of 2023.[50] If enacted, these efforts not only enshrine anti-LGBTQ+ sentiments into law—which, in turn, has the reifying effect of legitimizing anti-LGBTQ+ prejudice,[51] but also promote stigma with potentially deadly consequences.

---

46 *LGBTQ Curricular Laws*, MOVEMENT ADVANCEMENT PROJECT (June 13, 2023). https://www.lgbtmap.org/equality-maps/curricular_laws [https://perma.cc/SZL2-JT5J] (reporting that five states—Arizona, Arkansas, Florida, Montana, and Tennessee—require parental notification and the ability to opt-out of any curricula inclusive of LGBTQ+ issues, and ten states outright censor discussions of LGBTQ+ people in schools, including Alabama, Arkansas, Iowa, Florida, Indiana, Kentucky, Louisiana, Mississippi, Oklahoma, and Texas).

47 140 S. Ct. 1731 (2020).

48 Pub. L. 88-352, Title VII, § 703, 78 Stat. 255 (1964) (codified as amended at 42 U.S.C. § 2000e-2 (2021)).

49 For a discussion of the limited reach of the *Bostock* decision, see Reed, *supra* note 33, *passim*.

50 Fradella & Rowland, *supra* note 44. This eclipsed the record set the prior year, which had set a record up to that point. Kelsey Butler, *Anti-LGBTQ Proposals Are Flooding U.S. State Legislatures at a Record Pace*, BLOOMBERG (Apr. 8, 2022, 5:00 AM), https://www.bloomberg.com/news/articles/2022-04-08/mapping-the-anti-lgbtq-proposals-flooding-u-s-state-legislatures [https://perma.cc/65QN-EJ4A]. This phenomenon has not been limited to Congress and state legislatures. Municipalities have also been targeting LGBTQ+ rights. *See, e.g.*, *Not in Our Town*, THE ADVOCATE, Mar.–Apr. 2022, at 9 (reporting that Chambersburg became the first local government in Pennsylvania to repeal a nondiscrimination ordinance that had been inclusive of LGBTQ+ people).

51 Sobel, *supra* note 40, at 1178–79 (noting that backlash efforts that harness law and policy to subordinate LGBTQ+ people "operate explicitly or implicitly to maintain social, economic, and political dominance by one group over another" and there create or reinforce "existing social hierarchies that tell outgroup members that they are inferior"); *cf.* Henry F. Fradella, *Legal, Moral, and Social Reasons for Decriminalizing Sodomy*, 18 J. CONTEMP. CRIM. JUST. 279, 292–93 (2002) (summarizing arguments that sodomy laws "create criminals," reinforce hostility toward LGBTQ+ persons by labeling them as criminals, and perpetuate legal and moral stigma against LGBTQ+ people); Michele Goodwin & Erwin Chemerinsky, *The Transgender Military Ban: Preservation of Discrimination Through Transformation*, 114 NW. U. L. REV. 751, 757

> Data has shown that restrictive legislation has consequences on the mental and physical health of the queer and trans community, especially youth. A 2021 study shows that LGBTQ+ teens in states with homophobic and transphobic policies were more likely to attempt suicide than those in states with inclusive policies. In March, the CDC released data that one in five LGBTQ+ youth seriously considered attempting suicide in the in the [twelve] months before the survey. Advocates fear legislation like "Don't Say Gay" will only exacerbate these consequences for queer and trans youth.[52]

As if the uptick in discriminatory legislation were not worrisome enough threats to the promises of equality, liberty, and dignity for LGBTQ+ people, a key foundation of their civil rights were gutted by the U.S. Supreme Court's decision in *Dobbs v. Jackson Women's Health*

(2019) (stating that ban on transgender people serving in the military "reifies a social construction of LGBTQ persons being mentally ill or diseased"); Nancy J. Knauer, *Historical Contingency and the Limits of Identity: Implications for Law and Policy*, 28 S. CAL. INTERDISC. L.J. 387, 416 (2019) (arguing that religious exemptions "insulate religious objectors from the increased legal and social acceptance of LGBTQ[+] individuals and their families" and "signal that there is something different about LGBTQ[+] rights from other type of civil rights that merits caution").

52 Alexandra Martinez, *Hate Crimes Are Rising as Anti-LGBTQ+ Legislation Passes and Misinformation Thrives*, PRISM (Apr. 20, 2022), https://prismreports.org/2022/04/20/hate-crimes-rise-anti-lgbtq-legislation/ [https://perma.cc/J8AL-CJTF] (citing Christina Aivadyan, Melissa N. Slavin & Elwin Wu, *Inclusive State Legislation and Reduced Risk of Past-Year Suicide Attempts Among Lesbian, Gay, Bisexual, and Questioning Adolescents in the United States*, 27 ARCHIVES SUICIDE RSCH. 63 (2023), https://doi.org/10.1080/13811118.2021.1967237); *see also* Sherry Everett Jones, Kathleen A. Ethier, Marci Hertz, Sarah DeGue, Vi Donna Le, Jemekia Thornton, Connie Lim, Patricia J. Dittus & Sindhura Geda, *Mental Health, Suicidality, and Connectedness Among High School Students During the COVID-19 Pandemic—Adolescent Behaviors and Experiences Survey, United States, January–June 2021*, 72 MORBIDITY & MORTALITY WKLY. REP. 16 (Apr. Supp. 2022), http://dx.doi.org/10.15585/mmwr.su7103a3.

Organization.[53] *Dobbs* overruled both *Roe v. Wade*[54] and *Planned Parenthood of Southeastern Pennsylvania v. Casey.*[55] Although abortion decisions, both *Roe* and *Casey* were substantive due process cases that rested upon the right to privacy.[56] As explored in Chapter 2, despite the *Lawrence* decision's emphasis on liberty more than privacy, the line of privacy cases, including *Roe* and *Casey*, were nonetheless important precedents underpinning the holding and rationale in *Lawrence.*[57] In the wake of *Dobbs*, what will happen to *Lawrence*—and LGBTQ+ civil rights more generally—remain open, important questions.[58]

---

53 142 S. Ct. 2228, 2242 (2022) ("We hold that *Roe* and *Casey* must be overruled. The Constitution makes no reference to abortion, and no such right is implicitly protected by any constitutional provision, including the one on which the defenders of *Roe* and *Casey* now chiefly rely—the Due Process Clause of the Fourteenth Amendment. That provision has been held to guarantee some rights that are not mentioned in the Constitution, but any such right must be 'deeply rooted in this Nation's history and tradition' and 'implicit in the concept of ordered liberty.'" (internal citation omitted).

54 410 U.S. 113, 153 (1973) (holding that the right to privacy "is broad enough to encompass a woman's decision whether or not to terminate her pregnancy," at least prior to fetal viability), *overruled by Dobbs*, 142 S. Ct. at 2242.

55 505 U.S. 833, 876 (1992) (reaffirming *Roe*'s central holding while rejecting its trimester framework in favor of one that disallows undue burdens on the decision to terminate a pregnancy), *overruled by Dobbs*, 142 S. Ct. at 2242.

56 *Roe*, 410 U.S. at 153; *Casey*, 505 U.S. at 883, 896.

57 *See infra* notes 151–173 and accompanying text.

58 Even before, the *Dobbs* decision was handed down, commentators warned that the fall of *Roe* and *Casey* could endanger LGBTQ+ civil rights. *See, e.g.*, Jeannie Suk Gersen, *If* Roe v. Wade *Is Overturned, What's Next?*, NEW YORKER (Apr. 17, 2022), https://www.newyorker.com/magazine/2022/04/25/if-roe-v-wade-is-overturned-whats-next [https://perma.cc/X67S-2BQC] ("Overturning *Roe* would almost certainly fuel the broader fight to get fundamental moral issues out of the realm of federal constitutional rights and under the control of the states."). After a draft majority opinion in *Dobbs* was leaked and published online, scholars chimed in that these warnings were not alarmist, but rather realistic assessments of the threats to *Lawrence*, *Windsor*, and *Obergefell*. *See, e.g.*, Kate Sosin & Orion Rummler, *What Happens If* Roe v. Wade *Is Overturned? LGBTQ+ Legal Experts Are Worried about Civil Rights*, THE 19TH (May 6, 2022), https://19thnews.org/2022/05/lgbtq-civil-rights-roe-supreme-court/ [https://perma.cc/HC48-N3WV] (quoting constitutional law professor Michael Kreis as saying, "The danger of overturning it is in the fact that you're tipping a major leg of the right-to-privacy stool out from underneath it[. . . .] If you take that critical component piece out, then it opens all these other things up to a greater degree of susceptibility."); Lauren Vella, *How* Roe v. Wade*'s Reversal Could Affect the LGBT Community*, THE HILL (May 8, 2022, 8:00 AM), https://thehill.com/news/state-watch/3479755-how-roe-v-wades-reversal-could-effect-the-lgbt-community/ [https://perma.cc/6MF6-Q9HU] (quoting law professor Melissa Murray as explaining,

As previously mentioned, several commentators—nearly all of whom wrote before *Obergefell* was decided—asserted that the *Lawrence* decision had limited jurisprudential impact.[59] Although such claims were supported by analysis of select cases, they were not empirically established via systematic methods. For instance, in the summer of 2010, law professor J. Kelly Strader, who specializes in criminal law and LGBTQ+ rights, supported that very observation by noting that a "quick Westlaw or Lexis search will identify dozens of judicial decisions declining to follow, declining to extend, or distinguishing *Lawrence*, but only a handful of decisions affirmatively relying on *Lawrence*."[60] Strader drew that conclusion six to seven years after *Lawrence* was decided. As of this writing, *Lawrence* has been the law of the land for roughly two decades. What has its impact been over this longer period of time? Put differently, what has been the reach of *Lawrence* beyond its immediate role decriminalizing certain sexual acts performed in private between consenting adults and its longer-term impact on marriage equality? The present study seeks to answer that question through a systematic content analysis of how state courts have interpreted and applied *Lawrence*.[61]

"All of these rights are unenumerated and you know, if you tug on the *Roe* thread it's like playing a really horrible game of Jenga."); Lindsay Whitehurst & Zeke Miller, *LGBTQ Advocates Worry Other Rights at Risk If Court Overturns* Roe v. Wade, PBS NEWS (May 4, 2022, 7:44 PM), https://www.pbs.org/newshour/politics/lgbtq-advocates-worry-other-rights-at-risk-if-court-overturns-roe-v-wade [https://perma.cc/UEK2-ZN3M] (noting that even if the Court were hesitant to overturn *Obergefell*, it might be sympathetic to marriage equality challenges on religious liberty grounds).

59 Black, *supra* note 25, at 330; Buchanan, *supra* note 25, at 1237; Reinheimer, *supra* note 25, at 505. Sparling made the same assertion even after the marriage equality cases in the mid-2010s, perhaps because the observation contained a caveat about *Lawrence*'s limited impact on "jurisprudence in the *lower* courts," which would exempt *Windsor* and *Obergefell* from the generalization since they were U.S. Supreme Court decisions. Sparling, *supra* note 25, at 82 (emphasis added).

60 J. Kelly Strader, *Resurrecting* Lawrence v. Texas *as a Basis for Challenging Criminal Prosecutions*, 25 CRIM. JUST. 30, 31 (2010).

61 For an in-depth discussion about how systematic content analysis is particularly well suited for the study of legal cases, see Mark A. Hall & Ronald F. Wright, *Systematic Content Analysis of Judicial Opinions*, 96 CALIF. L. REV. 63, 66 (2008). Hall and Wright maintained that well-established social science research methods of content analysis:

The present study focuses on state courts because *Dobbs* potentially heralds a significant retreat from federal constitutional protections for liberty and privacy rights. Understanding how state courts view these rights may help to provide insights that might inform future LGBTQ+ civil rights efforts—something that has taken on new urgency since *Dobbs* gutted key cases that had cemented privacy, autonomy, and liberty rights for half a century.

Chapter 2 contains a brief history of sodomy laws in Section A. Section B discusses how the regulation of sodomy changed in the post-World War II era. Section C provides an overview of the jurisprudential bases of the right to privacy. Section D summarizes how *Bowers v.*

> could form the basis for a uniquely legal empirical methodology. On the surface, content analysis appears simple, even trivial, to some. Using this method, a scholar collects a set of documents, such as judicial opinions on a particular subject, and systematically reads them, recording consistent features of each and drawing inferences about their use and meaning. This method comes naturally to legal scholars because it resembles the classic scholarly exercise of reading a collection of cases, finding common threads that link the opinions, and commenting on their significance. But content analysis is more than a better way to read cases. It brings the rigor of social science to our understanding of case law, creating a distinctively legal form of empiricism.

Id. at 64 (internal citations omitted).

Hall and Wright also noted that scholars began to use content analysis to study case law systematically in the late 1950s. *Id.* at 67 (citing Fred Kort, *Predicting Supreme Court Decisions Mathematically: A Quantitative Analysis of the "Right to Counsel" Cases*, 51 AM. POL. SCI. REV. 1, 11 (1957). Legal scholars began to rely on the method "in greater numbers in the 1990s" and its use has increased since then. *Id.* at 70. Hall and Wright noted that the author of the present study previously had used a qualitative version of the method often referred to as ethnographic content analysis. *Id.* at 81 n.70 ("Social scientists also use rigorous qualitative analysis, such as ethnography, but we found only one example based on case content analysis. *See* Henry F. Fradella, Adam Fogarty & Lauren O'Neill, *The Impact of ion the Admissibility of Behavioral Science Testimony*, 30 PEPP. L. REV. 403 (2002). Most qualitative analyses based on case coding use the looser, discursive style common to conventional legal scholarship, which is not regarded as scientific."). Indeed, I have used this method to study legal cases dozens of times, publishing results in both social science and law journals. *See, e.g.*, Henry F. Fradella, *In Search of Meritorious Claims: A Study of the Processing of Prisoner Civil Rights Cases in a Federal District Court*, 21 JUST. SYS. J. 23 (1999); Erin Lutes, James A. Purdon, & Henry F. Fradella, *When Music Takes the Stand: A Content Analysis of How Courts Use and Misuse Rap Lyrics in Criminal Cases*, 46 AM. J. CRIM. L. 77 (2019); Samuel G. Vickovic, Marie L. Griffin & Henry F. Fradella, *Depictions of Correctional Officers in Newspaper Media: An Ethnographic Content Analysis*, 26 CRIM. JUST. STUD. 455 (2013).

Hardwick, the 1986 U.S. Supreme Court case that upheld the constitutionality of sodomy laws, undercut this long line of privacy rights cases.[62] Section E examines select implications of *Lawrence v. Texas*'s overturning of *Hardwick*.[63] And Section F discusses the research questions addressed by the present study.

Chapter 3 contains details of the current study's research methodology. Chapter 4 presents the quantitative results while Chapter 5 contains the in-depth qualitative results. Chapter 6 evaluates the study's key findings and their implications before offering some concluding thoughts.

62 Bowers v. Hardwick, 478 U.S. 186, 192–93 (1986).

63 Lawrence v. Texas, 539 U.S. 558, 578 (2003).

Chapter 2:

The Path to *Lawrence*

A. Sodomy Laws in Historical Context[64]

Most historians agree that "no Western legal or moral tradition—civil or ecclesiastical, European, English, or Anglo-American—has ever attempted to penalize or stigmatize a 'homosexual person' apart from the commission of external acts."[65] Thus, nonnormative sexual orientation, per se, has not been condemned throughout history. Rather only particular sexual acts in which members of the same biological sex might engage—which are usually taken to include both oral and anal intercourse and subsumed under the general term "sodomy"—have been proscribed for centuries.

Sodomy laws have existed since biblical times. Even the term "sodomy" comes from the Bible, in the story of the destruction of Sodom.[66] Judaic law specifically prohibited sodomy.[67] There is scholarly literature which suggests that the biblical condemnation of same-sex relations may not be aimed at condemning same-sex relations.[68] But even

---

64 Portions of this section are adapted from my prior writings on sodomy laws. Fradella, *supra* note 51, at 280–82; Henry F. Fradella & Kenneth Grundy, *The Criminal Regulation of Sex: The Limits of Morality and Consent*, *in* FRADELLA & SUMNER , *supra* note 5, at 183, 186–87.

65 John Boswell, *On the History of Social Attitudes Toward Homosexuality from Ancient Greece to the Present*, *in* GAYS AND THE MILITARY: THE UNITED STATES VERSUS JOSEPH STEFFAN 40–48, 40 (Marc Wolinsky & Kenneth Sherrill eds., 1993).

66 *Genesis* 19:1–29.

67 *See* Arthur E. Brooks, Note, Doe *and* Dronenburg*: Sodomy Statutes Are Constitutional*, 26 WM. & MARY L. REV. 645, 648 (1985) (citing *Leviticus* 18:22).

68 JOHN BOSWELL, CHRISTIANITY, SOCIAL TOLERANCE & HOMOSEXUALITY (1980); Robert K. Gnuse, *Seven Gay Texts: Biblical Passages Used to Condemn Homosexuality*, 45 BIBLICAL THEOLOGY BULL. 68, 68 (2015).

if we accept the text as a condemnation of homosexuality, it is clear that sodomy has not always been considered a crime. For example, sodomy played a large part in ancient Greek and Roman culture since both societies not only condoned acts of sodomy, but also encouraged them under certain circumstances. [69] Under the tradition of *paiderastia* "ordained in law by Solon the lawgiver himself," male citizens before marrying "had the obligation to take as a lover and pupil a younger male and train him in the arts of war and citizenship."[70]

With the spread of Christianity in Europe, Western Civilization came to be revolted by homosexuality and punished sodomy as an ecclesiastical offense.[71] Sodomy was made a crime against the state, punishable by death, in the sixteenth century by Henry VIII.[72] The English law, which used the term "buggery," was interpreted as prohibiting bestiality (i.e., any sex act in which either a man or women engaged with an animal), anal sex between men and women, and anal sex between men.[73] Thus, the early English prohibition on buggery did not extend to acts of oral sex.[74] That changed, however, in 1885, when the mass suppression of sexuality of all types during the Victorian Era led Parliament to make it a crime, punishable by up to two years imprisonment, to be a party "to procur[ing]

---

69 HAVELOCK ELLIS, THE PSYCHOLOGY OF SEX: A MANUAL FOR STUDENTS 279 (1933) ("True love for the Greeks was nearly always homosexual."); BYRNE R.S. FONE, HOMOPHOBIA: A HISTORY 17–28 (2000).

70 FONE, *supra* note 69, at 19. Fone cautioned that *paiderastia* not be confused with pedophilia because the former, sanctioned practice involved males who had reached puberty. *Id.*; *see also* KENNETH J. DOVER, GREEK HOMOSEXUALITY 19 (1978).

71 RICHARD DAVENPORT-HINES, SEX, DEATH AND PUNISHMENT: ATTITUDES TO SEX AND SEXUALITY IN BRITAIN SINCE THE RENAISSANCE 59 (1990); Brooks, *supra* note 67, at 648.

72 Brooks, *supra* note 67, at 649 (citing 25 Henry VIII, ch. 6 (1533)). Queen Mary repealed the law, but Elizabeth I reinstated it. *Id.* (citing 1 Mary, ch. 1 (1553); 5 Eliz., ch. 17 (1562)); *see also* William N. Eskridge, Jr., *Law and the Construction of the Closet: American Regulation of Same-Sex Intimacy, 1880–1946*, 82 IOWA L. REV. 1007, 1012 (1997) (citing Francois Lafitte, *Homosexuality and the Law*, 9 BRIT. J. DELINQ. 8, 12 (1958)).

73 Eskridge, *supra* note 72, at 1012 (citing Stafford's Case, 77 Eng. Rep. 1318 (1607); King v. Wiseman, 92 Eng. Rep. 774 (K.B. 1718)); *see also* Lawrence v. Texas, 539 U.S. 558, 568, (2003) (citing *Wiseman*, 92 Eng. Rep. at 775).

74 Eskridge, *supra* note 72, at 1012 (citing Rex v. Jacobs, 168 Eng. Rep. 830 (1817) (holding that even forcible oral sex committed by an adult man upon a seven-year-old boy "did not constitute the offence of sodomy")).

the commission by any male person of any act of gross indecency with another male person," whether in public or private.[75]

The Puritans brought sodomy laws with them to the colonies, but expanded their reach to include other sex acts, including those attendant to "men lying with men" and "women lying with women."[76] The original thirteen states maintained laws against buggery (primarily in the south and mid-Atlantic regions) or sodomy (primarily in New England), although violations were not punishable by death in some jurisdictions.[77] Statutory provisions did not elaborate on the specific acts prohibited, "for this remained the 'unmentionable' sin against nature."[78] Some laws even used terminology such as "the infamous crime against nature" or the "abominable and detestable crime against nature,"[79] borrowing from the phrase coined by noted English jurist William Blackstone.[80]

As the United States grew, sodomy laws spread, largely as a function of "the natural law philosophy valorizing procreative sex within marriage."[81] The meaning of sodomy laws, however, varied over time.[82] Some states maintained the English approach of having laws that differentiated sodomy (which continued to be understood as targeting bestiality and anal sex), from oral sex (which was punishable under statutes punishing gross indecency, lewd and lascivious conduct, or oral copulation).[83] Other states amended their sodomy statutes to include oral

---

75 *Id.* at 1026 (citing 48 & 49 Vict. 69, cl. 11 (1885) (Eng.).

76 Eskridge, *supra* note 72, at 1013 (citing J. HAMMOND TRUMBULL, THE TRUE-BLUE LAWS OF CONNECTICUT AND NEW HAVEN 201 (1879)).

77 *Id.*

78 *Id.*

79 *See, e.g.*, JONATHAN NED KATZ, GAY/LESBIAN ALMANAC 121–22 (1983) (citing Acts and Laws, Passed by the Great and General Council or Assembly of the Province of Massachusetts-Bay in New England from 1692, to 1719, at 110 (1724); *see also* James Hampton, *Homosexuality: An Aggravating Factor*, 28 TUL. J.L. & SEXUALITY 25, 28 n.19 (2019) (citing Louis Crompton, *Homosexuals and the Death Penalty in Colonial America*, 1 J. HOMOSEXUALITY 278 (1976)).

80 4 WILLIAM BLACKSTONE, COMMENTARIES *125. Blackstone did not define the term "crime against nature" or delineate its limits.

81 Eskridge, *supra* note 72, at 1015.

82 *Id.* at 1013–15.

83 *Id.* at 1027 (citing, *inter alia*, 1903 Mich. Pub. Acts 198 (gross indecency between males); 1939 Mich. Pub. Acts 148 (gross indecency between females); MASS. GEN.

sex, many of which followed Pennsylvania's lead in detailing the prohibited conduct.[84] Still other states incorporated oral sex into their prohibitions against sodomy via judicial decisions that reasoned such sexual activity shared with anal sex both the inability to result in procreation and the "unnatural use . . . of body parts designed for breathing and excretion."[85]

Renowned legal scholar William Eskridge, Jr., explained that sodomy statutes were "the only formal regulations of same-sex intimacy in the United States before the 1880s."[86] Yet, the laws were almost never invoked for such purposes, at least not against consenting adults.[87] That quickly changed as the United States grew more urbanized, largely in response to two factors: (1) what the growing middle class viewed as the increasing perversions of city life—especially widespread prostitution;[88]

LAWS ch. 436, § 1 (1887) (lewd and lascivious acts); 1915 CAL. STAT. 586, *repealed and replaced by* 1921 CAL. STAT. 848 (containing a similar provision criminalizing oral copulation)).

84 *Id.* at 1027–28 (citing Act of June 11, 1879, § 1, 1879 Pa. Laws 156).

85 *Id.* at 1028 (citing, *inter alia*, Honselman v. People, 48 N.E. 304 (Ill. 1897)).

86 *Id.* at 1015 ("As far as I can tell, there is no reported case in the United States before 1880 where a sodomy conviction was upheld against a man apparently engaged in consensual intercourse with another man, or a woman engaged in intercourse with another woman.").

87 *Id.*; *see also* Ellen Ann Anderson, *The Stages of Sodomy Reform*, 23 T. MARSHALL L. REV. 283, 288 (1998) ("Although on the books, these laws were virtually never enforced against consenting adults in private, and virtually never within a marital relationship. Nonetheless, they served as the cornerstone for criminalizing homosexuality and legitimating discrimination against lesbian, gay, and bisexual people."). Eskridge reported that according to 1880 census data, only sixty-three people in the whole country were incarcerated for sodomy, the majority of whom "were males of color in the South." Eskridge, *supra* note 72, at 1015. Of the White prisoners, a third were from abroad. *Id.* Thus, Eskridge concluded that, "To the extent crime-against-nature laws were mechanisms of social control, their objects were people of color and foreign-born individuals, both 'alien' to a nervous white Anglo-Saxon America." *Id.*

88 *Id.* at 1017–28. Eskridge summarized several authoritative sources that explained how, as middle-class women became more active in public life, they sought to help women engaged in sex work for whom they had sympathy. *Id.* at 1019 (citing, *inter alia*, CARROLL SMITH-ROSENBERG, DISORDERLY CONDUCT: VISIONS OF GENDER IN VICTORIAN AMERICA 172–78 (1985)). But men, who grew uncomfortable with their wives' participation in politics, business, and the arts, usurped women's more helpful efforts by mobilizing governmental authority (which, of course, they controlled) to prosecute those engaged in prostitution, which included not only women, but also gay and gender-nonconforming men. *Id.*

and (2) a new medical vocabulary of degeneration (i.e., de-evolution or "evolutionary reversion") to refer to people with nonnormative sexual orientations and gender identities, many of whom flocked to growing urban areas where they could avoid the watchful eyes of family and close-knit community members in small towns.[89] Moral crusaders sounded the alarm that "the 'degenerate classes,' those 'persons of low grade and development, physically and mentally, with a defective understanding of their true relations to the social system in which they live' [spread] vice, crime, and disease."[90] As a result of the ensuing moral panic, vice squads

---

[89] Eskridge cited numerous authorities to explain that the medical establishment at the time labeled those who fell in the latter group, as well as those who sought their services, using terms such as "sexual inverts," "sexual perverts," and "sexual degenerates." Eskridge, *supra* note 72, at 1017, 1020–23 (citing, *inter alia*, ; RICHARD VON KRAFFT-EBING, PSYCHOPATHIA SEXUALIS, WITH SPECIAL REFERENCE TO ANTIPATHIC SEXUAL INSTINCT: A MEDICO-FORENSIC STUDY 581–85 (F.J. Rebman ed., Physicians & Surgeons Book Co. 1931) (1899); Havelock Ellis, *The Study of Sexual Inversion*, 12 MED.-LEGAL J. 148 (1894–1895); G. Frank Lydston, Clinical Lecture: *Sexual Perversion, Satyriasis and Nymphomania*, 61 MED. & SURGICAL REP. 253, 254 (1889)).

[90] Eskridge, *supra* note 72, at 1024 (quoting G. FRANK LYDSTON, THE DISEASES OF SOCIETY (THE VICE AND CRIME PROBLEM) 37 (1905)). Notably, this moral panic was imbued with racism:

> In an 1892 article, Dr. Irving Rosse associated sexual perversions with prehistoric "trogdolytes," barnyard animals, prostitutes, and people of color. His main contemporary example of perversion involved a "band of negro men" of "androgynous character" whose "rites" of phallic worship were raided by the Washington police. . . . Dr. Lydston's 1905 book on social disease devoted an entire chapter to the so-called degenerated practices of racial minorities and primitive cultures. "Physical and moral degeneracy—the latter involving chiefly the higher and more frequently acquired attributes—with a distinct reversion of type is evident in the Southern negro. This physical and moral degeneracy and atavism is especially manifest in the direction of sexual proclivities," Lydston wrote. "The removal by his liberation of certain inhibitions placed upon the negro by slavery itself . . . has been especially effective as a causal factor of sexual crimes among the blacks of the South."
> A third author was inspired by the drag balls in black St. Louis to suggest that perversion and cross-dressing were imported from Africa.

Id. (citing LYDSTON, *supra* note 90, at 395; C.H. Hughes, *Postscript to a Paper on Érotopathia*, 14 ALIENIST & NEUROLOGIST 731, 731-32 (1895); Irving C. Rosse, *Sexual Hypochondriasis and Perversion of the Genetic Instinct*, 17 J. NERVOUS & MENTAL DISEASE 795 (1892)).

emerged to step up vigorous enforcement of laws criminalizing prostitution and sodomy.[91]

Law enforcement zeal to arrest and prosecute morals offenses contributed to what Eskridge termed an "inexorable legal revolution" in the construction and application of sodomy laws.[92] Police and prosecutors used moral offenses to target persons with nonnormative sexual orientations and gender identities, including those criminalizing sodomy, lewd and lascivious conduct, indecent exposure, solicitation, public sexual indecency, obscenity, and even new crimes like appearing in public dressed in a manner incongruous with prevailing gender norms.[93] Moreover, public order offenses, like disorderly conduct, loitering, and vagrancy, were vigorously used not only to support general anti-prostitution efforts, but also in ways that targeted "male degeneracy" in ways that "created a multiplicity of elastic offenses that any kind of sexual nonconformist could be charged with violating."[94]

---

91 Eskridge, *supra* note 72, at 1025–26.

92 *Id.* at 1026.

93 *Id.* at 1032–38, 1040, 1067–70. In fact, obscenity laws were expanded to prohibit possession of ""any indecent or lewd book, picture or other thing whatever of an immoral or scandalous nature." *Id.* at 1070 (quoting Chicago, Ill., Charter and Ordinances ch. XXXVIII, art. I, § 6 (1856)).

94 Eskridge, *supra* note 72, at 1039. It should be noted that although state and municipal enforcement of morals legislation formed the backbone of the criminal regulation of sex, sexuality, and gender, the federal government also participated in such social control efforts, two of which had notable long-term effects. First, the military adopted regulations excluding "degenerates" and sodomy became a basis for court martial. *Id.* at 1052 (citing United States, Manual for Courts-Martial § 443 (1917)). Controversies about LGBTQ+ people serving in the military continue to this day. *See, e.g.*, Manuel, *supra* note 43, at 77–88 (summarizing the evolution of the military's exclusion of LGBTQ+ people, including the ban on military service for transgender people put into effect during the Trump administration).

Immigration laws and polices changed between the 1880s and 1920s to bar not only the "importation" of women for the purposes of prostitution, but also anyone with contagious diseases (including sexually-transmitted infections), people convicted of felonies, and people with misdemeanor convictions for crimes of moral turpitude (which included a range of sexual indecency laws, including sodomy). Eskridge, *supra* note 72, at 1045–47 (citing, *inter alia*, 1909 Immigr. Serv. Ann. Rep. 115 ("Nothing can be more important than to keep out of the country the anarchistically and criminally inclined and the degenerate in sexual morality.")). By 1917, immigration law included "'constitutional psychopathic inferiority' as a basis for exclusion or deportation," a category that includes "sexual perverts." *Id.* at 1048 (citing 39 Stat. 874). This, too, had long-standing effects. For instance, it took until 1990 for Congress to lift the

Targeted enforcement of morals offenses against LGBTQ+ people increased significantly in the early- to mid-twentieth century, partly as a function of the rise of psychiatry.[95] In the United States, society—including the legal establishment—largely misinterpreted Sigmund Freud's theory of psychosexual development[96] as evidence that "homosexuals" posed significant social threats, especially to minors.[97] The social construction of gay men, in particular, as child molesters and sexual psychopaths led to "draconian sanctions against same-sex intimacy."[98] As

---

psychopathic personality exclusion that included LGBTQ+ people. Immigration Act of 1990, Pub. L. No. 101-649, 104 Stat. 4978 (1990). And it took until after the *Windsor* decision before U.S. citizens could sponsor the same-sex partners for immigration benefits. *See generally* Victor C. Romero, *Reading (into)* Windsor*: Presidential Leadership, Marriage Equality, and Immigration Policy*, 23 S. CAL. REV. L. & SOC. JUST. 1 (2013) (arguing in favor of demonstrative actions the Obama administration took after *Windsor* to begin treating bi-national same-sex couples the same way that as opposite-sex couples were treated under U.S. immigration law). For a broader discussion of how turn-of-the-twentieth century immigration law changes impacted LGBTQ+ persons, see Shannon Minter, *Sodomy and Public Morality Offenses Under U.S. Immigration Law: Penalizing Lesbian and Gay Identity*, 26 CORNELL INT'L L.J. 771 (1993).

95 Eskridge, *supra* note 72, at 1054–59.

96 Freudian theory offered one of the first fully-developed theories of sexual orientation. *Id.* at 1058. Contrary to the social construction of same-sex attraction as evidence of psychopathology, Freud did not see "the inverted" as either "degenerates" (in the neurological, evolutionary, or popular-use sense) or as a symptom of mental illness. SIGMUND FREUD, THREE ESSAYS ON SEXUALITY 9 (A.A. Brill trans., Global Grey e-book ed. 2021) (1905), https://www.globalgreyebooks.com/ebooks1/sigmund-freud/three-essays-on-the-theory-of-sexuality/three-essays-on-the-theory-of-sexuality.pdf [https://perma.cc/8BCT-QKNH] (noting that "inversion is found among persons who otherwise show no marked deviation from the normal . . . whose capabilities are not disturbed, who on the contrary are distinguished by especially high intellectual development and ethical culture"). Freud viewed all humans an innately bisexual who, as a function of normal development, mature into socially appropriate unisexual orientations. FREUD, *supra*, at 11. But for those who early childhood development did not result in successful resolution of the either the Oedipal complex (for males) or Electra complex (for females) due to environmental factors (like parenting styles) or biological factors (natural variation in hormone levels), *Id.* at 10–12, Freud viewed same-sex attraction as nature outcome. *Id.* at 49–55.

97 Eskridge, *supra* note 72, at 1058 (explaining that key figures in U.S. psychiatry at the time "emphasized features of Freud's theories that suited them, such as the functional (curable) rather than hereditary (incurable) causes of perversion, and deemphasized other features, such as Freud's relatively pro-sex hedonism").

98 *Id.* at 1059 (citing Estelle B. Freedman, "*Uncontrolled Desires": The Response to the Sexual Psychopath, 1920-1960*, J. AM. HIST., June 1987, at 83). It is important to

the myth of gay predators became woven into the fabric of society and its collective conscience, the need for social control of nonnormative sexual orientations and gender identities grew exponentially.[99]

> The new discourse combined themes of sodomy (criminal acts), inversion (violation of social gender norms), and sexual psychopathy (dangerous and uncontrollable desires) to produce a mythic figure—The Homosexual—who could be regulated for any of three reasons: committing illegal acts, challenging gender roles associated with her or his sex, or having specified sexual desires, or "homosexual tendencies."[100]

It should be unsurprising, then, that all U.S. jurisdictions had adopted sodomy laws in their criminal codes by the middle of the twentieth century.[101] On their face, these laws were neutral such that they applied to

---

emphasize that the medical establishment in the United States was more heavily influenced by the moralist movement against "degeneracy" than it was by psychoanalytic theory. Contrary to Freud's position, medicine selected only parts of Freudian theory to link moral degeneracy with crime in ways that perpetuated anti-LGBTQ+ prejudice by falsely equating "sexual perverts" with psychopathy. *Id.* at 1063 (quoting PAUL E. BOWERS, A SURVEY OF TWENTY-FIVE HUNDRED PRISONERS IN THE PSYCHOPATHIC LABORATORY AT THE INDIANA STATE PRISON 33 (n.d.) ("[I]t may be safely said that the majority of sexual perverts are psychopathic individuals . . . an exceedingly dangerous and demoralizing class which should be permanently isolated to prevent their mingling with others.")).

99 Eskridge, *supra* note 72, at 1068–69.

100 *Id.* at 1069.

101 Bowers v. Hardwick, 478 U.S. 186, 193–94 (1986) ("[U]ntil 1961, all [fifty] States outlawed sodomy, and today, [twenty-four] States and the District of Columbia continue to provide criminal penalties for sodomy performed in private and between consenting adults."); MODEL PENAL CODE § 213.2 cmt. 1 (AM. L. INST. 1980), at 360 ("At the time the Model Code was under consideration, all jurisdictions maintained some criminal prohibition on deviate sexual intercourse. . . .").

Various authorities similarly contain assertions about a fifty-state ban. *E.g.*, Christopher R. Leslie, *Creating Criminals: The Injuries Inflicted by "Unenforced" Sodomy Laws*, 35 HARV. C.R.-C.L. L. REV. 103, 106 (2000) (noting that "all fifty states and the District of Columbia had sodomy laws on their books in the mid-twentieth century"); Yao Apasu-Gbotsu et al., *Survey on the Constitutional Right to Privacy in the Context of Homosexual Activity*, 40 U. MIAMI L. REV. 521, 526 (1986) ("Until the early 1960s, homosexual behavior was prohibited in all fifty states and the District of Columbia through some form of sodomy statute" (citing James J. Rizzo, Note, *The Constitutionality of Sodomy Statutes*, 45 FORDHAM L. REV. 553, 554–57 (1977))). But none of these authorities actually list statutory provisions totaling to fifty-one—one for each state and the District of Columbia. The *Bowers* decision listed thirty-eight states

people of all sexes, sexual orientations, and gender identities. Enforcement of these laws, however, disproportionately targeted consensual acts between members of the same sex.[102] Indeed, there is little question that

---

that had adopted sodomy laws in effect in 1868. *Bowers*, 478 U.S. at 193 n.6 (listing statutes). The *Bowers* decision went on to make the fifty-state assertion and cited Apasu-Gbotsu and colleagues' survey of the law in support of that proposition. *Bowers*, 478 U.S. at 193–94 (citing Apasu-Gbotsu et al., *supra*, at 524 n.9). The authors of the University of Miami survey of the law, however, did not list fifty-one statutes either; rather, they cited Rizzo's note. Apasu-Gbotsu et al., *supra*, at 526 n.23. But Rizzo never asserted that sodomy had been a crime in all U.S. jurisdictions. Rather, he said that as of the time he wrote in 1977, "private consensual sodomy [was] a criminal offense in the large majority" of states. Rizzo, *supra*, at 553. In support of that statement, Rizzo listed the laws of thirty-two states. *Id.* at 553 n.1. He noted, however, that seven states had repealed their sodomy statutes prior to 1973 and ten more states had either repealed or invalidated their sodomy laws between 1973 and 1977. Rizzo, *supra*, at 592 (listing statutes and citing WILLIAM BARNETT, SEXUAL FREEDOM AND THE CONSTITUTION (1973)). Rizzo also pointed out that in 1968, Heffner had documented the forty-nine states that had sodomy laws as of 1968. Rizzo, *supra*, at 592 (citing Hugh Hefner, *The Legal Enforcement of Morality*, 40 U. COLO. L. REV. 199, 210 (1968)). If Heffner's assertion was correct, because Illinois had repealed its consensual sodomy statute in 1961, see 961 Ill. Laws 1983, § 11-2 (eff. Jan. 1, 1962), it would appear that all fifty states and the District of Columbia criminalized had adopted laws between the late 1800s and the 1950s. However, Heffner only cited select laws, rather than providing a comprehensive listing. Heffner, *supra*, at 210–15 (citing Robert C. Bensing, *Comparative Study of American Sex Statutes*, 42 J. CRIM. L. 57 (1951)). He also cited authority for his assertion, directing readers to a survey of laws published by Bensing in 1951. Bensing did compile a comprehensive listing of statutory authority for forty-eight states, but he asserted that neither New Hampshire nor Vermont has such laws. Bensing, *supra*, at 63. But New Hampshire did, in fact, have a sodomy law that dated back to 1679 which was expanded in 1899 to include oral sex. *See* WILLIAM N. ESKRIDGE, JR., DISHONORABLE PASSIONS 398 (2008) (citing 1899 N.H. Laws ch. 33). And Vermont had adopted a sodomy law inclusive of oral sex by 1923. *See id.* (citing 1937 Vt. Pub. Acts No. 211). So, the assertion that all U.S. states and the District of Colombia criminalized sodomy seems to be correct despite the fact that most authorities failed to fully document their sources. The only comprehensive source I have been able to locate is Professor's Eskridge's 2008 book *Dishonorable Passions*, which contains an appendix of all such laws in U.S. history. *See* ESKRIDGE, *supra*, at 388–406.

102 Eskridge, *supra* note 72, at 1080–83; Marie-Amélie George, *The Harmless Psychopath: Legal Debates Promoting the Decriminalization of Sodomy in the United States*, 24 J. HIST. SEXUALITY 225, 236 (2015) (citing Stephen Robertson, *Shifting the Scene of the Crime: Sodomy and the American History of Sexual Violence*, 19 J. HIST. SEXUALITY 240, 240–42 (2010)). Police raids of "spaces for same-sex socializing and cruising . . . [including] music halls, cafes and restaurants, private flats, public parks, streets, public toilets, the local YMCA lobby, theatres, public baths, and subways" become commonplace, starting in 1910. Eskridge, *supra* note 72, at 1080; *see also* Anderson, *supra* note 87, at 294 ("In the early morning hours of June 28, 1969, the

despite their wording, sodomy laws "in fact apply only to homosexual sodomy."[103]

B. The Competing Values During the Era of Kinsey and McCarthy

During the late 1940s and early 1950s, pioneering research by Alfred Kinsey and his colleagues began to dispel many of the then-common misconceptions about human sexual behavior, including sexual activity between people of the same sex.[104] Kinsey's groundbreaking, albeit controversial work, stirred "new popular interest in the status of our sex law"[105] that presented "a rare opportunity for re-examining a portion of the criminal law in the light of a factual study of the relevant social

---

police raided the Stonewall Inn, a gay bar in New York City's Greenwich Village. Raids of this sort were not uncommon at the time; establishments catering to lesbian, gay, and bisexual customers were often subject to police harassment."). Such police practices continued, largely unabated, through the post-Stonewall era, even as organizations aimed at LGBTQ+ civil rights grew exponentially and legal reforms to decriminalize sodomy accelerated. *Id.* at 296; *see also* Matt Baume, *51 Years After Stonewall, Police Raided Two Gay Bars Aiding Protestors*, Them (June 5, 2020), https://www.them.us/story/ police-raided-two-gay-bars-aiding-george-floyd-protestors [https://perma.cc/34PR-RDGL] (detailing how police raided gay bars in Des Moines and Raleigh because people in them were providing medical care to people injured in protests against the policing killing of George Floyd); Jacob Ogles, *30 Infamous Police Raids of Gay Bars and Bathhouses*, THE ADVOCATE (Mar. 1, 2017), https://www.advocate.com/politics/ 2017/3/01/30-infamous-police-raids-gay-bars-and-bathhouses#media-gallery-media-29 [https://perma.cc/3EGW-68HN] (documenting a series of police raids between 1903 and 2016).

103 RICHARD A. POSNER, SEX AND REASON 291 (1994).

104 *See generally* ALFRED C. KINSEY, WARDELL B. POMEROY & CLYDE E. MARTIN, SEXUAL BEHAVIOR IN THE HUMAN MALE 392, 895 (1948) (reporting that 37% of males had at least one sexual encounter with another male); ALFRED C. KINSEY, WARDELL B. POMEROY, CLYDE E. MARTIN & PAUL H. GEBHARD, SEXUAL BEHAVIOR IN THE HUMAN FEMALE (1953) (reporting that 13% of females at least one sexual encounter with another female).

105 Note, *Post-Kinsey: Voluntary Sex Relations as Criminal Offenses*, 17 U. CHI. L. REV. 162, 163 (1949–50). In arguing for the decriminalization of several consensual sex offenses, the editors of the *University of Chicago Law Review* noted that the Kinsey report indicated a "substantial proportion"—perhaps as high as 95%—of men between sixteen and sixty was "engaging in illicit sex conduct at any given time." *Id.* at 169–70.

behavior."[106] The supreme courts of Utah and Hawai'i both questioned the legitimacy of sodomy laws in light of the Kinsey studies, although neither court voided their state laws criminalizing such acts.[107] Several state commissions similarly expressed concerns about laws criminalizing certain consensual sex acts.[108] This led to a handful of states decreasing the penalties for sodomy,[109] removing consensual sodomy from the scope of sexual psychopath laws,[110] or removing "sexual perverts" from the ambit of sterilization laws.[111]

---

106 *Id.* at 162; *see also* George, *supra* note 102, at 227 (explaining the shift from "the widespread implementation of sexual psychopath statutes to the decriminalization of sodomy . . . emerged out of debates around sexual psychopath laws and Alfred Kinsey's reports on male and female sexual behavior, which questioned many of the assumptions underlying both sexual psychopath statutes and criminal code provisions on consensual sodomy").

107 State v. Cooper, 201 P.2d 764, 767 (Utah 1949) ("Congenital homosexuals, and to a certain extent, psychopathic homosexuals, may be wholly unresponsible for their homosexual acts. They are motivated by biological and physiological factors which may be beyond their power to combat or control. And while such persons cannot be left to prey upon society, and particularly upon young children, the wisdom of declaring their conduct to be criminal may be seriously questioned . . . ."); Territory v. Bell, 43 Haw. 23 (1958) ("There is much criticism of making a crime out of homosexual or other unnatural sexual relations, this criticism being particularly widespread in England at this time, but the remedy, if any, is a matter for the legislature.").

108 Marie-Amélie George, *Bureaucratic Agency: Administering the Transformation of LGBT Rights*, 36 YALE L. & POL'Y REV. 83, 106 (2017) ("Commissions in Illinois, Pennsylvania, Michigan, New Jersey, New York, and Virginia all questioned whether—in light of Kinsey's findings—criminal laws could effectively be enforced.").

109 California abolished its twenty-year maximum sentence and replaced it with an indeterminate sentence as judicially imposed. 1952 Cal. Laws ch. 24, p. 382. Nevada reduced the minimum penalty from five years, see NEV. REV. LAWS § 6459 (1911), to one year, although the maximum penalty remained a potential life sentence. 1951 Nev. Laws ch. 318, p. 524–25 (codified at NEV. REV. STAT. § 2010.190 (1951); *compare Ex parte* Benites, 140 P. 436, 436 (Nev. 1914) (citing then-applicable statute and upholding conviction for its violation), *with* Hogan v. State, 441 P.2d 620, 621 (Nev. 1968) (same). New York, for example, reduced sodomy between consenting adults from being a felony, see N.Y. PENAL LAW § 690 (1909), to a misdemeanor. *See* 1950 N.Y. Laws ch. 525, § 151, p. 1271, 1278–79; *see also* People v. Randall, 203 N.Y.S.2d 372, 373 (1960) (noting the change to the state's sodomy statute), *aff'd*, 9 N.Y.2d 413, 174 N.E.2d 507 (1961).

110 George, *supra* note 108, at 106–07 (citing 1955 Ill. Laws 1144, 1144–46).

111 1909 CAL. STATS., ch. 720, § 1, pp. 1093–94, *replaced by* 1913 CAL. STATS. ch. 363, § 1, pp. 775–76, *partially repealed and replaced by* 1951 CAL. STATS. ch. 552, § 1, pp. 1706–07 (removing sexual "perversion" as a basis for sterilization).

Importantly, the American Law Institute ("ALI") omitted sodomy from its highly influential Model Penal Code,[112] noting the "absence of harm to the secular interests of society occasioned by atypical sexuality between consenting adults."[113] The ALI recognized that its decision to omit "deviate sexual intercourse" occurring in private between consenting adults represented a "fundamental departure from prior law."[114] As a function of Illinois reorganizing its criminal laws by adopting nearly all of Model Penal Code in 1961, it became the first state to decriminalize sodomy.[115] Idaho enacted a similar statutory overhaul, "but when the legislature discovered it had repealed the sodomy law, it repealed the entire reform package instead."[116]

---

[112] For insights into how the Model Penal Code came to be, see the works of one the Code's primary architects, Herbert Wechsler. *E.g.*, Herbert Wechsler, *The Challenge of A Model Penal Code*, 65 HARV. L. REV. 1097 (1952); Herbert Wechsler, *Codification of Criminal Law in the United States: The Model Penal Code*, 68 COLUM. L. REV. 1425 (1968). For insights on the Code's achievements and impact, see Herbert L. Packer, *The Model Penal Code and Beyond*, 63 COLUM. L. REV. 594 (1963); Paul H. Robinson & Markus D. Dubber, *The American Model Penal Code: A Brief Overview*, 10 NEW CRIM. L. REV. 319 (2007).

[113] MODEL PENAL CODE § 213.2 cmt. at 369 (AM. L. INST., Proposed Official Draft 1962). For an in-depth discussion of the Code's treatment of morals offenses, including sodomy, see Louis B. Schwartz, *Morals Offenses and the Model Penal Code*, 63 COLUM. L. REV. 669 (1963). Schwarz noted that the Kinsey studies contributed to the views expressed in the comments on tentative drafts of the Model Penal Code:

> The Code does not attempt to use the power of the state to enforce purely moral or religious standards. We deem it inappropriate for the government to attempt to control behavior that has no substantial significance except as to the morality of the actor. Such matters are best left to religious, educational and other social influences. Apart from the question of constitutionality which might be raised against legislation avowedly commanding adherence to a particular religious or moral tenet, it must be recognized, as a practical matter, that in a heterogeneous community such as ours, different individuals and groups have widely divergent views of the seriousness of various moral derelictions.

Id. at 674 (quoting MODEL PENAL CODE § 207.1 cmt. at 207 (AM. L. INST., Tent. Draft No. 4, 1955)).

[114] MODEL PENAL CODE § 213.2 cmt. 2 at 369 (AM. L. INST., Proposed Official Draft 1962).

[115] Act of July 28, 1961, § 35-1, 1961 Ill. Laws 1983, 2044 (codified at 983 ILL. COMP. STAT. 5/11-2 (1962) (repealed 1984); *see also* George, *supra* note 108, at 109.

[116] *Getting Rid of Sodomy Laws: History and Strategy that Led to the Lawrence Decision*, ACLU, https://www.aclu.org/other/getting-rid-sodomy-laws-history-and-strategy-led-lawrence-decision [https://perma.cc/A56D-TTUZ] (last visited Aug. 31, 2022).

Some states, however, *increased* their penalties for sodomy at that time, largely in response to the renewed moral panic over "homosexuality" that was attendant to Cold War politics, which viewed all types of nonconformity as threats to national security.[117] Conservative politicians, especially Joseph McCarthy, crusaded against communism and homosexuality.[118] Not only did this cause some states to increase criminal punishments for select moral offenses, but also resulted in the "Lavender Scare"—the widespread persecution of LGBTQ+ people in governmental jobs.[119] Perhaps as a result of the antigay sentiments of the era, no states other than Illinois repealed their sodomy laws between 1950 and 1969 as applied to private acts between consenting adults despite Kinsey's research and advocacy.[120] Most jurisdictions—including the federal government—refocused enforcement efforts in ways that targeted gay

---

117 For instance, Congress enacted a sodomy law governing the District of Columbia that included oral sex and provided for a penalty of up to ten years in prison. Pub. L. No. 615-428, 62 Stat. 346, 347 (1948). Both Arizona and Wyoming increased their penalties for violating their sodomy laws. ARIZ. CODE ANN. § 43–406 (1939), *revised by* 1951 Laws Ariz. ch. 134, § 1 (codified at ARIZ. REV. STAT. § 13-651 (1955) (changing the name of the crime from sodomy to the "infamous crime against nature" and increasing the punishment from a term of incarceration from one to five years to a term of five to twenty years); Laws Wyo. 1890, ch. 73, p. 127 (five-year penalty), *amended by* 1955 Wyo. Laws ch. 209, p. 230 (codified at WYO. COMP. STAT. § 9-520) (1957)) (increasing penalty to a maximum term of imprisonment of ten years).

118 George, *supra* note 102, at 230 (explaining that governmental "investigations into security risks and disloyalty targeted homosexuals in particular, based on the belief that homosexuals lacked emotional stability and were susceptible to blackmail"); *see also* JOHN D'EMILIO, SEXUAL POLITICS, SEXUAL COMMUNITIES: THE MAKING OF A HOMOSEXUAL MINORITY IN THE UNITED STATES, 1940–1970, at 32, 40–41 (2d ed. 1998); *see generally* DAVID M. OSHINSKY, A CONSPIRACY SO IMMENSE: THE WORLD OF JOE MCCARTHY (1983) (examining McCarthy's life and the impact of his politics).

119 *See* DAVID K. JOHNSON, THE LAVENDER SCARE: THE COLD WAR PERSECUTION OF GAYS AND LESBIANS IN THE FEDERAL GOVERNMENT (2004) (exploring McCarthy's pivotal role in the long-lasting search for and purge of homosexuality from the ranks of U.S. government).

120 In fact, despite law reform commissions in many states successfully pushing for adoption of the Model Penal Code, opposition to the decriminalization of sodomy from law enforcement and religious organizations caused most state legislatures to refuse to exclude criminal prohibits against sodomy as a function of not wanting to be seen as tolerating, if not endorsing, homosexuality. William N. Eskridge, Jr., Hardwick *and Historiography*, 1999 U. ILL. L. REV. 631, 662 (1999). As a result, "[n]o other state decriminalized consensual sodomy until Connecticut did so in its 1969 criminal code revision." *Id.* at 663.

men, in particular.[121] Such anti-LGBTQ+ animus was not limited to how police and prosecutors enforced consensual sex crimes. Indeed, it might best be exemplified by how legislatures changed sodomy laws themselves. Consider that in response to the work of Kinsey, Wilhelm Reich, Masters and Johnson, and other sex researchers, society became more open to sexuality in general during the sexual revolution of 1960s and 1970s.[122] As a result, a number of states altered their statutes so that acts of sodomy between opposite-sex partners (i.e., "heterosexual sodomy") would be beyond the reach of the criminal law, but acts between members of same-sex remained criminalized.[123] A constitutional attack on one such sodomy law during the 1980s led to one of the most shameful U.S. Supreme Court decisions of the twentieth century: *Bowers v. Hardwick*.[124]

---

[121] George, *supra* note 102, at 231 ("The widespread depiction of homosexuals as national security risks and moral perverts gave police forces around the country a license to harass homosexual men and women, leading to brutal crackdowns throughout the 1950s" (citing D'EMILIO, *supra* note 118, at 49)); *see also* JOHNSON, *supra* note 119, at 61; *see also* James Gleason, *LGBT History: The Lavender Scare*, NAT'L LGBT CHAMBER OF COM. (Oct. 3, 2017), https://www.nglcc.org/blog/lgbt-history-lavender-scare [https://perma.cc/F3SN-HTBL] (reporting that when the United States Park Police created a program of enforcement aimed at the elimination of "sex perversion" in 1947, at least 500 five hundred people were arrested and seventy-six were charged).

[122] Jeffrey Escoffier, *The Sexual Revolution, 1960–1980*, THE GLBTQ ENCYCLOPEDIA PROJECT ARCHIVES 2 (Claude Summers ed., 2004), http://www.glbtqarchive.com/ssh/sexual_revolution_S.pdf [https://perma.cc/6XV4-GCBQ]; *see generally* DAVID ALLYN, MAKE LOVE, NOT WAR – THE SEXUAL REVOLUTION: AN UNFETTERED HISTORY (2016) (exploring the full scope of the sexual revolution).

[123] *See, e.g.*, ARK. STAT. ANN. § 41-1813 (1975), *invalidated by* Jegley v. Picado, 80 S.W.3d 332, 350, 353–54 (2002) (finding the law violated the state constitutional guarantees of privacy and equal protection); KAN. STAT. ANN. § 21-3505 (1969); KY. REV. STAT. ANN. § 510.100 (1974), *invalidated by* Commonwealth v. Wasson, 842 S.W.2d 487, 496, 501–02 (1992) (finding the law violated the state constitutional guarantees of privacy and equal protection); MO. ANN. STAT. § 566.090(3) (1977); TEX. PENAL CODE ANN. § 21.06 (1973). In the mid-1980s, the Court of Criminal Appeals of Oklahoma limited its facially neutral law to criminalizing sodomy only between members of the same sex. Post v. State, 717 P.2d 1151, 1152 (Okla. 1986) (holding OKLA. STAT. § 21-886 could not constitutionally reach "private, consensual and non-commercial heterosexual acts between adults").

[124] 478 U.S. 186 (1986). I previously referred to *Bowers v. Hardwick* as "the *Plessy v. Fergusson* of our time." Fradella, *supra* note 4, at 606 (citing Plessy v. Fergusson, 163 U.S. 537, 551–52 (1896) (permitting segregation under the racist "separate but equal" doctrine)); *see also* Kris Franklin, *Homophobia and the "Matthew Shepard Effect" in* Lawrence v. Texas, 48 N.Y.L. SCH. L. REV. 657, 691 (2004) (equating the homophobia in *Bowers* to the racism that "undergird[e]d segregation" before *Brown v. Board of*

C. The Right to Privacy Leading Up to *Bowers v. Hardwick*

Bowers v. Hardwick held that the right to privacy did not protect consensual sexual acts of sodomy between members of the same sex.[125] The 1986 decision was not the first, however, to reject a constitutional challenge to sodomy laws. In 1926, for example, the Wisconsin Supreme Court upheld a sodomy conviction of a woman for allegedly engaging in the act with a man in her home. After determining that the police were lawfully in the woman's apartment, the court dispensed with her challenge to the law saying that "uphold[ing] defendant's contention would seriously embarrass the enforcement of law, and license the defendant and her kind to continue their abominable practices under the protection of the law."[126] In 1944, an Arizona man specifically challenged his sodomy conviction for engaging in oral sex with another man on the grounds that "the privacy of his home" had been invaded.[127] The Arizona Supreme Court simply ignored his argument when upholding his conviction.[128] Unlike in these

---

Educ. of Topeka, 347 U.S. 483 (1954), overturned *Plessy*). For other critiques of the homophobia in *Bowers* and the flawed reasoning in the decision, see Mary C. Dunlap, *Gay Men and Lesbians Down by Law in the 1990's USA: The Continuing Toll of* Bowers v. Hardwick, 24 GOLDEN GATE U. L. REV. 1, 10 (1994) ("The inescapable conclusion is that the result in *Hardwick* is about homophobia, and, given that cause of the result, playing with the facts will not change the outcome; only a frontal address of the homophobia will do so."); Janet E. Halley, *Reasoning About Sodomy: Acts and Identity in and After* Bowers v. Hardwick, 79 VA. L. REV. 1721, 1770 (1993) (describing the decision as an "exercise of homophobic power"); Darren Lenard Hutchinson, *The Majoritarian Difficulty: Affirmative Action, Sodomy, and Supreme Court Politics*, 23 LAW & INEQ. 1, 36 (2005) ("The *Bowers* decision is highly flawed and harmful to justice claims because it rests on explicitly homophobic language, construes liberty in an extremely narrow fashion, contains gross misstatements of history, and permits states to satisfy rational basis review by simply asserting that their laws advance some undefined, ambiguous conception of "morality.").

125 *Bowers*, 478 U.S. at 191–96 .

126 Edwards v. State, 208 N.W. 876, 877 (Wis. 1926).

127 Faber v. State, 521 P.2d 671, 673 (Ariz. 1944).

128 Courts in other states, including California, Iowa, Minnesota, and Oregon, also upheld sodomy convictions without regard for the privacy implications of doing so. *See, e.g.*, State v. Edwards, 412 P.2d 526, 527–28 (Or. 1966) (upholding sodomy conviction after a neighbor reported the defendant, a person assigned the male gender at birth, who used the name Joyce and dressed in women's clothing, living with a man whom Joyce married in a civil ceremony); People v. Manicap, 260 P.2d 137, 137 (Cal. 1953)

early cases, the outcome in *Bowers v. Hardwick* was surprising in light of a series of U.S. Supreme Court cases concerning the right to privacy. The remainder of this section traces the jurisprudence of this constitutional right as a backdrop to *Bowers*.

1. Early Origins of the Right to Privacy

The right to privacy is not specifically enumerated in the U.S. Constitution.[129] In fact, the word "privacy" appears nowhere throughout the document.[130] Commentors often cite an influential *Harvard Law Review* article that Samuel D. Warren and Louis D. Brandeis authored in 1890 in which they advocated for recognition of a right to privacy that encompasses the "right to be let alone," largely in response to the press availing themselves of then-new technologies that allowed tabloid journalists to capture and publish salacious photos.[131] Others have suggested that judicial recognition of the right to privacy in the United States has roots that predate the article by Warren and Brandeis.[132] For instance, in *Union Pacific Railway Co. v. Botsford*, the Court upheld a determination that courts cannot compel surgical examinations in personal injury actions of those claiming injuries.[133] Although the Court did not

---

(upholding convictions of women seen entering a motel room and subsequently seen by police because they had "pushed the blind aside" to see them in bed together); State v. Nelson, 271 N.W. 114, 115 (Minn. 1937) (upholding convictions based on a "confession" contained in letters that a postal inspector had opened); People v. Funtas, 182 P. 785, 785 (Cal. 1919) (upholding conviction obtained after a mother "caused to be bored two auger-holes in a wall" of her son's bedroom, allowing her to witness the act); State v. Gage, 116 N.W. 596 (Iowa 1908) (upholding conviction of man who witnesses, peering through a keyhole, observed engaging in oral sex while in a locked water closet on a train).

129 *See generally* U.S. CONST, *passim*.

130 *Id.*

131 Samuel D. Warren & Louis D. Brandeis, *The Right to Privacy*, 4 HARV. L. REV. 193, 195 (1890) (quoting THOMAS M. COOLEY, A TREATISE ON THE LAW OF TORTS, OR THE WRONGS WHICH ARISE INDEPENDENT OF CONTRACT 29 (2d ed. 1888)).

132 Eugene McCarthy, *In Defense of* Griswold v. Connecticut: *Privacy, Originalism, and the Iceberg Theory of Omission*, 54 WILLAMETTE L. REV. 335, 339 (2018) (citing Boyd v. United States, 116 U.S. 616 (1886)).

133 141 U.S. 250, 251 (1891) ("No right is held more sacred, or is more carefully guarded by the common law, than the right of every individual to the possession and control of his own person, free from all restraint or interference of others, unless by clear and

specifically reference privacy, per se, it clearly was concerned with bodily autonomy as illustrated by its statement that "[t]he right to one's person may be said to be a right of complete immunity; to be let alone."[134] Indeed, the Court invoked the very same language from a leading torts treatise by Judge Thomas M. Cooley that Warren and Brandeis had quoted in their article the year before *Botsford* was decided.[135]

Professor Eugene McCarthy argued that *Boyd v. United States* was one of the first U.S. Supreme Court decisions to "tackle[] the right to privacy from a constitutional perspective."[136] That case invalidated a statutory provision allowing for court orders, akin to subpoenas *duces tecum*, compelling the production of customs invoices that the government could use to build criminal cases.[137] In so holding, the Court wrote:

> [I]nvasions on the part of the government and its employees of the sanctity of a man's home and privacies of life. It is not the breaking of his doors, and the rummaging of his drawers, that constitutes the essence of the offense; but it is the invasion of his indefeasible right of personal security, personal liberty and private property.[138]

Brandeis was confirmed as an Associate Justice on the U.S. Supreme Court in 1916.[139] During his tenure, he participated in two cases that turned

---

unquestionable authority of law."). Notably, the majority in *Roe v. Wade* the cited *Botsford* as "perhaps" its earliest privacy rights case. 410 U.S. 113, 152 (1973).

134 *Botsford*, 141 U.S. at 251 (quoting COOLEY, *supra* note 131, at 29).

135 *Id.*; *see also* COOLEY, *supra* note 131, at 29.

136 McCarthy, *supra* note 132, at 339 (citing *Boyd*, 116 U.S. 616).

137 *Boyd*, 116 U.S. at 636–38. Of course, *Boyd*'s view regarding the compelled production of evidence has been repudiated. *See, e.g.*, Warden, Md. Penitentiary v. Hayden, 387 U.S. 294, 301 (1967). Still, *Boyd*'s recognition of privacy rights stemming from both the Fourth and Fifth Amendments illustrates the notion of rights via constitutional "penumbras" long predates the Court's explicit use of such an approach in *Griswold v. Connecticut*, 381 U.S. 479, 484 (1965) (stating that "specific guarantees in the Bill of Rights have penumbras, formed by emanations from those guarantees that help give them life and substance"—including those from the First, Third, Fourth, Fifth, and Ninth Amendments that create "zones of privacy").

138 McCarthy, *supra* note 132, at 339 (quoting *Boyd*, 116 U.S. at 630).

139 *Louis D. Brandeis, 1916–1939*, SUP. CT. HIST. SOC'Y, https://supremecourthistory.org/associate-justices/louis-d-brandeis-1916-1939/ [https://perma.cc/EGS6-9WJ2].

out to be key precedents in subsequent privacy cases despite the fact that the word "privacy" is not used in either case. In *Meyer v. Nebraska*, the Court reversed the conviction of a school teacher who had provided foreign language instruction in violation of a state law prohibiting the teaching of foreign languages to grammar school students.[140] In invalidating the law on due process grounds, the Court said that the Fourteenth Amendment's protection of liberty

> denotes not merely freedom from bodily restraint but also the right of the individual to contract, to engage in any of the common occupations of life, to acquire useful knowledge, to marry, establish a home and bring up children, to worship God according to the dictates of his own conscience, and generally to enjoy those privileges long recognized at common law as essential to the orderly pursuit of happiness by free men.[141]

Applying such reasoning, the Court found that the restriction on foreign language instruction interfered with the protected liberty interests of teachers' rights to instruct and parents' rights to direct the upbringing and education of their children.[142] Two years later in *Pierce v. Society of the Sisters of the Holy Names of Jesus & Mary*,[143] the Court applied the same logic when it unanimously invalidated an Oregon law that mandated children attend public schools, rather than private or parochial schools.[144]

Thirty-eight years after the publication of his highly influential article with Warren, Brandeis again used the phrase "the right to be left alone" in his dissent from an opinion in *Olmstead v. United States*, which upheld the warrantless use of telephone wiretaps.[145] His approach ultimately prevailed years after his death,[146] perhaps due, in part, to Brandeis' efforts

---

140 262 U.S. 390, 396–97, 403 (1923) (citing Laws Neb. 1919, ch. 249).

141 *Id.* at 399.

142 *Id.* at 400.

143 268 U.S. 510, 530, 534–35 (1925).

144 *Id.* at 529 (citing Laws Or. 1923, p. 9).

145 *See* Olmstead v. United States, 277 U.S. 438, 466, 478 (1928) (Brandeis, J., dissenting), *abrogated, in part, by* Katz v. United States, 389 U.S. 347 (1967).

146 *Katz*, 389 U.S. at 350.

to persuade other Justices to recognize the right to privacy as a way of protecting "personal liberty rights against government intrusion."[147]

Professor McCarthy noted that Brandeis' efforts to get the Court to recognize a right to privacy even extended to him selecting and vetting William O. Douglas, another privacy rights proponent, as his successor on the Court.[148] Douglas assumed the mantle, using his dissents in several key cases to inform his fellow Justices about privacy rights.[149] A modified version of the Brandeis/Douglas approach to the right to privacy eventually won the day in the landmark 1965 case of *Griswold v. Connecticut*.[150]

---

147 McCarthy, *supra* note 132, at 341 (citing *Katz*, 389 U.S. at 350).

148 *Id.* at 341–42 (citing Richard A. Posner, *The Anti-Hero*, NEW REPUBLIC, Feb. 24, 2003, at 27 (book review)); *see also* DARIEN A. MCWHIRTER & JON D. BIBLE, PRIVACY AS A CONSTITUTIONAL RIGHT 91 (1992).

149 McCarthy, *supra* note 132, at 343–44 (citing Poe v. Ullman, 367 U.S. 497, 521 (1961) (Douglas, J., dissenting from a dismissal of a declaratory judgment action brought by married couples who challenged a law preventing them from accessing contraceptives on the basis that they lacked standing and, in doing so, emphasizing that such laws were "an invasion of the privacy that is implicit in a free society"); On Lee v. United States, 343 U.S. 747, 762–63 (1952) (Douglas, J., dissenting from upholding the warrantless use of a wire by an undercover agent); Beauharnais v. Illinois, 343 U.S. 250, 285 (1952) (Douglas, J., dissenting from upholding a racist pamphlet as libelous on First Amendment grounds and, in doing so, equating the freedom of speech to the right to privacy as "equally sacred"); Pub. Utils. Comm'n v. Pollak, 343 U.S. 451, 467–69 (1952) (Douglas, J., dissenting from an opinion upholding a private bus company's ability to broadcast a radio station for compensation on the ground that passengers were a "captive audience" whose rights to privacy were infringed by being forced to list to the radio station's message)).

150 Griswold v. Connecticut, 381 U.S. 479, 481–86 (1965). It should be noted that prior to *Griswold*, the Court issued at least three two decisions that broadly interpreted the liberty interests protected by substantive due process. First, in *Skinner v. Oklahoma*, 316 U.S. 535, 541–43 (1942), the Court invalidated a law that compelled the sterilization of people convicted of three felony offenses from a select list. Although technically decided on equal protection grounds (due to the nature of the included and excluded felony offenses), *Skinner* used language implicating substantive due process:

> We are dealing here with legislation which involves one of the basic civil rights of man. Marriage and procreation are fundamental to the very existence and survival of the race . . . . There is no redemption for the individual whom the law touches. Any experiment which the State conducts is to his irreparable injury. He is forever deprived of a basic liberty.

Id. at 541. By referencing marriage and procreation as "basic civil rights" and by classifying infringements of these rights as deprivations of "basic liberty," the Court recognized unenumerated rights that were directly at issue in subsequent right to

2. *Griswold v. Connecticut*

Griswold invalidated a Connecticut statute that prohibited the use of contraceptives, even by married couples.[151] Unlike in his previous dissents in which Justice William O. Douglas moored the right to privacy in the Fourteenth Amendment's protection of liberty, in *Griswold*, Douglas grounded the right to privacy in the penumbral emanations of specific, enumerated constitutional rights:

> [S]pecific guarantees in the Bill of Rights have penumbras, formed by emanations from those guarantees that help give them life and substance. Various guarantees create zones of privacy. The right of association contained in the penumbra of the First Amendment is one, as we have seen. The Third Amendment in its prohibition against the quartering of soldiers "in any house" in time of peace without the consent of the owner is another facet of that privacy. The Fourth Amendment explicitly affirms the "right of the people to be secure in their persons, houses, papers, and effects, against unreasonable searches and seizures." The Fifth Amendment in its Self-Incrimination Clause enables the citizen to create a zone of privacy which government may not force him to surrender to his detriment. The Ninth Amendment provides: "The enumeration in the Constitution, of certain rights, shall not be construed to deny or disparage others retained by the people."
>
> * * *
>
> We have had many controversies over these penumbral rights of "privacy and repose." These cases bear witness that the right of privacy which presses for recognition here is a legitimate one.[152]

---

privacy cases. *Id.* Then, in both *Kent v. Dulles*, 357 U.S. 116, 125, 130 (1958), and *Aptheker v. Secretary of State*, 378 U.S. 500, 505 (1964), the Court invalidated restrictions on the right to travel. Like the right to privacy, the right to travel is not specified in the U.S. Constitution. These cases, therefore, illustrate the Court's willingness to protect unenumerated rights that implicate personal liberty. "In the light of *Skinner*, *Kent*, and *Aptheker*, *Griswold* was, in effect, a decision waiting to happen." G. Sidney Buchanan, *The Right of Privacy: Past, Present, and Future*, 16 OHIO N.U. L. REV. 403, 418 (1989).

151 *Griswold*, 381 U.S. at 485–86.

152 *Id.* at 484–85 (internal citations omitted).

Douglas' majority opinion went on to conclude that the anticontraception law at issue in the case violated the right to privacy in ways that could intrude into the "sacred precincts of marital bedrooms."[153] As the next

---

[153] *Id.* at 485. *Griswold* sparked a backlash among conservatives to which some commentators trace the contemporary movement for originalism. McCarthy, *supra* note 132, at 348 (citing SCOTT DOUGLAS GERBER, FIRST PRINCIPLES: THE JURISPRUDENCE OF CLARENCE THOMAS 57 (1999)). Originalism is a doctrine which posits words should be interpreted in accordance with their commonly understood meanings at the time they were written. Put differently, those who subscribe to originalism adhere to a "canon that a legal text should be interpreted through the historical ascertainment of the meaning that it would have conveyed to a fully informed observer at the time when the text first took effect." *Originalism*, BLACK'S LAW DICTIONARY (11th ed. 2019). Because the Constitution neither specifically guarantees a right to privacy nor prohibits any ban on access to contraceptives, originalists—including the two dissenters in *Griswold*, Justices Hugo Black and Potter Stewart—maintain that the challenge to the anticontraceptive law at issue in *Griswold* "does not raise a constitutional issue and is not a matter upon which the Court is authorized to make a determination." McCarthy, *supra* note 132, at 349–50 (citing *Griswold*, 318 U.S. at 507–27)).

There are originalists, however, who defend *Griswold* and its logic. McCarthy, for instance, argued that the right to privacy was "foremost . . . among self-evident liberties" that the public understood at the time the framers were striving to form a free society. *Id.* at 360 (quoting JOHN W. JOHNSON, *GRISWOLD V. CONNECTICUT*: BIRTH CONTROL AND THE CONSTITUTIONAL RIGHT OF PRIVACY 192 (2005)). Thus, he concluded that the "*Griswold* opinion—and its articulation of the constitutional right to privacy—adheres meticulously to the tenets of judicial originalism and accurately captures the original public meaning of the Constitution." *Id.* at 359; *see also* Suzanna Sherry, *The Founders' Unwritten Constitution*, 54 U. CHI. L. REV. 1127, 1162 (1987) (explaining that the Ninth Amendment was included in the Bill of Rights to allay the concerns of many of the Founders were opposed to enumerating specific rights for fear that doing so "would inaccurately imply that the rights themselves were limited to those enumerated").

> Justice Douglas's *Griswold* opinion simply engages in a plain, close reading of the constitutional text, which is precisely the starting point upon which any originalist analysis should begin. Indeed, Randy Barnett reinforces this plain reading argument, noting that the "Ninth Amendment's public meaning in the founding era is identical to what ordinary readers take it to mean today (until they enter law school and are told otherwise)." That is, it means just what it says: the Constitution contemplated additional unenumerated rights that would be retained in the people.
>
> Judicial originalists inexplicably resist this plain reading of the text. They refuse to adhere to the prime directive of their own interpretive model. The typical originalist response to this plain reading is that such an open-ended construction of the Ninth Amendment turns it into a "bottomless well," from which the Court can dip for undreamed of rights at their limitless discretion. They attest that the Ninth Amendment's "certain rights" is an expression too vague and open to interpretation to mean anything at all. As such, judicial

section in this chapter illustrates, *Griswold* was the first in an important line of cases the Court decided in the eight-year period between 1965 and 1973 that either explicitly turned on the right to privacy or its related guarantee of liberty under the Fourteenth Amendment.

3. *Loving*, *Stanley*, *Eisenstadt*, and *Roe*

Two years after *Griswold*, the Court issued the landmark decision of *Loving v. Virginia*, which invalidated the nation's then-remaining miscegenation laws on both substantive due process and equal protection grounds.[154] The Court did not use the word "privacy" in its unanimous decision, but it nonetheless captured dimensions of the right to privacy when it held that laws banning interracial marriage "deprive all the State's citizens of liberty without due process of law" because "the freedom to marry or not marry . . . resides with the individual and cannot be infringed by the State."[155]

Two years after *Loving*, the Court decided *Stanley v. Georgia*.[156] The case overturned a law that had criminalized the "private possession of

---

> originalists declare the Ninth Amendment to be an "inkblot" on the constitutional text—something that, due to its obscurity, we should ignore entirely. However, to erase the Ninth Amendment is to engage in an act of violence to both the Constitution and the drafters' original intent behind the Ninth Amendment. Every word in the Constitution must have had some original public meaning.

McCarthy, *supra* note 132, at 360–61 (quoting Randy E. Barnett, *The Ninth Amendment: It Means What It Says*, 85 TEX. L. REV. 1, 5 (2006) (other internal citations omitted). *But see* Russell L. Caplan, *The History and Meaning of the Ninth Amendment*, 69 VA. L. REV. 223, 259–65 (1983) (arguing that the Ninth Amendment was intended to protect rights contained in state law (i.e., state constitutions, statutes., and common law) and, therefore, cannot appropriately form an independent federal basis for invalidating state laws).

154 Loving v. Virginia, 388 U.S. 1, 12 (1967).

155 *Id.* As law professor Sydney Buchanan noted, the *Loving* opinion did not directly link its holding to the right to privacy or even cite the *Griswold* decision, which was then just two years old. Buchanan, *supra* note 150, at 454. But the Court subsequently made that link explicit in *Zablocki v. Redhail*, in which the Court cited *Griswold* in support of its statement that "the right to marry is part of the fundamental 'right to privacy.'" 434 U.S. 374, 384 (1978) (invalidating a law that required people paying child support to getting married without first obtaining permission from a judicial officer)).

156 394 U.S. 557, 568 (1969).

obscene material."[157] The Court reasoned that, although there are important governmental interests at stake in regulating the creation, distribution, and sale of materials that may be obscene and, therefore, not subject to First Amendment protections, the same is not true regarding the possession of such materials in the privacy of one's own home.[158] Importantly, the case was not strictly decided on privacy grounds, as it presented concerns under the First and Fourth Amendments, as well.[159] With regard to the former, the Court emphasized that "[i]f the First Amendment means anything, it means that a State has no business telling a man, sitting alone in his own house, what books he may read or what films he may watch. Our whole constitutional heritage rebels at the thought of giving government the power to control men's minds."[160] Still, despite the confluence of different constitutional rights, the location of defendant's possession of obscene movies "in the *privacy* of [his] own home" contributed an "added dimension" to the case.[161]

Three years later, the Court extended *Griswold*'s central holding to unmarried couples in *Eisenstadt v. Baird*.[162] Although the Court stated in *Eisenstadt* that the right to privacy includes the individual's interest in making certain decisions that fundamentally affect his or her person "free from unwarranted governmental intrusion,"[163] the Justices did not rely on due process for their decision; rather, *Eisenstadt* was decided on equal protection grounds.[164]

---

157 *Id.* at 559.

158 *Id.* at 565.

159 *Id.* at 572.

160 *Id.*

161 *Id.* at 564 (emphasis added) ("For also fundamental is the right to be free, except in very limited circumstances, from unwanted governmental intrusions into one's privacy.").

162 405 U.S. 438, 453 (1972).

163 *Id.*

164 *Id.* at 453 ("[W]hatever the rights of the individual to access to contraceptives may be, the rights must be the same for the unmarried and the married alike. . . . If the right of privacy means anything, it is the right of the individual, married or single, to be free from unwarranted governmental intrusion into matters so fundamentally affecting a person as the decision whether to bear or beget a child.").

One year after its decision in *Eisenstadt*, the Court extended the right to privacy to "include[] the abortion decision" in *Roe v. Wade*.[165] Relying on a "line of decisions" recognizing a constitutional right to personal privacy—including *Botsford*, *Boyd*, *Meyer*, *Pierce*, *Griswold*, *Loving*, *Stanley*, and *Eisenstadt*[166]—*Roe* invalidated laws prohibiting abortions during the first trimester of pregnancy.[167] By contrast, the Court reasoned that the State's interest in the protection of "the potentiality of human life" during the third trimester of pregnancy (i.e., after a fetus is viable),[168] permits the regulation and even proscription of abortions "except when it is necessary to preserve the life or health of the mother."[169] The Court subsequently abandoned the trimester framework in *Planned Parenthood of Southeastern Pennsylvania v. Casey*,[170] but nonetheless reaffirmed *Roe*'s core holding that "a State may not prohibit any woman from making the ultimate decision to terminate her pregnancy before viability."[171] Although the Supreme Court overruled *Roe* and *Casey* in *Dobbs v. Jackson Women's Health Organization*,[172] those cases were "good law" at the time the Court reviewed and upheld the constitutionality of Georgia's sodomy law in *Bowers v. Hardwick*.[173]

D. Sodomy Laws and *Bowers v. Hardwick*'s Retreat from the Right to Privacy

In 1986, the U.S. Supreme Court strikingly departed from the line of privacy cases previously discussed when it notoriously upheld the constitutionality of sodomy laws in *Bowers v. Hardwick*.[174] The factual

---

165 410 U.S. 113, 154 (1973), *overruled by* Dobbs v. Jackson Women's Health Org., 142 S. Ct. 2228, 2242 (2022).

166 *Id.* at 152–53; *see generally supra* notes 133–164 and accompanying text.

167 *Roe*, 410 U.S. at 162–65.

168 *Id.* at 162.

169 *Id.* at 164.

170 505 U.S. 833, 874–76 (1992), *overruled by Dobbs*, 142 S. Ct. at 2242.

171 *Id.* at 879.

172 142 S. Ct. at 2242.

173 478 U.S. 186, 196 (1986).

174 *Id.*

background of the case suggests that homophobia played a significant role in the Justices' reasoning.[175]

1. Background Facts

To say the *Bowers v. Hardwick* decision is skimpy on the salient facts of the case would be quite the understatement. The Court simply stated that "[i]n August 1982, respondent Hardwick . . . was charged with violating the Georgia statute criminalizing sodomy by committing that act with another adult male in the bedroom of respondent's home."[176] But as Leslie Huff explained, the "little-known facts" of the case are important.[177] Relying on Peter Iron's interview with Michael Hardwick,[178] Huff reported that a police officer known for targeting LGBTQ+ people cited Hardwick for having an open can of beer by the doorway to the gay bar where he worked as a bartender.[179] The officer wrote conflicting information on the ticket. In one area, he underlined a hearing date on a Wednesday, but in smaller print on another part of the citation, he wrote a date corresponding to one day earlier, which fell on a Tuesday.[180] Thinking he did not need to be in court until Wednesday, Hardwick inadvertently missed his hearing on Tuesday, prompting the citing officer to obtain an arrest warrant for Hardwick.[181] Hardwick subsequently went to court to show the conflicting dates on the ticket and paid the fine due.[182]

---

175 *See supra* note 124 and accompanying text; *see also* Amy D. Ronner, *Homophobia: In the Closet and in the Coffin*, 21 LAW & INEQ. 65, 102–03 (2003) ("While the Georgia statute itself was gender-neutral, proscribing both homosexual and heterosexual sodomy, the *Bowers* Court read it as singling out only homosexual conduct. What the *Bowers* Court did was engraft criminalized conduct onto what it perceived as a homogenous group—homosexuals. In so doing, it personified sexual orientation as a menace to a wholesome society.").

176 *Bowers*, 478 U.S. at 187–88.

177 Leslye M. Huff, *Deconstructing Sodomy*, 5 AM. U. J. GENDER & L. 553, 561 (1997).

178 Peter Irons, *Interview with Michael Hardwick*, *in* LESBIANS, GAY MEN AND THE LAW 125, 125–31 (William Rubenstein ed., 1993).

179 Huff, *supra* note 177, at 561 (citing Irons, *supra* note 178, at 126).

180 *Id.* (citing Irons, *supra* note 178, at 126).

181 *Id.* (citing Irons, *supra* note 178, at 126).

182 *Id.* at 562 (citing Irons, *supra* note 178, at 126).

A few weeks later, the officer showed up at Hardwick's home at approximately 8:30am.[183] Because it was a hot morning during August, Hardwick had left his front door open for ventilation. The officer availed himself of that fact to enter the home, found Hardwick in his bedroom engaging in oral sex with his partner, and arrested them both.[184] The American Civil Liberties Union (ACLU) contacted Hardwick and convinced him to challenge the constitutionality of the Georgia's sodomy law, especially since the arrest took place in the privacy of his home.[185]

Prosecutors refused to move forward with the case in an attempt to prevent the ACLU from challenging the state's sodomy law.[186] Hardwick then filed a declaratory judgment action in federal district court in which he claimed he lived in fear of prosecution under the sodomy statute which, he argued, violated his rights to privacy, due process, and freedoms of expression and association.[187] The district court dismissed his complaint "for failure to state a claim, relying on *Doe v. Commonwealth's Attorney for the City of Richmond*," a 1975 federal district court case in which a three-judge panel upheld the constitutionality of Virginia's sodomy law and was summarily affirmed by the Supreme Court.[188] The U.S. Court of Appeals for the Eleventh Circuit reversed the district court, concluding that Georgia's sodomy law violated the rights to privacy and intimate association.[189] The State of Georgia then petitioned for certiorari and the U.S Supreme Court granted review.[190]

---

183 *Id.* (citing Irons, *supra* note 178, at 126).

184 *Id.* (citing Irons, *supra* note 178, at 127).

185 *Id.* at 563 (citing Irons, *supra* note 178, at 128).

186 *Id.* at 564 (citing Irons, *supra* note 178, at 128).

187 Brief of Petitioner Michael J. Bowers at *3, Bowers v. Hardwick, No. 85-140, 1985 WL 667939 (U.S. Dec. 17, 1985).

188 Bowers v. Hardwick, 478 U.S. 186, 188 (1986) (citing Doe v. Commonwealth's Att'y, 403 F. Supp. 1199 (E.D. Va. 1975), *summarily aff'd*, 425 U.S. 901 (1976)).

189 *Id.* (citing Hardwick v. Bowers, 760 F.2d 1202, 1212–13 (11th Cir. 1985), *rev'd*, 478 U.S. 186 (1986)). The Eleventh Circuit distinguished Hardwick's challenge from the one brought by the *Doe* plaintiffs by noting that they "had neither been arrested nor threatened with prosecution," unlike Michael Hardwick. Hardwick v. Bowers, 760 F.2d at 1207.

190 Bowers v. Hardwick, 474 U.S. 943 (1985) (granting certiorari). Some commentators were surprised by this "unexpected grant." Yao Apasu-Gbotsu et al., *supra* note 101, at 521. The editors of the *University of Miami Law Review* went on to say that "[i]t is

2. The *Bowers* Decision

The *Bowers* decision began by explaining that the issue presented in the case was not covered by the Court's privacy line of cases.[191] The Court distinguished cases like *Pierce*, *Meyer*, *Griswold*, *Loving*, and *Roe* as being limited to privacy rights as they impact child rearing, education, family relationships, marriage, and procreation.[192] Reasoning that "homosexual sodomy" did not concern any of these issues, the *Bowers* Court concluded such conduct lies outside the realm of the constitutional right to privacy those cases collectively represented.[193]

Having removed the case from the protections of the right to privacy, the majority in *Bowers* then cast the issue in the case as whether there was a "fundamental right to engage in homosexual sodomy."[194] The Court answered that question in the negative, reasoning that fundamental rights are those either "'implicit in the concept of ordered liberty,' such that 'neither liberty nor justice would exist if [they] were sacrificed'"[195] or those which are "deeply rooted in this Nation's history and tradition."[196] The Court concluded that neither formulation supported answering the question in the affirmative, especially since "proscriptions against that conduct have ancient roots."[197]

The dissenting Justices criticized the majority opinion in *Bowers* for having framed the issue much too narrowly:

> This case is no more about "a fundamental right to engage in homosexual sodomy[]" . . . than *Stanley v. Georgia* . . . was about a fundamental right to watch obscene movies, or *Katz v. United States* . . . was about a fundamental right to place interstate bets

---

our hope that what at first came as an unexpected surprise to our editorial board will result in an opinion offering greater insight into the proper scope of the right to privacy and its possible continued expansion into other areas of individual freedoms." *Id.* at 523. Their hopes were not realized.

191 *Bowers*, 478 U.S. at 190.

192 *Id.* (internal citations omitted)

193 *Id.* at 190, 191–92.

194 *Id.* at 191.

195 *Id.* at 191–92 (quoting Palko v. Connecticut, 302 U.S. 319, 325 (1937)).

196 *Id.* at 192 (quoting Moore v. City of E. Cleveland, 431 U.S. 494, 503 (1977)).

197 *Id.*

> from a telephone booth. Rather, this case is about "the most comprehensive of rights and the right most valued by civilized men," namely, "the right to be let alone." [198]

The dissent persuasively argued that the majority had failed to consider how sodomy laws infringe important privacy rights.[199] Many scholars were similarly critical of the Court's bizarrely narrow framing of the issue in the case.[200] Had the Court examined the issue through a broader right to privacy lens, it easily could have situated the case within the protections of *Griswold* and its progeny to conclude that consenting adults have a right "to engage in non-procreative sexual relations, even outside the traditional setting of marriage."[201]

---

198 *Id.* at 199 (Blackmun, Brennan, Marshall, and Stevens, J.J., dissenting) (internal citations omitted).

199 *Id.* at 206 ("[W]hat the Court really has refused to recognize is the fundamental interest all individuals have in controlling the nature of their intimate associations with others.").

200 *E.g.*, Richard D. Mohr, *Mr. Justice Douglas at Sodom: Gays and Privacy*, 18 COLUM. HUM. RTS. L. REV. 43, 44 (1986–1987) (arguing "why privacy should be viewed as a fundamental, substantive and quite general constitutional right, why gay sex falls under that right, and why it is important that this should be so recognized by the courts"); Thomas B. Stoddard, Bowers v. Hardwick*: Precedent by Personal Predilection*, 54 U. CHI. L. REV. 648, 651–52 (1987) ("[T]he majority went out of its way to reformulate the issue presented by the case in order to rebuke homosexual—an only homosexual—'sodomy.' The Georgia statutes covers oral or anal intercourse committed by any two people—homosexual or heterosexual, unmarried or married. . . . The Supreme Court, however, characterized the case as one concerning 'the fundamental rights of homosexuals,' and specifically postponed the issue of the statute's application to 'other acts of sodomy.' It reframed *Hardwick*, converting it from a 'sexual privacy' case to a 'gay rights' case.").

201 Fradella, *supra* note 51, at 282–83 (quoting B.J. Williamson, *The Constitutional Privacy Doctrine after* Bowers v. Hardwick*: Rethinking the Second Death of Substantive Due Process*, 62 S. CAL. L. REV. 1297, 1310 (1989)); *see also* Daniel O. Conkle, *The Second Death of Substantive Due Process*, 62 IND. L.J. 215, 236 (1987) ("In addressing 'deviant' sexual practices, the Supreme Court in *Bowers v. Hardwick* rendered a deviant judicial decision. The Court's decision is deviant because it is blatantly inconsistent with the Court's own precedents . . . . It is also perverse, because the constitutional claim rejected in *Bowers* was not merely of the same strength as the claim the Court accepted in *Roe*; it was substantially stronger."); David A.J. Richards, *Constitutional Legitimacy and Constitutional Privacy*, 61 N.Y.U. REV. 800, 860–61 (1986) ("Consistent with the Court's previous applications of constitutional privacy, blanket prohibitions on homosexual activity fail to satisfy the burden required for abridging the constitutional right to privacy. Like anti-contraception laws, the bans on homosexual sex force people to refrain from nonprocreative sex. The interest of

Scholars also criticized *Bowers* for resorting to a fundamental rights analysis that depends on what is deeply rooted in history and tradition.[202] After all, *Loving* invalided miscegenation laws despite the fact that such laws existed in many states for much of the nation's history.[203] *Griswold* and *Roe* similarly found behaviors to be within the scope of the right to privacy despite the fact that neither contraceptives nor abortion were rights deeply rooted in history and tradition.[204] The editors of the *Harvard Law Review* deconstructed this inconsistency as follows:

> [R]elying on history involves a value choice in that the Court selects which history it will base its decision on. The Court could have decided to rely on recent history: for example, a majority of states no longer outlaw sodomy, and homosexual leaders now occupy prominent positions in local, state, and federal elective office. The historic persecution of homosexuals should not have been used to deter the current societal trend of recognizing that individuals have a fundamental right to define their own sexual identities. Such reliance on past discrimination to justify future discrimination harkens back to the days when historical tradition was used to justify long-since condemned laws supporting slavery and the so-called separate but equal treatment of blacks.[205]

This criticism is well-taken because it illustrates how in the two decades preceding *Bowers*, "the mere longevity of a statute, even when the law fits into a legal pattern or 'tradition,' has never before been deemed a

---

autonomy in intimate homosexual relations is at least as strong as the reproductive autonomy in abortion decisions."); *cf.* Anne B. Goldstein, *History, Homosexuality, and Political Values: Searching for the Hidden Determinants of* Bowers v. Hardwick, 97 YALE L.J. 1073, 1079 (1988) ("If the Court understood Hardwick's sexual act as similar to other activities protected under the 'constitutional right of privacy,' his challenge should have succeeded.").

202 *E.g.*, Richards, *supra* note 201, at 850–51 ("The gravamen of Justice White's argument is an appeal to history. . . . It is difficult to regard this appeal to history as anything but disingenuous, since the Court's previous work in the area of constitutional privacy disavows such an anachronistic and indeed ahistorical interpretation of history.").

203 Stoddard, *supra* note 200, at 654.

204 Fradella, *supra* note 51, at 283; Stoddard, *supra* note 200, at 654.

205 Note, *Right to Privacy and Consensual Sodomy:* Bowers v. Hardwick, 100 HARV. L. REV. 210, 218–19 (1986).

bar to judicial intervention."[206] On the other hand, the criticism does not go far enough because it does not directly debunk the flawed presentation of history in *Bowers*' majority opinion.[207] As previously discussed, the alleged historical condemnation of sodomy—especially in the form of oral sex—is factually inaccurate.[208] It reflects one point in history while ignoring others. Consider philosopher Richard Mohr's criticism of the selective use of history in *Bowers*:

> Judges have no special insight to [history]; their job neither allows them time nor invokes the talents required for honing historical skills to a degree that might permit impartial findings—not even professional historians usually achieve that. Even for experts, [history] is controversial and as ideologically laden as any of the humanities and social sciences. Judges are as likely as any amateurs to pick and choose its variety in ways that fit their preconceived ends. Justice Burger's concurrence in *Bowers* provides a stellar case of this vice. He claims that "homosexual conduct [has] been subject to state intervention throughout the history of Western Civilization" and that to protect gay sex "would be to cast aside millennia of moral teaching." He cites but one historian and makes no mention of John Boswell's work on the history of gay people. Boswell thoroughly criticizes Burger's one source and shows that far from a uniform condemnation of gay sex "throughout the history of Western Civilization," over the largest stretch of that civilization—6th century [B.C.E.] to the 12th century [C.E.]—there were a large variety and considerable flux

206 Stoddard, *supra* note 200, at 655. In subsequent cases, the Court conceded that "[h]istory and tradition are the starting point but not in all cases the ending point of the substantive due process inquiry." Lawrence v. Texas, 539 U.S. 558, 572 (2003) (quoting Sacramento v. Lewis, 523 U.S. 833, 857 (1998) (Kennedy, J., concurring)).

207 In *Lawrence*, the Court acknowledged that in the wake of *Bowers*, scholars had written extensively about the "fundamental criticisms of the historical premises relied upon by the majority and concurring opinions" in Bowers as they related to assertions about the history of sodomy proscriptions. *Lawrence*, 539 U.S. at 567–68 (citations omitted).

208 Eskridge, *supra* note 72, at 1107 ("In truth, sodomy laws were rarely enforced before 1880, and almost never applied to sex between consenting adults, same-sex or otherwise; were understood as a regime for normalizing procreative sex, a goal now considered unconstitutional; and were authoritatively applied to oral sex (Michael Hardwick's crime) in not a single state before 1879."); *see also supra* notes 65–124 and accompanying text.

in the moral, social, legal and religious evaluation of gays and gay acts.[209]

3. The Aftermath

The decision in *Bowers* prompted an avalanche of criticism.[210] Scholars referred to its "venomous mean-spiritedness,"[211] called it "hateful and bigoted,"[212] described it as a "study of aggression" that serves as "a classic example of discrimination against a disfavored minority,"[213] and derided it as "rag[ing] irrationally against [homosexuality]" using rhetoric that "discursively makes and marks" sexual differences that "make[] homophobia possible."[214] Findlaw included *Bowers* on its list of the thirteen "most terrible, horrible, no good, very bad Supreme Court decisions" of all time.[215] Even the Supreme Court eventually

---

209 Mohr, *supra* note 200, at 67.

210 *E.g.*, James E. Fleming, *Constructing the Substantive Constitution*, 72 TEX. L. REV. 211, 270 (1993) ("In *Bowers*, however, the Court practically reduces the due process inquiry to a backward-looking question concerning historical practices . . . ."); Jamal Greene, *The Anticanon*, 125 HARV. L. REV. 379, 432 (2011) ("The analytic problems of the *B*owers majority opinion appear almost willful."); Andrea Sachs, *The Worst Supreme Court Decisions Since 1960*, TIME (Oct. 6, 2015, 11:36 AM), https://time.com/4056051/worst-supreme-court-decisions/ [https://perma.cc/6QLY-C26L] (quoting law professor Jamal Greene criticizing *Bowers* a saying "narrow-minded, cynical and offensive" and quoting law professor Kathryn Abrams as saying "it doesn't get much worse than this"); Stoddard, *supra* note 200, at 656 ("*Bowers v. Hardwick* is, fundamentally, lawmaking by personal predilection . . . a cavalier decision, without reference to either standard or principle and in blatant disregard of well-settled procedural rules.")

211 Valdes, *supra* note 14, 1391.

212 Sachs, *supra* note 210 (quoting law professor Ashutosh Bhagwat).

213 Janet Self, Bowers v. Hardwick*: A Study of Aggression*, 10 HUM. RTS. Q. 395, 395 (1988).

214 Kendall Thomas, *The Eclipse of Reason: A Rhetorical Reading of* Bowers v. Hardwick, 79 VA. L. REV. 1805, 1828 (1993).

215 Casey C. Sullivan, *13 Worst Supreme Court Decisions of All Time*, FINDLAW (Oct. 14, 2015 12:51 PM), https://www.findlaw.com/legalblogs/supreme-court/13-worst-supreme-court-decisions-of-all-time/ [https://perma.cc/B8ZE-X9QD]. This list places *Bowers* alongside other dubious cases, including *Dred Scott v. Sanford*, 60 U.S. (19 How.) 393, 393–94 (1857), which held that the U.S. Constitution did not grant citizenship to people of African descent, regardless of whether they were free or enslaved), *superseded by* U.S. CONST. amends. XIII & IV; *Buck v. Bell*, 274 U.S. 200, 207–08 (1927), which upheld the forced sterilization of intellectually disabled people; *Plessy v. Fergusson* , 163 U.S . 537, 551–52 (1896), *overruled by* Brown v. Board of

acknowledged that the "criticism of *Bowers* has been substantial and continuing, disapproving of its reasoning in all respects, not just as to its historical assumptions."[216]

Between 1961 and when *Bowers* was decided in 1986, about half of U.S. states decriminalized sodomy either through legislative repeal or through state court judicial action.[217] Beyond generating scathing critiques from scholars and commentators alike, *Bowers* triggered another, arguably more important response by mobilizing activists for LGBTQ+ rights.[218] As a result of their efforts, combined with advocacy that led some courts to invalidate their states' sodomy laws on state constitutional grounds,[219] twelve more states decriminalized sodomy between 1986 and 2003.[220] Thus, at the time *Lawrence v. Texas* was decided, thirteen states still

---

Educ. of Topeka, 347 U.S. 483, 495 (1954), which endorsed segregation; and *Korematsu v. United States*, 323 U.S. 214, 219–20 (1944), *abrogation recognized by* 584 F. Supp. 1406, 1420 (N.D. Cal. 1984) (grating Korematsu a writ of *coram nobis*, saying "Korematsu remains on the pages of our legal and political history. As a legal precedent it is now recognized as having very limited application. As historical precedent it stands as a constant caution that in times of war or declared military necessity our institutions must be vigilant in protecting constitutional guarantees."), which shamefully sanctioned internment camps for Japanese Americans during the Second World War.

216 Lawrence v. Texas, 539 U.S. 558, 560 (2003).

217 Bowers v. Hardwick, 478 U.S. 186, 193–94 (1986) ("[T]oday, [twenty-four] States and the District of Columbia continue to provide criminal penalties for sodomy performed in private and between consenting adults."(citing Yao Apasu-Gbotsu et al., *supra* note 101, at 524, n.9)); *see also* Fradella, *supra* note 51, at 285–86 tbl.1 (listing the status of sodomy laws).

218 *See, e.g.*, Melinda D. Kane, *Social Movement Policy Success: Decriminalizing State Sodomy Laws, 1969-1998*, 8 MOBILIZATION 313 (2003); Mitchell Lloyd Pearl, Note, *Chipping Away at* Bowers v. Hardwick: *Making the Best of an Unfortunate Decision*, 63 N.Y.U. L. REV. 154, 155 (1988) (citing *Antisodomy Laws Targeted for Repeal After High Court Ruling*, WASH. POST, Feb. 4, 1987, at A16)).

219 *See* Fradella, *supra* note 51, at 285–86 tbl.1 (citing, *inter alia*, Powell v. State, 510 S.E.2d 18, 26 (Ga. 1998) (invalidating the very law that *Bowers* had upheld); Commonwealth v. Wasson, 842 S.W.2d 487, 491–92 (Ky. 1992)).

220 Fradella, *supra* note 4, at 600; *see also Lawrence*, 539 U.S. at 573 ("The [twenty-five] States with laws prohibiting the relevant conduct referenced in the *Bowers* decision are reduced now to [thirteen]. . . .").

criminalized sodomy.[221] Those laws fell with the Supreme Court's decision in *Lawrence v. Texas.*[222]

E. *Lawrence v. Texas* Overturns *Bowers* and Ushers In a New Age of Liberty

Lawrence concerned two men who had been convicted of violating Texas' sodomy law after police entered John Lawrence's apartment and allegedly found him having sex with Tyron Garner.[223] Police showed up and entered the apartment in response to a complaint of a weapons disturbance.[224] It turns out there was no such disturbance. The story was fabricated by someone trying to harass Garner, perhaps out of a combination of jealousy and racism.[225] How the case unfolded is subject to debate, but there is credible evidence which suggests that the two men pled "no contest" to violating Texas' "homosexual conduct" law[226] and, through their attorneys, arranged to pay a fine just high enough to allow for an appeal in the hopes of the case being used to challenge the constitutionality of the statute.[227] The Court of Appeals of Texas affirmed their convictions over due process and equal protection challenges under the state and federal constitutions.[228] The Supreme Court reversed and, in

---

221 Fradella, *supra* note 4, at 600 ("This is fairly remarkable since, in the wake of the European Convention on Human Rights calling for the decriminalization of sodomy, many other countries in the free world—even former Soviet republics—had invalidated their sodomy laws in the last decade. Even staunchly religious Ireland had done so!"); *see also Lawrence*, 539 U.S. at 573 (citing Dudgeon v. United Kingdom, 45 Eur. Ct. H.R. (1981), at ¶ 52).

222 *Lawrence*, 539 U.S. at 578–79.

223 *Id.* at 562–63.

224 *Id.* at 562.

225 *See* Dale Carpenter, *The Unknown Past of* Lawrence v. Texas, 102 MICH. L. REV. 1464, 1479 (2004). Carpenter's article deconstructs the facts of the case by offering a convincing analysis as to why police accounts of what transpired are not credible. *Id.* at 1475–1508.

226 TEX. PENAL CODE ANN. § 21.06 (a) (West 2003).

227 Carpenter, *supra* note 225, at 1518–19.

228 Lawrence v. State, 41 S.W.3d 349 (Tex. App. 2001), *rev'd*, 539 U.S. 558 (2003), *dismissed on remand*, No. 14-99-00109-CR, 2003 WL 22453791, at *1 (Tex. App. Oct. 30, 2003) (reversing the original judgments of the trial court, ordering the complaints be dismissed, and entering judgments of acquittal).

doing so, invalidated the thirteen remaining sodomy laws in the United States.[229]

In the majority opinion, five Justices used sweeping language that evidenced strong support for LGBTQ+ rights. After a brief review of the landmark privacy cases summarized in Section C of this Chapter,[230] the *Lawrence* majority acknowledged that the framing of the issue in *Bowers* was mistaken in that it failed "to appreciate the extent of the liberty [interest] at stake."[231] *Lawrence* correctly recognized that sodomy laws do more than criminalize particular sex acts. They "have more far-reaching consequences, touching upon the most private human conduct, sexual behavior, and in the most private of places, the home," and, in doing so, such laws "seek to control a personal relationship that . . . is within the liberty of persons to choose without being punished as criminals."[232] The Court went on to state that "*Bowers* was not correct when it was decided" and, therefore, should be overruled.[233]

---

229 *Lawrence*, 539 U.S. at 574–75 (explaining that the Texas statute could be invalidated on equal protection grounds, but because such an approach would not reach more neutral sodomy laws—ones that are not just targeted at sexual activity between people of the same-sex, the Court opted to decide the case on due process grounds to protect "the substantive guarantee of liberty" infringed by all sodomy statutes).

230 *See supra* notes 133–171 and accompanying text.

231 *Lawrence*, 539 U.S. at 567.

232 *Id.*

233 *Id.* at 578. In overruling *Bowers*, the Court acknowledged that respect for precedent via "[t]he doctrine of *stare decisis* is essential to the respect accorded to the judgments of the Court and to the stability of the law. It is not, however, an inexorable command." *Id.* at 577 (citing Payne v. Tennessee, 501 U.S. 808, 828 (1991)).

> In *Casey* we noted that when a court is asked to overrule a precedent recognizing a constitutional liberty interest, individual or societal reliance on the existence of that liberty cautions with particular strength against reversing course. . . . The holding in *Bowers*, however, has not induced detrimental reliance comparable to some instances where recognized individual rights are involved. Indeed, there has been no individual or societal reliance on *Bowers* of the sort that could counsel against overturning its holding once there are compelling reasons to do so. *Bowers* itself causes uncertainty, for the precedents before and after its issuance contradict its central holding.

Id.

F. The Present Study: The Need to Evaluate the Impact of *Lawrence* as the U.S. Supreme Court Cuts Back on Privacy Rights by Overturning *Roe v. Wade*

As previously mentioned, the specific right announced in *Lawrence* is unclear.[234] Narrowly read, the liberty interest announced in *Lawrence* is for consenting adults to engage in acts of oral or anal sex, regardless of their marital status or sexual orientation. But the broad language used in the text of the opinion suggests a more far-reaching result. In 2003, I asked "did the Court really mean what it said with regard to morality not being a sufficient rational basis for upholding the constitutionality of legislation?"[235] I suggested the answer was probably "no," largely because of the Court's then-current stance on active euthanasia/assisted suicide, as well as the ongoing criminal regulation of incest, prostitution, and bigamy.[236] Since that time, others have written eloquent, in-depth analyses of how *Lawrence* impacts law criminalizing assisted suicide, incest, prostitution, and bigamy,[237] as well as its effect on other laws, regulations, and policies that might impinge on sexual privacy and intimate association rights.[238]

---

234 *See supra* notes 17–20 and accompanying text.

235 Fradella, *supra* note 4, at 604.

236 *Id.* at 604 –05 (citing Washington v. Glucksberg, 521 U.S. 702, 723–33 (1997)).

237 *See, e.g.*, Jonathan E. Amgott, *Post-*Windsor *Prospects for Morals Legislation: The Case of Polygamous Immigrants*, 26 STAN. L. & POL'Y REV. 513 (2015); Diana Hassel, *Sex and Death:* Lawrence*'s Liberty and Physician-Assisted Suicide*, 9 U. PA. J. CONST. L. 1003 (2007).

238 *See, e.g.*, J. Richard Broughton, *The Criminalization of Consensual Adult Sex After* Lawrence, 28 NOTRE DAME J.L. ETHICS & PUB. POL'Y 125, 132 (2014); H. Hunter Bruton, *The Questionable Constitutionality of Curtailing Cuckolding: Alienation-of-Affection and Criminal-Conversation Torts*, 65 DUKE L.J. 755 (2016); Richard Glover, *Can't Buy A Thrill: Substantive Due Process, Equal Protection, and Criminalizing Sex Toys*, 100 J. CRIM. L. & CRIMINOLOGY 555 (2010); LiJia Gong & Rachel Shapiro, *Sexual Privacy After* Lawrence v. Texas, 13 GEO. J. GENDER & L. 487 (2012); Matthew W. Green, Jr., Lawrence*: An Unlikely Catalyst for Massive Disruption in the Sphere of Government Employee Privacy and Intimate Association Claims,* 29 BERKELEY J. EMP. & LAB. L. 311 (2008); Y. Carson Zhou, *The Incest Horrible: Delimiting the* Lawrence v. Texas *Right to Sexual Autonomy*, 23 MICH. J. GENDER & L. 187 (2016); *cf.* Sara L. Dunski, *Make Way for the New Kid on the Block: The Possible Zoning Implications of* Lawrence v. Texas, 2005 U. ILL. L. REV. 847.

I similarly questioned how the case might impact LGBTQ+ rights under the Equal Protection Clause since *Lawrence* arguably invited the continued use of the lowest standard of review for constitutional scrutiny of laws making distinctions on the basis of sexual orientation.[239] Again, others have written insightfully on select cases raising such issues played out in the wake of *Lawrence*.[240] But as far as I can tell, no one has undertaken a systematic examination of *Lawrence*'s broad impact over the nearly two decades since it was decided. This study fills that void in the literature by examining the impact of *Lawrence v. Texas* in state courts beyond its immediate role decriminalizing certain sexual acts performed in private between consenting adults. Specifically, the study seeks to answer the following research questions:

1. What are the specific types of cases in which courts grapple with applying *Lawrence*? Are they limited primarily to cases presenting questions about sexual privacy or LGBTQ+ rights, or do the cases present other types of questions?
2. In what ways do courts accept litigants' attempts to broadly construe *Lawrence* in ways that embrace or expand privacy and liberty protections? Conversely, under what circumstances do courts reject such attempts by narrowly construing *Lawrence* in ways that limit privacy and liberty protections?
3. What extra-legal factors, if any, are related to how judges construe *Lawrence*? Are there geographical differences across the country? Are there differences by the sex, race, or political party of the judge?

Chapter 3 summarizes the research methods used to answer these research questions.

---

[239] Fradella, *supra* note 4, at 605–06.

[240] For instance, Strader and Hay examined how the discriminatory targeting of LGBTQ+ people in sting operations might run afoul *Lawrence*. J. Kelly Strader & Lindsey Hay, *Lewd Stings: Extending* Lawrence v. Texas *to Discriminatory Enforcement*, 56 AM. CRIM. L. REV. 465, 465 (2019).

Chapter 3:
Research Methods

A. Data Collection

This study examines the final outcomes in all civil and criminal cases, both published and unpublished, in U.S. state courts that cited *Lawrence v. Texas*. I included all cases decided after the release date of the decision in *Lawrence* in June of 2003 until December 31, 2021.[241] I obtained these cases using Westlaw by selecting the KeyCite "citing references" feature for *Lawrence* and then limiting the results to state court decisions.[242] That process yielded a total of 441 cases. All of these cases were read and coded by two researchers.[243]

I eliminated thirty cases because they were duplicates, often because the case was decided at multiple levels of the court system's hierarchy.[244]

---

241 The cut-off date was selected because data coding and analysis began during the spring of 2022, a process that continued through the summer of that year.

242 Because search results were limited to cases from U.S. state courts, this study does not analyze cases from tribal courts, U.S. commonwealths (Puerto Rico and the Northern Marianas Islands), and U.S. territories (Guam, American Samoa, U.S. Virgin Islands).

243 To ensure the reliability of my coding, a Ph.D. student employed as my research assistant also coded all of the cases. I reiterate my appreciation to Gerald Eastwood for his excellent assistance in this time-consuming and often tedious process.

244 State v. Arlene's Flowers, Inc., 389 P.3d 543 (Wash. 2017), *vacated and remanded*, 138 S. Ct. 2671 (2018); Brush & Nib Studio, LC v. City of Phoenix, 418 P.3d 426 (Ariz. Ct. App. 2018), *vacated in part*, 448 P.3d 890 (Ariz. 2019); Blumenthal v. Brewer, 24 N.E.3d 168 (Ill. App. Ct. 2014), *rev'd in part, vacated in part*, 69 N.E.3d 834 (Ill. 2016); Toghill v. Commonwealth, No. 2230–12–2, 2014 WL 545728 (Va. Ct. App. Feb.11, 2014), *aff'd* 768 S.E.2d 674 (Va. 2015); Jones v. Jones, 307 P.3d 598 (Utah Ct. App. 2013), *aff'd*, 359 P.3d 603 (Utah 2015); Fleming v. State, 376 S.W.3d 854 (Tex. App. 2012), *aff'd*, 455 S.W.3d 577 (Tex. Ct. Crim. App. 2014); Elane Photography, LLC v. Willock, 284 P.3d 428 (N.M. Ct. App. 2012), *aff'd*, 309 P.3d 53 (N.M. 2013), *cert. denied*, 572 U.S. 1046 (2014); People v. Hollins, No. 2–10–0051, (Ill. App. Ct. June 27, 2011), *aff'd*, 971 N.E.2d 504 (Ill.), *cert denied*, 568 U.S. 1002 (2012); State v. Hunt, 710 S.E.2d 339, 347 (N.C. Ct. App. 2011), *rev'd*, 722 S.E.2d 484

For example, I removed the decision of an intermediate court of appeals whenever a state court of last resort reviewed the case and issued a subsequent decision.[245] Similarly, even when a case remained at the same

---

(2012); Commonwealth v. Carey, 947 N.E.2d 1124 (Mass. App. Ct. 2011), *aff'd*, 974 N.E.2d 624 (Mass. 2012); Fleming v. State, 323 S.W.3d 540 (Tex. App. 2010), *vacated and remanded*, 341 S.W.3d 415 (Tex. Ct. Crim. App. 2011); State v. Coman, 214 P.3d 1198 (Kan. Ct. App. 2009), *rev'd*, 273 P.3d 701 (Kan. 2012); State v. Limon, 83 P.3d 229, 249 (Kan. Ct. App. 2004), *rev'd*, 122 P.3d 22 (Kan. 2005), *appeal after remand*, No. 96,013, 2007 WL 1042154 (Kan. Ct. App. Apr. 6 2007); People v. Scott, 54 Cal. Rptr. 3d 674 (Cal. Ct. App.), *vacated and remanded*, 169 P.3d 95 (Cal. 2007); *In re* Marriage Cases, 49 Cal. Rptr. 3d 675 (Cal. Ct. App. 2006), *superseded by* 149 P.3d 737 (Cal. 2006), *rev'd*, 183 P.3d 384 (Cal. 2008); *In re* R.L.C., 635 S.E.2d 1 (N.C. Ct. App. 2006), *aff'd*, 643 S.E.2d 920 (N.C.), *cert. denied*, 552 U.S. 1024 (2007); McDonald v. Commonwealth, 630 S.E.2d 754 (Va. Ct. App. 2006), *aff'd*, 645 S.E.2d 918 (Va. 2007); Hernandez v. Robles, 805 N.Y.S.2d 354 (Sup. Ct. App. Div. 2005), *aff'd*, 855 N.E.2d 1 (N.Y. 2006), *abrogated by* Obergefell v. Hodges, 576 U.S. 644 (2015); State v. Lowe, No. 2004CA00292, 2005 WL 1983964 (Ohio Ct. App. Aug. 15, 2005), *aff'd*, 861 N.E.2d 512 (Ohio), *cert. denied*, 552 U.S. 845 (2007); Lewis v. Harris, 875 A.2d 259 (N.J. Super. Ct. App. Div. 2005), *aff'd as modified*, 908 A.2d 196 (N.J. 2008); People v. Hofsheier, 11 Cal. Rptr. 3d 762 (Cal. Ct. App.); *superseded by* 91 P.3d 163 (Cal. 2004), *aff'd in part, rev'd in part*, 129 P.3d 29 (Cal. 2006); State v. Limon, 83 P.3d 229 (Kan. Ct. App. 2004), *rev'd*, 122 P.3d 22 (Kan. 2005); Deane v. Conaway, No. 24-C-04-005390, 2006 WL 148145, at *1 (Md. Cir. Ct. Jan. 20, 2006), *rev'd*, 932 A.2d 571 (2007), *opinion extended after remand*, (Md. Cir. Ct. 2008); Hernandez v. Robles, 794 N.Y.S.2d 579 (Sup. Ct.), *rev'd and vacated*, 805 N.Y.S.2d 354 (App. Div., 2005), *aff'd*, 855 N.E.2d 1 (N.Y. 2006); *In re* Coordination Proceeding, Special Title Rule 1550(c), No. 4365, 2005 WL 583129, at *9 (Cal. Super. Ct. Mar. 14, 2005), *aff'd in part, rev'd in part sub nom. In re* Marriage Cases, 49 Cal. Rptr. 3d 675 (Ct. App. 2006), *superseded by* 149 P.3d 737 (Cal. 2006), *rev'd*, 183 P.3d 384 (2008); Howard v. Child Welfare Agency Rev. Bd., No. CV 1999-9881, 2004 WL 3154530 (Ark. Cir. Ct. Dec. 29, 2004), *aff'd sub nom.* Dep't of Hum. Servs. & Child Welfare Agency Rev. Bd. v. Howard, 238 S.W.3d 1 (2006); Castle v. State, No. 04-2-00614-4, 2004 WL 1985215 (Wash. Super. Ct. Sept. 7, 2004), *rev'd sub nom.* Andersen v. King Cnty., 138 P.3d 963 (Wash. 2006); Andersen v. King County, No. 04–2–04964–4–SEA, 2004 WL 1738447 (Wash. Super. Ct. Aug. 4, 2004), *rev'd*, 138 P.3d 963 (Wash. 2006); Lewis v. Harris, No. MER–L–15–03, 2003 WL 23191114 (N.J. Super. Ct. Nov. 5, 2003).

245 For instance, the trial court in *Andersen v. King County* invalidated marriage laws as violative of the privileges and immunities clause and due process rights under the Washington State Constitution. 2004 WL 1738447, *11–12. That decision was reversed on direct appeal to the Washington Supreme Court. 138 P.3d 963 (2006), *abrogated by* Obergefell v. Hodges, 576 U.S. 644 (2015). The trial court's decision in *Anderson* briefly (and positively) discussed *Lawrence* as an example of how shifting societal views on sexuality call for re-evaluation of freedoms "in the context of 'an emerging awareness that liberty gives substantial protection to adult persons in deciding how to conduct their private lives in matters pertaining to sex.'" 2004 WL 1738447 at *2 (quoting Lawrence v. Texas, 139 U.S. 553, 52 (2003)). On appeal, the court cited *Lawrence* for the proposition that LGBTQ+ people were not a suspect class

level in a court system's hierarchy, I removed opinions that were superseded due to the original one being withdrawn or vacated and replaced by a subsequent decision of the same court.[246] After the removal of all such duplicates, 411 cases remained.

B. Data Coding and Analyses

Each of the 411 cases was analyzed using both quantitative and ethnographic content analysis.[247] Content analysis, broadly speaking, is "a formal system for doing something we all do informally rather frequently—draw conclusions from observations of content."[248] In contrast to informal observations, however, content analysis uses a systematic set of procedures "for making replicable and valid inferences from data to their context."[249]

Content analysis can be quantitative or qualitative. Quantitative content analysis involves an *a priori* design in which the manifest content of source material (here, judicial opinions) are coded for the presence or absence of predefined variables—or even the degrees to which those variables are manifest—and then those data are analyzed.[250] The approach is particularly useful for measuring the frequency and extent to which key

---

and, therefore, the rational basis test applied to the plaintiffs' challenge of the state's marriage laws. 138 P.3d 976 (citing *Lawrence*, 139 U.S. at 572). Because the latter decision was the final one in the case, it is the one coded in the present study; the trial court decision is not included in the study.

246 For instance, I removed *People v. Scott*, 54 Cal. Rptr. 3d 674 (2007), because it was superseded by *People v. Scott*, 68 Cal. Rptr. 3d 592 (2007); *see also* State v. Arlene's Flowers, Inc., 389 P.3d 543 (Wash. 2017) (removed due to subsequent history), *vacated*, 138 S. Ct. 2671 (2018), *aff'd on remand*, 441 P.3d 1203 (Wash. 2019) (included as final decision on merits), *cert. denied*, 141 S. Ct. 2884 (2021).

247 DAVID L. ALTHEIDE & CHRISTOPHER J. SCHNEIDER, QUALITATIVE MEDIA ANALYSIS (2d ed. 2013) (detailing the phases of qualitative content analysis); KIMBERLY A. NEUENDORF, THE CONTENT ANALYSIS GUIDEBOOK (2d ed. 2017).

248 Guido Hermann Stempel, III, *Content Analysis*, *in* MASS COMMUNICATION RESEARCH AND THEORY 209 (Guido Hermann Stempel, David Hugh Weaver & G. Cleveland Wilhoit eds., 2003).

249 KLAUS KRIPPENDORFF, CONTENT ANALYSIS: AN INTRODUCTION TO ITS METHODOLOGY 21 1980).

250 NEUENDORF, *supra* note 247, at 18.

variables are related.[251] This approach also offers the benefits of allowing for hypothesis testing and easy replicability.[252] By contrast, ethnographic content analysis is inductive; it is particularly appropriate when multiple cases are reviewed in an attempt to discover emergent patterns and differing emphases among and between the cases.[253] The present study employs both of these types of content analysis to provide comprehensive and rich insights into how state courts have applied *Lawrence*.

1. Exclusion of Irrelevant Cases

Of the 411 distinct state court cases, two researchers agreed that 104 should be excluded because, even though these cases cited *Lawrence*, they did so for reasons that had nothing to do with any of the research questions. These cases fell into one of the exclusion categories described in the remainder of this subsection.

a. *Lawrence* as an Example of an Invalided Criminal Law ($n = 12$)

In *Ibenyenwa v. State*,[254] a judge, who was concurring in part and dissenting in part, made the point that reasons of judicial economy would not justify convicting and punishing someone for an unconstitutional offense simply because the defendant had not made a facial challenge to the law at the trial court level.[255] That judge then wrote: "Surely this Court would not, after the Supreme Court's decision in *Lawrence v. Texas*, uphold a sodomy conviction today even though the defendant had not complained in the trial court about the unconstitutionality of the 'still in the books' sodomy statute."[256] The citation to *Lawrence* had nothing to do

---

251 *Id.* at 96–119 (discussing variable coding); *Id.* at 121–62 (discussing variable measurement).

252 *Id.* at 19–20.

253 ALTHEIDE & SCHNEIDER, *supra* note 247, at 12–13.

254 Ibenyenwa v. State, 367 S.W.3d 420, 422 (Tex. App. 2012) (stating holding that "a defendant may not raise for the first time on appeal a facial challenge to the constitutionality of a statute").

255 *Id.* at 427 (Dauphinot, J., concurring in part and dissenting in part).

256 *Id.* ; *see also* Karenev v. State, 281 S.W.3d 428, 440 (Tex. Crim. App. 2009) (using the identical language).

with the substance of the *Ibenyenwa* decision and, therefore is coded as "irrelevant" for the purposes of the present study.[257]

b. *Lawrence* as an Example of a "New Rule" Qualifying for Retroactive Application ($n = 8$)

When criminal laws or processes are declared unconstitutional, the retroactivity of such decisions may give rise to claims for collateral relief from convictions that predate the invalidation of the law at issue.[258] Cases presenting such claims by relying on *Lawrence*, even in part, are certainly be relevant to the present study and, therefore, would be included in the

---

[257] *See also* Hunsucker v. Fallin, 408 P.3d 599, 628 (Okla. 2017) (citing *Lawrence* as the sole example of a law invalidated under rational basis review of a substantive due process claim) (Wyrick, J., concurring in part and dissenting in part); *Ex parte* Chance, No. WR–81,136–01, 2014 WL 1796648, at *4 (Tex. Crim. App. May 7, 2014) (Keller, P.J., dissenting) (citing *Lawrence* as an example of a case involving conduct that cannot be constitutionally criminalize); Gillmor v. Summit Cnty., 246 P.3d 102, 111 (Utah 2010) (using sodomy laws as an example of an unconstitutional law that lingered on the books for many years before being invalidated in a case in which law caused harm to a particular plaintiff); Herrington v. United States, 6 A.3d 1237, 1244 (D.C. 2010) (citing *Lawrence* as an example of the facial invalidation of a law that lacks any "plainly legitimate sweep"); *Ex parte* Masonheimer, 220 S.W.3d 494, 515 (Tex. Crim. App. 2007) (citing *Lawrence* in a strong of cases to illustrate that the U.S. Supreme Court "is not averse to reassessing its prior precedent when appropriate"); State v. T.M., No. 35957-3-III, 2019 WL 5838086, at *9 (Wash. Ct. App. 2019) (citing *Lawrence* after saying that "courts have always reserved for the judiciary the prerogative to declare some crimes or criminal behavior unconstitutional"); People v. Smith, 89 N.E.3d 960, 967 (Ill. Ct. App. 2017) (using sodomy as an example of conduct that "was once criminalized and is now recognized as protected"), *abrogated by In re* N.G., 115 N.E.3d 102 (Ill. 2018); *In re* Care & Treatment of Williams, No. 99,235, 2009 WL 2762455, at *3 (Kan. Ct. App. 2009) ("[S]odomy is no longer a crime between consenting adults."), *rev'd*, 253 P.3d 327 (Kan. 2011); Gilliam v. McGrady, 673 S.E.2d 474, 480 (Va. Ct. App. 2009), *aff'd in part, rev'd in part*, 691 S.E.2d 797 (Va. 2010) (noting that the state's fornication law had previously been invalidated under *Lawrence*); Commonwealth v. Coleman, 854 A.2d 978, 983 (Pa. Super. Ct. 2004), *appeal granted in part, decision vacated in part*, 874 A.2d 1150 (Pa. 2005) (noting that at the time, the military could proscribe oral sex in private between consenting adults, whereas states could not do that after *Lawrence*); *cf.* N.G., 115 N.E.3d 102, 121 (Ill. 2018) (noting that another court had granted relief from a twenty-five year-old conviction for sodomy after the decision in *Lawrence* ruled such consensual conduct was constitutionally protected).

[258] *See* Teague v. Lane, 489 U.S. 288, 311 (1989) (stating that "a new rule should be applied retroactively if it places 'certain kinds of primary, private individual conduct beyond the power of the criminal law-making authority to proscribe'" (internal citations omitted)).

cases analyzed. However, sometimes arguments about retroactivity cite *Lawrence* as an example even though the holding and rationale of *Lawrence* have nothing to do with the claim being adjudicated. For instance, in *Commonwealth v. Reid*, the court grappled with whether the U.S. Supreme Court's decision in *Williams v. Pennsylvania*,[259] which concerned the due process implications of when a judge previously "had significant, personal involvement as a prosecutor in critical decisions regarding a defendant's case," qualified as a substantive rule such that it needed to be given retroactive effect on collateral review.[260] By way of example, the court cited *Muth v. Frank*, a Seventh Circuit decision holding that *Lawrence* had announced a substantive rule that must be given retroactive effect.[261] But nothing in *Reid* had anything to do with *Muth* or *Lawrence*, rendering *Reid* irrelevant to the present study.[262]

---

259 Williams v. Pennsylvania, 579 U.S. 1, 8 (2016).

260 Commonwealth v. Reid, 235 A.3d 1124, 1181–82 (Pa. 2020) ("The remaining question is whether the precise due process rule established in *Williams* qualifies as a substantive rule within the meaning of *Teague*. The clearest example of a substantive rule is one holding that certain conduct cannot be criminalized. . . . [But there] is no doubt that Reid was convicted for conduct that the States may validly punish.").

261 *Id.* at 1182 ("Muth v. Frank, 412 F.3d 808, 817 (7th Cir. 2005) (recognizing that the decision in *Lawrence v. Texas* . . . barring criminalization of sodomy would apply retroactively under *Teague*).").

262 *See also* Commonwealth v. Olson, 218 A.3d 863, 871 (Pa. 2019) (distinguishing blood test refusal from sodomy and flag burning as examples of behaviors "beyond the government's power to criminalize" that would trigger retroactivity under *Teague*); *In re* N.G., 115 N.E.3d 102 (Ill. 2018); Schwartz v. State, 361 P.3d 1161, 1186 (Haw. 2015) (describing *Lawrence*'s overruling of *Bowers* as the "paradigm" case that creates a new rule); Bush v. State, 428 S.W.3d 1, 17 (Tenn. 2014) (distinguishing procedural change in rule governing statute of limitations tolling from *Lawrence*'s rule that "private individual conduct [was] beyond the power of the criminal law-making authority to proscribe"); Shrove v. State, 329 So. 3d 93, 99 (Ala. Crim. App. 2020) (citing *Lawrence* as an example when the court would "apply retroactively on collateral review a new rule that prohibits the punishment of certain primary conduct"); Sayles v. State, No. E2018-00141-CCA-R3-PC, 2019 WL 1417873, at *7 (Tenn. Crim. App. Mar. 28, 2019) (same); Kemmer v. State, No. A04-1913, 2005 WL 2277253, at *3 (Minn. Ct. App. Sept. 20, 2005) (rejecting a challenge to a sodomy law conviction because a privacy-rights challenge would not have been a "novel" claim justifying post-conviction relief under state law retroactivity principles and case law).

c. *Lawrence* as a General Example of Fourteenth Amendment Principles ($n = 32$)

Jones v. Jones cited *Lawrence* in a footnote following this sentence: "When the court has recognized a due process right it deems 'fundamental," it consistently has applied a standard of strict scrutiny to the protection of such a right.'"[263] Any U.S. Supreme Court case explaining that fundamental rights are reviewed using strict scrutiny could have been cited here. Indeed, the court in *Jones* also cited *Reno v. Flores* immediately after the cite to *Lawrence*.[264] Such citations stand in contrast to cases adjudicating Fourteenth Amendment claims by substantively relying on *Lawrence*. For instance, if a court ruled that the rational basis test was applicable because *Lawrence* did not announce a fundamental right for due process purposes, or because *Lawrence* did not declare LGBTQ+ people to be either suspect or quasi-suspect classes for equal protection analyses, then such cases are relevant and included in the study.[265] But when courts cite *Lawrence* for merely announcing general Fourteenth Amendment principles for which other cases could have been cited instead, as in *Jones*, those cases were excluded from the study.[266]

---

[263] 359 P.3d 603, 609 n.5 (Utah 2015) ("*See, e.g.*, Lawrence v. Texas, 539 U.S. 558, 593 . . . (2003) ('Our opinions applying the doctrine known as "substantive due process" hold that the Due Process Clause prohibits States from infringing fundamental liberty interests, unless the infringement is narrowly tailored to serve a compelling state interest.')").

[264] *Id.* (citing Reno v. Flores, 507 U.S. 292, 301–02 (1993)); *see also* Doe v. Phillips, 194 S.W.3d 833, 844 n.8 (Mo. 2006) ("The right to privacy is fundamental. *Lawrence* . . . .").

[265] *See, e.g.*, Hawkins v. Grese, 809 S.E.2d 441, 447 (Va. Ct. App. 2018); *see generally infra* Chapter 5.

[266] *See also* Rowitz v. McClain, 138 N.E.3d 1241, 1257 (Ohio 2019); State v. Webb, 144 So. 3d 971, 977–78 (La. 2014); Raynor v. State, 99 A.3d 753, 772 (Md. 2014); Vision Mining, Inc. v. Gardner, 364 S.W.3d 455, 483 (Ky. 2011); Neifert v. Dep't of Env't, 910 A.2d 1100, 1112 (Md. 2006); State v. Seering, 701 N.W.2d 655, 664 (Iowa 2005); Ferdon *ex rel.* Petrucelli v. Wisconsin Patients Comp. Fund, 701 N.W.2d 440, 460 (Wis. 2005), *overruled by* Mayo v. Wisconsin Injured Patients & Fams. Comp. Fund, 914 N.W.2d 678 (Wis. 2018); Wagner v. AGW Consultants, 114 P.3d 1050, 1063 (N.M. 2005); Montoy v. State, 120 P.3d 306, 317 (Kan. 2005); Woods v. Commonwealth, 142 S.W.3d 24, 55 (Ky. 2004); Nixon v. Commonwealth, 839 A.2d 277, 287 (Pa. 2003); *In re* Detention of Cubbage, 671 N.W.2d 442, 447 (Iowa 2003); Harrison v. Vanderkooi, No. 330537, 2017 WL 2262889, at *8 (Mich. Ct. App. May 23, 2017), *rev'd in part sub nom.* Johnson v. Vanderkooi, 918 N.W.2d 785 (Mich.

d. *Lawrence* Cited as an Example of *Stare Decisis* Principles ($n = 36$)

As previously discussed, *Lawrence* overruled *Bowers v. Hardwick.*[267] Courts sometimes cite *Lawrence* as an example of a case in which the U.S. Supreme Court overturned one of its own precedents, often quoting from

---

2018); People v. Noyan, 181 Cal. Rptr. 3d 601, 610 (Ct. App. 2014); People v. Novie, 976 N.Y.S.2d 636, 646 (Sup. Ct. App. Term 2013); People v. Martinez, No. H033918, 2009 WL 3777413, at *8 (Cal. Ct. App. Nov. 12, 2009); People v. Delacy, 122 Cal. Rptr. 3d 216, 231 (Ct. App. 2011); People v. Rotroff, 100 Cal. Rptr. 3d 558, 569 (Ct. App. 2009), *review granted and opinion superseded*, 223 P.3d 1 (Cal. 2010); People v. Castellanos, No. H032865, 2009 WL 2438434, at *19 (Cal. Ct. App. Aug. 11, 2009); State *ex rel.* Branson v. Fabian, No. A09-0814, 2009 WL 2447531, at *2 (Minn. Ct. App. Aug. 11, 2009); Cendant Corp. v. Dep't of Revenue, 226 P.3d 1102, 1111 (Colo. App. 2009); State Route 4 Bypass Auth. v. Superior Ct., 64 Cal. Rptr. 3d 286, 299 (Ct. App. 2007); Buckner v. Fam. Servs. of Cent. Fla., Inc., 876 So. 2d 1285, 1288 (Fla. Dist. Ct. App. 2004).

In addition to mere mention of Fourteenth Amendment standards of review, this category also includes cases that simply reference—but do not apply—the fact that, at the time a case was decided, due process protected the right to privacy as it relates to "personal decisions relating to marriage, procreation, contraception, family relationships, child rearing, and education." People v. Calderon, No. H030215, 2007 WL 1683576, at *6 (Cal. Ct. App. June 12, 2007) (upholding the admission of inculpatory statements a father made to a social worker about his sexual abuse of a toddler); *see also* Gutraj v. Dep't of Fin. & Pro. Regul., No. 4–12–1096, 2013 WL 5777170, at *5 (Ill. Ct. App. Oct. 24, 2013) (differentiating privacy due process cases from plaintiff's claim that he was entitled to a hearing before the termination of his certified public accounting license); State v. Odell, No. 105,311, 2013 WL 310335, *15 (Kan. Ct. App. Jan. 18, 2013) (citing *Lawrence* as an example of a substantive due process decision in a case raising both procedural and substantive due process concerns for failing to have provided correctional officer with written notice of prohibited conduct that would give rise to potential criminal liability); People v. Gonzales, 120 Cal. Rptr. 3d 911, 927 (Ct. App. 2011) (listing, in an informational privacy dispute involving the release of psychotherapy records, the ways in which courts have applied the right to privacy), *rev'd*, 296 P.3d 945 (Cal. 2013); *In re* J.R., 171 S.W.3d 558, 570 n.5 (Tex. App. 2005); Proceeding for the Appointment of a Guardian for Leon, No. 2016–XXXX, 2016 WL 5724234, at *3 (N.Y. Sur. Ct. 2016) (noting the appointment of a guardian engenders the potential loss of fundamental liberty interests regarding "self-determination, privacy, and autonomy" and, therefore, warrants the appointment of counsel); *In re* Zhuo, 53 Misc. 3d 1121, 1127 (N.Y. Sur. Ct. 2016) (same); *In re* V.R., No. NN 5616-04, 2004 WL 3029874, at *5 (N.Y. Fam. Ct. 2004) (directing the reader to compare the leading privacy rights cases in a decision ordering an unfit mother to conceive no more children until such time as she remained those in the care of others); *In re* Bobbijean P., No. 03626-03, 2004 WL 834480 (N.Y. Fam. Ct. 2004), *vacated in part*, 842 N.Y.S.2d 826 (App. Div. 2007) (same).

267 *See supra* notes 231–233 and accompanying text.

Lawrence that although *stare decisis* is important, it is not "an inexorable command."[268] But *Lawrence* was not the first case to use such language. For instance, courts could cite *Payne v. Tennessee*, which stated "[*s*]*tare decisis* is not an inexorable command; rather, it 'is a principle of policy and not a mechanical formula of adherence to the latest decision.'"[269] Cases in which courts cited *Lawrence* in this manner were removed because such citations are not relevant to any of this study's research questions.[270]

---

268 Lawrence v. Texas, 539 U.S. 558, 577 (2003).

269 Payne v. Tennessee, 501 U.S. 808, 828 (1991) (quoting Helvering v. Hallock, 309 U.S. 106, 119 (1940)).

270 *See In re* Commitment of C.S., 940 N.W.2d 875, 895 (Wis. 2020) (Bradley, J., dissenting); Hilburn v. Enerpipe Ltd., 442 P.3d 509, 517 (Kan. 2019); Ray v. Swager, 903 N.W.2d 366, 393 (Mich. 2017) (Wilder, J., dissenting); State v. Lynch, 885 N.W.2d 89, 104 (Wis. 2016); State v. Peeler, 140 A.3d 811, 876 (Conn. 2016); Quinn v. Quinn, 137 A.3d 423, 438 (N.J. 2016) (Albin, J., dissenting); State v. Witt, 126 A.3d 850, 868 (N.J. 2015); Hernandez v. Banks, 65 A.3d 59, 65 (D.C. 2013); Miller v. Johnson, 289 P.3d 1098, 1141 (Kan. 2012) (Beier, J., concurring in part and dissenting in part), *abrogated by* Hilburn v. Enerpipe Ltd., 442 P.3d 509 (Kan. 2019); League of Women Voters Minn. v. Ritchie, 819 N.W.2d 636, 684 (Minn. 2012) (Anderson, J., dissenting); State v. Swick, 279 P.3d 747, 754 (N.M. 2012); Home Paramount Pest Control Companies, Inc. v. Shaffer, 718 S.E.2d 762, 766 (Va. 2011); O'Neal v. St. John Hosp. & Med. Ctr., 791 N.W.2d 853, 868 (Mich. 2010) (Weaver, J., concurring); Regents of Univ. of Mich. v. Titan Ins. Co., 791 N.W.2d 897, 908 (Mich. 2010), *overruled by* Joseph v. Auto Club Ins. Ass'n, 815 N.W.2d 412 (Mich. 2012); Bezeau v. Palace Sports & Ent., Inc., 795 N.W.2d 797, 808 n.3 (Mich. 2010) (Weaver, J., concurring); McCormick v. Carrier, 795 N.W.2d 517, 535 (Mich. 2010); Lansing Sch. Educ. Ass'n v. Lansing Bd. of Educ., 792 N.W.2d 686, 696 (Mich. 2010); People v. Feezel, 783 N.W.2d 67, 84 (Mich. 2010); People v. Petrenko, 931 N.E.2d 1198, 1212 (Ill. 2010); State v. Bodyke, 933 N.E.2d 753, 762 (Ohio 2010); State v. Pena-Flores, 965 A.2d 114, 140 (N.J. 2009), *abrogated by* State v. Witt, 126 A.3d 850 (N.J. 2015); Oberhand v. Dir., Div. of Tax'n, 940 A.2d 1202, 1213 (N.J. 2008); State v. Lawrence, 920 A.2d 236, 265 (Conn. 2007); State v. Brown, 919 A.2d 107, 118 (N.J. 2007); Matheney v. Commonwealth, 191 S.W.3d 599, 625 (Ky. 2006); State v. Marsh, 102 P.3d 445, 463 (Kan. 2004), *rev'd and remanded*, 548 U.S. 163 (2006); State v. J.P., 907 So. 2d 1101, 1109 (Fla. 2004); State v. Brown, 156 S.W.3d 722, 731 (2004); Vitro v. Mihelcic, 806 N.E.2d 632, 640 (Ill. 2004) (Fitzgerald, J., dissenting); Westfield Ins. Co. v. Galatis, 797 N.E.2d 1256, 1268 n.5 (Ohio 2003); Ramirez v. Bank of America, N.A., 627 S.W.3d 486, 493 (Tex. App. 2021); Durden v. State, 290 S.W.3d 413, 423 (Tex. App. 2009); Hammon v. State, 809 N.E.2d 945, 950 n.2 (Ind. Ct. App. 2004), *vacated*, 829 N.E.2d 444 (Ind. 2005), *rev'd and remanded sub nom.* Davis v. Washington, 547 U.S. 813 (2006); Harvey v. City of Newark, No. CIV. A. 5023-VCS, 2010 WL 4240625, at *7 n.43 (Del. Ch. Oct. 20, 2010).

e. **Other Irrelevant Cases** ($n = 16$)

Several cases cited *Lawrence* for "one-off" reasons that were not repeated in a significant number of other cases. Such citations include using *Lawrence* as an example of (1) a court rejecting the framing of an issue as being too narrow;[271] (2) a case that relied on social science research;[272] (3) a rare case in which en banc reconsideration had been granted by a state appellate court;[273] (4) substantive due process being used to invalidate a law;[274] (5) a case in which a *pro se* prisoner cited *Lawrence* in support of a post-conviction petition without connection to the facts of the case;[275] (6) how perceptions of legality change over time;[276] (7) the importance of being represented by counsel in misdemeanor

---

[271] Mays v. Governor of Mich., 954 N.W.2d 139, 138 n.1 (Mich. 2020) (McCormack, C.J., concurring).

[272] State v. Brown, 945 N.W.2d 584, 606 n.7 (Wis.), *cert. denied*, 141 S. Ct. 881 (2020) (Dallet, J., dissenting); State v. Roberson, 935 N.W.2d 813, 834 n18 (Wis. 2009) (Dallet, J., dissenting); State v. Trammell, 928 N.W.2d 564, 586 (Wis. 2019) (Dallet, J., concurring).

[273] Texas Dep't of Fam. & Prot. Servs. v. Grassroots Leadership, Inc., NO. 03-18-00261-CV, 2019 WL 6608700, *2 (Tex. App. Dec. 5, 2019) (Triana, J., dissenting).

[274] Palmer v. Atl. Coast Pipeline, LLC, 801 S.E.2d 414, 421 (Va. 2017).

[275] State v. Tom, No. 2 CA-CR 2016-0088-PR, 2016 WL 1601706, at *1–2 (Ariz. Ct. App. Apr. 20, 2016) ("[Petitioner] claimed his prosecution was 'time barred by the statute of limitations,' no reasonable jury could have found him guilty beyond a reasonable doubt, and there had been several significant changes in the law applicable to his case, specifically . . . *Lawrence* . . . [but] has not developed on review any argument that *Lawrence* . . . appl[ies] to his case.").

[276] In *Nonhuman Rts. Project, Inc. ex rel. Hercules & Leo v. Stanley*, 49 Misc. 3d 746, 772–73, 16 N.Y.S.3d 898, 917 (N.Y. Sup. Ct. 2015), animal rights activists sought a writ of habeas corpus on behalf of two chimpanzees held in custody of a university. In denying the writ, the court wrote:

> The similarities between chimpanzees and humans inspire the empathy felt for a beloved pet. Efforts to extend legal rights to chimpanzees are thus understandable; some day they may even succeed. Courts, however, are slow to embrace change, and occasionally seem reluctant to engage in broader, more inclusive interpretations of the law, if only to the modest extent of affording them greater consideration. As Justice Kennedy aptly observed in *Lawrence v. Texas*, albeit in a different context, "times can blind us to certain truths and later generations can see that laws once thought necessary and proper in fact serve only to oppress."

Id. (quoting Lawrence v. Texas, 539 U.S. 558, 579 (2003)).

proceedings;[277] (8) how appellate rulings on state constitutions provisions have impacted subsequent U.S. Supreme Court decisions;[278] (8) courts having noted that sex offender registration requirements are not trivial collateral consequences of sex crime convictions;[279] (9) a victimless crime;[280] (10) asking a rhetorical question;[281] (11) the fact that legislatures do not need to draft statutes with logical consistency in every application;[282] and (12) the impropriety of a dismissal with prejudice when a police officer is late to court in a case where there had been no prior continuances;[283] and (13) a criminal statute with a history of nonenforcement.[284]

---

[277] State v. Young, 863 N.W.2d 249, 280 (Iowa 2015) (citing *Lawrence* as an example supporting the assertion that "the history of our jurisprudence is rife with very complicated and important legal questions arising in the context of misdemeanor prosecutions. . . .").

[278] State v. Baldon, 829 N.W.2d 785, 819 (Iowa 2013) (noting that a Georgia Supreme Court ruling contributed to the *Lawrence*'s overruling of *Bowers*).

[279] Barnes v. State, 31 A.3d 203, 211 (Md. 2011).

[280] State v. Matthews, No. M2010-02601-CCA-R3CD, 2011 WL 3798873, at *5 (Tenn. Crim. App. Aug. 26, 2011).

[281] Gunn v. Mariners Church, Inc., No. G032304, 2005 WL 1253953, at *11 (Cal. Ct. App. May 27, 2005) ("Pray tell, is Justice Scalia 'known to be homophobic" for having dissented in *Lawrence* . . .? Try that at your next dinner party if you don't want to tackle the question of whether the Catholic Church, or any other sector of traditional Judaism, Islam, or Christianity is 'homophobic.'").

[282] Carl J. Battaglia, M.D., P.A. v. Alexander, 177 S.W.3d 893, 914 (Tex. 2005) (quoting Justice Scalia's dissent in *Lawrence* that "people, unlike judges, need not carry things to their logical conclusion").

[283] State v. Toll, No. 95,713, 2007 WL 519040, at *1 (Kan. Ct. App. Feb. 16, 2007) (reversing dismissal in a case where the defendant was charged with sodomy, but the decision had nothing to do with the crime, but rather a determination that a dismissal with prejudice was an abuse of discretion because the trial court did not consider any less severe means of sanctioning the prosecution, "like granting a continuance with a warning, or dismissing the case without prejudice.").

[284] State v. Johnson, 425 S.W.3d 542, 553 (Tex. App. 2014), *aff'd*, 475 S.W.3d 860 (Tex. Crim. App. 2015) (nothing that "a lack of challenged convictions (or arrests for that matter)" did not necessary "disprove that the statute's scope has had a chilling effect on individuals' decisions to engage in what is known as constitutionally protected conduct").

2. Quantitative Coding and Analyses

After the removal of the irrelevant cases, the number of relevant state court cases stood at 307. All of these cases relied on *Lawrence* for a substantive reason—meaning that one party to the litigation sought to have a court apply *Lawrence* to the facts of the case at bar or, alternatively, that a court felt *Lawrence*'s holding or rationale provided some support, if meaningful guidance, to deciding the particular case. Each of these judicial opinions was coded for all of the variables presented in Table 1.

TABLE 1: STUDY VARIABLES

VARIABLE NAME	DESCRIPTION
Dependent Variables	
Outcome	Dichotomous variable indicating resolution of a criminal or quasit-criminal case in favor of (1) prosecution, or (2) defense
Treatment	Trichotomous variable: (1) neutral, (2) narrow/limiting, (3) broad/expansive

TABLE 1: STUDY VARIABLES (con't)

Independent Variables	
Case Type	Civil or criminal
Depth	Dichotomous variable indicating the depth of treatment *Lawrence* received as being either (1) mentioned in passing, or (2) key to case
Party	Dummy categories were created to indicate whether the judge writing an opinion (1) ran for office in a nonpartisan election, or either ran for partisan officer or was appointed by a (2) democrat or (3) republican
Race	Dummy categories were created to indicate the race and ethnicity of the judge writing an opinion: (1) Non-Hispanic White; (2) Asian/Pacific Islander; (3) African-American/Black; (4) Hispanic/Latino; and (5) Native American
Region	Dummy categories were created for the geographical region of the country based on U.S. Census regions: (1) Northeast,[285] (2) Midwest,[286] (3) South,[287] and (4) West[288]
State Political Identity	Dummy categories were created for the "color" of a state based on the candidate for whom the state voted in the 2008, 2012, 2016, and 2020 presidential elections: (1) deep red,[289] (2) light red,[290] (3) purple,[291] (4) light blue,[292] and (5) deep blue[293]
Sex	Dummy categories were created for the sex of the judge writing an opinion: (1) male or (2) female[294]

---

285 The Northeast includes New England (CT, MA, ME, NH, RI, VT) and the Mid-Atlantic (NJ, NY, and PA). *Census Regions and Divisions of the United States*, U.S. CENSUS BUREAU, https://www2.census.gov/geo/pdfs/maps-data/maps/reference/us_regdiv.pdf [https://perma.cc/LT7J-EUE8] [hereinafter *Census Regions*] (last visited June 13, 2022), at 1.

286 The Midwest includes the East North Central division (IL, IN, MI, OH, and WI) and the West North Central division (IA, KS, MN, MO, NE, ND, and SD). *Id.* at 1.

287 The South includes the South Atlantic division (DC, DE, FL, GA, MD, NC, SC, VA, and WV), the East South-Central division (AL, MS, KY, TN), and the West South-Central division (AR, LA, OK, and TX). *Id.* at 1.

288 The West include the Mountain division (AZ, CO, ID, MT, NV, NM, UT, and WY)) and the Pacific division (AK, CA, HI, OR, and WA). *Id.* at 1.

289 AK, AL, AR, ID, KS, KY, LA, MO, MS, MT, ND, NE, OK, SC, SC, TN, TX, UT, WV, and WY.

290 AZ, GA, IN, and NC.

291 FL, IA, and OH.

292 MI, PA, and WI.

293 CA, CO, CT, DC, DE, HI, IL, MA, MD, ME, MN, NH, NJ, NM, NV, NY, OR, RI, VA, VT, and WA.

294 I respectfully acknowledge that this coding scheme has the potential to erase nonbinary and intersex people. But as far as I could tell, none of the judges writing any of the opinions analyzed in the current study identified as either. The Victory Fund, an LGBTQ+ political advocacy organization, reports that it the first nonbinary person ever

a. Coding of Variables

The *outcome* variable refers to the outcome of a case—namely whether an opinion ruled in favor of one party or the other. In criminal cases, the data are evident from the text of the cases themselves. Although the same is true in civil cases, it is unclear what an outcome in favor of the plaintiff or defense means, depending on who filed the cause of action and what they were seeking. For instance, in collateral attacks on criminal convictions or declaratory judgment actions seeking the invalidation of criminal laws, the plaintiff is someone who was or could be a defendant in a criminal case and an outcome in favor of such a plaintiff has the effect of an outcome for a criminal defendant in direct appeals. Accordingly, the outcome in all such civil cases that are quasi-criminal in nature are coded such that an outcome that favors the state are coded as wins for the prosecution and outcomes that favor plaintiff/petitioners challenging a criminal conviction or the constitutionality of criminal laws are coded as defense victories.

In contrast to criminal and quasi-criminal cases where the outcome clearly benefits the state or a criminal defendant, the outcome of civil cases that do not involve questions of criminal law or procedure do not indicate much. For instance, the plaintiffs in some of the civil cases sought expansion of civil rights in ways that benefited LGBTQ+ people—often by arguing for broad or expansive interpretations of *Lawrence*. But in family law disputes, the plaintiff is whoever filed first, some of whom sought narrow constructions of *Lawrence*. Thus, the coding for the outcomes of civil cases is meaningless; the *treatment* variable is far more salient in such cases than which party prevailed.

As for *treatment*, cases were coded in one of three ways. Cases were coded as having "narrow" treatment of *Lawrence* if a judicial opinion narrowly construed *Lawrence* such that it was either (1) unwilling to

---

elected to judicial office in the United States did not occur until November of 2021 and that person did not author any of the opinions in the current study. *See Xander Orenstein Is First Non-Binary Person Elected to a Judicial Position in the United States*, LGBTQ+ VICTORY FUND (Nov. 2, 2021), https://victoryfund.org/news/xander-orenstein-is-first-non-binary-person-elected-to-a-judicial-position-in-the-united-states/ [https://perma.cc/NWR5-TH8J]. Additionally, I could identify no news source reporting that an openly nonbinary person had been appointed to judicial office.

extend *Lawrence* to protect claims of liberty or privacy rights, (2) criticized or disregarded *Lawrence*, or (3) distinguished *Lawrence* to render it inapplicable to claims of liberty or privacy rights. Cases were coded as having "broad" treatment of *Lawrence* if a judicial opinion expansively interpreted *Lawrence* to protect liberty or privacy rights. Finally, cases coded as "neutral" either involved (1) a straightforward application of *Lawrence*'s specifically articulated exclusions from its central holding—such as alleged claims of sexual privacy involving minors, nonconsensual acts, commercial sex, or sex acts in public; or (2) those in which *Lawrence* was cited or briefly discussed, but not relied upon in any outcome-determinative manner. Again, to ensure the reliability of this coding scheme, my research assistant and I coded these cases independently.

b. Coding of Independent Variables

Some of this coding was accomplished simply by reading the cases, including whether the case was a civil or criminal one. The jurisdiction in which a case was decided is also evident from a judicial decision and was coded, as applicable, using the corresponding region of the country as defined by the U.S. Census Bureau.[295]

As for the *depth* variable, cases discussing *Lawrence* in ways not central to the holding were coded as "mentioned in passing." By contrast, cases involving decisions in which *Lawrence* was central to the decision at issue were coded as "key to case." To ensure the reliability of this coding scheme, my research assistant and I coded these cases independently. Moreover, we verified our own coding against the depth indicator in Westlaw's KeyCite feature. In KeyCite, one star indicates a case was mentioned, usually in a string citation; two stars means a case was discussed in a few sentences, but usually not more than a full paragraph; three stars indicates a case was substantively discussed for more than a paragraph, but less than a page; and four stars means a case was examined

[295] *Census Regions*, *supra* note 285, at 1.

in depth, usually for more than a full page of printed text.[296] All of the cases we coded as "key to case" were coded in KeyCite with two, three, or four stars.[297] All of the cases we removed as irrelevant had one or two

[296] WESTLAW, GUIDE TO LAW REVIEW RESEARCH 20 (2007), http://lscontent.westlaw.com/images/banner/documentation/LawReviewResearchGuide.pdf [https://perma.cc/5LSH-95AX].

[297] The coding system in this study differs from KeyCite's because it does not reply on the number of lines in a judicial opinion, but rather the centrality of *Lawrence* to the disposition of a subsequent case. For example, *Jacobson v. State*, No. 63293, 2013 WL 7167806 (Nev. Nov. 13, 2013), is a very short decision—so much so that the slip opinion fits on a single page. The entirety of the court's rationale consists of a single paragraph. Hence, KeyCite awards only two stars in its depth rating as relating to *Lawrence*. Yet, *Lawrence* was outcome determinative and, therefore, coded as "key to case":

> Appellant argues that he is innocent because "it is unconstitutional to prohibit sexual conduct between prisoners" . . . under *Lawrence* . . . . We disagree. *Lawrence* did not concern the sexual conduct of prisoners. A prisoner's constitutional rights are limited by the fact of incarceration and by valid penological objectives, including deterrence of crime, prisoner rehabilitation, and institutional security.

Id. at *1; *see also, e.g.*, People v. Perez, 961 N.Y.S.2d 51, 52 (Sup. Ct. App. Div. 2013) (similarly refusing to extend *Lawrence* to the prison setting in a matter of just two sentences); State v. Jones, No. 95,558, 2007 WL 656367, at *1 (Kan. Ct. App. Mar. 2, 2007) (dispensing with a constitutional attack on a rape statute by citing *Lawrence* and saying it was "clearly not applicable here" because unlike the case at bar, *Lawrence* "involved consensual activity by adults"); Hobbs v. Smith, No. 05 CVS 267, 2006 WL 3103008 (N.C. Super. Ct. Aug. 25, 2006) (declaring fornication statute unconstitutional under *Lawrence* in a single sentence).

stars in KeyCite, except for one.[298] And all of the cases coded as "mentioned in passing" had either two or three stars in KeyCite.[299]

The *state political identity* variable represents the "color" of a state based on the party of the candidate for whom the state's Electoral College votes were cast in the 2008, 2012, 2016, and 2020 presidential elections. States where the republican candidate won four times are coded as "deep red" and those in which the republican candidate won three times are coded as "light red. The "purple" states were won by each party twice in the past four elections. The "light blue" states are those won by democratic candidates three times, and democrats won the "deep blue" states in all of the past four elections.

The name of the judge or justice writing an opinion is clearly evident in most cases, but demographic information about those judicial officers is not. For instance, the race, sex, and political affiliation of judges is not contained in judicial opinions. Such data were obtained by consulting the

---

298 That one exception is *State v. Peeler*, 140 A.3d 811 (Conn. 2016), a per curiam decision by the Supreme Court of Connecticut that reversed a death sentence. A concurring justice wrote about when a case should be overruled despite the principle of *stare decisis*. That justice noted that *stare decisis* does not "explain why we should be restrained from overruling a case that was demonstrably wrong when decided, has not engendered any reliance, and imposes significant costs on society simply because a justice who decided it has been replaced." *Id.* at 876. The concurring opinion then cited *Lawrence*'s overruling of *Bowers* as an example. *Id.* Given the length of this part of the opinion, KeyCite classified *Peeler* as warranting three stars for its depth of discussion about *Lawrence*. By contrast, my research assistant and I both classified *Peeler* as irrelevant because nothing about *Lawrence*'s holding was applied in the *Peeler* case and, therefore, *Peeler* does not help answer any of the research questions in the present study. *See also, e.g.*, Westfield Ins. Co. v. Galatis, 797 N.E.2d 1256, 1268 (Ohio 2003) (citing *Lawrence* for its "trifold *stare decisis* test").

Other times, KeyCite just appears to be wrong. For instance, a KeyCite of *Lawrence* identified *League of Women Voters Minnesota v. Ritchie*, 819 N.W.2d 636, 684 (Minn. 2012), as warranting three stars for depth. However, the discussion of *Lawrence* is limited to two sentences in a footnote in which the case is cited, yet again, as an example of the fact that *stare decisis* is not "an inexorable command." *Id.* at 684 n.26 (quoting Lawrence v. Texas, 539 U.S. 558, 577 (2003)). In short, the coding scheme used in the present study is designed to provide a more meaningful framework for depth of coverage than KeyCite does.

299 In KeyCite, three stars simply indicates a paragraph or two of discussion. That does not automatically indicate, however, that the discussion of *Lawrence* was central to a case's holding. It is that criterion—being the linchpin of a court's rationale for its decision—that warrants being coded as "key to case" in the present study.

websites for the courts on which each state court judge or justice sits or sat,[300] as well as BallotPedia's database on state court judges.[301] On the rare occasion that the salient demographic information about a particular judge could not be gleaned from one of these two sources, Google searches were used to track down the information as needed. These methods are reliable ways of obtaining judges' or justices' biographies, including their sex, political party affiliation, and education. The same, however, cannot be said about the race and ethnicity of any judge. Sometimes that information is provided in judicial biographies; other times, it needed to be obtained from news sources;[302] and still other times, determinations about this demographic characteristic needed to be determined from people's names and photos.[303] Finally, when judicial candidates ran for

300 For instance, the website for the Supreme Court of New Mexico contains a page listing the current justices with hyperlinks to pages presenting photos and biographies for each sitting justice. *Supreme Court, Current Supreme Court Justices*, N.M. CTS., https://supremecourt.nmcourts.gov/supreme-court/supreme-court-justices/current-supreme-court-justices/ [https://perma.cc/BV8W-X259] (last visited June 13, 2022). That website also contains a similar database for former justices on the court. *Supreme Court, Former Supreme Court Justices*, N.M. CTS., https://supremecourt.nmcourts.gov/supreme-court/supreme-court-justices/former-supreme-court-justices/ [https://perma.cc/LU6D-266J] (last visited June 13, 2022).

301 *Courts and Judges by State*, BALLOTPEDIA, https://ballotpedia.org/Courts_and_judges_by_state [https://perma.cc/C4GJ-YFAK] (last visited June 13, 2022).

302 For instance, neither BallotPedia nor the California Supreme Court website state that Associate Justice Patricia Guerreo is Latina. *See Patricia Guerrero*, BALLOTPEDIA, https://ballotpedia.org/Patricia_Guerrero [https://perma.cc/Z7ZD-D32J] (last visited June 13, 2022); *Patricia Guerrero, Associate Justice*, CAL. CTS., https://www.courts.ca.gov/38044.htm [https://perma.cc/5F85-LA89] (last visited June 13, 2022). However, a Google search for Justice Guerreo revealed her ethnic heritage. *E.g.*, *Governor Newsom Swears in Justice Patricia Guerrero to California Supreme Court, the First Latina to Serve on State's Highest Court*, CAL. OFF. OF GOVERNOR (Mar. 28, 2022), https://www.gov.ca.gov/2022/03/28/governor-newsom-swears-in-justice-patricia-guerrero-to-california-supreme-court-the-first-latina-to-serve-on-states-highest-court/ [https://perma.cc/E3UD-D2Z9].

303 This is a limitation of the study. As other researchers have acknowledged, "'eyeballing' race is far from ideal, given there are considerable differences in skin tone between—and within—White, Latino, and Black communities." Danielle Slakoff & Pauline K. Brennan, *White, Black, and Latina Female Victims in U.S. News: A Multivariate and Intersectional Analysis of Story Differences*, 13 RACE & JUST. 155 (2023), https://doi.org/10.1177/2153368720961837; *see also* Aliya Saperstein, *Double-Checking the Race Box: Examining Inconsistency Between Survey Measures of Observed and Self-Reported Race*, 85 SOC. FORCES 57 (2006),

office via partisan elections, I coded their political party affiliation as reported by BallotPedia as either “democrat” or “republican”; nonpartisan candidates are coded as “other.” When judicial officers were appointed to the bench, I coded for the political affiliation of the appointing entity, typically a governor.

c. Analytic Strategy

The ethnographic content analysis, described more fully in the next subsection, is used to qualitatively address the first two research questions. The third research question, however, poses empirical questions regarding the relationship between extralegal factors and the use of *Lawrence*. I use both bivariate and multivariate analyses to determine whether there are significant differences between case outcomes and the categorical independent variables. Specifically, I used Pearson’s chi-square tests to analyze if there are any significant differences between treatment of *Lawrence* and factors such as the geographic region in which the case was decided and judicial officers’ demographic characteristics. The chi-square test of independence is used to examine if two categorical variables are truly independent of each other.[304] Where applicable, I report the probabilities for statistically significant relationships using Fisher Exact

---

https://doi.org/10.1353/sof.2006.0141. To address this methodological concern, I followed the lead of Slakoff and Brennan in that whenever photographs were used to determine race, a second coder verified the coding. The two coders agreed each time, resulting in 100% inter-rater reliability for this variable.

304 *See* ALAN AGRESTI, AN INTRODUCTION TO CATEGORICAL DATA ANALYSIS 36–41 (3d ed. 2019); *Using Chi-Square Statistic in Research*, STAT. SOLS., https://www.statisticssolutions.com/using-chi-square-statistic-in-research/ [https://perma.cc/9Q3Q-8WEK] (last visited Apr. 16 2021).

tests[305] and I also report Cramer's V statistics to assess the strength of such associations.[306]

Bivariate analyses do not provide the same level of insight as multivariate analyses. That is because multivariate analyses can examines several variables at the same time to see if one or more of them predict a certain outcome.[307] Thus, to examine what factors might predict how judges treat *Lawrence*, I employed logistic regression. Regression is a statistical procedure that assesses whether independent variables—such as the geographical region of the country or judicial race, sex, and political party affiliation—are associated with some outcome (i.e., the dependent variable).[308] Regression analyses are able to identify which particular

---

305 The Fisher Exact test serves the same purpose as chi-squares, but is more appropriate with sample sizes less than 1,000 or when 20% of expected frequencies in cross-tabulation cells are less than or equal to five. *See* Matthias Döring, *Testing Independence: Chi-Squared vs Fisher's Exact Test*, DATA SCI. BLOG (Oct. 17, 2018), https://www.datascienceblog.net/post/statistical_test/contingency_table_tests/ [https://perma.cc/C36Q-4WG8]. Because this study analyzes fewer than 1,000 cases and because some of the chi-square analyses had expected cell frequencies less than five, both the chi-square and Fisher's Exact statistics are reported as confirmatory of each other.

306 *Nominal Variable Association*, STAT. SOLUTIONS, https://www.statisticssolutions.com/free-resources/directory-of-statistical-analyses/nominal-variable-association/ [https://perma.cc/9R2Y-C5J6] (last visited Aug. 19, 2022). Note that I use Cramer's V, rather than a Phi coefficient, because the latter is used only for two-by-two tables, whereas Cramer's V is appropriate for both a two-by-two table and larger ones such as many of those reported in Chapters 4 and 5. *Id.*

Cramer's V results range from 0.00 to 1.00. Some authorities make three divisions for interpreting the strength of associations values. *Id.* (describing values less than 0.10 as weak, 0.10 to 0.30 as moderate, and 0.31 or higher as strong). Other sources refine interpretation across five levels with values less than 0.05 indicating a very weak relationship; values between 0.05 and 0.10 indicating weak associations; values between 0.10 and 0.15 representing moderate associations; values between 0.15 and 0.25 indicating strong associations; and values of 0.25 or higher indicating very strong relationships. Haldun Akoglu, *User's Guide to Correlation Coefficients*, 18 TURK. J. EMERGENCY MED. 91, 92 tbl.2 (2018).

307 *See generally* Joshua Bush, *The Difference Between Bivariate & Multivariate Analyses*, SCIENCING (June 4, 2018), https://sciencing.com/difference-between-bivariate-multivariate-analyses-8667797.html [https://perma.cc/7BKR-LFZ8].

308 *What Is Linear Regression?*, STAT. SOLUTIONS [hereinafter *Regression*], https://www.statisticssolutions.com/free-resources/directory-of-statistical-analyses/what-is-linear-regression/ [https://perma.cc/3FYP-NK2K] (last visited June 13, 2022).

independent variables "are significant predictors of the outcome variable" and the degree to which they do so as "indicated by the magnitude and sign of the beta estimates."[309] When all of the independent variables are categorical in nature, as is the case for all of the independent variables in this study, and the dependent variable is also categorical, then logistic regression is the appropriate type of regression analysis.[310]

3. Qualitative Coding and Analyses

Consistent with the research method as set forth by Altheide and Schneider, the qualitative portion of this research project focuses on narrative data in which both categorical and unique data were obtained from each case studied.[311] The content analysis was conducted in three phases, the completion of which allowed for the creation of a typology based on the patterns that emerged during the analyses of cases.

a. Phase One: Preliminary Protocol Development

The first phase of the qualitative content analysis involved two researchers independently reviewing forty cases in an attempt to discern distinctive patterns in ways that courts were applying *Lawrence*. This allowed each of the researchers to develop a preliminary protocol containing categories against which other cases could be assessed. Importantly, this phase involves a collaborative, discoursive process to identify categories that capture the richness of narrative descriptions without any predefined categories.[312] Then, after independently identifying emergent themes, two researchers compared their own assessments of the forty cases and then harmonized their conceptualizations so that cases presenting similar themes could be more reliably coded as falling within a particular category.

---

[309] *Id.*

[310] *Id.*; *see also* AGRESTI, *supra* note 304, at 89–102; *What Is Logistic Regression?*, STAT. SOLUTIONS [hereinafter *Logistic Regression*], https://www.statisticssolutions.com/free-resources/directory-of-statistical-analyses/what-is-logistic-regression/ [https://perma.cc/UC6Z-FEJ2] (last visited June 13, 2022).

[311] ALTHEIDE & SCHNEIDER, *supra* note 247, at 23–73.

[312] *Id.* at 44–45.

b. Phase Two: Case Classification into Typology Categories

The second phase of the content analysis involved two researchers independently coding all 307 relevant cases in a manner responsive to the first two research questions concerning the different ways in which courts apply *Lawrence*. When a particular case fell within one of the themes developed as part of the preliminary data analysis protocol, it was added to the previously-identified category. By contrast, when a case presented a substantially different use of *Lawrence*, a new category was created, thereby allowing for the emergence of central themes that are explored in detail in Chapters 4 and 5.

c. Phase Three: Case Studies

In the third and final phase of the content analysis, I compared and contrasted the cases within each of the categories that emerged in phase two. Specifically, I sought to make generalizations not only about the ways that litigants sought to use *Lawrence*, but also about how courts ultimately ruled on such attempts to answer the third research question.

d. Inter-Rater Reliability

During the first phase, the two coders reached 77.5% agreement, which exceeds the typical threshold of 75% agreement required in the social sciences.[313] We met, talked through our different approaches to coding, and then proceeded to code all of the cases independently during phase two. That allowed us to increase our inter-rater reliability, largely as a function of having solidified our themes. Specifically, both researchers coded all but nine (2.9%) of the 307 cases identically during the second phase of coding, yielding an impressively high concurrence rate of 97.1%, which exceeds the level of agreement typically required in medical sciences.[314] A third person then reviewed and independently coded each of the nine cases on which the two other researchers disagreed. In essence,

---

313 *See, e.g.*, *Inter-rater Reliability IRR: Definition, Calculation*, STAT. HOW TO (July 17, 2016), https://www.statisticshowto.com/inter-rater-reliability/ [https://perma.cc/RG46-XFSH].

314 *Id.* (reporting that medicine typically expects 90% or higher levels of inter-rater reliability).

that researcher's coding served as a tie-breaking vote on the coding of those cases. That person's tie-breaking vote is how the final nine cases were ultimately coded.

Chapter 4:

Quantitative Results

A. Descriptive Statistics

1. The Cases

More than two-thirds of the cases were either criminal ($n = 195$, 94.1%) or quasi-criminal in nature ($n = 18$, 5.9.%), while the remainder were civil disputes ($n = 94$, 30.6%). Comparably few ($n = 26$, 8.5%) decisions were issued by trial courts; the balance represented decisions from intermediate appellate courts ($n = 191$, 62.2%) and state high courts of last resort ($n = 90$, 29.3%).

The cases fell into one of nine primary themes that emerged during the qualitative analysis of the data. They include, in alphabetical order, (1) business operations and employment law; (2) family law; (3) LGBTQ+ civil rights; (4) noncommercial, consensual sex crimes (e.g., adultery, fornication, and sodomy); (5) obscenity and pornography; (6) other types of sexual privacy claims (e.g., bigamy, incest, lewdness, indecent exposure, voyeurism, revenge porn, and knowing transmission of sexually-transmitted infections); (7) post-conviction claims filed by sex offenders; (8) prostitution and related commercial sex offenses; and (9) sexual assault and statutory rape. In addition to these nine substantive categories, a miscellaneous category presents cases that used *Lawrence* in ways that differed from one of the other categories that emerged during data analysis. Figure 1 illustrates the number of cases in each category along with the corresponding percentage of the 307 total cases in the study.

FIGURE 1: CATEGORY FREQUENCIES

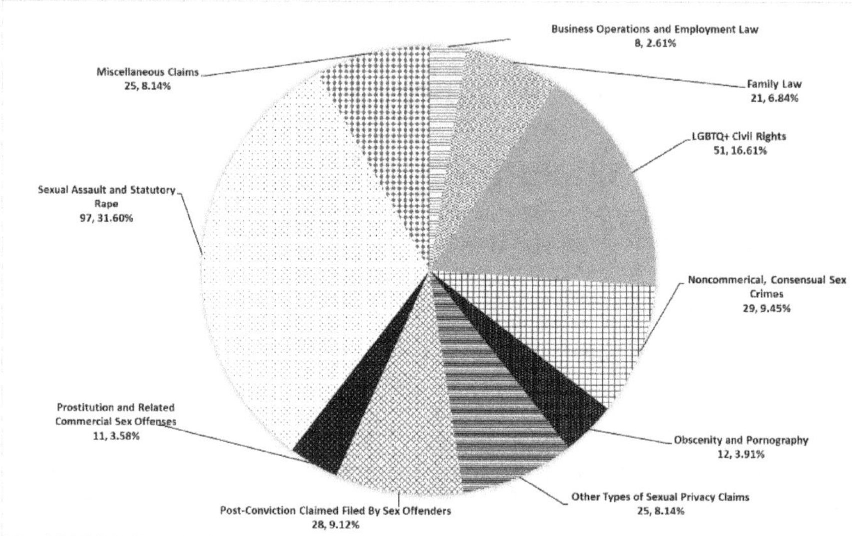

a. Depth of *Lawrence* Analysis

Overall, judges cited *Lawrence* in passing in 169 (55.5%) of the cases. *Lawrence* was key to case outcomes in 138 (45.0%) of the cases. Perhaps unsurprisingly since *Lawrence* was a criminal case, it was more likely to be key to the outcome in criminal cases than it was in civil cases ($\chi^2_{(1, 307)}$ = 22.971; p <0.001; Fisher exact = 0.001; Cramer's V = 0.274). Table 2 illustrates a crosstabulation of the depth of analysis across the case categories, illustrating that *Lawrence* was more likely to be key to a case outcome, to a statistically significant degree, in noncommercial consensual sex crimes (adultery, fornication, and sodomy), other criminal cases involving claims of sexual privacy, and sexual assault cases than any other type of claims, including those centering around LGBTQ+ civil rights.

TABLE 2: CROSSTABULATION OF DEPTH BY CATEGORY

Case Category	Depth of Analysis		
	Mentioned in Passing	*Key to Case*	*Total*
Business Operations and Employment Law	7 (2.3%)	3 (1.0%)	10 (3.3%)
Family Law	20 (6.5%)	2 (0.7%)	22 (7.2%)
LGBTQ Civil Rights	35 (11.4%)	14 (4.6%)	49 (16.0%)
Noncommercial Consensual Sex Crimes	12 (3.9%)	17 (5.5%)	29 (9.4%)
Obscenity and Pornography	5 (1.6%)	7 (2.3%)	12 (3.9%)
Other Claims of Sexual Privacy	9 (2.9%)	16 (5.2%)	25 (8.1%)
Post-Conviction Claims Filed By Sex Offenders	20 (6.5%)	8 (2.6%)	28 (9.1%)
Prostitution and Related Commercial Sex Offenses	4 (1.3%)	7 (2.3%)	11 (3.6%)
Sexual Assault and Statutory Rape	37 (12.1%)	60 (19.5%)	97 (31.6%)
Miscellaneous Claims	20 (6.5%)	4 (1.3%)	24 (7.8%)
Total	169 (55.0%)	138 (45.0%)	307 (100.0%)

$\chi^2_{(9, 307)} = 47.992$; $p < 0.001$; Fisher exact = 0.001; Cramer's V = 0.395

b. Treatment of *Lawrence*

Courts applied *Lawrence* straightforwardly in just over half of all of the cases ($n = 163$, 53.1%). As Table 3 shows, when judges interpreted and applied *Lawrence* in ways that went beyond a neutral application of its central holding, they gave the case a narrow construction more frequently than a broad one, although there are salient differences depending on the type of case.

TABLE 3: CROSSTABULATION OF TREATMENT BY CASE TYPE

Case Type	Treatment of *Lawrence*			
	Neutral	*Narrow Construction*	*Broad Construction*	*Total*
Civil	42 (13.7%)	16 (5.2%)	33 (11.7%)	94 (30.6%)
Criminal & Quasi-Criminal	121 (39.4%)	66 (21.5%)	26 8.5%)	213 (67.8%)
Total	163 (53.1%)	8 (26.7%)	62 (20.2%)	307 (100.0%)

$\chi^2_{(2, 307)} = 28.552$; $p < 0.001$; Fisher exact = 0.001; Cramer's V = 0.305[315]

When judges interpreted and applied *Lawrence* in criminal cases in ways that went beyond a neutral application of its central holding, they gave the case a narrow construction far more frequently than a broad one, which, as Table 4 shows, overwhelming aided the prosecution in criminal cases.

TABLE 4: CROSSTABULATION OF TREATMENT BY CRIMINAL CASE OUTCOME

Criminal & Quasi-Criminal Case Outcome	Treatment of *Lawrence*			
	Neutral	*Narrow Construction*	*Broad Construction*	*Total*
Prosecution	109 (51.2%)	59 (27.7%)	1 (6.6%)	182 (85.4%)
Defense	12 (5.6%)	7 (3.3%)	12 (5.6%)	31 (16.6%)
Total	121 (56.8%)	66 (31.0%)	26 (12.2%)	213 (100.0%)

$\chi^2_{(2, 213)} = 23.796$; $p < 0.001$; Fisher exact = 0.001; Cramer's V = 0.334[316]

---

315 When a chi-square analysis is run on a crosstabulation of case outcome and judicial treatment using only those cases in which judges did not straightforwardly apply *Lawrence* (i.e., negative and positive cases included, but neutral cases excluded), the results remain statistically significant: $\chi^2_{(1, 144)} = 22.745$; $p < 0.001$; Fisher exact = 0.001; Cramer's V = 0.397.

316 When a chi-square analysis is run on a crosstabulation of criminal case outcomes and judicial treatment of *Lawrence* using only those cases in which judges did not

c. Region and Regional Politics

As Table 5 reveals, cases from southern states were disproportionately represented in comparison to other census regions of the country. The geographical region in which cases were decided was significantly related to how courts applied *Lawrence*, with judges in the northeastern region having interpreted the case broadly by a margin of more than three-to-one over narrow constructions, while judges in other regions gave *Lawrence* a narrower reading in roughly twice as many cases as they applied the case expansively.

straightforwardly apply *Lawrence* (i.e., negative and positive cases included, but neutral cases excluded), the results remain statistically significant: $\chi^2_{(1, 92)} = 14.383$; $p < 0.001$; Fisher exact = 0.001; Cramer's V = 0.395.

TABLE 5: TREATMENT BY CENSUS REGION OF CASES

Census Region	Treatment of *Lawrence*			
	Neutral	*Narrow Construction*	*Broad Construction*	*Total*
Northeast				
New England	13 (4.2%)	3 (1.0%)	10 (3.3%)	26 (8.5%)
Mid-Atlantic	14 (4.6%)	5 (1.6%)	15 (4.9%)	34 (11.1%)
Subtotal	27 (8.8%)	8 (2.6%)	25 (8.1%)	60 (19.5%)
South				
South-Atlantic	22 (7.2%)	16 (5.2%)	8 (2.6%)	46 (15.0%)
East South Central	14 (4.6%)	3 (1.0%)	0 (0.0%)	17 (5.5%)
West South Central	32 (10.4%)	11 (3.6%)	6 (2.0%)	49 (16.0%)
Subtotal	68 (22.1%)	30 (9.8%)	14 (4.6%)	112 (36.5%)
Midwest				
East North Central	10 (3.3%)	11 (3.6%)	5 (1.6%)	26 (8.5%)
West North Central	19 (6.2%)	9 (2.9%)	4 (1.3%)	32 (10.4%)
Subtotal	29 (9.4%)	20 (6.5%)	9 (2.9%)	58 (18.9%)
West				
Mountain	16 (5.2%)	8 (2.6%)	6 (2.0%)	30 (9.8%)
Pacific	23 (7.5%)	16 (5.2%)	8 (2.6%)	47 (15.3%)
Subtotal	39 (12.7%)	24 (7.8%)	14 (4.6%)	77 (25.1%)
Total	163 (53.1%)	82 (26.7%)	62 (20.2%)	307 (100.0%)

Four Regions: $\chi^2_{(6, 307)} = 29.269$; $p < 0.001$; Fisher exact = 0.001; Cramer's V = 0.220[317]

Nine Subdivisions: $\chi^2_{(16, 307)} = 36.406$; $p < 0.003$; Fisher exact = 0.001; Cramer's V = 0.244[318]

---

317 When a chi-square analysis is run on a crosstabulation of case outcome and judicial treatment using only those cases in which judges did not straightforwardly apply *Lawrence* (i.e., negative and positive cases included, but neutral cases excluded), the results remain statistically significant: $\chi^2_{(3, 144)} = 18.968$; $p < 0.001$; Fisher exact = 0.001; Cramer's V = 0.363.

318 When a chi-square analysis is run on a crosstabulation of case outcome and judicial treatment using only those cases in which judges did not straightforwardly apply *Lawrence* (i.e., negative and positive cases included, but neutral cases excluded), the

The political affiliation of nearly two-thirds of the judges ($n = 199$, 64.9%) could not be determined because they had achieved judicial office by winning nonpartisan elections or through other nonpartisan means. Of the judges who were elected in partisan races or appointed via partisan political processes, forty-two (14.0%) were affiliated with the Democratic party and sixty-seven (21.8%) with the Republican party. The political affiliation of the judge writing an opinion was not statistically significantly related to the treatment of *Lawrence* ($\chi^2_{(4, 301)} = 2.113$; $p > 0.05$, n.s.). But given the high percentage of judges whose political affiliation is unknown, cross-tabulations were run comparing the treatment of *Lawrence* to the "color" of the state in which the case was decided. Table 6 demonstrates that while "blue" and "purple" states do not differ significantly in the rate in which *Lawrence* is narrowly or broadly interpreted, decisions from "red" states apply *Lawrence* narrowly at least twice as frequently as they apply it broadly.

TABLE 6: TREATMENT OF *LAWRENCE* BY POLITICS OF THE STATE IN WHICH CASES WERE DECIDED

State Political Climate	**Treatment of *Lawrence***			
	Neutral	*Narrow Construction*	*Broad Construction*	*Total*
Deep Red	72 (23.5%)	22 (7.2%)	11 (3.6%)	105 (34.2%)
Light Red	11 (3.6%)	13 (14.2%)	5 (1.6%)	29 (9.4%)
Purple	7 (2.3%)	5 (1.6%)	5 (1.6%)	17 (5.50%)
Light Blue	8 (2.6%)	3 (1.0%)	3 (1.0%)	14 (14.6%)
Deep Blue	65 (21.2%)	39 (12.7%)	38 (24.4%)	142 (46.3%)
Total	163 (53.1%)	82 (26.7%)	62 (20.2%)	307 (100.0%)

$\chi^2_{(8, 307)} = 21.807$; $p < 0.010$; Fisher exact = 0.005; Cramer's V = 0.188[319]

---

results remain statistically significant: $\chi^2_{(8, 144)} = 20.653$; $p < 0.008$; Fisher exact = 0.009; Cramer's V = 0.379.

319 When a chi-square analysis is run on a crosstabulation of case outcome and judicial treatment using only those cases in which judges did not straightforwardly apply

2. The Judges

Courts issued per curiam decisions in thirteen cases (4.2%). Of the remaining opinions, men authored 195 (66.3%) and women wrote ninety-nine (32.27). The sex of the judge writing an opinion was not statistically significantly related to the outcomes in criminal and quasi-criminal cases ($\chi^2_{(1, 202)} = 0.050$; $p > 0.05$, n.s.), even when the analyses excluded neutral applications of *Lawrence* ($\chi^2_{(1, 88)} = 0.517$; $p > 0.05$, n.s.). As Table 7 illustrates, however, the sex of the judge writing an opinion was statistically significantly related to the treatment of *Lawrence*. Specifically, there were moderate sex differences between narrow and expansive constructions of *Lawrence*, with women being more likely than men to apply the case broadly.

TABLE 7: TREATMENT BY SEX

Judge's Sex	**Treatment of *Lawrence***			
	Neutral	*Narrow Construction*	*Broad Construction*	*Total*
Male	99 (33.7%)	60 (20.4%)	36 (12.2%)	195 (66.3%)
Female	57 (19.4%)	17 (5.8%)	25 (8.5%)	99 (33.7%)
Total	156 (53.1%)	77 (26.2%)	61 (20.7%)	294 (100.0%)

$\chi^2_{(2, 294)} = 6.668$; $p < 0.036$; Fisher exact = 0.038; Cramer's V = 0.151[320]

The racial/ethnic distribution of state court judges authoring opinions citing *Lawrence* in the past two decades is presented in Table 8. Given that people of color account for comparatively few of the judges represented in the study, it is necessary to collapse the categories in Table 8 into White ($n = 254$, 82.7%), Nonwhite ($n = 39$, 12.7%), and Not

---

Lawrence (i.e., negative and positive cases included, but neutral cases excluded), the results were no longer statistically significant: $\chi^2_{(4, 144)} = 4.545$; $p > 0.05$, n.s.)

320 When a chi-square analysis is run on a crosstabulation of the sex of the judge and judicial treatment using only those cases in which judges did not straightforwardly apply *Lawrence* (i.e., negative and positive cases included, but neutral cases excluded), the results remain statistically significant: $\chi^2_{(1, 138)} = 5.746$; $p < 0.017$; Fisher exact = 0.025; Cramer's V = 0.204.

Applicable/Unknown ($n = 14$, 4.6%) to avoid there being too few observations for meaningful statistical analyses.

TABLE 8: RACE/ETHNICITY OF JUDGES

	n	%
African-American/Black	17	5.5%
Asian/Pacific Islander	6	2.0%
Hispanic	16	5.2%
White	254	82.7%
Not Applicable (per curiam)	13	4.2%
Unknown	1	0.3%

There were no statistically significantly differences between White and Nonwhite judges with regard to the treatment of *Lawrence* ($\chi^2_{(4,\ 307)} = 1.521$; $p > 0.05$, n.s.).

B. Logistic Regression

When neutral cases are excluded such that only cases in which judges interpreted *Lawrence* and applied it to fact that went beyond the express holding or limitations of the case, the logistic regression results presented in Table 9 indicate that case type, depth of treatment, and region of the country were all significantly related to how *Lawrence* was interpreted. Specifically, *Lawrence* being broadly or expansively interpreted is associated with 76.7% lower odds in criminal and quasi-criminal cases compared to civil ones, 65.6% lower odds when key to the case outcome compared to when mentioned in passing, and 88.2% and 87.0% lower odds in the South and Midwest compared to in the Northeast. And although the sex of a judge was not a statistically significant predictor in the model at the 0.05 alpha level, it approached significance at that level such that the odds of women judges interpreting *Lawrence* broadly were 2.5 times more than their male counterparts.

TABLE 9: BINARY LOGISTIC REGRESSION PREDICTING BROAD TREATMENT OF *LAWRENCE*

N = 144								
Omnibus Test of Model Coefficients: $\chi^2 = 52.770_{(16, 144)}$, $p < 0.001$								
Hosmer & Lemeshow Test: $\chi^2 = 8.014_{(8, 144)}$, $p > 0.05$								
Nagelkerke Pseudo-$R^2 = 0.412$								
	B	S.E.	Wald	df	Sig.	Exp(B)	95% CI for Exp(B)	
							Lower	Upper
Type [a]	-1.458	.465	9.840	1	.002***	.233	.094	.579
Depth [b]	-1.067	.437	5.970	1	.015**	.344	.146	.810
Region [c]			7.596	3	.055			
South	-2.136	.804	7.050	1	.008***	.118	.024	.572
Midwest	-2.040	.900	5.138	1	.023**	.130	.022	.759
West	-1.282	.654	3.845	1	.051*	.277	.077	.999
State Politics [d]			2.505	4	.644			
Deep Red	.955	.702	1.852	1	.174	2.598	.657	10.274
Light Red	.479	.788	.369	1	.544	1.614	.344	7.568
Purple	1.302	.983	1.754	1	.185	3.677	.535	25.268
Light Blue	.749	1.254	.356	1	.550	2.114	.181	24.694
Judge's Sex [e]			3.811	2	.149			
Female	.918	.470	3.811	1	.051*	2.504	.996	6.294
N/A (per curiam)	-23.094	40192.973	.000	1	1.000	.000	.000	.
Judicial Party [f]			1.088	3	.780			
Democrat	.155	.653	.056	1	.813	1.167	.325	4.194
Republican	-.235	.559	.177	1	.674	.790	.264	2.363
Unknown	-1.059	1.169	.821	1	.365	.347	.035	3.430
Constant	1.927	.603	10.206	1	.001	6.870		

Reference categories:

[a] = Civil [b] = Mentioned in Passing [c] = Northeast [d] Deep Blue [e] Male [f] Nonpartisan

Significance: * $p < 0.10$ ** $p < 0.05$ *** $p < 0.01$

Chapter 5:

Mixed-Methods Analyses of Cases

A. Noncommercial, Consensual Sex Offenses ($n = 29$, 9.4%)

Twenty-eight of the twenty-nine cases in this category concerned the constitutionality of laws either directly criminalizing sodomy, adultery, or fornication, or alternatively raised claims that depended, in part, on the validity or scope of such laws.[321] Of these, eleven (37.9%) applied *Lawrence* in a straightforward manner, thirteen (44.8%) construed the precedent narrowly, and only five (17.2%) gave the case a broad reading. Table 10 details the characteristics of the cases in this category across all of the dependent variables in the study, none of which were significantly related to how courts applied *Lawrence* in this context.

---

[321] The other case merely noted that the state had repealed its sodomy law after *Lawrence* was decided. Dixon v. Missouri State Highway Patrol, 583 S.W.3d 521, 524 (Mo. Ct. App. 2019) ("In 2006, the General Assembly removed the language which criminalized deviate sexual intercourse with another person of the same sex . . . [p]resumably . . . in response to the decision in *Lawrence* . . . .").

TABLE 10: VARIABLE FREQUENCIES AND RELATIONSHIPS TO TREATMENT OF *LAWRENCE* IN NONCOMMERCIAL, CONSENSUAL SEX OFFENSE CASES

Category	Treatment of *Lawrence* *n* (%)				Chi-Square	Sig.	Cramer's V
Type	*Neutral*	*Narrow*	*Broad*	*Total*			
Civil	3 (10.3%)	2 (6.9%)	0 (0.0%)	5 (17.2%)	1.849 (2, 29)	$p > 0.050$	N/A
Criminal	8 (27.6%)	11 (37.9%)	5 (17.2%)	24 (82.8%)			
Depth	*Neutral*	*Narrow*	*Broad*	*Total*			
Mentioned in Passing	7 (24.1%)	4 (13.8%)	1 (3.4%)	12 (41.4%)	3.792 (2, 29)	$p > 0.050$	N/A
Key to Case	4 (13.8%)	9 (31.0%)	4 (13.8%)	17 (58.6%)			
Outcome	*Neutral*	*Narrow*	*Broad*	*Total*			
Prosecution	7 (24.1%)	9 (31.0%)	3 (10.3%)	19 (65.5%)	3.538 (4, 29)	$p > 0.050$	N/A
Defense	1 (3.4%)	2 (6.9%)	2 (6.9%)	5 (17.2%)			
Not Relevant (Civil)	3 (10.3%)	2 (6.9%)	0 (0.0%)	5 (17.2%)			
State Politics	*Neutral*	*Narrow*	*Broad*	*Total*			
Deep Red	3 (10.3%)	1 (3.4%)	2 (6.9%)	6 (20.7%)	2.932 (4, 29)	$p > 0.050$	N/A
Light Red	2 (6.9%)	4 (13.8%)	1 (3.4%)	7 (24.1%)			
Purple	0 (0.0%)	0 (0.0%)	0 (0.0%)	0 (0.0%)			
Light Blue	0 (0.0%)	0 (0.0%)	0 (0.0%)	0 (0.0%)			
Deep Blue	6 (20.7%)	8 (27.6%)	2 (6.9%)	16 (55.2%)			
Region	*Neutral*	*Narrow*	*Broad*	*Total*			
Northeast	0 (0.0%)	0 (0.0%)	0 (0.0%)	0 (0.0%)	4.195 (4, 29)	$p > 0.050$	N/A
South	9 (31.0%)	8 (27.6%)	4 (13.8%)	21 (72.4%)			
Midwest	1 (3.4%)	0 (0.0%)	0 (0.0%)	1 (3.4%)			
West	1 (3.4%)	5 (17.2%)	1 (3.4%)	7 (24.1%)			
Judge's Sex	*Neutral*	*Narrow*	*Broad*	*Total*			
Male	4 (13.8%)	7 (24.1%)	4 (13.8%)	15 (55.6%)	3.504 (4, 28)	$p > 0.050$	N/A
Female	6 (22.2%)	5 (18.5%)	1 (3.7%)	12 (44.4%)			
Not Applicable (per curiam)	0 (0.0%)	1 (3.6%)	0 (0.0%)	1 (3.6%)			
Judge's Race/Ethnicity	*Neutral*	*Narrow*	*Broad*	*Total*			
White	9 (31.0%)	9 (31.0%)	5 (17.2%)	23 (79.3%)	2.557 (4, 29)	$p > 0.050$	N/A
Nonwhite	1 (3.4%)	3 (10.3%)	0 (0.0%)	4 (13.8%)			
Not Applicable or Unknown	1 (3.4%)	1 (3.4%)	0 (0.0%)	2 (6.9%)			
Judge's Political Affiliation	*Neutral*	*Narrow*	*Broad*	*Total*			
Nonpartisan	9 (31.0%)	7 (24.1%)	2 (6.9%)	18 (62.1%)	4.383 (4, 29)	$p > 0.050$	N/A
Democrat	0 (0.0%)	3 (10.3%)	1 (3.4%)	4 (13.8%)			
Republican	2 (6.9%)	3 (10.3%)	2 (6.9%)	7 (24.1%)			

1. Sodomy and Solicitation to Engage In It

Lawrence, of course, decriminalized noncommercial acts of oral or anal sex if they occur in private between consenting adults.[322] Some states repealed their criminal sodomy laws after the decision in *Lawrence*.[323] Other states retained their sodomy laws, enforcing them in ways not covered by *Lawrence*.[324] For instance, sodomy laws that include criminal prohibitions against bestiality may still be constitutionally enforced.[325] Courts reason that even if *Lawrence* removed morality as a basis for criminalizing sex acts between humans and animals, there are at least two rational bases for the continued prohibition of such acts: the prevention of cruelty to animals and the protection of public health.[326]

---

322 Lawrence v. State, No. 14-99-00109-CR, 2003 WL 22453791, at *1 (Tex. App. Oct. 30, 2003) (reversing the original judgments of the trial court, ordering the complaints be dismissed, and entering judgments of acquittal after remand from the U.S. Supreme Court). As a result, an adult soliciting another person over the age of consent to engage in noncommercial acts of oral or anal sex, in private, under circumstances in which no vulnerability impacts the ability to consent, may not be constitutionally enforced.

323 Notably, at least one court rejected an attempt to reinstate sodomy as a criminal offense after the *Lawrence* decision. In *McLaughlin v. Becerra*, the plaintiff had proposed ballot measure titled the "Sodomite Suppression Act," which would have made the "touch[ing of] another person of the same gender for purposes of sexual gratification" punishable by "death by bullets to the head or by any other convenient method." No. B280529, 2018 WL 654556, at *1 (Cal. Ct. App. Feb. 1, 2018). The state attorney general sought and was granted a declaratory judgment that the proposed ballot initiative was unconstitutional under *Lawrence*, thereby relieving her office of its usual obligations to summarize and circulate the proposed ballot initiative. *Id.* The California Court of Appeals upheld a lower court's grant of the declaratory judgment. *Id.* at *6.

324 Watson v. State, 750 S.E.2d 143, 146–47 (Ga. 2013) ("[A]n individual violates the solicitation of sodomy statute if he (1) solicits another individual (2) to perform or submit to a sexual act involving the sex organs of one and the mouth or anus of the other and (3) such sexual act is to be performed (a) in public; (b) in exchange for money or anything of commercial value; (c) by force; or (d) by or with an individual who is incapable of giving legal consent to sexual activity.").

325 *See, e.g.*, Louisiana Electorate of Gays & Lesbians, Inc. v. Connick, 902 So. 2d 1090, 1096 (La. Ct. App.), *writ denied*, 916 So. 2d 1062 (2005) ("We conclude that the two types of behavior are severable, because the prohibition against human/human portion can be removed without affecting the validity or intent of the human/animal prohibition.").

326 Warren v. Commonwealth, 822 S.E.2d 395, 402 (2019) ("Bestiality can be considered animal abuse because the sexual molestation of animals by humans may physically injure or kill the animal victim." Emily Malhiot, *Chapter 86: Nevada Finally Outlaws Bestiality*, 49 U. PAC. L. REV. 555, 561 (2018) (internal alterations omitted)); *id.* ("Scientists estimate that more than [six] out of every [ten] known infectious diseases

Sodomy laws may also be constitutionally applied to commercial sex (i.e., sex in exchange for compensation)[327] or when the acts occur in public.[328] Notably, most courts not only consider communal areas inside correctional facilities to be "public" spaces which lie outside the scope of *Lawrence*'s protections,[329] but also reason that consensual sexual activities occurring in inmates' cells are also not constitutionally protected because judges reason that "prisoners have no cognizable right to sexual privacy" in their cells as a function of their diminished expectations of privacy while incarcerated.[330]

---

in people are spread from animals, and [three] out of every [four] new or emerging infectious diseases in people are spread from animals." (*Zoonotic Diseases*, CTRS. FOR DISEASE CONTROL & PREVENTION, https://www.cdc.gov/onehealth/basics/zoonotic-diseases.html [https://perma.cc/9XHW-LZ6H] (last updated July 1, 2121)).

327 Because prostitution and related crimes involve commercial activity, cases involve those offenses are presented in their own category in Part B of this chapter. *See infra* notes 356–363 and accompanying text.

328 *See, e.g.*, Waller v. Commonwealth, 833 S.E.2d 484, 486 (Va. Ct. App. 2019) (dismissing petition for actual innocence on the grounds that *Lawrence* and state cases applying it voided a conviction for solicitation to commit sodomy based on acts that took place in a public park, reasoning that the petitioner "only advance[d] an argument on the legal effect of subsequent judicial decisions, a ground not contemplated by" state law, which limited writs of actual innocence to newly discovered nonbiological evidence (internal quotations and citations omitted)); State v. Gentle, 817 S.E.2d 833, 839 (N.C. Ct. App. 2018) (upholding sodomy conviction for act that the defendant unsuccessfully claimed had occurred "well outside the public view in an area . . . described as 'dark' and 'wooded'"), *aff'd*, 822 S.E.2d 616 (N.C. 2019); Singson v. Commonwealth, 621 S.E.2d 682, 688 (Va. Ct. App. 2005) ("[B]ecause Singson's [solicitation of sodomy from an undercover police officer] proposed conduct occurred in a public [restroom], . . . the circumstances of this case do[] not implicate [his] constitutionally-protected right to engage in private, consensual acts of sodomy."); Tjan v. Commonwealth, 621 S.E.2d 669, 673 (Va. Ct. App. 2005) (same); *see also* State v. Thomas, 891 So. 2d 1233, 1236 (La. 2005) (reversing dismissal of solicitation of oral sex charges against a sex worker because the *Lawrence* decision specifically stated it did "not disturb state statutes prohibiting public sexual conduct or prostitution."); State v. Pope, 608 S.E.2d 114, 116 (N.C. Ct. App. 2005) (same).

329 *See, e.g.*, McClary v. Commonwealth, No. 0240-13-4, 2014 WL 1707377, at *2 (Va. Ct. App. Apr. 29, 2014), *aff'd*, No. 140785, 2015 WL 10945036 (Va. Feb. 26, 2015) (upholding conviction for sodomy that occurred in a public area of a correctional facility); Askew v. Commonwealth, No. 0235-03-1, 2004 WL 234810, at *2 (Va. Ct. App. Feb. 10, 2004) (refusing to find "good cause" that would excuse the defendant's failure to object to the sodomy law at the trial court level because the oral sex "occurred the openness of the recreation area and was readily observable").

330 *See* People v. Groux, No. F059366, 2011 WL 2547022, at *11 (Cal. Ct. App. June 28, 2011); *see also* Jacobson v. State, No. 63293, 2013 WL 7167806 (Nev. Nov. 13, 2013)

Because laws targeting sodomy with minors also fall outside of *Lawrence*'s scope, they, too, have been upheld as valid exercise of the state's police power.[331] As a result, inchoate offenses related to sodomy, such as the solicitation of a minor to engage in oral or anal sex, may be prosecuted without running afoul the constitution.[332] Additionally, courts have held that convictions for sodomy against children that predate *Lawrence* may be used for sentencing enhancement purposes for other sex crimes committed after *Lawrence* was decided.[333] Moreover, sodomy laws

---

(upholding conviction for "conspiracy to commit voluntary sexual conduct between a prisoner and another person" without identifying the planned location). *But see* Vann v. Pixley, No. CL13000066–00, 2013 WL 9564167, at *2 (Va. Ct. App. 2013) (granting habeas corpus petition from inmate convicted of attempted sodomy for trying to engage in anal intercourse in a correctional courtyard, a public location, on the grounds that *Lawrence* rendered the sodomy law void ab initio).

The result in *Vann v. Pixley*, *id.*, is curious. The conduct in question occurred in a public location and, therefore, the conviction did not implicate *Lawrence*'s central holding. Nonetheless, the court felt constrained to grant the petition on the grounds that the U.S. Court of Appeals for the Fourth Circuit had declared the state law void under analogous circumstances—namely as applied to a solicitation of a minor to engage in oral sex. *See* MacDonald v. Moose, 710 F.3d 154, 165 (4th Cir. 2013) (stating that "although the Virginia General Assembly might be entitled to enact a statute specifically outlawing sodomy between an adult and an older minor, it has not seen fit to do so" and, therefore, the court would not rewrite the law to conform it to constitutional requirements). That same logic did not affect a direct appeal of a conviction for sodomy that occurred in a public area of a correctional facility in *McClary*, 2014 WL 1707377, at *2, presumably because Virginia state courts "construe the plain language of a statute to have limited application if such a construction will tailor the statute to a constitutional fit." Virginia Soc'y for Hum. Life v. Caldwell, 500 S.E.2d 814, 817 n.3 (1998).

331 McDonald v. Commonwealth, 645 S.E.2d 918, 924 (Va. 2007); People v. Fields, 178 Cal. Rptr. 3d 425, 434 (Ct. App. 2014), *review granted and opinion superseded*, 340 P.3d 1043 (Cal. 2015), *app. dismissed* 348 P.3d 875 (2015); Saunders v. Commonwealth, 753 S.E.2d 602, 608 (Va. Ct. App. 2014), *aff'd*, No. 140507, 2015 WL 10945236 (Va. Feb. 26, 2015); State v. Torres, No. COA07-156, 2007 WL 3256856, at *4 (N.C. Ct. App. Nov. 6, 2007).

332 Toghill v. Commonwealth, 768 S.E.2d 674, 678–80 (2015); Blackington v. Commonwealth, No. CL–2013–18691, 2015 WL 10521382, at *1 (Va. Cir. Ct. Mar. 3, 2015) (applying *Toghill* as "dispositive").

333 The Texas Court of Appeals determined otherwise in *Fisk v. State*, 538 S.W.3d 763, 776 (Tex. App. 2017), *rev'd*, 574 S.W.3d 917 (Tex. Crim. App. 2019). In that case, the defendant was convicted of three counts of sexual indecency with a child. *Fisk*, 538 S.W.3d at 766 (citing TEX. PENAL CODE ANN. § 22.011 (2009)). He was sentenced to three life sentences as a habitual defender, in part, because he had been convicted of sodomy while in the military during the time when former Article 125 of the Uniform

targeting sexual activity with minors may engender differential punishments than other forms of sex with minors. The California Court of Appeals reasoned that it was "not irrational" for the state legislature to have granted judges more discretion for imposing potentially harsher sentences for oral sex than for sexual intercourse between adults and certain teenagers because it may have wanted to "deter offenses it perceives as more common, more difficult to detect, and more likely to be committed than similar offenses, by imposing more severe punishment for them, even if the less common offenses involve a greater risk of harm."[334]

Military Code of Justice criminalized all forms of sodomy. *Id.* at 767 (citing UNITED STATES, MANUAL FOR COURTS-MARTIAL pt. IV, ¶ 87 (1982)). On appeal, he argued that his military conviction was not substantially similar to the state law offenses and, therefore, should not trigger the provision imposing automatic life sentences on habitual offenders. *Id.* at 771–75. The court agreed the military's former sodomy statute "was designed to protect against a certain type of sexual activity—penetration of the mouth or anus by the sexual organ of another—regardless of whether that activity was between consenting adults, between adults and children, or between persons and animals," whereas the state penal code protected "against nonconsensual contact or penetration of the mouth, anus, or sexual organ of an adult or any sexual acts against children." *Id.* at 776. The Texas Court of Criminal Appeals reversed, reasoning as follows:

> With respect to children, Article 125 contains elements that are substantially similar to the elements of sexual assault of a child under [our sexual assault statute]. They both prohibit the penetration of a child's mouth or anus by a person's sexual organ or the penetration of a person's mouth or anus by a child's sexual organ. The one-year age difference in the definition of child—16 vs. 17—does not defeat the substantial similarity. . . . Nor does Article 125's inclusion of carnal copulation "in any opening of the body" defeat a finding of substantial similarity because its prohibitions against sodomy with a child do not encompass a markedly different range of conduct than the Texas offenses [do].

Fisk, 574 S.W.3d at 923.

334 *Fields*, 178 Cal. Rptr. 3d at 434; *see also* People v. Garza, No. E041547, 2008 WL 187982, at *6 (Cal. Ct. App. Jan. 23, 2008); People v. Sintay, No. B177202, 2005 WL 2789322, at *7 (Cal. Ct. App. Oct. 27, 2005). *But see* People v. Hofsheier, 129 P.3d 29, 41–42 (Cal. 2006) (holding that mandatory lifetime sex offender registration for a twenty-two-year-old convicted of engaging in oral sex with a sixteen-year-old violated equal protection because vaginal sexual intercourse between people of those same ages was not subject to a mandatory registration requirement), *overruled by* Johnson v. Dep't of Just., 341 P.3d 1075 (Cal. 2015) (find that the potential for teenage pregnancy provided a rational basis to allow judges discretion in placing offenders on the registry, while mandating registration for those convicted of other nonforcible sex crimes).

Finally, acts of oral or anal sex that are not mutually consensual fall outside of *Lawrence*'s scope.[335]

2. The Criminal Regulation of Adultery and Fornication

Shortly after *Lawrence*, activists moved quickly to seek the invalidation of laws criminalizing fornication and adultery. They were unsuccessful in the first such case because the court found that the fear of possible criminal prosecution did not give rise to a "distinct and palpable injury" that would confer standing to challenge such laws.[336] But within two years of the *Lawrence* decision, the Virginia Supreme Court declared the state's fornication law unconstitutional in *Martin v. Ziherl*.[337] The court reasoned that *Lawrence* was dispositive:

> We find no principled way to conclude that the specific act of intercourse is not an element of a personal relationship between two unmarried persons or that the Virginia statute criminalizing intercourse between unmarried persons does not improperly abridge a personal relationship that is within the liberty interest of persons to choose. Because [the law] . . . is an attempt by the state to control the liberty interest which is exercised in making these personal decisions, it violates the Due Process Clause of the Fourteenth Amendment.[338]

The court in *Martin* noted that because *Lawrence* did not apply strict scrutiny, it would apply the rational basis test.[339] Even under this deferential standard, the court rejected the notion that any valid public reasons justified the fornication law's "encroachment on personal

---

335 Incest and bigamy could arguably be included in this category, but because consent is often questionable in many cases involving those offenses, they are presented in Section E of this chapter. *See infra* notes 505–538 and accompanying text. Other cases presenting questions of consent are discussed in Section D of this chapter. *See infra* notes 394–500 and accompanying text.

336 Berg v. State, 100 P.3d 261, 265 (Utah 2004).

337 607 S.E.2d 367, 371 (Va. 2005). The Virginia fornication law designated sex outside of marriage a low-level misdemeanor punishable by a fine case. VA. CODE § 18.2–344 (1975 & 2004 Supp.) (repealed by Va. Acts 2020, ch. 122).

338 *Martin*, 607 S.E.2d at 370.

339 *Id.*

liberty."[340] Commentators previously noted that the *Martin* court rejected several state arguments—including the promotion of marriage, raising children in family with married parents, and the dubious notion that extra-marital intercourse increases public health risks—that prior to *Lawrence*, would likely have satisfied the rational basis test.[341] In light of *Lawrence*, there can be little doubt that the outcome in *Martin* represents both an "acceptance of reality" regarding contemporary views on extramarital sex and a recognition of "the proper limits of the law."[342]

The *Martin* case is well-known. Indeed, the "citing references" feature in Westlaw reveals that at the time of this writing in mid-June of 2023, the case had been cited by fifty-five courts and 151 secondary sources.[343] It is, therefore, somewhat surprising that few states have followed *Martin*'s lead. In fact, only four cases since *Martin* have applied *Lawrence* to fornication or adultery statutes and only one, *Hobbs v. Smith*, similarly declared a fornication statute unconstitutional on due process grounds.[344]

3. The Civil Law Reach of Constitutionally Questionable Laws Criminalizing Adultery or Fornication

In *York v. Longlands Plantation*, the court refused to consider the constitutionality of South Carolina's fornication statute in a civil case for workers compensation survivor benefits because the claimant was unable to show she had been dependent on the deceased for the "reasonable

---

340 *Id.*

341 ESKRIDGE, *supra* note 101, at 344; Carpenter, *supra* note 18, at 1159.

342 Robert E. Rains, *The Future of Justice Scalia's Predictions of Family Law Doom*, 29 BYU J. PUB. L. 353, 370 (2015).

343 For an extensive analysis of adultery and fornication laws before and after *Lawrence*, including a discussion of the *Martin* case, see, e.g., Joanne Sweeny, *Undead Statutes: The Rise, Fall, and Continuing Uses of Adultery and Fornication Criminal Laws*, 46 LOY. U. CHI. L.J. 127 (2014).

344 Hobbs v. Smith, No. 05 CVS 267, 2006 WL 3103008, at *1 (N.C. Super. Ct. Aug. 25, 2006) ("The Court has reviewed the pleadings, the submissions of the parties, and has heard the arguments of counsel and is of the opinion that N.C.G.S. § 14–184 violates plaintiff's substantive due process right to liberty as explained in *Lawrence* . . . [and is therefore] declared unconstitutional, both on its face and as applied to the plaintiff, because it is in violation of the Fourteenth Amendment to the United States Constitution and Article I Section 19 of the North Carolina Constitution.").

necessities of life" and, therefore, would not qualify as a dependent for death benefits.[345] Other cases, though, provide insight into how some courts limit *Lawrence*'s reach.

In *Robinson v. Salvation Army*, the plaintiff filed a common law wrongful termination claim against her former employer in which she alleged that she had been fired for refusing to engage in sex with her manager.[346] Despite the fact that *Martin* had invalidated Virginia's fornication law, the plaintiff argued that because it remained "on the books," it represented the state's public policy; thus, she argued that terminating her employment-at-will for refusal to commit a violation of the law was actionable.[347] Both a trial court and the Supreme Court of Virginia rejected her argument, reasoning that for her claim to be cognizable, her manager would have to had encouraged her to engage in conduct that fell outside the realm of *Lawrence* by engaging in "public fornication, prostitution, or other such crimes."[348] Absent such facts, the court held that demands for extramarital sex "can no longer provide the basis for a valid allegation of wrongful termination whether the employee accedes to the demands or is terminated for refusing the demands." But this is quite a narrow interpretation of *Lawrence*. At-will employees who are subject to termination for refusing to engage in sexual activity with a supervisor could easily fall within *Lawrence*'s exclusion for those "who are situated in relationships where consent might not easily be refused."[349] Indeed, a lower court in Virginia cited that very sentence in *Lawrence* when ruling that a wrongful termination claim stemming from an alleged refusal to engage in acts of adultery, fornication, or sodomy did, in fact, violate the public policy of the state.[350] Curiously, that case was not cited

---

[345] 840 S.E.2d 544, 578 n.5 (S.C. 2020) ("While we are cognizant of *Lawrence* . . . and case law from other states casting doubt on the constitutionality of section 16-15-60, we need not address this issue in light of our decision.").

[346] 791 S.E.2d 577, 578 (Va. 2016).

[347] *Id.* at 578–80.

[348] *Id.* at 580.

[349] Lawrence v. Texas, 539 U.S. 558, 578 (2003).

[350] *See, e.g.*, Bomar v. Chesapeake Bay Steakhouse, Inc., No. CL12–2415, 2013 WL 9564168 (Va. Cir. Ct. 2013).

in *Robinson v. Salvation Army* despite the fact that it had been decided three years earlier.

Malecek v. Williams involved the constitutionality of two "common law causes of action—alienation of affection and criminal conversion—that permit litigants to sue the lovers of their unfaithful spouses."[351] The court acknowledged these "aging" torts "were born out of misogyny and in modern times are often used as tools for enterprising divorce lawyers seeking leverage over the other side."[352] Yet, the court rejected the defendant's challenge to these causes of action, reasoning that they deterred and compensated for personal injuries while fostering "the promise of monogamy that accompanies most marriage commitments."[353] In so holding, the court rejected the defendant's argument that these torts infringed on the constitutionally protected liberty interest for consenting adults to engage in private sexual relations. The court noted *Lawrence* applies only to activity that did not inflict "injury to a person" or "abuse . . . an institution the law protects."[354] Because marriage is an "obvious choice" of an important human institution the law protects, the court held that the two torts at issue in the case served a legitimate—even a substantial—governmental interest in compensating aggrieved spouses for the injuries caused by marital infidelity.[355]

B. Prostitution and Related Commercial Sex Offenses ($n = 11$, 3.6%)

All eleven of the prostitution and related cases (e.g., pimping) were criminal in nature. Three judicial opinions (27.3%) applied *Lawrence* straightforwardly, one dissenting opinion applied the precedent broadly, and all of the rest construed *Lawrence* narrowly in this context ($n = 7$, 63.6.7%). Table 11 illustrates that all of the cases were resolved in favor of the prosecution; none of the other variables were significantly related to how *Lawrence* was applied in these cases.

---

351 804 S.E.2d 592, 594 (N.C. Ct. App. 2017).

352 *Id.*

353 *Id.*

354 *Id.* at 595.

355 *Id.* at 595–96.

TABLE 11: VARIABLE FREQUENCIES AND RELATIONSHIPS TO TREATMENT OF *LAWRENCE* IN PROSTITUTION CASES

Category	**Treatment of *Lawrence*** ***n* (%)**				**Chi-Square**	**Sig.**	**Cramer's V**
Depth	*Neutral*	*Narrow*	*Broad*	*Total*	1.946 (2, 11)	p > 0.050	N/A
Mentioned in Passing	2 (18.2%)	2 (18.2%)	0 (0.0%)	4 (36.4%)			
Key to Case	1 (9.1%)	5 (45.5%)	1 (9.1%)	7 (63.6%)			
Outcome	*Neutral*	*Narrow*	*Broad*	*Total*	No statistics can be computed because all case outcomes (*n* = 11, 100.0%) favored the prosecution		
Prosecution	3 (27.3%)	7 (63.6%)	1 (9.1%)	11 (65.5%)			
Defense	0 (0.0%)	0 (0.0%)	0 (0.0%)	0 (0.0%)			
State Politics	*Neutral*	*Narrow*	*Broad*	*Total*	5.587 (6, 11)	p > 0.050	N/A
Deep Red	0 (0.0%)	3 (27.3%)	0 (0.0%)	3 (27.3%)			
Light Red	1 (9.1%)	0 (0.0%)	0 (0.0%	1 (9.1%)			
Purple	0 (0.0%)	1 (9.1%)	0 (0.0%)	1 (9.1%)			
Light Blue	0 (0.0%)	0 (0.0%)	0 (0.0%)	0 (0.0%)			
Deep Blue	2 (18.2%)	3 (27.3%)	1 (9.1%)†	6 (54.4%)			
Region	*Neutral*	*Narrow*	*Broad*	*Total*	7.543 (4, 11)	p > 0.050	N/A
Northeast	0 (0.0%)	0 (0.0%)	0 (0.0%)	0 (0.0%)			
South	0 (0.0%)	3 (27.3%)	0 (0.0%)	3 (27.3%)			
Midwest	0 (0.0%)	3 (27.3%)	0 (0.0%)	3 (27.3%)			
West	3 (27.3%)	1 (9.1%)	1 (9.1%)	5 (45.5%)			
Judge's Sex	*Neutral*	*Narrow*	*Broad*	*Total*	0.629 (2, 11)	p > 0.050	N/A
Male	3 (27.3%)	6 (54.5%)	1 (9.1%)	10 (90.9%)			
Female	0 (0.00%)	1 (9.1%)	0 (0.0%)	1 (9.1%)			
Judge's Race/Ethnicity	*Neutral*	*Narrow*	*Broad*	*Total*	3.317 (2, 11)	p > 0.050	N/A
White	2 (18.2%)	6 (54.5%)	0 (0.0%)	8 (72.7%)			
Nonwhite	1 (9.1%)	1 (9.1%)	1 (9.1%)	3 (27.3%)			
Judge's Political Affiliation	*Neutral*	*Narrow*	*Broad*	*Total*	7.857 (4, 29)	p > 0.050	N/A
Nonpartisan	3 (27.3%)	3 (27.3%)	0 (0.0%)	6 (54.6%)			
Democrat	0 (0.0%)	1 (9.1%)	1 (9.1%)	2 (18.2%)			
Republican	0 (0.0%)	3 (27.3%)	0 (0.0%)	3 (27.3%)			

† Dissenting opinion

Justice Scalia's dissent in *Lawrence* warned that the majority decision in the case threatened the validity of laws against prostitution, but his concerns did not materialize.[356] Courts have uniformly held that *Lawrence* specifically excluded commercial conduct from its holding and, therefore, laws criminalizing prostitution—including solicitation of prostitution and pimping—have uniformly withstood constitutional challenges.[357] Indeed,

356 Lawrence v. Texas, 539 U.S. 558, 590 (Scalia, J., dissenting).

357 *E.g.*, People v. Conroy, 145 N.E.3d 537, 541–44 (2019); State v. Romano, 155 P.3d 1102, 1110–1115 (2007); Robles v. State, 585 S.W.3d 591, 595–96 (Tex. App. 2019).

the lack of any statistically significant results in Table 11 lends support to the fact that judges are unified in their approaches to applying *Lawrence* in prostitution cases (and hence there are no significant differences to be detected). Specifically, regardless of extralegal case characteristics, courts uniformly rejected arguments that *Lawrence* "recognized any fundamental right to privacy concerning consensual adult sexual activity" and, therefore, laws criminalizing commercial sex needed only to survive rational basis review.[358] Reasoning such laws were rationally related to the legitimate governmental interests of deterring related crimes, "such as human trafficking and sexual assault" as well as curbing "the spread of infectious diseases," courts consistently upheld such laws in the name of public health, safety, and welfare.[359] Laws specifically targeting pimping were also upheld on the grounds that they prevent exploitation of others and the expansion of the potential supply of those engaging in prostitution.[360]

Although all majority decisions unanimously rejected the notion that *Lawrence* protects commercial sex, not all judges agreed. For example in *State v. Romano*, after acknowledging *Lawrence*'s specific exclusion of prostitution from its holding, a dissenting justice on the Hawai'i Supreme Court wrote the following:

> No further explanation of prostitution's exclusion was forthcoming, but the thrust of the *Lawrence* majority's analysis supports the conclusion that the Court was focused on addressing only private sexual activity among adults capable of consenting and, therefore, to the extent that prostitution involves public solicitation, it departed from the realm of the private and, hence, from the scope of the *Lawrence* analysis. However, where two consenting adults swap money for sex in a transaction undertaken

---

358 Jackson v. State, No. 05-10-00561-CR, 2011 WL 2320819, at *2 (Tex. App. June 14, 2011).

359 Cardoso-Reyna v. State, No. 03-19-00050-CR, 2021 WL 219303, at *4 (Tex. App. Jan. 22, 2021); People v. Ford, No. B300811, 2020 WL 5687501, at *4–5 (Cal. Ct. App. Sept. 24, 2020); State v. Green, 989 N.E.2d 1088, 1090 (Ohio Ct. App. 2013); State v. Freitag, 130 P.3d 544, 546 (Ariz. Ct. App. 2006); People v. Williams, 811 N.E.2d 1197, 1198–99 (Ill. Ct. App. 2004).

360 People v. Miller, No. B267728, 2016 WL 6835497, at *4 (Cal. Ct. App. Nov. 21, 2016); People v. Grant, 123 Cal. Rptr. 3d 840, 844–48 (2011).

> entirely in seclusion, the analysis of the *Lawrence* majority, despite the majority's attempt to avoid the notion, leads inexorably to the conclusion that the state may not exercise its police power to criminalize a private decision between two consenting adults to engage in sexual activity, whether for remuneration or not.[361]

Justice Steven H. Levinson therefore would have applied strict scrutiny to the prostitution law as applied to the defendant.[362] Because he viewed potential threats to marriage and the possible transmission of sexually-transmitted infections as being "speculative and attenuated," Justice Levinson argued that for private activities involving sex for compensation, less restrictive time, plane, and manner restrictions would be more constitutionally appropriate than those applicable to prostitution in the public sphere, including "streetwalking" and advertisements for escort services.[363] To date, no appellate courts applying *Lawrence* to laws criminalizing prostitution or related offenses have agreed with his perspective on this matter.

C. Obscenity and Pornography (n = 12, 3.9%)

Sexually-explicit expression that is indecent, but not obscene, is protected by the First Amendment, whereas obscene materials are not. Since 1973, the test for obscenity has been governed by the U.S. Supreme Court's decision in *Miller v. California*.[364] *Miller* held that work is obscene if three criteria are met: (1) the average person, applying contemporary community standards, must find that the work, taken as a whole, appeals to the prurient interest (i.e., a shameful or morbid interest in nudity, sex, or excretion); (2) it must depict, in a patently offensive way, sexual conduct specifically defined by the applicable state law; and (3) taken as a whole, the work must lack serious literary, artistic, political, or scientific value.[365]

---

361 *Romano*, 155 P.3d at 1118–19 (Levinson, J., dissenting).

362 *Id.* at 1124.

363 *Id.*

364 413 U.S. 15, 24 (1973).

365 *Id.* at 24–25.

Although states may criminalize the production and distribution of obscene materials, it may not criminally regulate the personal possession of such materials pursuant to the U.S. Supreme Court's decision in *Stanley v. Georgia*, in which the Court reasoned that "[w]hatever the power of the state to control public dissemination of ideas inimical to the public morality, it cannot constitutionally premise legislation on the desirability of controlling a person's private thoughts."[366] The scope of *Stanley*'s protections, however, does not extend to the possession of child pornography because "safeguarding the physical and psychological well-being of a minor" constitutes a compelling government interest and banning the possessing of such materials is narrowly tailored to achieve that end.[367]

Courts have been called upon to apply these principles of obscenity law in cases in which litigants argued that *Lawrence* somehow altered the landscape of these leading precedents. Judges overwhelmingly disagreed with such arguments at illustrated by the criminal case outcome distribution in Table 12, which also presents frequencies for the other variables and their relationships to how courts applied *Lawrence* in the cases in this category. Notably, courts in the South and Midwest construed *Lawrence* narrowly in this context, to a statistically significant degree, compared to alternative applications of the precedent.

---

366 394 U.S. 557, 566 (1969).

367 Osborne v. Ohio, 495 U.S. 103, 109 (1990).

TABLE 12: VARIABLE FREQUENCIES AND RELATIONSHIPS TO TREATMENT OF *LAWRENCE* IN OBSCENITY AND PORNOGRAPHY CASES

Category	**Treatment of *Lawrence* *n* (%)**				**Chi-Square**	**Sig.**	**Cramer's V**
Depth	*Neutral*	*Narrow*	*Broad*	*Total*	1.714 (2, 12)	p > 0.050	N/A
Mentioned in Passing	1 (8.3%)	3 (25.0%)	1 (8.3%)	5 (41.7%)			
Key to Case	1 (8.3%)	6 (50.0%)	0 (0.0%)	7 (58.3%)			
Outcome	*Neutral*	*Narrow*	*Broad*	*Total*	12.000 (2, 12)	Fisher Exact p = .008	0.999
Prosecution	2 (16.7%)	9 (75.0%)	0 (0.0%)	11 (91.7%)			
Defense	0 (0.0%)	0 (0.0%)	1 (9.1%)	1 (8.3%)			
State Politics	*Neutral*	*Narrow*	*Broad*	*Total*	5.926 (4, 12)	p > 0.050	N/A
Deep Red	2 (16.7%)	7 (58.3%)	0 (0.0%)	0 (75.0%)			
Light Red	0 (0.0%)	0 (0.0%)	0 (0.0%	0 (0.0%)			
Purple	0 (0.0%)	1 (8.3%)	0 (0.0%)	1 (8.3%)			
Light Blue	0 (0.0%)	0 (0.0%)	0 (0.0%)	0 (0.0%)			
Deep Blue	0 (0.7%)	1 (8.3%)	1 (8.3%)	2 (16.7%)			
Region	*Neutral*	*Narrow*	*Broad*	*Total*	13.524 (4, 12)	Fisher's Exact p = 0.041	0.751
Northeast	0 (0.0%)	0 (0.0%)	0 (0.0%)	0 (0.0%)			
South	2 (16.7%)	5 (41.7%)	0 (0.0%)	7 (58.3%)			
Midwest	0 (0.0%)	4 (33.3%)	0 (0.0%)	4 (33.3%)			
West	0 (0.0%)	0 (0.0%)	1 (8.3%)	1 (8.3%)			
Judge's Sex	*Neutral*	*Narrow*	*Broad*	*Total*	0.917 (2, 11)	p > 0.050	N/A
Male	1 (9.1%)	6 (54.5%)	1 (9.1%)	8 (72.7%)			
Female	1 (9.1%)	2 (18.2%)	0 (0.0%)	4 (33.3%)			
Judge's Race/Ethnicity	*Neutral*	*Narrow*	*Broad*	*Total*	5.926 (4, 12)	p > 0.050	N/A
White	2 (16.7%)	7 (58.3%)	0 (0.0%)	9 (75.0%)			
Nonwhite	0 (0.0%)	1 (8.3%)	1 (8.3%)	2 (16.7%)			
Not Applicable or Unknown	0 (0.0%)	1 (8.3%)	0 (0.0%)	1 (8.3%)			
Judge's Political Affiliation	*Neutral*	*Narrow*	*Broad*	*Total*	2.333 (6, 12)	p > 0.050	N/A
Nonpartisan	1 (8.3%)	2 (16.7%)	0 (0.0%)	3 (25.0%)			
Democrat	0 (0.0%)	2 (16.7%)	0 (0.0%)	2 (16.7%)			
Republican	1 (8.3%)	4 (33.3%)	1 (8.3%)	6 (50.0%)			
Unknown	0 (0.0%)	1 (8.3%)	0 (0.0%)	1 (8.3%)			

1. Child Pornography

Courts uniformly rejected arguments from defendants who asserted that *Lawrence*'s recognition of a protected liberty interest for adults to engage in private, consensual sexual conduct extends to the possession or creation of materials that fall within the definition of child pornography.

> [I]n this case the defendant engaged in sex with a minor and pressured him to pose nude for photographs, one of which was sent over the internet. We find no support in *Lawrence* to prevent

> the defendant's prosecution . . . . The defendant's privacy argument also fails, for his activities related to child pornography are not protected by a constitutional right of privacy.[368]

Importantly, this logic applied to child pornography cases in which the minors depicted in photos or videos had reached the age of consent and, therefore, were old enough to engage in sexual activity lawfully under state law.[369] Courts explained that laws barring child pornography are aimed at different types of harm than those targeted by statutory rape laws.[370]

> Even for those who record an intimate act and intend for it to remain secret, a danger exists that the recording may find its way into the public sphere, haunting the child participant for the rest of his or her life. It is reasonable to conclude that persons [sixteen] and [seventeen] years old, although old enough to consent to sexual relations, may not fully appreciate that today's recording of a private, intimate moment may be the Internet's biggest hit next week.[371]

In contrast to courts' unanimous rejection of *Lawrence* as protecting the possession or creation of child pornography, at least one court held that *Lawrence* limited the terms of probation that could be imposed on a defendant convicted of possessing such materials. The defendant in *People v. Kinley* appealed his sentence for possession of child pornography because it included a condition that required him to "not establish an intimate/romantic relationship or cohabit with a person, whether or not that person is responsible for the care of minor children, without having fully

---

368 Cochran v. State, 111 So. 3d 148, 157 (Ala. Crim. App. 2012) (internal citations and alterations omitted); *see also* State v. Horn, No. 91,692, 2005 WL 823896, at *2 (Kan. Ct. App. Apr. 8, 2005) ("[*Lawrence*] specifically excluded children from its determination and pointed out that the only legitimate historical precedent for a state regulating sexual practices involved predatory acts, such an adult victimizing a child . . . . Because an individual has no constitutionally protected interest in engaging in sexual contact with minors, we reject [defendant's] due process challenge.").

369 *Cochran*, 111 So. 3d at 157; *Ex parte* Dehnert, 605 S.W.3d 885, 892 (Tex. App. 2020) (differentiating *Lawrence* as involving the privacy rights of two consenting adults" from those of minors "who might be injured or coerced").

370 *E.g.*, State v. Senters, 699 N.W.2d 810, 817 (2005).

371 *Id.*; *see also* People v. Hollins, 971 N.E.2d 504, 510–11 (Ill. 2012) (relying on *Senters*).

disclosed to that person the nature of your conviction, probation status and necessity for their written informed consent."[372] The court agreed with the defendant that the provision was overbroad because it infringed on his constitutionally-protected privacy rights by forcing him to disclose his criminal history with potential partners who have no children while not serving any rehabilitative purpose.[373]

2. Pornography Involving Adults

Only one case in the study concerned a constitutional question about pornography that did not involve children. In *Baird v. State*, although the defendant had been convicted of possessing child pornography,[374] he challenged the use of pornographic material involving adults that had been found on his computer during his sentencing. The prosecution offered such images purportedly to give the judge "a full picture" of his sexual interests and "the extent to which he will go to indulge in those sexual proclivities" so the court could evaluate the defendant's "redeemability" and "danger to the community."[375] On appeal, the defendant argued that because those images were not illegal, they were constitutionally protected under *Lawrence* and, therefore, should not have been used as evidence at his sentencing hearing.[376] Because the admissibility of evidence used at sentencing lies within the discretion of a trial court, the appellate court did not meaningfully address the constitutional issue, but rather applied the abuse of discretion standard to hold that "it was within the zone of reasonable disagreement for the trial court to admit this evidence."[377]

3. Sale, Distribution, and Promotion of Adult-Oriented Materials

In cases narrowly construing *Lawrence*, courts rejected assertions that *Lawrence* recognized a fundamental right to sexual privacy, thereby

---

372 No. A130550, 2011 WL 6099374, at *5 (Cal. Ct. App. Dec. 8, 2011).

373 *Id.* at *5–6.

374 Baird v. State, 379 S.W.3d 353, 354 (Tex. App. 2012), *aff'd*, 398 S.W.3d 220 (Tex. Crim. App. 2013).

375 *Id.* at 359.

376 *Id.*

377 *Id.* at 360.

paving the way to uphold laws criminalizing the sale of adult materials, including sex toys, using the deferential rational basis standard of review.[378] Consider *1568 Montgomery Highway, Inc. v. City of Hoover*, a case in which the Alabama Supreme Court upheld the constitutionality of a state statute that criminalized the sale or distribution of "any device designed or marketed as primarily useful for the stimulation of human genital organs . . . ."[379] Following the lead of the Eleventh Circuit in *Williams v. Prior*, a pre-*Lawrence* federal case upholding that same law,[380] the Alabama Supreme Court reasoned that there were rational bases for such a prohibition, including the protection of public morality.[381] But *Lawrence* should have led to the rejection of that particular justification. Yet, the court embraced Justice Scalia's dissent in *Lawrence*—which, of course, was not controlling law—when it stated that "to hold that public morality can never serve as a rational basis for legislation after *Lawrence* would cause a 'massive disruption of the current social order.'"[382] The court quoted heavily from the federal district court decision in the remand of the *Williams* case, which conflated *Lawrence*'s due process and equal protection implications when it upheld the Alabama law, reasoning that *Lawrence*'s statements about morality were not aimed at ending all morals legislation, but rather were limited to the criminalization of conduct that targeted a class of people out of animus, hostility, or moral condemnation.[383] Because the Alabama law applied to all adults—married or unmarried, regardless of sex or sexual orientation, the court distinguished the case from the morals-laden regulation of sodomy at issue

---

378 1568 Montgomery Highway, Inc. v. City of Hoover, 45 So. 3d 319, 329 (Ala. 2010).

379 *Id.* at 330 (citing ALA. CODE § 13A-12-200.2 (1999)).

380 Williams v. Pryor, 240 F.3d 944, 950 (11th Cir. 2001).

381 *1568 Montgomery Highway*, 45 So. 3d at 341.

382 *Id.* at 334–35 (quoting Williams v. King, 420 F. Supp. 2d 1224, 1249–50 (N.D. Ala. 2006) (quoting Lawrence v. Texas, 539 U.S. at 591 (2003) (Scalia, J., dissenting)), *aff'd*, 478 F.3d 1316 (11th Cir. 2007)).

383 *1568 Montgomery Highway*, 45 So. 3d at 334–35.

in *Lawrence*.[384] It also distinguished the case as bar from *Lawrence* in that the Alabama law regulated commercial activity, not private conduct.[385]

By contrast, other courts invalidated laws banning the sale of adult materials by interpreting *Lawrence* more broadly. One of the leading cases to do so was *Reliable Consultants, Inc. v. Earle*, a federal case in which the Fifth Circuit stated that *Lawrence* was not just concerned with the constitutionality of a particular act, "but instead a right to be free from governmental intrusion regarding the most private human contact, sexual behavior."[386] In a far more accurate reading of *Lawrence* than the one given to it in *1568 Montgomery Highway*, the Fifth Circuit specifically rejected the argument that the general applicability of the law banning the sale of sex toys somehow removed the statute from the scope of *Lawrence*'s protection by not targeting a specific class of people because *Lawrence*'s central holding rested on due process, not equal protection grounds.[387]

> An individual who wants to legally use a safe sexual device during private intimate moments alone or with another is unable to legally purchase a device in Texas, which heavily burdens a constitutional right. This conclusion is consistent with the decisions in *Carey* and *Griswold*, where the Court held that restricting commercial transactions unconstitutionally burdened the exercise of individual rights. Indeed, under this statute it is

---

384 *Id.*

385 *Id.* at 336 (quoting *Williams*, 478 F.3d at 1322–23); *see also Ex parte* Dave, 220 S.W.3d 154, 158–59 (Tex. App. 2007) (rejecting the argument that *Lawrence* expanded the right to privacy "into the public sphere of commercial transactions between consenting adults"); State v. Acosta, No. 08-04-00312-CR, 2005 WL 2095290, at *3 (Tex. App. Aug. 31, 2005) (rejecting that *Lawrence* encompasses the commercial sale of sexual devices); State v. Jenkins, No. C–040111, 2004 WL 3015091, at *5 (Ohio Ct. App. Dec. 30, 2004) ("[E]ven though the Supreme Court has recognized a person's right to sit alone in the privacy of his own home and view obscene matter, . . . the Court has never articulated a correlative right to transport, distribute, mail, or sell such materials." (internal citations omitted)); *cf.* Varkonyi v. State, 276 S.W.3d 27, 38 (Tex. App. 2008) (upholding obscenity conviction for showing undercover officers a video depicting bestiality on the grounds that *Lawrence* did not protect the "promotion of obscene material").

386 Reliable Consultants, Inc. v. Earle, 517 F.3d 738, 744 (5th Cir. 2008) (internal quotations omitted).

387 *Id.*

> even illegal to "lend" or "give" a sexual device to another person. This further restricts the exercise of the constitutional right to engage in private intimate conduct in the home free from government intrusion. It also undercuts any argument that the statute only affects public conduct.[388]

Thus, by applying *Lawrence* more faithfully than the Eleventh Circuit or the Alabama Supreme Court were willing to do in similar cases, the Fifth Circuit rejected public morality as a basis for upholding the statute at issue in *Reliable Consultants*.[389] The court also rejected the protection of children as a rational basis for the law, reasoning that such an aim was not logically connected to prohibiting consenting adults from accessing such materials.[390]

In *1568 Montgomery Highway,* the Alabama Supreme Court found the Eleventh Circuit's reasoning in *Williams* to be more persuasive than the Fifth Circuit's reasoning in *Reliable Consultants*, largely because the Alabama statute reached "public commercial activity, not the regulation of private sexual conduct."[391] But the Texas statute that the Fifth Circuit invalidated also reached commercial activity by banning the selling or advertising of sexual devices.[392] Because the Alabama Supreme Court did not fully explain its reasons beyond that one, flawed justification, the decision in *568 Montgomery Highway* does not satisfactorily explain why the Fifth Circuit's more expansive view of *Lawrence* is less persuasive than the then Eleventh Circuit's.

D. Sexual Assault and Statutory Rape ($n = 97$, 31.6%)

As previously discussed, the scope of *Lawrence*'s constitutional protections concerns private sexual conduct between consenting adults. There is no protected due process liberty interest in any nonconsensual sex acts, including those involving participants whose capacity to consent is impaired. These facts notwithstanding, discussions of *Lawrence* were

---

388 *Id.* at 744.

389 *Id.* at 745–46.

390 *Id.* at 746.

391 1568 Montgomery Highway, Inc. v. City of Hoover, 45 So. 3d 319, 341 (Ala. 2010).

392 *See Reliable Consultants*, 517 F.3d at 741 (citing TEX. PENAL CODE § 43.21 (1994)).

more prevalent in sexual assault cases than in any other category in the study—the overwhelming majority of which ($n = 79$, 81.4%) simply called for a straightforward application of *Lawrence*'s so-called exclusion paragraph.[393] In the remaining cases, eleven (11.3%) construed *Lawrence* narrowly and seven (7.2%) construed the case broadly. Table 13 summarizes the characteristics of the cases in this category across the other dependent variables in the study.

Table 13 shows that two variables were statistically significantly related to the treatment of *Lawrence* in sexual assault cases. First, when *Lawrence* was mentioned in passing or briefly discussed, it was neutrally interpreted in twenty-six (26.8%) of cases, and nearly evenly divided in the others, with five cases interpreting it narrowly and six interpreting it broadly. But when *Lawrence* was key to the outcome in case, its central holding or specified exclusions were dispositive in fifty-three (54.6%) cases, while narrow interpretations outnumbered broad interpretations by a ratio of six to one. Second, neutral application of *Lawrence* resulted in an outcome favorable to the prosecution in seventy-three cases compared to just five with outcomes favoring the defense. When judges had to go beyond *Lawrence*'s holding and articulated exclusions, narrow constructions of the precedent occurred in eight cases that ended in favor of the prosecution, compared to only two that gave *Lawrence* broad interpretations but nonetheless resulted in a conviction being upheld. In cases with outcomes ultimately favoring defendants, broad interpretations of *Lawrence* were more common than narrow constructions. These data show a very strong association between the treatment of *Lawrence* and the ultimate outcome in sexual assault cases. The qualitative analyses of cases illustrate the reasons why this is true.

393 Lawrence v. Texas, 539 U.S. 558, 578 (2003) (excluding minors, public conduct, position, and "persons who might be injured or coerced or who are situated in relationships where consent might not easily be refused").

TABLE 13: VARIABLE FREQUENCIES AND RELATIONSHIPS TO TREATMENT OF *LAWRENCE* IN SEXUAL ASSAULT CASES

Category	Treatment of *Lawrence* *n* (%)				Chi-Square	Sig.	Cramer's V
Type	*Neutral*	*Narrow*	*Broad*	*Total*	0.230 (2, 97)	p > 0.050	N/A
Civil	1 (1.0%)	0 (0.0%)	0 (0.0%)	1 (1.0%)			
Criminal	78 (80.4%)	11 (11.3%)	7 (7.2%)	96 (99.0%)			
Depth	*Neutral*	*Narrow*	*Broad*	*Total*	7.880 (2, 97)	Fisher's Exact p = 0.014	0.285
Mentioned in Passing	26 (26.8%)	5 (5.2%)	6 (6.2%)	37 (38.1%)			
Key to Case	53 (54.6%)	6 (6.2%)	1 (1.0%)	60 (61.9%)			
Outcome	*Neutral*	*Narrow*	*Broad*	*Total*	25.643 (4, 97)	Fisher's Exact p = 0.001	0.364
Prosecution	73 (75.3%)	8 (8.2%)	2 (2.1%)	83 (85.6%)			
Defense	5 (5.2%)	3 (3.1%)	5 (5.2%)	13 (13.4%)			
Not Relevant (Civil)	1 (1.0%)	0 (0.0%)	0 (0.0%	1 (1.0%)			
State Politics	*Neutral*	*Narrow*	*Broad*	*Total*	13.899 (8, 97)	p > 0.050	N/A
Deep Red	38 (39.2%)	2 (2.1%)	2 (2.1%)	42 (4.3%)			
Light Red	6 (6.2%)	4 (4.1%)	0 (0.0%	10 (10.3%)			
Purple	3 (3.1%)	0 (0.0%)	1 (1.0%)	4 (4.1%)			
Light Blue	5 (5.2%)	1 (1.0%)	1 (1.0%)	7 (7.2%)			
Deep Blue	27 (27.8%)	4 (4.1%)	3 (3.1%)	34 (35.1%)			
Region	*Neutral*	*Narrow*	*Broad*	*Total*	5.719 (6, 97)	p > 0.050	N/A
Northeast	10 (10.3%)	2 (2.1%)	2 (2.1%)	14 (14.4%)			
South	34 (35.1%)	3 (3.1%)	2 (2.1%)	39 (40.2%)			
Midwest	17 (17.5%)	5 (5.2%)	1 (1.0%)	23 (23.7%)			
West	18 (18.6%)	1 (1.0%)	2 (2.1%)	21 (21.6%)			
Judge's Sex	*Neutral*	*Narrow*	*Broad*	*Total*	0.990 (4, 93)	p > 0.050	N/A
Male	47 (50.5%)	8 (8.6%)	4 (4.3%)	59 (63.4%)			
Female	26 (28.0%)	3 (3.2%)	3 (3.2%)	32 (34.4%)			
Not Applicable (per curiam)	2 (2.2%)	0 (0.0%)	0 (0.0%)	2 (2.2%)			
Judge's Race/Ethnicity	*Neutral*	*Narrow*	*Broad*	*Total*	2.925 (4, 97)	p > 0.050	N/A
White	66 (68.0%)	11 (11.3%)	6 (6.2%)	83 (85.6%)			
Nonwhite	7 (7.2%)	0 (0.0%)	1 (1.0%)	8 (8.2%)			
Not Applicable or Unknown	6 (6.2%)	0 (0.0%)	0 (0.0%)	6 (6.2%)			
Judge's Political Affiliation	*Neutral*	*Narrow*	*Broad*	*Total*	5.711 (6, 97)	p > 0.050	N/A
Nonpartisan	51 (52.6%)	6 (6.2%)	4 (4.1%)	61 (62.9%)			
Democrat	11 (11.3%)	1 (1.0%)	1 (1.0%)	13 (13.4%)			
Republican	16 (16.5%)	3 (3.1%)	1 (1.0%)	20 (20.6%)			
Not Applicable or Unknown	1 (1.0%)	1 (1.0%)	1 (1.0%)	3 (3.1%)			

1. Sexual Assaults Involving Force, Threats of Force, or Clear Nonconsent

A straightforward application of *Lawrence* results in courts unanimously rejecting claims that *Lawrence* somehow shields defendants' actions when a trier-of-fact concludes that the victim either did not consent to the acts in question in any given case,[394] or withdrew consent during the

---

[394] *E.g.*, State v. Music, No. 33285–3–III, 2016 WL 1704687, at *4–5 (Wash. Ct. App. Apr. 28, 2016) (reversing declaration that state sodomy law was facially unconstitutional since the conviction at issue was for forcible, not consensual sodomy from a time that predated the update of rape statutes to include nonconsensual oral sex); Gilbert v. State, 220 So. 3d 1099, 1105 (Ala. Crim. App. 2016) (upholding sodomy conviction the absence of consent); Wesson v. State, 208 So. 3d 1160, 1163 (Ala. Crim. App. 2015) (same); *In re* J.F., 766 S.E.2d 341, 348 (N.C. Ct. App. 2014) (reversing sodomy conviction for insufficiency of the evidence that any penetration occurred, but noting that had there been oral penetration, *Lawrence* would not be a bar to delinquency liability for a fourteen-year-old convincing a seven-year-old to engage in oral sex); People v. Garza, No. E041547, 2008 WL 187982, at *6 (Cal. Ct. App. Jan. 23, 2008) (rejecting claim that *Lawrence* prohibits differential punishments for sexual assault and sodomy on a child by someone over a certain age); State v. Schrader, No. 97,206, 2007 WL 4577915, at *2–3 (Kan. Ct. App. Dec. 21, 2007) (rejecting constitutional challenge to sodomy law in a case involving attempt on presumed fourteen-year-old who was actually a police officer posing as such in a chat room); State v. Irby, No. 95,349, 2007 WL 219971, at *1 (Kan. Ct. App. Jan. 26, 2007) (upholding convictions for forcible rape and sodomy of a child over defendant's claim that such conduct was protected by *Lawrence*); State v. Tillman, No. 92,850, 2005 WL 3579258, at *5 (Kan. Ct. App. Dec. 30. 2005) (upholding constitutionality of child rape statute on the grounds that it served the legitimate state interest of protecting children from adult sexual predators); People v. Sanches, No. G032738, 2004 WL 2757435, at *6 (Cal. Ct. App. Dec. 2, 2004) ("We further dismiss out of hand defendant's contention that his spousal rape conviction infringed on the right to privacy between a marital couple. This is not a victimless case where the state has charged mutually consenting adults with committing a sexual act prohibited by state law in the privacy of their home."); *cf.* State v. Goewey, 135 A.3d 1220, 1224 (Vt. 2015) (upholding maximum sentence for aggravated sexual assault imposed on sixty-one year-old-man for having performed oral sex on a "young man" over the defendant's objections that the trial court biasedly referred to the victim as having been "repeatedly sodomized," thereby expressing a purportedly "religious view or moral judgment by the judge about sexual practices, which impermissibly tainted the sentencing hearing"); House v. State, No. 1717 Sept. Term 2013, 2015 WL 6087609, at *2 (Md. Ct. Spec. App. July 21, 2015) (rejecting appeal from defendant convicted of forcible rape and sodomy over his objection to a pattern jury instruction that had not been updated to reflect *Lawrence*'s holding, yet he had requested at trial); State v. Franco, 319 P.3d 551, 556–57 (Kan. Ct. App. 2014) (upholding conviction for forcible sodomy over defendant's argument that the judge should have provided a lesser include offense jury instruction for nonforcible sodomy even though that offense had been effectively decriminalized by *Lawrence*).

encounter.[395] By contrast, when defendants are acquitted at trial for sexual assaults for which consent is a defense, sodomy laws can no longer be used as a catch-all offense.[396] Consider the decision *Williams v. State*.[397]

The defendant in *Williams* had been charged with forcible sodomy. He was acquitted, but convicted of the lesser included offense of sexual misconduct—an offense that Alabama law defined at the time as "engag[ing] in deviate sexual intercourse with another person under circumstances other than those [constituting forcible sodomy or nonforcible sodomy on a teenager between the ages of twelve and sixteen]. Consent is no defense to a prosecution under this subdivision."[398] On appeal, he argued that the sexual misconduct law was unconstitutional as applied to him in light of *Lawrence*. The court agreed with the defendant that because a jury had acquitted him of engaging in nonconsensual sodomy, a conviction for sexual misconduct violated his due process rights.[399]

---

395 Commonwealth v. Sherman, 116 N.E.3d 597, 605 (Mass. 2019) ("[C]onsensual sexual intercourse between adults is not only lawful, but also a private act of intimacy so important that it is constitutionally protected as a liberty interest[, but . . .] consensual sexual intercourse can become unlawful where the victim withdraws consent after the initial act of penetration has occurred.").

396 *E.g.*, State v. Whiteley, 616 S.E.2d 576, 583 (2005) (finding sodomy law unconstitutional as applied to defendant whom the jury acquitted on nonconsensual sexual assault charges); *cf.* State v. Hunt, 728 S.E.2d 409, 413 (N.C. App. 2012) (vacating sodomy conviction on double jeopardy grounds after jury had been instructed only about lack of consent, rather than on additional grounds that would have justified a conviction based on the fact that the victim was a minor, thereby rendering the "crime against nature" charge a lesser-included offense of a second-degree sexual offense under the particular facts of the case), *aff'd in part*, 766 S.E.2d 288 (N.C. 2014).

397 184 So. 3d 1064 (Ala. Crim. App. 2015).

398 *Id.* at 1069 (quoting ALA. CODE § 13A-6-65 (1977 & 2010 Supp.)).

399 *Id.* at 1070. The court also held that double jeopardy prevented the defendant from being retried.

> Williams was acquitted of sodomy in the first degree, an offense for which consent was a defense. Williams was, therefore, acquitted of sodomy. Accordingly, to reverse the conviction [for sexual misconduct] and remand this case for a new trial on a charge of nonconsensual sex based on the same facts presented during the first trial would violate double-jeopardy principles.

Id. at 1071; *cf. In re* Care & Treatment of Williams, 253 P.3d 327, 337 (Kan. 2011) (mentioning, in dicta, in an option upholding a determination that a defendant was a sexually dangerous person, that one prior charge originally filed as rape, then reduced to sodomy, and subsequently dismissed without prejudice, was unsubstantiated).

Even in cases in which *Lawrence* clearly offers no constitutional protections from criminal liability for the underlying acts due to the absence of consent, it nonetheless has implications for what evidence or arguments might be proper during sexual assault trials or how convicted defendants should be sentenced. For instance, in *People v. Cassala*, the defendant was convicted of sexually assaulting a fifteen-year-old victim for having forced her to submit to anal intercourse.[400] Given his use of force and the age of his victim, *Lawrence* offered the defendant no recourse concerning criminal liability. But during trial, the prosecution called the defendant's former wife who testified as to his "preference for anal intercourse during their consensual sexual relationship."[401] An appellate court agreed with the defendant that defense counsel's performance was constitutionally deficient for having failed to object to such testimony or to have requested a limiting instruction which, in turn, allowed the jury to consider constitutionally-protected intimacy between husband and wife as impermissible propensity evidence under factually dissimilar circumstances.[402]

Similarly, in *Commonwealth v. Baran*, an appellate court in Massachusetts upheld the granting of a new trial on the grounds of ineffective assistance of counsel.[403] The defendant had been convicted of multiple counts of raping children at a daycare center where he had been employed.[404] His trial was significantly flawed—seemingly tainted by judicial errors in admitting unreliable evidence, prosecutorial misconduct that appears to have included *Brady* violations, and by his attorney's "grievous failure to have investigated and prepared his case."[405] One of the many deficiencies that both a trial court judge and an appellate panel

---

400 15 N.Y.S.3d 479, 481 (Sup. Ct. App. Div. 2015).

401 *Id.* at 484.

402 *Id.*; *see also* People v. Garcia, 177 Cal. Rptr. 3d 231, 240 (Ct. App. 2014) (overturning conviction for sexual abuse of a six-year-old girl by her babysitter on the grounds that the prosecution had repeatedly referenced the defendant's sexual orientation, tying it to motive, thereby impermissibly telling "the jury the reason appellant chose to victimize A.G. is because she is gay").

403 905 N.E.2d 1122, 1126–48 (Mass. Ct. App. 2009).

404 *Id.* at 1126.

405 *Id.* at 1128.

of judges noted was defense counsel's "treatment of certain irrelevant and highly prejudicial evidence," which included the defendant's homosexuality.[406] The court juxtaposed prevailing social attitudes when the defendant was convicted with those today, first by noting that [i]n 1984, when the trial occurred, private consensual homosexual sex was criminalized in many States, and homosexuality, particularly male homosexuality, often described as a "crime against nature," was routinely linked with criminality, child molestation, indecency, deviance, pathology, uncontrolled urges, moral turpitude, and pedophilia."[407] The court then quoted from *Lawrence* with a "compare" signal: "The petitioners are entitled to respect for their private lives. The State cannot demean their existence or control their destiny by making their private sexual conduct a crime."[408] When added to the fear of LGBTQ+ people at the height of the AIDS crisis, the court in *Baran* concluded that failing to keep the defendant's sexuality from the jury added to a list of errors that "compound[ed] the already significant prejudice that . . . likely had a material effect on the jury and gave rise to a substantial risk that justice miscarried."[409]

The way the Massachusetts Court of Appeals treated the evidence of homosexuality in *Baran* differed markedly from the way the North Carolina Court of Appeals treated such evidence in *State v. Oakley*.[410] As with *Baran*, there was no question in *Oakley* about the fact that the defendant's actions were not shielded by *Lawrence*, as the case not only involved a minor, but also one who lived with the defendant while the latter served in the capacity as a "substitute parent."[411] Yet, the defendant allegedly exploited the minor, trading sex for money while he was supposed to be caring for the teenage victim.[412] At trial, and over the defense objection that they were unduly prejudicial, the court admitted

---

406 *Id.* at 1145.

407 *Id.* at 1147.

408 *Id.* at 1147–48 (quoting Lawrence v. Texas, 539 U.S. 558, 578 (1993)).

409 *Id.* at 1148.

410 605 S.E.2d 215 (N.C. Ct. App. 2004).

411 *Id.* at 217

412 *Id.*

fifteen photos depicting some shirtless males, some males in uniform, and some handcuffed males.[413] On appeal, the defendant argued that these photos unfairly biased the jury against him on the basis of his sexual orientation in violation of his rights under *Lawrence*. The appellate court disagreed, reasoning that the jury already knew about the defendant's sexuality because he admitted to engaging in sex with his male victim and because other witnesses referred to his sexual orientation before the photos were introduced.[414] But in light of that, why were the photos even needed? The state claimed they helped to corroborate the victim's testimony, but since the defendant admitted to engaging in sexual acts with the minor in his care, they seem to have served little probative value. Given the fact this case took place in North Carolina only one year after *Lawrence* was decided, anti-gay bias may account for the different treatment of sexuality evidence in *Oakley* than the Massachusetts Court of Appeals' treatment of it in *Baran*.

2. Sexual Assaults Testing the Limits of Consent Between Adults

The majority opinion in *Lawrence* was careful to note that case did "not involve persons who might be injured or coerced."[415] Courts grapple with the extent to which this sentence calls into question the degrees to which people can consent to injuries when the parties engaged in acts of bondage and discipline/sado-masochism (BDSM). In the context of BDSM, consent appears to constitute a valid defense to minor assaults that do not cause serious physical injury, such as spanking. But courts consistently find that people are not legally capable of granting effective legal consent to more serious harms, "even when the injuries are not permanent, seriously debilitating, or harmful enough that they cause a risk of death."[416]

---

413 *Id.*

414 *Id.* at 218.

415 Lawrence v. Texas, 539 U.S. 558, 578 (2003).

416 Ryan G. Fischer, Henry F. Fradella & Connie E. Ireland, *Sex, Violence, and the Boundaries of the Defense of Consent*, 45 CRIM. L. BULL. 1137, 1146 (2009). For a comprehensive discussion about some of the paradoxes in the way the criminal law

The cases that applied *Lawrence* in this context did not present genuine issues about the degrees to which people can knowingly and voluntarily grant consent to injury during BDSM sex. Rather, the facts of the cases turned on whether consent was present at all,[417] or, alternatively, the scope of such consent.[418] In all the cases, courts sided with the prosecution.

---

treats consent as a defense, see Cheryl Hanna, *Sex is Not a Sport: Consent and Violence in Criminal Law*, 42 B.C. L. REV. 239 (2001).

417 In *Commonwealth v. Carey*, 974 N.E.2d 624 (Mass. 2012), the defendant attempted to argue that consent could be a defense to armed home invasion, attempted murder, and assault with a dangerous weapon because the actions giving rise to these offenses stemmed from a consensual sexual encounter. But the evidence of nonconsent was overwhelming:

> [H]e attacked the victim, wrapping a necktie around her neck and pulling it from both ends. The victim managed to place her hands between the tie and her throat as the defendant continued to pull on the ligature. The two struggled, and the victim knocked over a heavy chair before falling to the floor.
>
> As the victim "began to fade out," she heard her son run downstairs. The son testified that, on reaching the kitchen area, he saw the defendant choking his mother, who was on the floor and trying to free herself from the defendant's grasp. When the son yelled, "What are you doing?" the victim told him to "[g]et a knife and stab him." The son went to the kitchen, retrieved a small knife, and stabbed the defendant in the back. When he did so, the blade of the knife separated from the handle. The son then dropped the handle, grabbed the defendant, and attempted to pull the defendant away from his mother.
>
> At some point, the defendant released his hold on the victim's throat and advanced toward the son. When he saw that the victim had risen to her feet, however, the defendant moved back toward her and punched her in the forehead and mouth.3 The victim, her son, and the defendant then ran from the house. The victim ran to one neighboring house, and her son fled to another. The defendant got into his vehicle and drove away

Id. at 628; *see also* State v. Christel, No. 2020AP1127-CR, 2021 WL 5828953, at *4 (Wis. Ct. App. 2022) (rejecting argument in post-conviction relief petition that *Lawrence* created a "right to engage in strangulation or suffocation in the privacy of one's bedroom" in a case in which the defendant claimed he and wife engaged in consensual erotic asphyxiation during sex).

418 *E.g.*, State v. Van, 688 N.W.2d 600, 614–15 (Neb. 2004) (upholding convictions for assault, false imprisonment, and terroristic threats in a "no limits" BDSM situation in which the submissive participant "expected to be tortured, humiliated, and to eventually die as a result of [the] relationship" over a *Lawrence* challenge on the basis that the case only provided constitutional protection for sexual relationships "absent injury to a person or abuse of an institution the law protects." (quoting Lawrence v. Texas, 539 U.S. 558, 567 (2003)); *cf.* State v. Jensen, 118 P.3d 762, 770 (N.M. Ct. App. 2005) (Robinson, J., concurring, in part, and dissenting, in part). In *Jenson*, a husband was

In *People v. Davidson*, the defendant was convicted of several crimes that the victim had repeatedly reported as domestic violence.[419] Indeed, one time she needed to be transported via ambulance to a hospital where "emergency room personnel observed extensive bruising throughout her body, including on her face, neck, extremities, torso, abdomen, and pelvic area; a perforated ear drum; two bite marks (on her leg and chest); and a previously stitched lip laceration."[420] By the time of trial, she recanted and claimed her injuries were a result of consensual BDSM activities. But given her prior statements to family, friends, medical personnel, and police, a jury convicted the defendant of torture, corporal injury to a cohabitant, and criminal threats. An appellate court upheld the verdict, stating that "[u]nlike the circumstances in *Lawrence*, the conduct at issue in this case involve[d] serious physical injury and terrorizing behavior."[421]

The defendant in *People v. Febrissy* appealed a conviction for "infliction of corporal injury upon a cohabitant" stemming from acts of BDSM.[422] Although his partner had consented to certain acts, she claimed that he exceeded the scope of her consent when he beat her with a whip

---

convicted of raping his wife. His defense was consent. He sought and was denied an instruction that would have told the jury that if they found evidence of consent, the state had to prove nonconsent beyond a reasonable doubt. The majority rejected his appeal, but a dissenting judge wrote the following:

> If an affirmative defense of consent is not a true defense, the effect is to make legal activity illegal. If a party cannot consent to sex involving force or violence, then each act of "rough sex" in the State of New Mexico before 2005 was illegal. There are cases in which consensual actions are prohibited for a good purpose. In the case of statutory rape, the public has a proper interest in the protection of persons under the age of consent, who cannot be said to have the ability to consent themselves. . . . With the issue at hand, what would be the public interest in prohibiting an intimate activity between consenting adults? [citing *Lawrence*]

Id.

419 No. D064880, 2015 WL 4751166, at *1 (Cal. Ct. App. Aug. 12, 2015).

420 *Id.* at *2.

421 *Id.* at *8; *cf.* People v. Schneider, No. A145308, 2016 WL 4183943, at *6 (Cal. Ct. App. Aug. 8, 2016) (upholding the exclusion of videos showing prior consensual activities between boyfriend and girlfriend in his domestic violence trial on the ground that they were more prejudicial than probative and did not show any sexual violence that could support the defendant's claim that victim's injuries on the date in question had occurred during consensual BDSM sexual activity).

422 No. C049033, 2006 WL 2006161, at *1 (Cal. Ct. App. July 19, 2006).

and a riding crop, resulting in welts on her body.[423] He asserted that his conviction should be set aside because it violated a protected liberty interest under *Lawrence*.[424] The court declined to consider whether *Lawrence* applies to BDSM in cases involving physical injury because the jury's verdict "necessarily reflect[ed] a rejection of any claim that the victim consented or the defendant reasonably could have believed in her consent."[425] It affirmed his conviction, reasoning that for any sexual activities to fall with *Lawrence*'s scope, it must involve private acts between adults who grant "full and mutual consent" to each other.[426]

State v. Dudas involved a series of violent sexual encounters between husband and wife that the latter claimed were sometimes nonconsensual.[427] The wife testified that when she declined to engage in a particular sex act, her husband would suffocate her until she submitted: "He would strangle me until I obeyed what he said to do."[428] In addition to multiple counts of sexual assault in varying degrees, the state also charged him with eleven counts of strangulation and suffocation—a distinct offense under Wisconsin law.[429] As part of his defense, the husband sought to introduce evidence that the two consensually engaged in BDSM and that the strangulation was part of their consensual sexual activities.[430] Among other arguments he raised on appeal after a jury convicted him, the defendant relied on *Lawrence* to argue that "[i]nstructing the jury that strangulation occurred during sexual relations when [she] performed oral sex on [him] and not requiring the jury to evaluate whether [she] consented to sexual intercourse improperly broaden[ed] the scope of the statute, and create[d] criminal liability for

---

423 *Id.* at *3.

424 *Id.* at *5.

425 *Id.*

426 *Id.* (quoting Lawrence v. Texas, 539 U.S. 558, 578 (2003)).

427 No. 2016AP2443-CR, 2020 WL 770083, at *2 (Wis. Ct. App. 2020).

428 *Id.*

429 WIS. STAT. ANN. § 940.235(1) (2008) ("Whoever intentionally impedes the normal breathing or circulation of blood by applying pressure on the throat or neck or by blocking the nose or mouth of another person is guilty of a Class H felony.").

430 *Dudas*, 2020 WL 770083, at *2

acts that are not criminal."[431] The court distinguished the case as involving someone who "might be injured" and reasoned that "*Lawrence* does not support an argument that [the strangulation statute] infringes upon a constitutional right, regardless of whether ten percent of the population engages in consensual BDSM sex."[432]

Collectively, *Davidson*, *Febrissy*, and *Dudas* illustrate that courts are highly skeptical of criminal defendants who attempt to avoid criminal liability by claiming that injuries to sexual partners occurred as a result of constitutionally protected BDSM activities. Of course, that distrust of defendants self-serving arguments is particularly well-founded in cases in which the alleged evidence of consent was highly circumspect, at best. If someone sought medical attention for injuries sustain during BDSM activities that both parties credibly maintained were truly consensual, it remains to be seen whether courts would find *Lawrence* applicable under such circumstances.

3. Statutory Factors Vitiating Consent

In many states, statutory provisions carve-out criteria that render a person without the legal capacity to consent to sexual activity. The most common of such factors is the youthful age of post-pubescent teenagers, but other statutory factors vitiating consent include an actor's unconsciousness, intoxication, or cognitive deficits.[433] Numerous cases raised questions about the capacity to consent under one of these circumstances.

a. Youthful Age: The Capacity of Minors to Consent

Perhaps the most well-known type of statutory rape law criminalizes sex between adults and minors under a certain age.

> The crime was first codified in English law in 1275, when the Statute of Westminster provided "[T]he King prohibiteth that

---

[431] *Id.* at *6.

[432] *Id.*

[433] *See generally* HENRY F. FRADELLA, CRIMINAL LAW: AN INTRODUCTION TO KEY CASES AND COMMENTS 205–07 (2022); Fradella & Grundy, *supra* note 64, at 201–03; *see also, e.g.*, ARIZ. REV. STAT. § 13-1401(A)(7)(b) (2021); OHIO REV. CODE § 2907.03(A)(2)–(3) (2019); TEX. PENAL CODE § 22.011(4)–(6) (2021).

> none do ravish, nor take away by force, any Maiden within Age." The age of consent was initially twelve years of age, but it was lowered to ten in 1576. That same age of ten years was incorporated into early American laws, but rose to eighteen or even twenty- one during the 1800s. Today, all US jurisdictions continue to have criminal laws penalizing sexual conduct with someone under their specified age of consent.[434]

Approximately thirty states and the District of Columbia currently set the age of consent at sixteen, eight states set the age of consent at seventeen, and the remaining twelve states use eighteen years of age.[435] Courts unanimously uphold these laws over due process challenges that attempted to extend *Lawrence*'s protections of private sexual activity between consenting adults into the realm of sex with teenagers who had not reached the statutory age of consent: "Certainly, the State has a significant interest in prohibiting sex between adults and minors not only because of the potentially coercive effect of an adult's influence but also because of concern regarding the minor's ability to arrive at an informed consent."[436]

Most states maintain the common law's treatment of statutory rape as a strict liability crime, an approach that courts have upheld since *Lawrence*

---

[434] FRADELLA, *supra* note 433, at 216 (citing Catherine L. Carpenter, *On Statutory Rape, Strict Liability, and the Public Welfare Offense Model*, 53 AM. U. L. REV. 313, 334 n.122 (2003); Michelle Oberman, *Turning Girls into Women: Re-Evaluating Modern Statutory Rape Law*, 8 DEPAUL J. HEALTH CARE L. 109 (2004–2005)); *see also* 3 Edw. 1, c. 13 (1275).

[435] FRADELLA, *supra* note 433, at 216 fig. 8.1.

[436] Crooks v. State, No. 93,759, 2006 WL 90104, at *10 (Kan. Ct. App. Jan. 13, 2006) (quoting State v. Limon, 122 P.3d 22, 35–36 (Kan. 2005)); *see also* Saunders v. Commonwealth, 753 S.E.2d 602, 608 (Va. Ct. App. 2014) ("[T]he case at bar involved actions between an adult and minors, removing it, therefore, from the ruling in *Lawrence*."), *aff'd*, No. 140507, 2015 WL 10945236 (Va. Feb. 26, 2015); Maxwell v. State, 895 A.2d 327, 336 (Md. Ct. Spec. App. 2006) ("[W]e see nothing in *Lawrence* that would apply to a statute properly drawn to protect minors from adult sexual predators."). And, as previously mentioned in the section on sodomy laws, the same logic applies when no act takes place, but it is solicited or attempted. Toghill v. Commonwealth, 768 S.E.2d 674, 678–80 (2015); Blackington v. Commonwealth, No. CL–2013–18691, 2015 WL 10521382, at *1 (Va. Cir. Ct. Mar. 3, 2015) (applying *Toghill* as "dispositive"); State v. Rung, 774 N.W.2d 621, 630 (Neb. 2009) (rejecting *Lawrence* as a basis to invalidate law criminalizing the use of a computer to entice a child—or a peace officer believed to be a child—for sexual purposes).

was decided.[437] By contrast, other states have changed their laws to require some proof of *mens rea* such that "an honest and reasonable mistake regarding the age of the victim can be a complete defense to statutory rape in approximately thirteen states and the District of Columbia."[438]

---

437 Courts continue to uphold the constitutionality of a strict liability approach to statutory rape. *See, e.g.*, Fleming v. State, 455 S.W.3d 577, 580–83 (Tex. Crim. App. 2014).

> It is clear that the Texas legislature intends for age to be an aggravating element in certain offenses and does not intend for the State to be required to prove that the defendant knew the age of the victim. . . . Because this statute serves the legitimate state objective of protecting children, we will not read a mens rea element into the statute and do not believe that failure to require mens rea as to the victim's age violates the federal or state constitution. . . . If the adult chooses not to ascertain the age of a sexual partner, then the adult assumes the risk that he or she may be held liable for the conduct if it turns out that the sexual partner is underage.

Id. at 581–82; *see also* State v. Holmes, 920 A.2d 632, 636 (N.H. 2007) (rejecting the argument that *Lawrence* requires proof a *mens rea* element with respect to a minor's age for statutory rape liability); Campos v. State, No. 03-18-00788-CR, 2020 WL 6834216, at *3 (Tex. App. Nov. 20, 2020) (same); State v. Valdez, No. 2 CA-CR 2013-0463, 2015 WL 428358, at *2–3 (Ariz. Ct. App. Jan. 30, 2015) (same); Jacobs v. State, 355 S.W.3d 99, 101 (Tex. App. 2011) (same); State v. Browning, 629 S.E.2d 299, 303 (N.C. Ct. App. 2006) (same).

438 *See, e.g.*, ARIZ. REV. STAT. § 13–1403(B) (2019) ("A person commits public sexual indecency to a minor if the person intentionally or knowingly engages in any of the acts listed in subsection A of this section and such person is reckless about whether a minor who is under fifteen years of age is present."); 18 PA. CON. STAT. § 3102 (2018) ("When criminality depends on the child's being below a critical age older than 14 years, it is a defense for the defendant to prove by a preponderance of the evidence that he or she reasonably believed the child to be above the critical age."); WYO. STAT. ANN. § 6-2-308(a) (2018) ("Except as provided by subsection (b) of this section, if criminality of conduct in this article depends on a victim being under sixteen (16) years of age, it is an affirmative defense that the actor reasonably believed that the victim was sixteen (16) years of age or older.").

An honest and reasonable mistake as to a minor's age may also be a defense to select crimes that are often thought of as precursors to illicit sexual activity with minor, such a "luring a child into a motor vehicle." *See, e.g.*, Commonwealth v. Gallagher, 874 A.2d 49, 50 (Pa. Super. Ct. 2005), *aff'd*, 924 A.2d 636 (Pa. 2007) (holding that for criminal liability to attach for luring, the state must prove defendants either intentionally sought out victims under the age of eighteen, knew their victims were under that age, or were reckless as to their victims' ages). *Gallagher* was among the cases in the study because a concurring judge criticized the prosecutor for bringing charges against the defendant for a host of reasons, one of which caused the judge to cite *Lawrence*:

> [I]f Appellant was prosecuted for luring due to the fact that the encounter actually led to consensual sex, then by rights every individual, including other minors, who have engaged in consensual sex with a minor in a car or after

The final resolution of *Estes v. State* illustrates how statutory rape laws typically operate, but the intermediate court of appeals decision in the case demonstrates how courts grapple with *Lawrence*'s impact on the validity of statutory rape laws.[439] The defendant in *Estes* was the father of a teenage boy whose teenage girlfriend frequently slept over their home.[440] Unbeknownst to his wife and his son, the defendant and his son's girlfriend engaged in sexual intercourse and other sex acts together over approximately a one-year period of time during which she was too young to grant consent.[441] The girl disclosed the abuse after one encounter during which she felt particularly scared in light of the defendant's roughness.[442] He was tried and convicted of five counts of sexual assault, among other charges.[443] On appeal, there was no question about the validity of a statutory rape conviction under such circumstances. But he nonetheless challenged the constitutionality of the statute for its sentencing provisions on the grounds that it treated "married people more harshly than unmarried

---

> driving the minor in a car to another place to have sex, should similarly be prosecuted for luring . . . . Also, the prosecution and potential punishment imposed here is incongruous when one considers that had Appellant lived near the convenience store and been on foot when he met the complainant, and had the two met and a consensual sexual encounter followed, no criminal liability would have attached to the incident. Why should Appellant, or anyone else similarly situated, be subject to two to four years' imprisonment simply because the encounter started in a motor vehicle?
>
> If the prosecution was motivated due to a discrepancy in age, it should be remembered that Appellant was found to have been operating under a reasonable belief that the complainant was 18 years of age or older . . . . Whatever the prosecutor may think of men or woman interested in partners much younger than they, any disdain for such a preference cannot be thought of as criminal and deserving of two to four years' imprisonment. Lastly, if the prosecution was motivated because of Appellant's sexual orientation, such a stance would certainly be unconstitutional in light of *Lawrence* . . . . In short, to the extent Appellant is guilty of luring a child into a motor vehicle, it is clear that a great many other individuals are also guilty of the offense, yet there is no effort expended to prosecute those individuals. As such, Appellant is clearly the victim of a selective prosecution.

Id. at 63 (Bender, J., concurring).

439 487 S.W.3d 737 (Tex. App. 2016), *rev'd*, 546 S.W.3d 691 (Tex. Crim. App. 2018).

440 *Id.* at 744.

441 *Id.* at 744–45.

442 *Id.* at 744.

443 *Id.* at 745.

people and therefore violate[d] his due process and equal protection rights."[444] The defendant made that argument because sexual assault is typically a second-degree felony under Texas law, but such an offense is elevated to a felony in the first degree "if the victim was a person whom the actor was prohibited from marrying or purporting to marry or with whom the actor was prohibited from living under the appearance of being married."[445] Because the defendant was legally married to his wife at the time of his sexual assaults on the victim, he was subjected to harsher penalties than an unmarried person would have been for the exact same conduct. The Texas Court of Appeals agreed with him, citing Justice O'Connor's concurring opinion in *Lawrence* for the proposition that "equal protection may be violated when a penal statute 'treats the same conduct differently based solely on the participants.'"[446] Because the court could not discern any rational basis for such a classification, it affirmed the substance of his convictions, but remanded for resentencing on second-degree felony charges.[447] After the state sought further appellate review, Texas Court of Criminal Appeals revised the intermediate appellate court's decision without citation to *Lawrence*, finding that the state had rational bases for the classification at issue in the case, namely "advancing both the narrow goal of deterring sexually-assaultive polygamous practices and the broader goal of providing 'more protection to children' from sexually exploitative practices generally."[448]

---

444 *Id.*

445 *Id.* at 746 (citing TEX. PENAL CODE ANN. § 22.011(f) (2009)).

446 *Id.* at 747–48 (quoting Lawrence v. Texas, 539 U.S. 558, 581 (2003) (O'Connor, J., concurring)).

447 *Id.* at 750.

448 Estes v. State, 546 S.W.3d 691, 700 (Tex. Crim. App. 2018); *see also* State v. Pryes, No. 2009AP2–CR, 2009 WL 1606746 (Wis. Ct. App. June 10, 2009) (rejecting equal protection challenge to statutory rape law that differentiates between married and unmarried sixteen-and seventeen-year-olds because many of the state interests in criminalizing statutory rape "are addressed when a minor has obtained permission to marry—most obviously the lack of considered consent, heightened vulnerability to physical and psychological harm, the lack of mature judgment, the potential for sexual exploitation and the potential for a minor bearing a child outside of a marital relationship"); State v. Jones, No. 95,558, 2007 WL 656367, at * 2 (Kan. Ct. App. Mar. 2, 2007) (same); People v. Downin, 828 N.E.2d 341, 348 (Ill. Ct. App. 2005) (same);

b. Statutory Rape Age-Gap Provisions

The overwhelming majority of U.S. states have enacted so-called "Romeo and Juliet" age-gap provisions, statutory exceptions that either reduce the age of consent to as low as twelve years of age when the sexual activity occurs between two youths close in age, or alternatively reduce the penalties for such acts.[449] Courts have consistently upheld the constitutionality of these provisions over age-based equal protection challenges by defendants too much older than their teenage victims to fall within the scope of the protections. In doing so, courts typically first differentiate *Lawrence* from the cases under consideration on the grounds that *Lawrence* did not involve minors.[450] Applying rational basis review, these courts go on to uphold the differential treatment of people close in age from others outside the applicable age difference range, often reasoning as follows:

> By permitting the affirmative defense, the legislature has recognized that individuals with less than a three-year age differential are still children in the eyes of the law and, because of that lack of maturity, their conduct should not be punished in the same manner as that of an adult like Arias, who at the time of the offense was twenty-four years old. . . . The recognition of a difference in judgment, maturity, and in an ability to control conduct between underage juveniles and significantly older, more

---

State v. Moore, 606 S.E.2d 127, 131–132 (N.C. Ct. App. 2004) (same); State v. Clark, 588 S.E.2d 66, 69 (N.C. Ct. App. 2003) (same).

449 FRADELLA, *supra* note 433, at 216–17; *see also* Steve James, Comment, *Romeo and Juliet Were Sex Offenders: An Analysis of the Age of Consent and A Call for Reform*, 78 UMKC L. REV. 241 (2009) (critiquing the often inconsistent and biased application of age-gap provisions and advocating for reforms). *Compare* N.J. REV. STAT. 2C:14-2(c)(4) (2022) ("An actor is guilty of sexual assault if he commits an act of sexual penetration with another person . . . [and the] victim is at least 13 but less than 16 years old and the actor is at least four years older than the victim"), *with* GA. CODE ANN. § 16-6-3(c) (2022) (reducing statutory rape from a felony to a misdemeanor if "the victim is at least 14 but less than 16 years of age and the person convicted of statutory rape is 18 years of age or younger and is no more than four years older than the victim").

450 *E.g.*, Arias v. State, 503 S.W.3d 523, 528 (Tex. App. 2016) ("*Lawrence*, however, applies to consenting adults and "does not involve minors. . . ." There is no fundamental liberty interest in having a consensual intimate relationship with a child.").

> sophisticated adults is a matter well within the peculiar province of the legislature.[451]

Notably, defendants raising constitutional challenges to the prescribed ages in statutory rape laws and corresponding age-gap provisions are not limited to adults who are older than their victims. For instance, *In re R.L.C.* involved a fourteen-year-old boy who had engaged in oral sex with his twelve-year-old girlfriend and was subsequently adjudicated a delinquent for violating the state's sodomy law.[452] He appealed, arguing that age-gap provisions in other state statutes should apply to the sodomy law and, further, that the sodomy was unconstitutional as applied to two juveniles. The court dispensed with the former argument that the sodomy law needed to be analyzed *in pari materia* (on the same subject) "with other statutes that criminalize similar activity," such as statutory rape and a few other sex crimes in the state.[453] If the two juveniles had engaged in vaginal sexual intercourse, there would have been no liability because they were within the age-gap that would exempt close-in-age youth from statutory rape liability.[454] Despite the merits of an *in pari materia* argument, the court simply stated it would "not judicially impose an age differential element into the crime against nature statute."[455] It then went on to dispense with the juvenile's due process argument by noting that *Lawrence* did not involve minors and that "[b]esides the goal of promoting proper notions of morality among our State's youth, the government's desire for a healthy young citizenry underscores the legitimacy of the government's interest in prohibiting the commission of crimes against nature by minors."[456] But as Professor Strader previously noted, the court's assertion that the criminalization of oral sex serves a legitimate state interest promoting "'a healthy young citizenry' is factually incorrect" because there is "substantial evidence that engaging in unprotected vaginal

---

451 *Id.* at 529.

452 *In re* R.L.C., 643 S.E.2d 920, 921 (N.C. 2007).

453 *Id.* at 923. "When determining the meaning of a statute, the purpose of viewing the statute *in pari materia* with other statutes is to harmonize statutes of like subject matter and, if at all possible, give effect to each." *Id.* at 924.

454 N.C. GEN. STAT. § 14-27.2(a)(1) (2004).

455 *R.L.C.*, 643 S.E.2d at 924.

456 *Id.* at 925.

intercourse carries a substantial risk of transmitting HIV, while engaging in oral sex carries little or no risk of HIV transmission, and zero risk of pregnancy."[457] Moreover, court cited no evidence—"no studies, no expert testimony, nothing"— to support its dubious assertion that oral sex poses some greater risk to the psychological health of teenagers than vaginal sexual intercourse.[458] Accordingly, it appears that the court upheld the delinquency determination on morality grounds that ought to been deemed invalid after *Lawrence*.[459]

One might attempt to explain *In re R.L.C.* as a remnant of outdated decision-making that had yet to catch up with the times shortly after *Lawrence* was decided. But in 2021, the Supreme Court of Kansas similarly upheld a delinquency adjudication against a juvenile, but in that case, the two teenagers were the same age![460] The state initially charged a fourteen-year-old girl in *In re A.B.* with "unlawful voluntary sexual relations" for having had sex with a fourteen-year-old boy.[461] That charge

---

457 Strader, *supra* note 10, at 82.

458 *Id.*

459 *Id.* at 82–83 ("Of course, the North Carolina court might have been bending over backwards to sustain a criminal law in order to punish the fourteen-year-old defendant for having sex with a twelve-year-old girl . . . . In any event, the decision's precedential impact reaches far beyond the facts of the case and ensnares all minors who engage in oral or anal sex in that state."); *see also* McDonald v. Commonwealth, 645 S.E.2d 918, 942 (Va. 2007) (upholding sodomy conviction against a forty-five-year-old man who engaged in oral sex with a sixteen- and seventeen-year-old girl, even though both teenagers were over the age of consent for vaginal intercourse, on the grounds that the sodomy statute did not contain an age limitation).

460 *In re* A.B., 484 P.3d 226, 229 (2021).

461 *Id.* Kansas law defined that offense as follows:

> (a) Unlawful voluntary sexual relations is:
>
> (1) Engaging in any of the following acts with a child who is 14 or more years of age but less than 16 years of age:
>
> (A) voluntary sexual intercourse;
>
> (B) voluntary sodomy; or
>
> (C) voluntary lewd fondling or touching;
>
> (2) when the offender is less than 19 years of age;
>
> (3) when the offender is less than four years of age older than the child;
>
> (4) when the child and the offender are the only parties involved; and
>
> (5) when the child and the offender are members of the opposite sex.

KAN. STAT. ANN. § 21-5507 (2011).

was dismissed because she was actually a few months younger than the boy and previous case law held that the statute required that the offender be older than the victim.[462] The state then charged the girl with having taken "aggravated indecent liberties with a child."[463] She appealed her delinquency adjudication, arguing the statute was unconstitutionally vague and overbroad. The court easily dispensed with the former, finding that there is nothing vague about a statute criminalizing sexual intercourse with a minor who is fourteen or fifteen years of age.[464] With regard to the overbreadth claim, the girl argued that under *Lawrence*, sexual intercourse between fourteen- or fifteen-year-old minors was "constitutionally protected activity" and that the statute was "designed to infringe on the right of privacy of young teenagers by preventing them from engaging in

---

462 *A.B.*, 484 P.3d at 229 (citing *In re* E.R., 197 P.3d 870, 871 (Kan. Ct. App. 2008)).

463 *Id.* at Kansas law defined that offense as follows:

> (b) Aggravated indecent liberties with a child is:
>
> (1) sexual intercourse with a child who is 14 or more years of age but less than 16 years of age;
>
> (2) engaging in any of the following acts with a child who is 14 or more years of age but less than 16 years of age and who does not consent thereto:
>
> (A) any lewd fondling or touching of the person of either the child or the offender, done or submitted to with the intent to arouse or to satisfy the sexual desires of either the child or the offender, or both; or
>
> (B) causing the child to engage in any lewd fondling or touching of the person of another with the intent to arouse or satisfy the sexual desires of the child, the offender or another;
>
> (3) engaging in any of the following acts with a child who is under 14 years of age:
>
> (A) any lewd fondling or touching of the person of either the child or the offender, done or submitted to with the intent to arouse or to satisfy the sexual desires of either the child or the offender, or both; or
>
> (B) soliciting the child to engage in any lewd fondling or touching of the person of another with the intent to arouse or satisfy the sexual desires of the child, the offender or another.

KAN. STAT. ANN. § 21-5506 (2011).

464 *A.B.*, 484 P.3d at 232.

consensual sexual intercourse."[465] The court disagreed, emphasizing that *Lawrence*'s holding was limited to adults.[466]

The facts of *In re A.B.* are perplexing. Because both parties were the same age, the case is easily distinguishable from cases in which an older juvenile exploits a younger child.[467] Yet, nothing in the *In re A.B.* decision elucidates why delinquency proceedings were instituted in the first place. And because the justices said nothing remotely critical of the state for prosecuting a teenage girl for having sex with a boy of the same age, one is left to wonder if Professor Strader's observation about *In re R.L.C.* might be equally relevant to *In re A.B.* insofar as it "ignored *Lawrence*'s underlying theory and doctrine, rejecting *Lawrence*'s harm principle, and relying on *Hardwick*'s morality rationale to sustain the laws at issue."[468]

Finally, it should be noted that age-gap provisions for statutory rape liability have been applied in ways that disproportionately burden

---

[465] *Id.* at 233.

[466] *Id.* ("[W]hile the right to privacy in connection with decisions affecting procreation extends to minors as well as to adults, that alone does not support A.B.'s premise that younger teenagers' sexual intercourse with their close-in-age mates is constitutionally protected." (internal quotations and citations omitted)).

[467] Commonwealth v. Wilbur W., 95 N.E.3d 259, 268 (Mass. 2018). In that case, a twelve-year-old pressured an eight-year old into performing oral sex on him.

> [T]he facts . . . do not support the view, as the juvenile suggests, that this was a case of juvenile experimentation among peers rather than a case of sexual abuse. To the contrary, the record at trial indicates that the juvenile was the aggressor, who arranged the victim's position behind a dresser in order to avoid detection. The jury were warranted in finding that the victim, a boy four years younger than the juvenile, complied with the juvenile's commands to stand next to the bureau, pull down his pants, and perform oral sex on the juvenile because he was frightened and did not want to risk disobeying the juvenile's instructions. On the day after the incident, the victim displayed his immaturity by asking, "Well, what does it mean when someone tries to put their private into your butt?" Given this, the juvenile's characterization of the incident as that of consensual sexual experimentation is unavailing.

Id. at 268.

[468] Strader, *supra* note 10, at 85.

LGBTQ+ youth.[469] The most well-known case illustrating such discrimination is *State v. Limon.*[470]

The age-gap provision in Kansas law set the maximum penalty for sexual activity between teenagers close in age to fifteen months incarceration, whereas sexual activity with a minor for those outside the age-gap carried a maximum prison term of seventeen years.[471] Notably, however, it only applied to acts that occurred between members of the opposite sex, meaning it was "purposefully written to apply to 'Romeo and Juliet,' but not 'Romeo and Romeo' or 'Juliet and Juliet,' thereby illustrating the continued stigma and discrimination that gays and lesbians face under the law."[472]

> At the relevant time, Matthew Limon was a football player in his senior year of high school. Shortly after his eighteenth birthday, he engaged in a non-coercive act of oral sex with a fourteen-year-old boy who was also a student at the same high school. Limon's attorneys argued that limiting the age gap exception to opposite-sex encounters violated the Equal Protection Clause of the Fourteenth Amendment to the U.S. Constitution. The lower courts of Kansas rejected this argument and, as a result, Limon was sentenced to more than seventeen years in prison, rather than the fifteen-month maximum sentence that could be imposed if Limon had engaged in oral sex with a female. The Kansas intermediate court of appeals affirmed Limon's conviction. Limon served three years in prison before the [U.S. Supreme Court ordered a review of the case in light of *Lawrence* and the] Kansas Supreme Court

---

469 *See, e.g.*, Caitlyn Silhan, Comment, *The Present Case Does Involve Minors: An Overview of the Discriminatory Effects of Romeo and Juliet Provisions and Sentencing Practices on Lesbian, Gay, Bisexual, and Transgender Youth*, 20 LAW & SEXUALITY 97 (2011).

470 122 P.3d 22 (Kan. 2005).

471 *Id.* at 29 (citing KAN. STAT. ANN. § 21-3522 (2000), *repealed by* Laws 2010, ch. 136, § 307, eff. July 1, 2011, *recodified as amended at* KAN. STAT. ANN. § 21-5507 (2011)).

472 Diana Caraveo-Parra, Henry F. Fradella, Jessica Salerno & Cody W. Telep, *Does Homophobia Affect Prosecutorial Discretion in Ambiguous Statutory Rape Cases?*, 3 WILLAMETTE SOC. JUST. & EQUITY L.J. 1, 18 (2019) (citing Michael J. Higdon, *Queer Teens and Legislative Bullies: The Cruel and Invidious Discrimination Behind Heterosexist Statutory Rape Laws*, 42 U.C. DAVIS L. REV. 195, 226–52 (2008); Shulamit H. Shvartsman, *"Romeo and Romeo": An Examination of* Limon v. Kansas *in Light of* Lawrence v. Texas, 35 SETON HALL L. REV. 359 (2004)).

> reversed his conviction, holding that the state's age gap provision could not be limited to sex acts between opposite-sex partners without violating equal protection.[473]

No other cases in the study raised issues like those in *Limon.*

c. When the Capacity to Consent Is Limited

The defendant in *Hopkins v. State* admitted to performing oral sex on a twenty-three-year-old who had several intellectual impairments.[474] The central issue at trial concerned his capacity to consent. Testimony established that he functioned at a level consistent with that of someone in the fourth through sixth grade.[475] Accordingly, a jury convicted the defendant and he appealed. After affirming the sufficiency of the evidence, an appellate court quickly dispensed with the defendant's argument that *Lawrence* rendered the state's sexual assault law unconstitutional because it categorically established that intellectually disabled persons cannot grant effective legal consent to engage in sexual activity.[476] The court simply said, "[t]o the extent he relies on *Lawrence v. Texas*, we note that the consensual nature of the sexual relations in that case was undisputed . . . . *Lawrence* therefore is inapposite."[477] Courts reached the same result in cases in which the evidence established that the victim was too intoxicated to grant consent,[478] even if there were evidence that an unconscious victim had engaged in consensual sexual activity with the defendant on prior occasions.[479]

---

[473] *Id.* at 18–19 (internal citations omitted).

[474] Hopkins v. State, 615 S.W.3d 530, 534 (Tex. App. 2020).

[475] *Id.* at 538.

[476] *Id.* at 552.

[477] *Id.*; *see also* People v. Vukodinovich, 189 Cal. Rptr. 3d 126, 132–33 (2015); State v. Knutsen, 345 P.3d 989, 994 (Idaho 2015); Grabowski v. State, No. 04-15-00699-CR, 2016 WL 6473066, at *3–5 (Tex. App. Nov. 2, 2016); State v. Cook, 192 P.3d 1085, 1088 (Idaho Ct. App. 2008).

[478] State v. Gomez-Alas, 477 P.3d 911, 920 (Idaho 2020) ("*Lawrence*'s holding does not affect our state's legitimate interest and indeed, duty, to interpose when consent is in doubt." (internal citations and quotations omitted)).

[479] People v. Jones, No. C045990, 2005 WL 2160425, at *5 (Cal. Ct. App. Sept. 7, 2005).

> A decision to engage in sexual intercourse is necessarily an ad hoc decision made at a particular time with respect to a particular act. While a woman may expressly or impliedly consent to conscious sexual intercourse in advance, she

Some states also limit the capacity to consent to sexual activity if the participants are in a particular type of relationship—those involving positions of trust or supervision such that a difference in power calls into question whether voluntary consent can genuinely be given.[480] These relationships often include those between relatives not covered by incest statutes, such as stepsiblings, aunts and uncles by marriage, and the like;[481] civilians and certain public servants (e.g., between those under correctional supervision and correctional service providers);[482] students and their teachers, coaches, counselors, or tutors;[483] patients and those who

---

> remains free to withdraw that consent, and ordinarily has the ability to do so since she is conscious. Even if a woman expressly or impliedly indicates in advance that she is willing to engage in unconscious sexual intercourse, a man who thereafter has sexual intercourse with her while she is unconscious necessarily deprives her of the opportunity to indicate her lack of consent. The inherent risk that a man may misinterpret a woman's prior statements or conduct weighs strongly against recognizing "advance consent" as a defense to rape of an unconscious person since the woman's lack of consciousness absolutely precludes her from making her lack of consent known at the time of the act. It follows that a man who intentionally engages in sexual intercourse with a woman he knows to be unconscious harbors a "wrongful" intent regardless of whether he believes that she has (or she actually has) consented in advance to the act.

Id. (quoting People v. Dancy, 124 Cal. Rptr. 2d 898, 910–11 (2002)).

480 *See e.g.*, ARK. CODE ANN. § 5-14-126 (2021); OHIO REV. CODE § 2907.03(A)(6)–(13) (2019); TEX. PENAL CODE §§ 22.011(8)–(14), 21.12 (2021).

481 Stinson v. Commonwealth, 396 S.W.3d 900, 908–09 (Ky. 2013) (upholding conviction of an uncle by marriage for the statutory rape of his seventeen-year-old niece by marriage, who was one yea rover the age of consent in Kentucky, because she spent the summer living with him and could therefore exercise undue influence over her).

482 Sheesley v. State, 437 P.3d 830, 835 (Wyo. 2019) (upholding prohibition under rational basis to ensure the relationships between prisoners and correctional officials, as well as institutional order and discipline, are not undermined by sexual contact); Commonwealth v. Mayfield, 832 A.2d 418, 425 (Pa. 2003) (same); R.H. v. State, 849 N.E.2d 1165, 1169 (Ind. Ct. App. 2006) ("[S]service providers have the ability by virtue of their positions to coerce compliance or authorize privileges. It is apparent that favoritism toward certain detainees, or unfounded retaliation against them, could undermine the integrity of the correctional facility."). *But cf.* State v. Mole, 994 N.E.2d 482, 483 (Ohio Ct. App. 2013), *aff'd*, 74 N.E.3d 368 (Ohio 2016) (invalidating law as applied to peace officers, broadly),

483 State v. McKenzie-Adams, 915 A.2d 822, 837 (Conn. 2007), *overruled on other grounds by* State v. Payne, 34 A.3d 370 (Conn. 2012); ("[T]he legislature reasonably could have concluded that a sexually charged learning environment likely would confuse, disturb and distract students, thereby undermining the quality of education in the state."); State v. Murphy, No. 27801, 2018 WL 4190982, at *6 (Ohio Ct. App. Aug.

are or purport to be their health providers;[484] congregants seeking pastoral counseling from their clergy members;[485] and disabled persons and their

---

31, 2018) (upholding prohibition under rational basis review to prevent school personnel "from taking unconscionable advantage of students, no matter their age, by using their undue influence over the students in order to pursue sexual relationships"); Pruitt v. State, 272 So. 3d 732, 737 (Ala. Crim. App. 2018) (upholding prohibition even though the student attended a different school than the one at which the defendant taught); *see also* Johnson v. State, 626 S.W.3d 451, 456 (Ark. Ct. App. 2021); Sellers v. State, No. 13-18-00572-CR, 2019 WL 2042040, at *1 (Tex. App. May 9, 2019); State v. Solomon, 274 So. 3d 1017, 1027 (Ala. Crim. App. 2018); Ramirez v. State, 557 S.W.3d 717, 721 (Tex. App. 2018); Toledo v. State, 519 S.W.3d 273, 281 (Tex. App. 2017); Colleps v. State, No. 02-12-00396-CR, 2014 WL 1324422, at *4 (Tex. App. Apr. 3, 2014); State v. Edwards, 288 P.3d 494, 502–03 (Kan. Ct. App. 2012); *Ex parte* Morales, 212 S.W.3d 483, 494 (Tex. App. 2006); Berkovsky v. State, 209 S.W.3d 252, 254 (Tex. App. 2006); State v. Clinkenbeard, 123 P.3d 872, 879 (Wash. Ct. App. 2005); Commonwealth v. Batykefer, No. 520 WDA 2016, 2017 WL 1906100, at *6 (Pa. Super. Ct. May 8, 2017); Commonwealth v. Merklinger, No. 2195 MDA 2014, 2015 WL 6603444, at *6 (Pa. Super. Ct. Oct. 29, 2015). *But see* Paschal v. State, 388 S.W.3d 429, 434 (Ark. 2012) (invalidating provision as applied to teachers with students over the age of eighteen).

No sexual activity need be consummated for liability to attach on laws prohibiting sexual conduct between school personnel and students. For instance, a solicitation to that effect from a teacher to a student—even one over the age of consent—can still be criminalized to prevent "the sexual exploitation of students by educators" and preserve "an educational environment conducive to learning." Collins v. State, 479 S.W.3d 533, 543 (Tex. App. 2015).

484 McCoy v. People, 442 P.3d 379, 391 (Colo. 2019) (upholding provision vitiating consent "when an actor engages in treatment or examination of a victim for other than bona fide medical purposes or in a manner substantially inconsistent with reasonable medical practices" as applied to defendant who, after purporting to be a trained health provider, "examined" men in their late teens through early twenties as part of a fake job interview for positions ostensibly requiring physical fitness); State v. Hollenbeck, 53 A.3d 591, 598 (N.H. 2012) (upholding sexual assault conviction against licensed psychologist for having sex with a former client within one year of termination of their therapeutic relationship).

485 State v. Wenthe, 865 N.W.2d 293, 303–05 (Minn. 2015) (upholding statute vitiating consent over a claim that clergy member must know that the congregant is seeking or receiving spiritual counsel over a dissenting opinion arguing that without such mens rea, sexual activity between ministers and members of their flock would infringe on their constitutional rights under *Lawrence*); State v. Edouard, 854 N.W.2d 421, 444 (Iowa 2014), *overruled on other grounds by* Alcala v. Marriott Int'l, Inc., 880 N.W.2d 699 (Iowa 2016) (upholding a pastor's conviction for sexual exploitation by counselor or therapist, reasoning that the statute did not limit liability to those using modern psychological principles and methods or those licensed to provide mental health services); Talbert v. State, 239 S.W.3d 504, 511 (Ark. 2006) (upholding conviction against minister noting that he had "no liberty interest to engage in sexual activity by abusing his position of trust and authority"); *cf.* Bandstra v. Covenant Reformed

caregivers.[486] Nearly all courts reject defendants' attempts to use *Lawrence* to escape criminal liability for sexual activity under such circumstances because the parties in the more subordinate roles are situated in relationships where consent might not be easily refused, even if both parties were over the age of consent.

This held true even in a case in which both parties to a sexual coupling were residents in a care facility when the defendant, who had Autism Spectrum Disorder, engaged in sex with another resident who was intellectually disabled to the point that he did not understand the nature of the act.[487] Because the former knew that the latter could not "appraise the nature of such conduct or resist it due to mental disease or defect," the Texas Court of Appeals upheld his conviction over a challenge that the defendant was a part of the class the law was designed to protect.[488] But

---

Church, 913 N.W.2d 19, 35 (Iowa 2018) (rejecting civil claims for negligent supervision after pastor was criminally convicted of using his position to sexually exploit parishioners, but only because the claims were time-barred under the applicable statute of limitations).

486 People v. Lemons, No. D050763, 2008 WL 4335684, at *4 (Cal. Ct. App. Sept. 24, 2008); *see also, e.g.*, ARK. CODE ANN. § 5-14-126 (2021); OHIO REV. CODE § 2907.03(A)(6)–(13) (2019); TEX. PENAL CODE §§ 22.011(8)–(14), 21.12 (2021).

487 Painter v. State, No. 11-15-00318-CR, 2017 WL 6559653, at *4 (Tex. App. Dec. 21, 2017).

488 *Id.* at *4–5; *see also* State v. Hamlin, 324 P.3d 1006, 1015 (Idaho Ct. App. 2014) ("By its express terms, the statute prohibits 'any person' from sexually abusing and exploiting a vulnerable adult. That is, both mentally retarded persons and persons who are not mentally retarded are prohibited from sexual contact with a vulnerable adult. Accordingly, [defendant] cannot legitimately assert that the State is treating him differently on account of any classification. [He] is not requesting that we invalidate a law that treats him unfairly on the basis of some classification; he is requesting preferential treatment. That is not a cognizable equal protection claim."); *cf.* Haynes v. State, No. W201500919CCAR3PC, 2016 WL 750233, at *1 (Tenn. Crim. App. Feb. 26, 2016) (denying post-conviction relief from convictions for the rape of an intellectually disabled nineteen-year-old where petitioner claimed he was also intellectually disabled).

> If the petitioner's argument is that he was too mentally impaired to violate the statute, then that is an issue of the petitioner's capacity to be resolved on the facts with expert testimony. If the petitioner's argument is that he did not know the victims were mentally incapacitated, then that is a factual issue for the jury's determination and not a constitutional claim. . . . Finally, counsel actually made a constitutional claim on direct appeal . . . by arguing [the statute] violated a constitutionally protected action of intellectually disabled persons to engage in sexual activities under *Lawrence v. Texas* unless a

two cases carved-out an exception to criminal liability under *Lawrence* in circumstances that criminalized consensual sex between actors based on one of their statuses.

In *State v. Mole*, a thirty-six-year-old police officer had been convicted of the sexual battery of a fourteen-year-old that he met online in a chat room.[489] He appealed, arguing that the statutory provision under which he had been convicted was facially unconstitutional. The provision at issue stated that "no person shall engage in sexual conduct with another, not the spouse of the offender, when . . . the other person is a minor, the offender is a peace officer, and the offender is more than two years older than the other person."[490] Unlike the other sections in the sexual battery statute, the provision aimed at peace officers "is unique in that it: (1) has no *mens rea* requirement and (2) contains no relationship or occupational requirement between the offender and victim."[491] Accordingly, the defendant argued, and the Ohio Court of Appeals accepted, that the provision singled-out peace officers in an impermissible manner:

> This subsection prohibits a peace officer from having sexual conduct with a minor more than two years younger than the officer, without consideration given to whether (1) the peace officer used his or her position to facilitate the offense or the victim was in the custody, control, or under the supervision or influence of the peace officer; (2) the victim knew that the offender was a peace officer; or (3) the peace officer knew or should have known the victim was a minor. Moreover, not only does this statute punish relationships such as the one in this case where the age difference was great, but it also punishes relationships between a 17–year–old minor and a 19–year–old peace officer, so long as there is more than a two-year age difference.

> consent requirement was read into the statute. Accordingly, we agree with the post-conviction court that the petitioner failed to prove that counsel performed deficiently or that any deficiency caused him prejudice.

Id. at *5.

489 994 N.E.2d 482, 483 (Ohio Ct. App. 2013), *aff'd*, 74 N.E.3d 368 (Ohio 2016).

490 *Id.* at 484 (quoting OHIO REV. CODE § 2907.03(A)(13) (2009)).

491 *Id.* at 486.

* * *

> [T]he state might have a legitimate interest in protecting minors from police officers who use their profession to pursue inappropriate sexual relationships. But there exists no occupational connection or relationship requirement in [the statute].
>
> We agree with Mole that one's occupation as a peace officer alone, without more, does not provide a person with an "unconscionable advantage" over a minor.
>
> Consequently, because the state's method or means of achieving its interest is not rational, [the statute] fails the second prong of the rational-basis test.[492]

The Supreme Court of Ohio affirmed this holding, without any citation to *Lawrence*, calling-out the differential treatment of peace officers as "irrational" for not only "fail[ing] to include any relationship or other element that justifies the omission of a scienter requirement," but also for singling-out peace officers in a manner that "bears no rational relationship to the government's interest in protecting minors from sexual coercion by people in positions of authority who use that authority to compel submission."[493]

In *Paschal v. State*, a teacher had been convicted of second-degree sexual assault for engaging in a consensual sexual relationship with an eighteen-year-old student enrolled at the school at which the defendant worked.[494] He appealed his conviction, arguing that *Lawrence* recognized a fundamental right for consenting adults to engage in private, sexual

---

492 *Id.* at 487–88.

493 74 N.E.3d 368, 389 (Ohio 2016). *But see* State v. Mogler, 719 N.W.2d 201, 208 (Minn. Ct. App. 2006) (upholding conviction of police officer for sexual intercourse with a seventeen-year-old while he in his police vehicle over challenges that (1) the statute criminalizing such conduct when performed by someone in a position of authority" was unconstitutionally vague and (2) that *Lawrence* applied despite the fact that victim was a minor).

494 388 S.W.3d 429, 434 (Ark. 2012) (quoting ARK. CODE ANN. § 5–14–125(a)(6) (Supp. 2009), which provided, at that time, that "[a] person commits sexual assault in the second degree if the person [i]s a teacher in a public school in a grade kindergarten through twelve (K–12) and engages in sexual contact3 with another person who is [a] student enrolled in the public school and [l]ess than twenty-one (21) years of age").

relationships and the Supreme Court of Arkansas agreed.[495] Thus, the court applied strict scrutiny. The court accepted that the state has a compelling interest in preserving "the special learning environment" in a high school by protecting all students, "regardless of their age, from the sexual advances of teachers who have special authority and control over" them.[496] Nonetheless, the court invalidated the law because there were less restrictive means of achieving the governmental interests at stake than criminalizing what the court called "adult consensual sex."[497] The court's opinion does not make clear what those less restrictive means might be.

Arkansas courts rejected this approach when high school students were under the age of eighteen.[498] And, curiously, they rejected this approach in the context of congregants and clergy members. Consider, for instance, that *Talbert v. State* affirmed a pastor's conviction for engaging in sexual relationships with two congregants even though they were all adults.[499] The court reasoned that the pastor

> was being prosecuted for using his position of trust and authority over those individuals to engage in those acts. Substantive due process, including his right to engage in private, consensual sex, protects an individual's liberty interest under the United States Constitution (*Lawrence* . . .), but [he] has no liberty interest to engage in sexual activity by abusing his position of trust and authority. His substantive due process rights simply were not violated in this instance.[500]

---

[495] *Id.* at 436–37.

[496] *Id.* at 436.

[497] *Id.* at 437.

[498] *E.g.*, Akers v. State, 464 S.W.3d 483, 488 (Ark. Ct. App. 2015).

[499] 239 S.W.3d 504, 511 (Ark. 2006).

[500] *Id. But see* State v. Bussmann, 741 N.W.2d 79, 86 (Minn. 2007). In *Bussman*, the Supreme Court of Minnesota allowed an intermediate court decision to stand due to the justices on the higher court being equally divided in their views as to whether a statute criminalizing sexual relationships between clergy and congregants was constitutional. Some of the justices' logic mirrored that of the majority in *State v. Mole*, which invalidated a similar provision against peace officers. State v. Mole, 994 N.E.2d 482, 483 (Ohio Ct. App. 2013), *aff'd*, 74 N.E.3d 368 (Ohio 2016).

> [The] sexual conduct statute does not require proof of any causal connection between the sexual conduct and the position of the clergy or the mental or emotional state of the parishioner. There is no requirement of proof that the

Why this same logic did not apply to the teacher in *Paschal* is a mystery. But given that most courts reject the notion that *Lawrence* recognized any fundamental right, *Paschal*'s application of strict scrutiny is anomalous and curious. But even accepting the dubious proposition that strict scrutiny applies to such instances, if protecting adults seeking pastoral counsel satisfies a compelling state interest for criminalizing sex between adults, why wouldn't the same be true for protecting high school students who have reached the age of maturity—especially since they arguably are in a far more vulnerable position with their teachers than are adults who engage in sex with members of their clergy?

4. Other Cases

Two sexual assault cases cited *Lawrence* in passing, but did not meaningfully rely on its holding for any substantive reason.[501] One of these cases, however, demonstrates the continuing pervasive nature of anti-LGBTQ+ bias.[502]

In *Kupper v. State*, an appellate court refused to consider the appellant's argument that in light of *Lawrence*, photographs of the

---

> clergy member was in a position to influence the parishioner; that the clergy member abused any such position; that the parishioner sought or received religious or spiritual advice because of any mental or emotional need; or that the parishioner's consent was influenced to any degree by the religious or spiritual advice that was given. Thus, unlike a psychotherapist-patient relationship, where the patient seeks counseling as treatment for a mental or emotional need, a parishioner may seek religious or spiritual advice out of intellectual curiosity without any mental or emotional need that could be seen as vulnerability.

Bussmann, 741 N.W.2d at 86. These justices also would have invalidated the statute on First Amendment grounds because, in their opinion, the law was not religiously neutral, but rather "incorporate[d] religious doctrine" because the law it assumes that clergy members are "always in a position of power" over advisees and that any sexual relationships between such persons will always be "causally related to the religious and spiritual advice" the clergy member dispenses. *Id.* at 89. The other justices on the court disagreed with these premises or the conclusion that they burdened the free exercise of religion. *Id.* at 89–92. They argued the law was based on "secular legislative determinations, not church doctrine." *Id.* at 100 (Anderson, C.J., dissenting).

501 State v. Stevens, 323 P.3d 901, 910 (N.M. 2014) (holding that the offense of "criminal sexual penetration during the commission of a felony" requires proof that the penetration was unlawful, such as when it occurred without consent); Kupper v. State, No. 05-03-00486-CR, 2004 WL 60768, at *4 (Tex. App. Jan. 14, 2004).

502 *Kupper* 2004 WL 60768, at *4.

defendant engaged in "homosexual activity" should have been excluded from evidence on the grounds that their probative value was outweighed by their prejudicial effect because the defense had not objected to their admission.[503] Had the issue not be waived, it appears to present a bona-fide concern. The case involved a male defendant charged with the sexual assault of a middle-school girl under the age of fourteen.[504] Introducing photos of him during the punishment phase of his trial that depicted him engaging in consensual sexual activity with a male over the age of consent serves little purpose other than to use constitutionally-protected acts to play on anti-LGBTQ+ prejudices in an attempt to secure a particularly harsh sentence. Under the facts of that case, it may well be that this mistake constituted harmless error; nonetheless, it illustrates that the year after *Lawrence* was decided, prosecutors and courts may still have viewed sexual activity between members of the same sex as sufficiently deviant conduct such that it illustrated a defendant's purportedly bad character.

E. Privacy and Other Sex Crimes ($n = 25$; 8.1%)

More than two dozen cases in the study presented questions about the constitutional validity of criminal offenses or punishments for a range of other types of sexual offenses. Some of these involved crimes that have been around for hundreds of years, such as bigamy, incest, and variations on public sexual indecency. Others, however, involved relatively new offenses that were adopted with the past fifty years to ameliorate public health crises, such as the knowing transmission of sexually transmitted infections, or to address privacy concerns in the Digital Age, such as laws criminalizing revenge porn. Regardless of the comparable age of these offenses, defendants who tried to use *Lawrence* to shield or diminish their criminal liability were largely unsuccessful.

In-depth analysis of *Lawrence* was strongly associated with narrow interpretations of the case ($n = 11$, 44.0%), compared to only one case (4.0%) in which *Lawrence* was broadly interpreted as being key to the case outcome. Perhaps that is why final case outcomes favored the prosecution by a ratio of more than seven to one as Table 14 demonstrates. Notably, in

---

503 *Id.*

504 *Id.* at *1.

the Northeast, criminal cases raising issues of sexual privacy were more likely to be associated with expansive interpretations of *Lawrence* compared to narrow ones. This finding stands in contrast to the fact that overall, largely due to decisions in the Midwest and Western regions, narrow interpretations of *Lawrence* outnumbered broad interpretations by a two to one ratio, resulting in statistically significant differences that reveal strong associations between region of the country and the way judges construe *Lawrence* in the criminal cases in this category.

TABLE 14: VARIABLE FREQUENCIES AND RELATIONSHIPS TO TREATMENT OF *LAWRENCE* IN OTHER SEXUAL PRIVACY CRIMINAL CASES

Category	Treatment of *Lawrence* *n* (%)				Chi-Square	Sig.	Cramer's V
Depth	*Neutral*	*Narrow*	*Broad*	*Total*	9.964 (2, 25)	Fisher's Exact p = 0.005	0.631
Mentioned in Passing	3 (12.0%)	1 (4.0%)	5 (20.0%)	9 (36.0%)			
Key to Case	4 (16.0%)	11 (44.0%)	1 (4.0%)	16 (64.0%)			
Outcome	*Neutral*	*Narrow*	*Broad*	*Total*	3.580 (2, 25)	p > 0.050	N/A
Prosecution	5 (20.0%)	12 (48.0%)	5 (20.0%)	22 (88.0%)			
Defense	2 (8.0%)	0 (0.0%)	1 (4.0%)	3 (12.0%)			
State Politics	*Neutral*	*Narrow*	*Broad*	*Total*	7.606 (8, 25)	p > 0.050	N/A
Deep Red	4 (16.0%)	3 (12.0%)	2 (8.0%)	9 (36.0%)			
Light Red	0 (0.0%)	2 (8.0%)	1 (4.0%)	3 (12.0%)			
Purple	0 (0.0%)	3 (12.0%)	0 (0.0%)	3 (12.0%)			
Light Blue	0 (0.0%)	1 (4.0%)	0 (0.0%)	1 (4.0%)			
Deep Blue	3 (12.0%)	3 (12.0%)	3 (12.0%)	9 (36.0%)			
Region	*Neutral*	*Narrow*	*Broad*	*Total*	15.880 (6, 25)	Fisher's Exact p = 0.011	0.564
Northeast	1 (4.0%)	0 (0.0%)	3 (12.0%)	4 (16.0%)			
South	4 (16.0%)	1 (4.0%)	2 (8.0%)	7 (28.0%)			
Midwest	1 (4.0%)	5 (20.0%)	1 (4.0%)	7 (28.0%)			
West	1 (4.0%)	6 (24.0%)	0 (0.0%)	7 (28.0%)			
Judge's Sex	*Neutral*	*Narrow*	*Broad*	*Total*	2.158 (4, 25)	p > 0.050	N/A
Male	5 (20.0%)	8 (32.0%)	3 (12.0%)	16 (64.0%)			
Female	2 (8.0%)	3 (12.0%)	3 (12.0%)	8 (32.0%)			
Not Applicable (per curiam)	0 (0.0%)	1 (4.0%)	0 (0.0%)	1 (4.0%)			
Judge's Race/Ethnicity	*Neutral*	*Narrow*	*Broad*	*Total*	2.307 (4, 25)	p > 0.050	N/A
White	5 (20.0%)	10 (40.0%)	5 (20.0%)	20 (80.0%)			
Nonwhite	2 (8.0%)	1 (4.0%)	1 (4.0%)	4 (16.0%)			
Not Applicable or Unknown	0 (0.0%)	1 (4.0%)	0 (0.0%)	1 (4.0%)			
Judge's Political Affiliation	*Neutral*	*Narrow*	*Broad*	*Total*	2.545 (4, 25)	p > 0.050	N/A
Nonpartisan	5 (20.0%)	11 (44.0%)	4 (16.0%)	20 (80.0%)			
Democrat	1 (4.0%)	0 (0.0%)	1 (4.0%)	2 (8.0%)			
Republican	1 (4.0%)	1 (4.0%)	1 (4.0%)	3 (12.0%)			

1. Bigamy

Justice Scalia's dissent in *Lawrence*, in which he eschewed LGBTQ+ people's equal treatment under law,[505] warned that the decriminalization

505 Justice Scalia's comments about LGBTQ+ people, some of which compared members of that community to child molesters, have previously been described as "breathtaking

of sodomy would lead to the fall of legal prohibitions against plural marriage.[506] His fears were overblown. In all cases in which people charged with violating laws against bigamy attempted to use *Lawrence* to shield their actions, they were unsuccessful.

---

in their bigotry." Jeet Herr, *Antonin Scalia Does Not Understand the Difference Between Gay People and Child Abusers*, NEW REPUBLIC (Nov. 17, 2005), https://newrepublic.com/article/124002/antonin-scalia-not-understand-difference-gay-people-child-abusers [https://perma.cc/LMC5-ZH4Z]. In his *Romer v. Evans* dissent, Scalia compared homosexuality to murder and or cruelty to animals. Romer v. Evans, 517 U.S. 620, 644 (1995) (Scalia, J., dissenting). For an analysis of his animus toward LGBTQ+ people, see, e.g., Daniel Gordon, *Symptoms for Scalia and Texas: Gay Rights and American Nationalism*, 35 GOLDEN GATE U. L. REV. 111, 125 (2005); *see also* Barney Frank, *Justice Scalia Is a Homophobe*, POLITICO (June 26, 2015), https://www.politico.com/magazine/story/2015/06/justice-scalia-gay-marriage-ruling-119480/ [https://perma.cc/NB38-9298]. For a more general discussion of Justice Scalia's often vitriolic style, especially when in dissent, see J. Lyn Entrikin, *Disrespectful Dissent: Justice Scalia's Regrettable Legacy of Incivility*, 18 J. APP. PRAC. & PROCESS 201, 202 (2017) ("His dissents frequently reflected uncloaked scorn for the majority.").

Given social changes toward greater acceptance of LGBTQ+ people, at least one scholar opined that Justice Scalia's dissent in *Lawrence* was more muted than his fiery dissent in *Romer*. Nancy J. Knauer, Lawrence v. Texas: *When "Profound and Deep Convictions" Collide with Liberty Interests*, 10 CARDOZO WOMEN'S L.J. 325 (2004).

> The majority's synopsis of the state regulation of same-sex desire in *Lawrence* directly challenged the notion of a trans-historical and universally condemned homosexual and took Chief Justice Burger to task for his unreflective reference to "Western civilization." Perhaps surprisingly, this evolution of understanding is also evident in Justice Scalia's dissent. The homosexual-as-sodomite reasoning has not simply failed to garner a majority of the Supreme Court, it has receded from socially acceptable discourse.

Id. at 332 (internal citations and alterations omitted).

Despite his slightly more civil tone in *Lawrence*, Justice Scalia still argued on behalf of those who "do not want persons who openly engage in homosexual conduct as partners in their business, as scoutmasters for their children, as teachers in their children's schools, or as boarders in their home" because "they view this as protecting themselves and their families from a lifestyle that they believe to be immoral and destructive." Lawrence v. Texas, 539 U.S. 558, 602 (2003) (Scalia, J., dissenting).

506 *Lawrence*, 539 U.S. at 590 (Scalia, J., dissenting) ("State laws against bigamy, same-sex marriage, adult incest, prostitution, masturbation, adultery, fornication, bestiality, and obscenity are likewise sustainable only in light of *Bowers'* validation of laws based on moral choices. Every single one of these laws is called into question by today's decision. . . .").

a. Laws Criminalizing Plural Marriage

One of the leading cases dealing with the criminalization of bigamy is *State v. Holm.*[507] The defendant in that case argued that the State of Utah could not constitutionally criminalize bigamy because, under *Lawrence*, polygamy implicates a "fundamental liberty interest" that cannot be infringed absent compelling governmental interests.[508] The Utah Supreme Court dismissed this argument by recognizing the protection of monogamous marital relationships as a compelling governmental interest.[509]

> [T]his case implicates the public institution of marriage, an institution the law protects . . . . First, the behavior at issue in this case is not confined to personal decisions made about sexual activity, but rather raises important questions about the State's ability to regulate marital relationships and prevent the formation and propagation of marital forms that the citizens of the State deem harmful. . . . Our State's commitment to monogamous unions is a recognition that decisions made by individuals as to how to structure even the most personal of relationships are capable of dramatically affecting public life . . . .
>
> [A] marriage license significantly alters the bond between two people because the State becomes a third party to the marital contract . . . It is precisely that third-party contractual relationship that gives the State a substantial interest in prohibiting unlicensed marriages when there is an existing marriage. Without this contractual relationship, the State would be unable to enforce important marital rights and obligations.[510]

Holm also rejected an equal protection challenge to the state's bigamy law on the grounds that it violated protections of the free exercise of religion. The court reasoned that the law was neutral with regard to religion: "One could engage in polygamy out of animus for religion and

---

[507] 137 P.3d 726, 744–45 (Utah 2006) (citing UTAH CODE § 76–7–101 (2003)).

[508] *Id.* at 742.

[509] *Id.* at 744 (quoting Potter v. Murray City, 760 F.2d 1065, 1070 (10th Cir. 1985) ("[T]he State is justified, by a compelling interest, in upholding and enforcing its ban on plural marriage to protect the monogamous marriage relationship.").

[510] *Id.* at 743–44.

still be considered in violation of the statute. Quite simply, the statute is designed to punish behavior regardless of the motivations giving rise to that behavior."[511]

b. Criminalizing Sex with Underage "Spouses"

The *Holm* case involved a thirty-two-year-old man who, after being legally married to a woman, subsequently participated in a religious marriage ceremony to a sixteen-year-old girl.[512] In addition to bigamy, the state also charged the defendant with unlawful sexual conduct with a sixteen- or seventeen-year-old, a particular variation of statutory rape that excluded those within ten years of each other's age, as well as those who were lawfully married to each other.[513] The defendant argued that such a statutory scheme impermissibly discriminated based on marital status.[514] The court found that there were valid reasons for treating married and unmarried minors in that age bracket differently:

> The protections afforded persons who are married in the eyes of the law include rights, vis-à-vis their spouses, to support and maintenance, . . . to the fulfillment of certain procedural requirements before the union can be dissolved, . . . to a fair distribution of property and debt obligations in the event such a dissolution occurs, . . . and to inherit all or a portion of the spouses' estates in the event of their death . . . . These examples represent only a few of the instances in which marital status is legally relevant.[515]

Additionally, the court reasoned that the state possesses legitimate interests in protecting minors from sexual exploitation at the hands of "older, more experienced persons until they reach the legal age of consent and can more maturely comprehend and appreciate the consequences of their sexual acts."[516]

---

[511] *Id.* at 745.

[512] *Id.* at 730.

[513] *Id.* at 731 (citing UTAH CODE § 76–5–401.2 (2003)).

[514] *Id.* at 750–51.

[515] *Id.* at 752 (internal citations omitted).

[516] *Id.* at 752 (quoting State v. Elton, 680 P.2d 727, 732 (Utah 1984)).

The Utah Supreme Court's decision in *Holm* is not unique. In the other cases in which criminal defendants charged with sexual abuse of minors had argued their polygamous marriages shielded them from criminal liability, courts unanimously rejected their attempted contortion of *Lawrence* to such effect.[517]

2. Incest

Justice Scalia's dissent in *Lawrence* opined that the decriminalization of sodomy would lead the country down a slippery slope such that prohibitions against adult incest would no longer be valid.[518] But as with his fears concerning bigamy and prostitution laws, his warning turned out to be bluster rather than prescience. Courts uniformly distinguished *Lawrence* in cases in which defendants attempted to avoid liability for incest.[519]

a. Incest Generally

The defendant in *Fergusson v. Commonwealth* appealed his conviction for incest for having engaged in sexual intercourse with stepdaughter.[520] In upholding Virginia's law criminalizing incest, the court reasoned that the defendant's "sexual relationship with his eighteen-year-old stepdaughter is not protected by the liberty interest recognized in

---

[517] *E.g.*, State v. Bateman, No. 1 CA-CR 07-0043, 2008 WL 4516447, at *7 (Ariz. Ct. App. Oct. 2, 2008) ("Th[e state] interest in protecting minors is rationally related to the distinction between minors entering into non-plural marriages and minors entering into plural marriages because of the evidence of pressure the [Fundamentalist Church of Jesus Christ of Latter-Day Saints] community places on young girls to consent to these plural marriages, including the evidence that a refusal to enter into the marriage would result in their having sinned and becoming outcasts from the only community they know."); State v. Fischer, 199 P.3d 663, 669 (Ariz. Ct. App. 2008) (rejecting both due process and equal protection challenges to statutory rape convictions).

[518] Lawrence v. Texas, 539 U.S. 558, 590 (2003) (Scalia, J., dissenting).

[519] Indeed, some courts did so with very little analysis. For instance, in a case in which a prisoner convicted of incent sought to toll the statutory period for seeking post-conviction relief on the grounds that *Lawrence* had established a constitutional right that would have provided him with a defense if it had been recognized at the time of his trial, the court simply stated that *Lawrence* did "not address the crime of incest" and did not alter any prior case law establishing that incestuous relationships were not constitutionally protected. Beard v. State, No. M200402227CCAR3PC, 2005 WL 1334378, at *2 (Tenn. Crim. App. June 7, 2005).

[520] 838 S.E.2d 75 (Va. Ct. App. 2020).

Lawrence . . . because it falls into one of the categories of relationships specifically excluded by *Lawrence*—[those] where one party 'might be injured or coerced' or 'where consent might not easily be refused.'"[521] The court also stated that laws criminalizing incest survived rational basis review for another reason, namely that they further the "legitimate state interest in protecting the family unit."[522] Other courts articulated these same reasons,[523] sometimes adding public health to the list of rational bases for upholding incest laws to prevent genetic abnormalities in the offspring of two closely-related people.[524] One court, however, disagreed with that final rationale.[525]

On equal protection grounds, the Connecticut Court of Appeals held in *State v. John M.* that the prevention of inbreeding did not provide a rational basis for criminalizing incest between opposite-sex partners closely-related either by consanguinity or affinity, such as those related only by marriage or adoption.[526] Additionally, the court found this proffered basis to be irrationally related to all opposite-sex couplings:

---

521 *Id.* at 82 (quoting *Lawrence*, 539 U.S. at 578).

522 *Id.* at 83.

523 State v. Lowe, 861 N.E.2d 512, 517–18 (Ohio 2007) (upholding incest ban as applied to stepparent and stepchild under rational basis review on the grounds of maintaining the integrity of the family unit); Morris v. State, No. 08-15-00249-CR, 2019 WL 396807, at *1, *66 (Tex. App. Jan. 31, 2019) (upholding conviction of father for sex with his estranged seventeen-year-old biological daughter in a state where the age of consent is seventeen, noting that the acts "took place against a backdrop of coercion and involved the active manipulation of a relationship where consent might not easily be refused"); *see also* Prather v. Commonwealth, No. 2012-CA-001725-MR, 2014 WL 2536866, at *4 (Ky. Ct. App. June 6, 2014); State v. Freeman, 801 N.E.2d 906, 909 (Ohio Ct. App. 2003) (noting that consent was questionable in incest case and that it can injure the psychological well-being of participants and disrupt the family unit).

524 People v. McEvoy, 154 Cal. Rptr. 3d 914, 923 (Ct. App. 2013) (upholding statute criminalizing incest between siblings on both genetic and family cohesion grounds); People v. Scott, 68 Cal. Rptr. 3d 592, 595 (2007) ("[T]here is a rational basis for criminalizing incest, specifically between consenting adults of the opposite sex who are related by consanguinity (e.g., fathers and daughters) as the present case involves . . . [including] in maintaining the integrity of the family unit, in protecting persons who may not be in a position to freely consent to sexual relationships with family members, and in guarding against in breeding.").

525 State v. John M., 894 A.2d 376 (Conn. Ct. App. 2006), *rev'd*, 940 A.2d 755 (Conn. 2008).

526 *Id.* at 391–92.

> Inbreeding is defined as "mating between organisms that are genetically more closely related than organisms selected at random from the population . . . ." It involves only persons related by consanguinity. Yet the degrees of kindred described in [the incest statute], by its express terms, plainly include persons related by affinity, and have for well over a century. . . . To accept the state's proffered basis would require us to turn a blind eye to the fact that the statute applies to persons incapable of inbreeding.
>
> The inescapable infirmity of the state's proffered basis for the classification here involved is that it pertains to only a portion of those relationships governed by the statute. . . . The breadth of [the incest statute] is sweeping. The classification contained therein includes not only heterosexual persons related by consanguinity, but persons related by affinity as well. Furthermore, [it] encompasses adopted relatives . . . . The dangers of inbreeding are inapplicable, and hence irrelevant, to sexual intercourse between persons related by affinity or adoption. Even more basic is the fact that certain persons are incapable of inbreeding, be it attributable to sterility or elderliness . . . . To conclude that the state's proffered basis is rational, it must be one that we may reasonably presume to have motivated an impartial legislature. In light of the foregoing, we conclude that the relationship of the classification to the proffered goal is so attenuated as to render the distinction arbitrary and irrational. Accordingly, the prevention of genetic defects due to inbreeding is not a rational basis for the classification . . . .[527]

Even though the State of Connecticut had only offered the prevention of inbreeding as a basis for upholding the classification affecting opposite-sex, but not same-sex relations, the court took it upon itself to also consider alternative arguments. Citing *Lawrence*, it rejected avoiding "the socially and morally undesirable consequences of sexual relations between persons within the prohibited degrees of relationship" as a basis for upholding the incest law.[528] Finally, the court rejected the preservation of tranquility within—and the integrity of—the family unit as a basis for the classification. It noted that reason should apply to sexual acts between all

---

[527] *Id.* at 391–92.

[528] *Id.* at 393.

related persons regardless of sexuality: "there is little justification for proscribing sexual intercourse between stepfather and stepdaughter, but not between stepfather and stepson."[529]

The state appealed the decision in *John M.* to the Connecticut Supreme Court.[530] That court scrutinized the wording of the incest prohibition in the penal code, which provided, in relevant part, "a person is guilty of sexual assault in the third degree when such person . . . (2) engages in sexual intercourse with another person whom the actor knows to be related to him or her within any of the *degrees of kindred* specified in section 46b–21."[531] The other statute referenced in that provision, contained in the family statutes, provided "no man may marry his mother, grandmother, daughter, granddaughter, sister, aunt, niece, stepmother or stepdaughter, and no woman may marry her father, grandfather, son, grandson, brother, uncle, nephew, stepfather or stepson. Any marriage within these degrees is void."[532] The court reasoned that the use of the term "degrees of kinship" in the criminal incest statute was not limited to "the precise male-female unions" set forth in the family law code, but rather incorporates "only the proximity of relation specified therein, namely, parent-child, grandparent-grandchild, sibling-sibling, aunt/uncle-niece/nephew and stepparent-stepchild."[533] Accordingly, the court concluded that the incest statute did not violate equal protection.[534]

Importantly, even if the Connecticut Supreme Court had upheld the decision of the intermediate court of appeals, that would not have been fatal to the penal social control of adult incest because the rationale for invalidating the statute was a classification on the basis of sexual orientation that lacked a rational basis.[535] Nothing in the opinion suggested that an incest statute of general applicability—one that applied regardless

---

529 *Id.* at 394.

530 940 A.2d 755 (Conn. 2008).

531 *Id.* at 766 (quoting CONN. GEN. STAT. ANN. § 53a-72a (2002) (emphasis in original)).

532 *Id.* at 766 (quoting CONN. GEN. STAT. ANN. § 46b-21 (1978)).

533 *Id.* at 767.

534 *Id.*

535 State v. John M., 894 A.2d 376, 391–92 (Conn. Ct. App. 2006), *rev'd*, 940 A.2d 755 (Conn. 2008).

of sex, sexuality, or gender identity—would be unconstitutional under *Lawrence* or any due process principles.

b. Incest When There Is Reasonable Doubt as to Consent for Other Sex Crimes

Courts have also upheld incest laws when applied as a fallback position for crimes to which consent is a defense. For instance, in *People v. McPhee*, the defendant, his wife, and her sixteen-year-old sister lived together. One night while the wife was out, the defendant served the minor so much alcohol that she vomited and eventually passed out.[536] She awoke in her sister's bed to find herself being sexually assaulted. At trial, the court instructed the jury on two different theories under which it could convict the defendant of criminal sexual conduct—"that defendant used force or coercion or that defendant was related to 'the complainant by blood or marriage within the third degree as a brother-in-law.'"[537] Because it was not known under which theory the jury convicted the defendant, an appellate court in Michigan reasoned it did not matter from a constitutional perspective:

> In contrast to a consensual sexual relationship between two adults . . . this case involved a 42-year-old married man's forced sexual contact with his intoxicated, 16-year-old sister-in-law to whom he acted as an authority figure. The familial relationship, the age discrepancy, the victim's alcohol consumption, and defendant's position as an authority figure in the victim's life certainly situated the victim in a position "where consent might not easily be refused . . . ." *Lawrence* does not extend to protect defendant's actions in this case. Applying rational-basis review, because there is no other authority cited and *Lawrence* does not stand for the proposition that defendant's asserted right is a fundamental right, we also conclude that [the statute] furthers the legitimate state interests of prohibiting sexual relationships that have traditionally been considered incestuous, as well as protecting the sanctity of the family.[538]

---

536 No. 258285, 2007 WL 912116, at *1 (Mich. Ct. App. Mar. 27, 2007).

537 *Id.*

538 *Id.* at *3.

3. Lewdness and Public Sexual Indecency

Many U.S. states have laws against "lewd" or "lascivious" conduct that fail to define these terms or, alternatively, define them tautologically by using phrases such as "lewd act" or "lascivious act" or "unnatural act" to define the *actus reus* of the crime.[539] Typically, these laws ban the commission of any act of sexual gratification, either by oneself or with another person, with knowledge or recklessness that the actions are "likely to be observed by others who would be affronted or alarmed."[540] Other states criminalize such conduct as public sexual indecency.[541]

The lack of definitional clarity in some lewdness laws can sometimes give rise to concerns that the statutes are unconstitutionally vague. Almost all courts reject such challenges by giving statutes narrow constructions in accordance with the rule of lenity,[542] but even that is not always the case.

---

539 *E.g.*, FLA. STAT. ANN. § 800.02 (1993 & 2022 Supp.); NEV. REV. STAT. § 201.210 (2017 & 2022 Supp.).

540 *E.g.*, ARIZ. REV. STAT. § 13-1403 (2011 & 2022 Supp.); MODEL PENAL CODE § 251.1 (AM. L. INST. Proposed Official Draft 1962); *see also* Berry v. State, 212 P.3d 1085, 1097 (Nev. 2009) (upholding jury instruction defining lewdness as "any act of sexual nature which actor knew was likely to be observed by victim who would be affronted by the act"), *abrogated on other grounds by* State v. Castaneda, 245 P.3d 550 (Nev. 2010). With regard to the variability in *mens rea*, compare Bruno v. Warren, 344 F. Supp. 97, 98 (E.D. Wis. 1972) (citing state stature defining lewd and lascivious behavior as including the commission of "an indecent act of sexual gratification with another with knowledge that they are in the presence of others"), with Commonwealth v. Heinbaugh, 354 A.2d 244, 467 (Pa. 1976) (interpreting lewdness statute as requiring intent element that the acts are "likely to be observed by others who would be affronted or alarmed").

541 *E.g.*, ARK. CODE ANN. § 5-14-111 (1975 & 2022 Supp.) ("A person commits public sexual indecency if he or she engages in any of the following acts in a public place or public view: (1) An act of sexual intercourse; (2) An act of deviate sexual activity; or (3) An act of sexual contact.").

542 People v. Graves, 368 P.3d 317, 328 n.12 (Colo. 2016) ("[T]he liberty interest . . . recognized in *Lawrence* . . . does not extend to public places such as the theater in this case).

> The theater in this case was a venue open to the public. In view of other patrons, [the defendant] stroked another man's erect penis through that man's pants. Such lascivious conduct of an overtly sexualized nature in a public venue meets any reasonable definition of "lewd" and falls well within the scope of the public indecency statute as we have construed it. In short, [the

Consider, for instance, that the Supreme Judicial Court of Massachusetts upheld a lewdness conviction over a vagueness challenge by a man who had pulled down his pants in front of four thirteen-year-old girls and "mooned" them by "exposing his buttocks along with a pair of red 'thong' underwear" he was wearing at the time.[543]

The lack of clarity in some lewdness statutes can also cause courts to struggle with how the elements of this offense intersect. For instance, a divided panel of the Indiana Court of Appeals upheld a felony conviction for "performing sexual conduct in the presence of a minor" against a man who masturbated in an alley while children were playing in the street.[544] The statute under which prosecutors charged the defendant prohibited anyone over the age of eighteen from "knowingly or intentionally . . . touch[ing] or fondl[ing] the person's own body . . . in the presence of a child less than fourteen (14) years of age with the intent to arouse or satisfy the sexual desires of the child or the older person."[545] The defendant maintained the children were unaware of the activity and, therefore, at most he was guilty of public indecency, a misdemeanor offense under the state's statutory scheme.[546] The majority disagreed with him, reasoning that its precedents established there need not be any

---

> defendant's] conduct in this case is so clearly within the ambit of [the statute] that he cannot claim that the statute failed to provide him fair warning.

Id. at 329.

[543] Commonwealth v. Quinn, 789 N.E.2d 138, 141 (Mass. 2003).

[544] Riddle v. State, No. 39A04-1712-CR-2975, 2018 WL 5274027, at *2 (Ind. Ct. App. Oct. 24, 2018).

[545] *Id.* (quoting IND. CODE § 35-42-4-5(c)(3) (2014)).

[546] IND. CODE § 35-45-4-1 (2014), which provides, in relevant part:

> (a) A person who knowingly or intentionally, in a public place:
> (1) engages in sexual intercourse;
> (2) engages in other sexual conduct (as defined in IC 35-31.5-2-221.5);
> (3) appears in a state of nudity with the intent to arouse the sexual desires of the person or another person; or
> (4) fondles the person's genitals or the genitals of another person;
> commits public indecency, a Class A misdemeanor.
>
> (b) A person at least eighteen (18) years of age who knowingly or intentionally, in a public place, appears in a state of nudity with the intent to be seen by a child less than sixteen (16) years of age commits public indecency, a Class A misdemeanor.

"nexus" between the act and the presence of children, but rather that it was sufficient that "a child under age fourteen be in the general area where the perpetrator is so that there is a reasonable prospect that children might be exposed to the perpetrator's conduct."[547]

A dissenting judge agreed with the defendant that the proper conviction was for public indecency. First, she distinguished the facts of the case from those the majority relied upon because those cases involved acts committed with knowledge of children being in the presence of the perpetrators, whereas in *Riddle*, "no children witnessed, or were near enough to witness, [the defendant's] conduct."[548] But the crux of her analysis centered on the fact that the public indecency statute did not require a child's presence "*with* the intent to arouse or satisfy the sexual desires."[549] Although her analysis centered on principles of statutory construction, Judge Robb noted that the majority's interpretation about the possibility of children being exposed to sexual conduct could "lead to absurd results."[550] She then inserted a footnote in which she said, "[a]lthough protecting children from the mere possibility of witnessing sexual conduct is a compelling governmental interest, I am not convinced this interpretation of the statute could pass constitutional scrutiny. See *Lawrence* . . . ."[551] She did not elaborate any further.

Although all courts upheld the validity of criminal laws targeting lewd and lascivious behaviors, not all judges agreed with those in the majority

---

547 *Riddle*, 2018 WL 5274027, at *2 (citing Glotzbach v. State, 783 N.E.2d 1221, 1227 (Ind. Ct. App. 2003) (interpreting the public indecency statute)).

548 *Id.* at *6 (Robb, J., dissenting). Judge Robb explained that the people who had witnessed the defendant were adults, and "only after a conscious attempt to do so." *Id.*

549 *Id.* at *7.

> Whereas the public indecency statute prohibits "appearing in the state of nudity with the intent to arouse the sexual desires of the person or another person in or on a public place *where* a child less than sixteen (16) years of age is present," . . . the performing sexual conduct in the presence of a minor statute requires the defendant's conduct occur "in the presence of a child . . . with the intent to arouse or satisfy the sexual desires of the child or the older person . . . ."

Id. at *8 (emphasis in original).

550 *Id.* at *8.

551 *Id.* at *8 n.4.

of such decisions.[552] For instance, *In re A.P.*, the Supreme Court of Vermont upheld a delinquency finding based on violation of the state's "open and gross lewdness and lascivious behavior" statute.[553] In that case, a high-school student groped the complainant's breast with his hand in the hallway of their school.[554] The court first rejected the petitioner's contention that the act was not "open" because no one else was present to observe the act, reasoning that a school hallway was "sufficiently public to meet its requirements" because "open" refers to "not concealed," rather than any occurrence in the presence of third-party witnesses.[555] Reasoning that the defendant's actions were "patently offensive," the court also rejected his argument that the act did not constitute gross lewdness because it involved an "unwanted touch over clothing for approximately one second."[556] Finally, the defendant challenged his adjudication on vagueness grounds, but the court cited its own precedent defining the meaning of lewd and lascivious conduct[557] and then held that the petitioner "should have known that groping a girl's breast without her consent in a school hallway constitutes prohibited conduct."[558] One justice, however, filed a dissent in which she explained her disagreement on two key points.[559]

Justice Robinson first argued that the use of the word "open" was targeted at preventing public sexual indecency, but in contravention of the

---

552 *E.g.*, People v. Graves, 368 P.3d 317, 328 (Colo. 2016) ("Sexual conduct in public is not constitutionally protected expressive activity. . . . Even assuming that some overtly sexual fondling or caressing may be expressive conduct protected under the First Amendment, the conduct potentially chilled by the legitimate enforcement of [the statute] is slight compared to the 'easily identifiable and constitutionally proscribable conduct' to which the statute applies.").

553 246 A.3d 399, 401 (Vt. 2020) (citing 13 VT. STAT. ANN. tit. 13, § 2601 (1981)), *cert. denied*, 141 S. Ct. 2630 (2021).

554 *Id.*

555 *Id.* at 402.

556 *Id.* at 403–04.

557 *Id.* at 407.

558 *Id.* at 404 ("[L]ewd and lascivious behavior means behavior that is sexual in nature, lustful, or indecent, that which offends the common social sense of the community, as well as its sense of decency and morality." (internal citations omitted)).

559 *Id.* at 407–19 (Robinson, J., dissenting) (quoting Lawrence v. Texas, 539 U.S. 558, 571 (2003)).

historical context of that word's meaning, an expansive definition of "open" no longer requires the presence of any person other than the actor and the victim, thereby allowing "the State to prosecute acts that the Legislature has not otherwise expressly criminalized, namely nonconsensual touching short of sexual assault."[560]

She also would have declared the statute unconstitutionally vague for three reasons. First, the meaning ascribed to the key terms in the statute refer to "ambiguous moralistic judgments" such that "murky and self-referential definition of lewdness invites prosecutors and courts to 'mandate our own moral code' by applying the statute to any sexual act that could be perceived as wrongful."[561] Second, she argued that the legislature needed to criminalize acts with more precise language. "We are no longer bound to respect the 'undesirability of the expression of certain words or thoughts within the chambers of Victorian society. If certain acts of a sexual nature are considered by our Legislature to be objectionable, then let such acts be enacted as crimes fully defined in clear, unequivocal language."[562] Finally, Justice Robinson maintained that "lascivious has no discernible meaning distinct from lewdness."[563] Applying that critique to the facts of the case, she noted that it was "not at all clear" the "unwanted touch over complainant's clothing was not only 'lewdness' but also 'lascivious behavior.'"[564] The distinction is not merely rhetorical, as lewd conduct alone is a misdemeanor under Vermont law, whereas lewd *and* lascivious behavior constitutes a felony.[565] Justice Robinson noted that "even though lasciviousness is the feature that elevates conduct from a misdemeanor to a felony within this statutory scheme, our statutes and

---

560 *Id.* at 410. "In fact, punishing nonconsensual touching has become a primary use of the statute, even though the statute is theoretically aimed at conduct that 'tends to affront the public conscience and debase the community morality,' and was not originally enacted to address invasions of individual privacy or bodily integrity." *Id.* at 411.

561 *Id.* at 412 (quoting Lawrence, 539 U.S. at 571).

562 *Id.* at 416 (internal quotations and citations omitted).

563 *Id.* at 417.

564 *Id.* at 419.

565 *Compare* 13 VT. STAT. ANN. tit. 13, § 2601a (2017) (punishing "open and gross lewdness" by up to one year in jail, a fine of up to $300, or both), *with* 13 VT. STAT. ANN. tit. 13, § 2601 (1981) (punishing "open and gross lewdness and lascivious behavior" by up to five years imprisonment, fine of up to $300, or both).

case law provide no clarity as to what 'lascivious' means, or how it is distinct from 'lewd.'"[566]

The position Justice Robinson took in her *In re A.P.* dissent was unique among the cases in the study. But her logic was mirrored by other courts that invalidated lewd and lascivious conduct statutes before *Lawrence* was decided.[567]

4. Public Nudity/Indecent Exposure

The lewd and lascivious conduct statutes in some U.S. states include indecent exposure.[568] But when so included, statutory language often limits liability for sexually-motivated exposures.[569] In some jurisdictions, however, indecent exposure constitutes a separate statutory offense that may or may not require any sexual motive. Either way, nearly all states today exempt breast-feeding from the definition of lewdness or indecent exposure.[570]

---

566 *A.P.*, 246 A.3d at 418 (Robinson, J., dissenting).

567 *See, e.g.*, D.C. v. City of St. Louis, 795 F.2d 652, 654–55 (8th Cir. 1986); Pryor v. Municipal Ct., 599 P.2d 636, 642 (Cal. 1979); State v. Kueny, 215 N.W.2d 215, 217–18 (Iowa 1974); District of Columbia v. Walters, 319 A.2d 332, 335 (D.C. 1974); Courtemanche v. State, 507 S.W.2d 545, 547 (Tex. Crim. App. 1974).

568 *E.g.*, KAN. STAT. ANN. § 21-5513(a)(2) (2011 & 2022 Supp.) ("Lewd and lascivious behavior is . . . publicly exposing a sex organ or exposing a sex organ in the presence of a person who is not the spouse of the offender and who has not consented thereto, with intent to arouse or gratify the sexual desires of the offender or another."); N.J. STAT. ANN. § 2C:14-4 (c) (1992 & 2022 Supp.) ("As used in this section, 'lewd acts' shall include the exposing of the genitals for the purpose of arousing or gratifying the sexual desire of the actor or of any other person."); N.Y. PENAL LAW 245.00 (2015 & 2022 Supp.) ("A person is guilty of public lewdness when he or she intentionally exposes the private or intimate parts of his or her body in a lewd manner or commits any other lewd act: (a) in a public place, or (b) (i) in private premises under circumstances in which he or she may readily be observed from either a public place or from other private premises, and with intent that he or she be so observed, or (ii) while trespassing, ...").

569 *See* statutes cited *supra* note 568.

570 *See, e.g.*, REV. CODE WASH. § 9A.88.010(1) (2004 & 2022 Supp.) ("A person is guilty of indecent exposure if he or she intentionally makes any open and obscene exposure of his or her person or the person of another knowing that such conduct is likely to cause reasonable affront or alarm. The act of breastfeeding or expressing breast milk is not indecent exposure.").

People v. Krause illustrates conduct that satisfies an indecent exposure statute that requires sexual motivation.[571] In that case, the defendant rented a room from the victim who told him when he moved in that they would be "strictly roommates and friends."[572] Within a few weeks of his moving in, however, he exposed himself to her several times (in addition to other actions that resulted in criminal liability). For the exposures, though, he was convicted of "willfully and lewdly . . . [exposing] his person, or the private parts thereof, in any public place, or in any place where there are present other persons to be offended or annoyed thereby."[573] On appeal, he conceded his acts were lewd and willful, but he argued that the statute could not reach exposure in one's own home just because the person with whom he lived was "not receptive to the overture."[574] The court disagreed, noting that the statute used the phrase "in any place" without limitation. The court also rejected the defendant's vagueness challenge to the statute, as well as his as-applied challenge on privacy grounds, noting that *Lawrence*'s scope required the mutual consent of parties even in the home.[575]

Krause involved a flagrant example of sexualized exposure to a nonconsenting victim. Indeed, some states would handle *Krause* thought lewd and lascivious conduct statutes. By contrast, in jurisdictions that separate nonsexual exposure from lewdness, action such as "(1) flashing a passerby for shock value, (2) streaking naked across a school campus, or (3) mooning someone out a window can all satisfy the *actus reus* of indecent exposure.[576] Several courts struggled to harmonize such broad indecent exposure laws with Fourteenth Amendment constitutional rights.

For instance, the defendant in *State v. Lilley* went topless while on a New Hampshire beach.[577] While there, she also did some yoga. Police were summoned and they asked her to cover up; she refused and was

---

[571] No. C050840, 2007 WL 1152688 (Cal. Ct. App. Apr. 19, 2007).

[572] *Id.* at *1.

[573] *Id.* at *4 (quoting CAL. PENAL CODE § 314 (1982)).

[574] *Id.*

[575] *Id.* at *5–6.

[576] State v. Murray, 416 P.3d 1225, 1229 (Wash. 2018).

[577] 204 A.3d 198, 203 (N.H. 2019).

therefore arrested for violating an ordinance that made it unlawful "for any person to knowingly or intentionally, in a public place . . . appear in a state of nudity."[578] Because the ordinance included exposure of females' breasts in its definition of nudity, but not males' chests, she argued the ordinance violated equal protection. The New Hampshire Supreme Court refused to apply heightened scrutiny, reasoning that the ordinance did not create a gender-based classification for two reasons. First, it prohibited public nudity by both men and women. Second, unlike with men, the court reasoned that "nudity in the case of women is commonly understood to include the uncovering of the breasts. The ordinance merely reflects the fact that men and women are not fungible with respect to the traditional understanding of what constitutes nudity."[579] The court also rejected a First Amendment challenge to the ordinance, finding it to be a content-neutral "general prohibition on public nudity" that regulates the "manner in which activities may be carried out in that they cannot be carried out in the nude."[580]

The dissent in *Lilley* disagreed with the majority that the ordinance did not create a gender-based classification that should trigger strict scrutiny under the provisions of the state constitution's Equal Rights Amendment.[581]

> That the ordinance classifies on the basis of gender is self-evident. The ordinance defines "nudity" differently for females and males. By the plain text of the ordinance, a person who appears in a public place showing "the female breast with less than a fully opaque covering of any part of the nipple" violates the ordinance; a male who appears in the same public place without such a covering does not. The challenged portion of the ordinance creates a public dress code which only one gender can violate. This is a gender-based classification.[582]

---

578 *Id.* (citing Laconia, N.H., Code of Ordinances ch. 180, art. I, §§ 180-2, 180-4).

579 *Id.* at 208 (internal quotations and citations omitted).

580 *Id.* at 213.

581 *Id.* at 218 (Bassett, J., dissenting) ; *see generally* N.H. CONST. pt. I, art. 2. ("Equality of rights under the law shall not be denied or abridged by this state on account of race, creed, color, sex, or national origin.").

582 *Lilley*, 204 A.3d at 218–19.

The dissent went on to argue that the majority's reasoned "upend[ed] the safeguards of equal protection" by relying on a physiological difference between men and women.

> [B]ecause women have a longer life expectancy than men, by the majority's reasoning, a hypothetical law that mandates that women work four years longer than men in order to qualify for a pension, or prevents women from retiring until age 70 as opposed to age 66 for men, or reduces a woman's social security benefits if she retires at the same age as a man, does not classify on the basis of gender.[583]

The dissent also noted that courts in some other jurisdictions agreed with the proposition that differential definitions of nudity create sex-based classifications for equal protection purposes.[584]

After determining that a sex-based classification was at issue, the dissent went on to analyze whether that classification was narrowly tailored to serve a compelling governmental interest and concluded the answer was no. The city argued that the ordinance served public safety because topless women could cause a "disturbance which has the potential for violence."[585] It also maintained that "because people think of female breasts in a sexualized manner, topless women may present other beachgoers with a mental health issue."[586] And finally, the city claimed the ordinance "supported morals as determined by the city council."[587]

The dissent first cited Justice O'Connor's concurrence in *Lawrence* for the proposition that moral disapproval, without more, is insufficient to allow discriminatory classifications.[588] Although the dissent questioned whether the purported protection of public sensibilities were "grounded in prejudice and unexamined stereotypes" and reflected "archaic prejudice,"

---

583 *Id.* at 220.

584 *Id.* at 219 (citing Tagami v. City of Chicago, 875 F.3d 375, 379–80 (7th Cir. 2017), *cert. denied*, 138 S. Ct. 1577 (2018); Craft v. Hodel, 683 F. Supp. 289, 299 (D. Mass. 1988); City of Tucson v. Wolfe, 917 P.2d 706, 707 (Ariz. Ct. App. 1995); Dydyn v. Department of Liquor Control, 531 A.2d 170, 175 (Conn. Ct. App. 1987)).

585 *Id.* at 225.

586 *Id.* (internal quotations omitted).

587 *Id.*

588 *Id.* (quoting Lawrence v. Texas, 539 U.S. 558, 582 (2003) (O'Connor, J., concurring)).

it nonetheless assumed, for the sake of argument, that the city's other proffered justifications constituted compelling governmental interests.[589] It then reasoned that the ordinance was not narrowly tailored to achieve these interests because it would be "perfectly lawful for a post-pubescent female to wear pasties with tassels" in the city streets, whereas a "four-year-old girl playing on the beach wearing only shorts, or an adult woman sunbathing without a top in her own back yard, engages in unlawful behavior if her nipples are 'visible to the public.'"[590] The dissent also questioned whether "a less restrictive ordinance, perhaps one more narrow in time or place"—presumably one limiting toplessness to certain areas of the beach or at certain times, rather than outright banning it—could sufficiently address the city's articulated concerns.[591]

In *State v. Legassie*, the Supreme Judicial Court of Maine invalidated the conviction of a twenty-one-year-old man who had sent a digital photo of his genitals to a fifteen-year-old-girl.[592] The statute under which he had been charged provided that one a "person is guilty of indecent conduct if . . . [i]n a private place, the actor exposes the actor's genitals with the intent that the actor be seen from a public place or from another private place."[593] The court agreed with the defendant that the statute required indecent exposure in the physical presence of a victim and, therefore, that sending nude photos of himself did not fall within the statutory parameters.[594]

> [T]he State's interpretation . . . which could subject to criminal liability any individual seen exposing his or her genitals by another in person or in a photograph, would present serious constitutional problems because [the statute] contains no "affront or alarm" requirement. The State's construction of [it] could therefore not only criminalize private behavior between consenting adults, but also subject to prosecution individuals who

---

589 *Id.* at 224.

590 *Id.* at 225.

591 *Id.*

592 171 A.3d 589, 592 (Me. 2017).

593 *Id.* at 594 (quoting ME. REV. STAT. ANN. tit. 17, § 854(1)(B) (2007)).

594 *Id.* at 595.

> appear in photographs, which could burden well-established free speech and due process rights. *See Lawrence* . . . .[595]

Of course, the holding in *Legassie* does not mean that states cannot regulate adults sending sexually-explicit photos or videos to minors. In fact, the Maine legislature enacted a law specifically criminalizing the dissemination of such images to people under the age of eighteen, a law the court in *Legassie* stated would not only be "more directly applicable" to the conduct in the case, but also weighed against the government's proffered interpretation of the indecent exposure statute. [596]

In short, few jurisdictions have retreated from the pre-*Lawrence* approaches that indecent exposure may be criminally regulated. But the scope of such laws continues to be debated, largely for reasons having little to do with *Lawrence*'s central holding.

5. Voyeurism

Voyeurism, broadly speaking, is commonly defined as "the practice of obtaining sexual gratification from observing others."[597] The law is concerned with such behaviors when they violate people's privacy vis-à-vis actors who, without consent, watch another people as they undress or engage in sexual activities.[598] Courts have interpreted *Lawrence* broadly

---

595 *Id.* at 596.

596 ME. REV. STAT. ANN. tit. 17, § 2911 (2011 & 2022 Supp.).

597 *Voyeurism*, MERRIAM-WEBSTER DICTIONARY, https://www.merriam-webster.com/dictionary/voyeurism [https://perma.cc/FL56-TWR2] (last visited Aug. 11, 2022); *cf. Voyeurism*, BLACK'S LAW DICTIONARY (11th ed. 2029) ("Gratification derived from observing the genitals or sexual acts of others, usu[ally] secretly.").

598 *E.g.*, TEX. PENAL CODE § 21.15(b) (2015), which provides:

> (b) A person commits an offense if, without the other person's consent and with intent to invade the privacy of the other person, the person:
>
> (1) photographs or by videotape or other electronic means records, broadcasts, or transmits a visual image of an intimate area of another person if the other person has a reasonable expectation that the intimate area is not subject to public view;
>
> (2) photographs or by videotape or other electronic means records, broadcasts, or transmits a visual image of another in a bathroom or changing room; or

in the context of protecting people from voyeurs or so-called "Peeping Toms" for the reasons the court explained in *Ex parte Metzger*:

> The right of privacy also includes rights to bodily integrity and sexual privacy. A person's fundamental interest in bodily integrity and sexual privacy have been recognized as liberty interests that are protected from unwarranted state interference by the Due Process Clause. . . . Those interests are invaded by a private actor who creates unconsented visual images of a person in a place such as a changing room or a bathroom where people are vulnerable, expose their bodies, and engage in highly private activities with the reasonable expectation they are not being photographed or recorded. A person's bodily integrity and sexual privacy is also violated when someone inside their home usurps the person's right to choose whether photographs may be taken of their intimate areas. . . . These types of "video voyeurism" "violate people's sexual privacy by denying their autonomy. It effectively takes dominion over their bodies, intimate activities, and sexual interactions without permission. It hijacks their ability to decide who has access to their body, bedroom, or bathroom. It undermines people's sense that they control their intimate lives. . . ." Likewise, "up-skirt" and "down-blouse" photographs violate sexual privacy by "undermining the victim's decision to shield her genitalia and breasts from the public—consent and sexual autonomy are no longer in victims' control. . . ."[599]

In light of these substantial rights, courts usually determined that the government has a compelling interest in protecting people from voyeurism.[600] Statutes that are narrowly tailored to achieve those interests survive strict scrutiny analysis over First Amendment challenges.[601]

> (3) knowing the character and content of the photograph, recording, broadcast, or transmission, promotes a photograph, recording, broadcast, or transmission described by Subdivision (1) or (2).

See also, e.g., 18 U.S.C. § 1801(a).

[599] 610 S.W.3d 86, 103–04 (Tex. App. 2020) (citing *Lawrence* and quoting Danielle Keats Citron, *Sexual Privacy*, 128 YALE L.J. 1870, 1909, 1914 (2019)) (other citations and internal alterations omitted).

[600] *Id.* at 104.

[601] *Id.* at 105–06.

6. Revenge Porn

Judges apply similar logic to the criminal regulation of nonconsensual pornography as they do to voyeurism. So-called "revenge porn" involves the unauthorized distribution of "sexually intimate images or videos of another person online in an effort to mentally damage the other person, derail his or her career or relationships, and/or profit from the views of the image."[602] Sometimes the distributed images are originally obtained consensually, such as when they are shared with sex partners, while other times they are obtained illegally by hackers or those engaged in illicit voyeurism.[603]

Nearly all states have enacted laws making it a crime to distribute such images without the consent of the person depicted.[604] But the two cases in the present study that cited *Lawrence* while evaluating the constitutionality of such laws both came from Texas. These courts both recognized that limits on such distribution constitute a content-based restriction on free speech and, therefore, apply strict scrutiny to evaluate the constitutionality of these laws.[605] But they also reasoned that the government has a compelling interest in protecting people from substantial invasions of privacy and that the Texas revenge porn law was narrowly

---

602 Seth Teleky, *You Know It When You See It: Punishments for and Regulation Against Revenge Porn*, 1 GEO. L. TECH. REV. 175, 175 (2016).

603 John A. Day, *A New Arrow in the Quiver to Fight Revenge Porn*, TENN. B.J., May/June 2022, at 38.

604 James J. Wilkerson, *Revenge Porn: State Laws, Constitutional Challenges, and the Progress of Federal Legislation*, 60 U. LOUISVILLE L. REV. 301, 302 (2021); Matt Stout, *In Less Than a Decade, Nearly Every State Has Outlawed 'Revenge Porn.' So Why Hasn't Massachusetts?*, BOS. GLOBE (Feb. 6, 2022, 4:22 PM), https://www.bostonglobe.com/2022/02/06/metro/less-than-decade-nearly-every-state-has-outlawed-revenge-porn-so-why-hasnt-massachusetts/ [https://perma.cc/FJN4-JP48].

The Stopping Harmful Image Exploitation and Limiting Distribution Act of 2022 (SHIELD Act), S.3777, 117th Cong. (2022), would make it a federal felony offense to "knowingly use any means or facility of interstate or foreign commerce to distribute an intimate visual depiction of an individual (1) with knowledge of or reckless disregard for (a) the lack of consent of the individual to the distribution; and (b) the reasonable expectation of the individual that the depiction would remain private; and (2) without an objectively reasonable belief that such distribution touches upon a matter of public concern."

605 *Ex parte* Fairchild-Porche, 638 S.W.3d 770, 782 (Tex. App. 2021).

tailored to protecting this interest if limited to circumstances in which the persons depicted are identified, have reasonable expectations of privacy in the images, and do not consent to their distribution, provided that the distributor acts intentionally with regard to their disclosure and at least recklessly with regard to whether the persons depicted consented to dissemination.[606] Consider the court's reasoning in *Ex parte Fairchild-Porche*:

> First, in addition to the requirement that the disclosure be intentional, the lack-of-consent element narrows the Statute's reach to an actor who intentionally discloses visual material despite knowing or being aware of a substantial and unjustifiable risk that the depicted person did not effectively consent to the disclosure. In those cases, the actor has, at the very least, some objective fair warning that the sensitive and potentially harmful speech the actor is about to utter is contrary to the wishes of the person who might be harmed by it. Providing criminal penalties for speech made in disregard of this fair warning is a narrowly tailored means to deter that speech—and only that speech—thereby vindicating, to the greatest extent constitutionally permissible, the depicted person's expectation of privacy.
>
> Second, the expectation-of-privacy element further narrows the Statute's scope, even without an express culpable mental state, because (1) the reasonable expectation of privacy requirement provides adequate protection; and (2) as a practical matter, the evidence needed to prove the circumstances under which the defendant obtained the material would necessarily satisfy a culpable mental state of knowledge. And, when this element is read with the lack-of-consent element, the Statute only punishes those who knew or were aware of but consciously disregarded a substantial and unjustifiable risk that the circumstances gave rise to a reasonable expectation by the depicted person that the material would be private.
>
> Third, the identification element narrows the Statute's reach to those who knowingly or recklessly reveal the identity of the depicted person through disclosure. Such a requirement means that the Statute does not apply to a person who intentionally

---

606 *Id.* at 784

> discloses visual material otherwise prohibited by the Statute if the depicted person is not identified or identifiable by future recipients . . . . Consequently, the Statute . . . is narrowly tailored to serve the government's compelling interest in protecting sexual privacy.[607]

Importantly, the initial dissemination of revenge porn is different than subsequent sharing of images by third parties. According to the Texas Court of Criminal Appeals' decision in *Ex parte Jones*, for liability to attach to such actors, the third parties would have to have

> (1) obtained the material under circumstances in which the depicted person had a reasonable expectation that the image would remain private; (2) knew or was aware of but consciously disregarded a substantial and unjustifiable risk that he did not have effective consent of the depicted person; and (3) knowingly or recklessly identified the depicted person and caused that person harm through the disclosure.[608]

The court acknowledged that such requirements exclude those "who receive intimate photos and forward them to others without knowing" that the initial disclosure lacked effective consent.[609] Despite such subsequent third-party disclosures falling outside the revenge porn statute's narrowed scope, the court nonetheless noted that copyright law and civil remedies may be available under such circumstances.[610]

7. Knowing Transmission of STIs

In 1990, Congress enacted the Ryan White Comprehensive AIDS Resources Emergency Act of 1990, which provided states with federal funding for the prevention and treatment of HIV/AIDS.[611] At that time, the HIV/AIDS epidemic was relatively young considering that the first known cases of AIDS occurred in 1981 and the virus that causes the disease was

---

607 *Id.* at 789–90.

608 No. PD-0552-18, 2021 WL 2126172, at *1 (Tex. Crim. App. May 26, 2021).

609 *Id.* at *13.

610 *Id.*

611 Ryan White Comprehensive AIDS Resources Emergency Act, Pub. L. No. 101-381, 104 Stat. 576 (1990) (codified as amended at 42 U.S.C. §§ 300ff (2022)).

discovered two years later.[612] Additionally, "effective treatments for HIV had not yet been discovered" at that time.[613] Perhaps that is why the legislation required that states certify their criminal laws were adequate to prosecute individuals who knowingly exposed another person to HIV. This requirement led many states to enact "HIV-specific criminal exposure laws [that] impose[d] criminal penalties on people living with HIV who know their HIV status and who potentially expose others to HIV."[614] As of 2021, thirty-five states had adopted either specific laws targeting HIV transmission, broader laws covering transmitting of a broader range of sexually transmitted infections (STIs), or sentencing enhancements for other crimes when the transmission of certain STIs are involved.[615] Most of these laws require someone who knows they have a STI covered by the applicable statute to disclose that information to potential sex partners before engaging in certain sexual conduct.[616] But some laws may not even recognize consent after disclosure as a possible defense, as exemplified by Alabama's statute criminalizing all persons with any STI from engaging in "any act which will probably or likely transmit such disease to another person."[617]

> The "prohibited conduct" contained in the *actus reus* of the offense includes more than vaginal or anal sex in many states, often including oral sex; needle-sharing; engaging in acts of prostitution; biting, spitting, and throwing bodily fluids, especially in correctional institutions; and donating blood, tissue, or bodily fluids. Four states also criminalize sharing sex objects/toys . . . .

---

612 Robert C. Gallo & Luc Montagnier, *The Discovery of HIV as the Cause of AIDS*, 349 NEW ENG. J. MED. 2283 (2003).

613 FRADELLA, *supra* note 433, at 219 (citing Ctrs. for Disease Control & Prevention, *HIV and AIDS–United States, 1981–2000*, 50 MORBIDITY & MORTALITY WEEKLY REPT. 430 (June 1, 2001), http://www.cdc.gov/mmwr/preview/mmwrhtml/mm5021a2.htm [https://perma.cc/LHV9-S89P]).

614 *HIV and STD Criminalization Laws*, CTRS. FOR DISEASE CONTROL & PREVENTION, https://www.cdc.gov/hiv/policies/law/states/exposure.html [https://perma.cc/DF3H-NL9G] (last updated Dec. 22, 2021).

615 *Id.*; *see also, e.g.*, FLA. STAT. ANN. § 384.24 (1986 & 2022 Supp.); IDAHO CODE § 39-608(3)(a) (1988 & 2022 Supp.); NEB. REV. STAT. § 28-934 (2011 & 2022 Supp.); TENN. CODE ANN. § 39-13-109 (1994 & 2022 Supp.).

616 FRADELLA, *supra* note 433, at 219–20.

617 ALA. CODE § 22-11A-21(c) (1987 & 2022 Supp.).

> Thus, many states fail to differentiate between high-risk (e.g., vaginal or anal intercourse) [and] low-risk (e.g., oral sex) . . . . Consider, for instance, that there are no documented cases of HIV transmission from spitting. And few states take into account behaviors that significantly reduce the risk of transmission, such as condom use (a defense in only four states), antiretroviral therapy, or pre-exposure prophylaxis.[618]

There are good reasons to question the wisdom of such laws today—and not just because HIV medications have evolved such that the diagnosis is now widely considered to be a chronic, treatable disease.[619] For one thing, research suggests these laws do little to change people's behavior.[620] But more importantly, these laws can be counterproductive to public health because they increase "stigma towards persons living with HIV"; reduce the "frequency of HIV testing since knowledge of status is required for culpability"; and flame "inflammatory or ill-informed media coverage that may perpetuate misinformation regarding modes of HIV transmission."[621] Thus, several scholars have called for the repeal or revision of knowing transmission laws to better serve public health interests and to prevent "overinclusive criminalization that potentially rises to the levels of due process violations."[622] A few courts analyzed due

---

618 FRADELLA, *supra* note 433, at 220 (citing J. Stan Lehman et al., *Prevalence and Public Health Implications of State Laws that Criminalize Potential HIV Exposure in the United States*, 18 AIDS BEHAV. 997, 1000–03 (2014) (internal quotations omitted)).

619 Dallas Swendemana, Barbara L. Ingramb & Mary Jane Rotheram-Borus, *Common Elements in Self-Management of HIV and Other Chronic Illnesses: An Integrative Framework*, 21 AIDS CARE 1321 (2009).

620 Carol L. Galletly & Stephen D. Pinkerton, *Preventing HIV Transmission Via HIV Exposure Laws: Applying Logic and Mathematical Modeling to Compare Statutory Approaches to Penalizing Undisclosed Exposure to HIV*, 36 J.L. & MED. ETHICS 577 (2008); Carol L. Galletly et al., *New Jersey's HIV Exposure Law and HIV-Related Attitudes, Beliefs, and Sexual and Seropositive Status Disclosure Behaviors of Persons Living with HIV*, 102 AM. J. PUB. HEALTH 2135 (2012); Keith J. Horvath, Richard Weinmeyer & Simon Rosser, *Should It Be Illegal for HIV-Positive Persons to Have Unprotected Sex Without Disclosure? An Examination of Attitudes Among US Men Who Have Sex with Men and the Impact of State Law*, 22 AIDS CARE 1221 (2010).

621 Lehman et al., *supra* note 618, at 999.

622 FRADELLA, *supra* note 433, at 221 (citing Isabel Grant, *Rethinking Risk: The Relevance of Condoms and Viral Load in HIV Nondisclosure Prosecutions*, 54 MCGILL L.J. 389 (2009); Ari Ezra Waldman, *Exceptions: The Criminal Law's Illogical Approach to HIV-Related Aggravated Assaults*, 18 VA. J. SOC. POL'Y & L. 550 (2011)).

process concerns in knowing transmission cases, one of which also addressed potential First Amendment concerns.

In *State v. Richardson*, the defendant knew he was HIV-positive and nonetheless, had sex with two different women.[623] The statute under which he was charged made it a crime for anyone who knows they are "infected with a life threatening communicable disease knowingly . . . [t]o engage in sexual intercourse or sodomy with another individual with the intent to expose that individual to that life threatening communicable disease."[624] The state argued that the statute required HIV-positive persons to be sexually abstinent because "any act of sexual intercourse or sodomy by an HIV-positive person, even utilizing a condom, creates some element of risk that the virus will be transmitted to the sex partner."[625] The court rejected this interpretation as "constitutionally suspect" under *Lawrence* and instead read the plain language of the statute as creating a specific intent crime.

> According to the State, "there is no conceivable means by which the State could prove, apart from the act of sexual intercourse itself, that an HIV positive individual who knowingly engages in sexual intercourse with another acts with 'intent to expose' the other to the virus." We disagree . . . . [C]ondom use can be germane to [a] defendant's specific intent . . . . [And p]roof that [victims] did not knowingly consent to engage in sexual intercourse with an HIV-infected partner . . . would [also] be a circumstance in furtherance of establishing . . . specific intent to expose [someone's] partners to HIV.[626]

At the preliminary hearing in the *Richardson* case, the prosecution established that neither woman was aware of the defendant's HIV status; indeed, he affirmably misrepresented to them that he was free from all

---

623 *E.g.*, State v. Richardson, 209 P.3d 696, 701 (Kan. 2009) (suggesting that due process requires defendants to know they are infected with a qualifying STI and then intentionally engage in sexual activity with the specific intent to expose a victim to that disease).

624 *Id.* at 700 (quoting KAN. STAT. ANN. § 21-3435(a)(1) (1999) (recodified as amended at KAN. STAT. ANN. § 21-5424 (2011 & 2022 Supp.)).

625 *Id.* at 701.

626 *Id.* at 704.

STIs.[627] The prosecution also established that the defendant did not use a condom while having sex with either woman.[628] Incredibly, though, the prosecution did not introduce "any of this information at trial" which resulted in the Supreme Court of Kansas overturning his conviction due to insufficiency of the evidence.[629]

Prosecutions for the knowing transmission of STIs that do not require specific intent do not have to clear the evidentiary hurdles that existed in *Richardson*. For example, the defendant in *State v. S.F.* was charged with violating a Missouri law that made it a felony for people who know they are HIV-positive from acting "in a reckless manner by exposing another person to HIV without the knowledge and consent of that person to be exposed to HIV . . . [t]hrough contact with blood, semen, or vaginal secretions in the course of oral, anal or vaginal sexual intercourse."[630] After testing positive for HIV, the defendant engaged in sexual intercourse with a man to whom she did not disclose her diagnosis.[631] After being convicted, she appealed arguing that the statute violated her rights "to free speech, privacy, and equal protection."[632]

The Supreme Court of Missouri dispensed with the First Amendment argument as follows:

---

627 *Id.*

628 *Id.*

629 *Id.*

630 483 S.W.3d 385, 387 (Mo. 2016) (quoting Mo. Rev. Stat. § 191.677 (2002)). Missouri amended that law in 2021 so that, as of the time of this wring, it reads as follows:

> 2. It shall be unlawful for any individual knowingly infected with a serious infectious or communicable disease to:
>
> * * *
>
> (2) Knowingly expose another person to such serious infectious or communicable disease through an activity that creates a substantial risk of disease transmission as determined by competent medical or epidemiological evidence; or
>
> (3) Act in a reckless manner by exposing another person to such serious infectious or communicable disease through an activity that creates a substantial risk of disease transmission as determined by competent medical or epidemiological evidence.

Mo. Rev. Stat. § 191.677 (2021).

631 *S.F.*, 483 S.W.3d at 386.

632 *Id.*

> [T]he statute seeks to prevent certain conduct that could spread HIV to unknowing or nonconsenting individuals. While individuals may have to disclose their HIV status if they choose to engage in activities covered by the statute, any speech compelled by [the statute] is incidental to its regulation of the targeted conduct and does not constitute a freedom of speech violation. "[I]t has never been deemed an abridgment of freedom of speech or press to make a course of conduct illegal merely because the conduct was in part initiated, evidenced, or carried out by means of language, either spoken, written, or printed." Because [the statute] regulates conduct and imposes only incidental burdens on speech, it does not violate the freedom of speech protections of the federal or state constitution.[633]

The court then dismissed the Fourteenth Amendment claims with even more brevity: "Unlike the statute struck down in *Lawrence*, [the statute] does not criminalize *consensual*, *non-harmful* sexual conduct. [It] regulates only sexual conduct that would expose another person to a life-jeopardizing disease when that person has not given consent to the conduct with knowledge of the risk of exposure."[634]

F. Post-Conviction Claims Filed by Sex Offenders ($n = 28$, 9.1%)

After people are convicted of one or more qualifying sex offenses, they are typically subjected to a range of social controls in the name of preventing recidivism.[635] Because people convicted of either violent sex crimes or those with child victims are "the most vilified of criminal offenders," they are often sentenced to harsh legal restrictions compared

---

[633] *Id.* at 388 (quoting Rumsfeld v. Forum for Acad. & Inst'l Rts., Inc., 547 U.S. 47, 62 (2006)).

[634] *Id.* at 389; *see also* State v. Musser, 721 N.W.2d 734, 748 (Iowa 2006) ("Surely it cannot be disputed that one considering having sexual intercourse with another would want to know whether the other person is infected with HIV prior to engaging in such intimate contact. Consent in the absence of such knowledge is certainly not a full and knowing consent as was present in *Lawrence*.").

[635] *See generally* D. RICHARD LAWS, SOCIAL CONTROL OF SEX OFFENDERS: A CULTURAL HISTORY (2016) (tracing the development of how the law, and society more broadly, perceives sex offenders and the impact of those evolving views on the mechanisms used to in the name of controlling their post-offense behaviors).

to offenders convicted of other serious, but nonsexual crimes.[636] Notably, many of the conditions to which sex offenders are sentenced after they are released from period of incarceration—such as registration and community notification requirements and restrictions on where they live and with whom they interact—are ineffective or even counterproductive, largely because they force offenders into criminogenic circumstances.[637] Research demonstrates that certain types of cognitive behavioral therapies and a range of informal social controls are far superior at facilitating rehabilitation and desistance that those to which offenders are typically sentenced.[638] Yet, judges routinely sentence those convicted of sex crimes to a range of post-incarceration restrictions of dubious efficacy, some of which have generated constitutional challenges from defendants. Perhaps

---

636 Karen Harrison, *Sentencing High-Risk Sex Offenders: Policy and Legislation*, *in* THE OXFORD HANDBOOK OF SEX OFFENCES AND SEX OFFENDERS 327–43 (Teela Sanders ed., 2017) [hereinafter SANDERS, OXFORD HANDBOOK]; John C. Navarro, *Sex Offenders, Policies, and Social Control*, *in* POLITICAL AUTHORITY, SOCIAL CONTROL AND PUBLIC POLICY 155 (Cara E. Rabe-Hemp & Nancy S. Lind eds., 2019).

637 LAWS, *supra* note 635, at 121–156; Navarro, *supra* note 636, at 155–68; Kristen M. Zgoba, *The Aftermath of Sex Offender Registration and Other Controls*, *in* SANDERS, OXFORD HANDBOOK, *supra* note 636, at 344–60.

638 Kimberly R. Kras, *Informal Social Control of Sex Offenders: The Family and Other Forms of Support*, *in* SANDERS, OXFORD HANDBOOK, *supra* note 636, at 415–36; Friedrich Lösel & Martin Schmucker, *Treatment of Sex Offenders: Concepts and Empirical Evaluations*, *in* SANDERS, OXFORD HANDBOOK, *supra* note 636, at 392–414.

unsurprisingly, most of these challenges fail.[639] A few, however, have been successful when the central holding in *Lawrence* is implicated.[640]

Before exploring the cases, several noteworthy quantitative findings should be noted. First, judges rejected expansive readings of *Lawrence* in all but four (14.3%) of the cases in this category, whereas they applied the

---

[639] *E.g.*, *In re* W.M., 851 A.2d 431, 450–51 (D.C. 2004) (upholding statutory scheme of sex offender registration and notification over a due process challenge); State v. Druktenis, 86 P.3d 1050, 1078 (N.M. 2004) (rejecting due process and equal protection challenges to sex offender registration and notification scheme, noting that "the concern about restrictions as to those convicted of criminally heinous acts harming non-consenting victims, often children, is simply not comparable to the protection of the privacy and dignity of those involved in the intimate decisions and relationships protected in Supreme Court cases [like] *Lawrence*"); *cf.* People v. Boston, No. C086940, 2021 WL 5027416, at *1 (Cal. Ct. App. Oct. 29, 2021), *review granted* (Jan. 26, 2022) (rejecting equal protection challenge to sentencing scheme making youthful forcible sex offenders ineligible for certain potential early release opportunities available to those convicted of other crimes, including homicides); People v. McCullon, No. B231429, 2012 WL 1548062, at *1 (Cal. Ct. App. May 3, 2012) (rejecting equal protection challenge to felony punishment for failing to register as a sex offender when misdemeanor punishments are imposed for failing to register for drug, arson, and gang offenses).

Courts have even upheld the constitutionality of sex offender registration and notification statutes when applied to defendants who commit certain nonsexual offenses involving child victims, such as the kidnapping or false imprisonment of a minor by a nonparent, on the view that such offenses can be precursors to sex crimes against children. People v. Knox, 903 N.E.2d 1149, 1154 (N.Y. 2009) ("In deciding not to exclude defendants and others similarly situated from the category of 'sex offenders,' the Legislature could have considered not only that cases where the term is unmerited are few, but also that the process of separating those cases from the majority in which it is justified is difficult, cumbersome and prone to error."); People v. Johnson, 870 N.E.2d 415, 426 (Ill. 2007); *cf.* People v. Moi, No. 1114–87, 2005 WL 1618124, at *10 (N.Y. Co. Ct. June 3, 2005) (upholding law under due process and equal protection facial challenges, but finding it unconstitutional as applied to the defendant, reasoning there was "no rational basis for having this defendant register as a sex offender when the crime for which he stands convicted has no sexual element whatsoever and Defendant has no history of committing sexual offenses"). Courts in other states, however, disagree with this proposition. *E.g.*, Am. Civ. Liberties Union of N.M. v. City of Albuquerque, 137 P.3d 1215, 1226 (N.M. 2006); State v. Robinson, 873 So. 2d 1205, 1217 (Fla. 2004); State v. Reine, No. 19157, 2003 WL 77174, at *3–4 (Ohio Ct. App., Jan. 10, 2003), *dismissed* 795 N.E.2d 686 (Ohio 2003).

[640] In *State v. LeBlanc*, No. 2020AP62-CR, 2021 WL 3234462, at *6 (Wis. Ct. App. July 30, 2021), the court remanded a case for resentencing. It did not reach the question of whether the sentencing judge had relied on an improper factor, but noted "to provide guidance on remand" that in light of *Lawrence*, it would be improper if the judge imposed a harsh sentence in light of the defendant's "permissive attitudes toward sex." *Id.* at *5.

precedent narrowly in fourteen (50.0%) such cases, with the remaining ten (35.7%) involving neutral applications. Table 15 reveals three more findings: unlike in many other categories, *Lawrence* was significantly more likely to be mentioned in passing in claims asserted by convicted sex offenders than it was to be key to a judicial opinion resolving such claims; cases presenting *Lawrence*-based arguments by sex offenders were far more common in the West than in other parts of the country; and consistent with many other categories, final case outcomes in favor of the prosecution were significantly more common than those favoring defendants, but not nearly by the same margin that existed in some other types of cases, such as those involving prostitution, obscenity, sexual assaults, and other sexual privacy claims. This held true even in "deep blue" states, where *Lawrence* was either neutrally or narrowly applied in these types of cases. Put differently, not a single case involving constitutional challenges by sex offenders brought in highly democratic states interpreted *Lawrence* broadly.

TABLE 15: VARIABLE FREQUENCIES AND RELATIONSHIPS TO TREATMENT OF *LAWRENCE* IN SEX OFFENDER CLAIMS CASES

Category	Treatment of *Lawrence* *n* (%)				Chi-Square	Sig.	Cramer's V
Depth	*Neutral*	*Narrow*	*Broad*	*Total*	8.575 (2, 28)	Fisher's Exact p = 0.008	0.553
Mentioned in Passing	10 (35.7%)	9 (32.1%)	1 (3.6%)	20 (71.4%)			
Key to Case	0 (0.0%)	5 (17.9%)	3 (10.7%)	8 (28.6%)			
Outcome	*Neutral*	*Narrow*	*Broad*	*Total*	2.240 (2, 28)	p > 0.050	N/A
Prosecution	7 (20.0%)	13 (44.6%)	3 (10.7%)	23 (82.1%)			
Defense	3 (10.7%)	1 (3.6%)	1 (3.6%)	5 (17.9%)			
State Politics	*Neutral*	*Narrow*	*Broad*	*Total*	12.900 (6, 28)	Fisher's Exact p = 0.032	0.480
Deep Red	4 (14.3%)	2 (7.1%)	2 (7.1%)	8 (28.6%)			
Light Red	0 (0.0%)	2 (7.1%)	1 (3.6%)	3 (10.7%)			
Purple	0 (0.0%)	0 (0.0%)	0 (0.0%)	0 (0.0%)			
Light Blue	0 (0.0%)	0 (0.0%)	1 (3.6%)	1 (3.6%)			
Deep Blue	6 (21.4%)	10 (35.7%)	0 (0.0%)	16 (57.1%)			
Region	*Neutral*	*Narrow*	*Broad*	*Total*	14.967 (6, 28)	Fisher's Exact p = 0.017	0.517
Northeast	3 (10.7%)	1 (3.6%)	0 (0.0%)	4 (14.3%)			
South	2 (7.1%)	3 (10.7%)	0 (0.0%)	5 (17.9%)			
Midwest	2 (7.1%)	2 (7.1%)	4 (14.3%)	8 (28.6%)			
West	3 (10.7%)	8 (28.6%)	0 (0.0%)	11 (39.3%)			
Judge's Sex	*Neutral*	*Narrow*	*Broad*	*Total*	4.781 (4, 28)	p > 0.050	N/A
Male	7 (25.0%)	12 (42.9%)	2 (7.1%)	21 (75.0%)			
Female	3 (10.7%)	1 (3.6%)	2 (7.1%)	6 (21.4%)			
Not Applicable (per curiam)	0 (0.0%)	1 (3.6%)	0 (0.0%)	1 (3.6%)			
Judge's Race/Ethnicity	*Neutral*	*Narrow*	*Broad*	*Total*	2.533 (4, 28)	p > 0.050	N/A
White	8 (28.6%)	12 (42.9%)	4 (14.3%)	24 (85.7%)			
Nonwhite	2 (7.1%)	1 (3.6%)	0 (0.0%)	3 (10.7%)			
Not Applicable or Unknown	0 (0.0%)	1 (3.6%)	0 (0.0%)	1 (3.6%)			
Judge's Political Affiliation	*Neutral*	*Narrow*	*Broad*	*Total*	2.297 (6, 28)	p > 0.050	N/A
Nonpartisan	8 (28.6%)	10 (35.7%)	3 (10.7%)	21 (75.0%)			
Democrat	0 (0.0%)	1 (3.6%)	0 (0.0%)	1 (3.6%)			
Republican	2 (7.1%)	2 (7.1%)	1 (3.6%)	5 (17.9%)			
Unknown	0 (0.0%)	1 (3.6%)	0 (0.0%)	1 (1.6%)			

1. Vacating Sex Offender Status for Applicable Persons

In the wake of the *Lawrence* decision, people who had been placed on sex offender registries for convictions related to sodomy, including solicitation to commit sodomy and attempted sodomy, sought their removal from such registries. Courts denied such petitions for offenders whose underlying convictions involved acts outside the scope of *Lawrence*'s protections—cases involving violence, nonconsent, minors, or public acts.[641] Presumably courts granted such requests for LGBTQ+ people who were declared criminal simply because they engaged in sex

---

641 *E.g.*, *In re* Commitment of Cleaveland, No. 09-12-00428-CV, 2014 WL 4364263, at *7 (Tex. App. Sept. 4, 2014) (upholding sexually violent predator determination and commitment for actions, among others, that involved biting a child on the buttocks); Guerra v. Lombardi, 336 S.W.3d 167, 171 (Mo. Ct. App. 2011) ("Guerra also argues that he cannot be required to register as a sex offender because sexual acts between two consenting adults is constitutionally protected conduct pursuant to *Lawrence* . . . [but t]his argument fails [because the] victim was not an adult capable of consenting to sexual conduct."); Green v. State, 692 S.E.2d 784, 785–86 (Ga. Ct. App. 2010) (upholding conviction for failure to register as a sex offender for a sodomy conviction involving conduct with a minor); People v. Westgarth, No. D044716, 2005 WL 1540137, at *4 (Cal. Ct. App. July 1, 2005) (upholding lifetime placement on sex offender registry for a defendant convicted of sex offenses involving oral and anal sex with a minor); *cf.* State v. Green, 706 S.E.2d 720, 722 (Ga. Ct. App. 2011) (declining, on procedural grounds, to reach the merits of whether an underlying sodomy charge was based on constitutionally-protected activities).

Similar logic applies for acts that occurred in violation of prison rules. *E.g.*, People v. Perez, 961 N.Y.S.2d 51, 52 (Sup. Ct. App. Div. 2013) (upholding a high level of sex offender classification based on points for "repeated instances of prohibited sexual activity in prison" because such acts demonstrated the "defendant's inability to refrain from forbidden sexual conduct [and, therefore,] was relevant to his potential for sexual recidivism").

As previously discussed in the section on the continued viability of sodomy laws in Section A.1 of this chapter, courts uphold differential requirements for sex offender registration those convicted of oral sex with minors compared to vaginal sex. Johnson v. Dep't of Just., 341 P.3d 1075, 1084 (Cal. 2015) ("There is, in fact, much more than a speculative possibility that sexual predators are more successful in manipulating minors to engage in oral copulation, as opposed to sexual intercourse. Studies indicate that pubescent minors may be more receptive to engaging in oral sex, which does not risk pregnancy and which many such minors believe is lower in risk for sexually transmitted diseases."); People v. McDermitt, No. C047482, 2005 WL 995520, at *2 (Cal. Ct. App. Apr. 29, 2005) (same). *But cf.* State v. Dykes, 744 S.E.2d 505, 510 (S.C. 2013) (invalidating statutory provision mandating lifetime satellite monitoring of persons convicted certain sex crimes against minors—with any opportunity for judicial review to assess a risk of re-offending—as being "arbitrary" and not rationally "related to the legislature's stated purpose of protecting the public from those with a high risk of re-offending"); State v. Coman, 273 P.3d 701, 709 (Kan. 2012) (resolving a statutory ambiguity by holding sex offender registration was not required for those convicted of misdemeanor criminal sodomy unless it involved a human under the age of eighteen, thereby exempting those convicted of bestiality from registration requirement).

with another consenting adult in private, but there were no cases in the study to attest to this conclusion.

Given the legal necessity of the closet prior to *Lawrence* time and the corresponding effect the closet had on cruising to meet other men,[642] the distinction between public and private acts is not always clearcut. Consider what occurred in *Keeney v. Fitch.*[643]

> In 1988, the St. Louis County Police Department received complaints that various men were engaging in homosexual sexual acts in open view of the public in the parking lot and bathrooms of a rest stop .... As a result of the complaints, the [police] conducted an undercover sting operation ... in which Detective Robert Bayes ... parked at the rest stop and sat in his car, waiting. While sitting in his car, undercover, Detective Bayes observed Appellant sitting in his car. Appellant started a conversation with Detective Bayes and asked Detective Bayes to sit in Appellant's car with him. Detective Bayes agreed and got in Appellant's car with him at the rest stop. Appellant and Detective Bayes talked for about ten minutes. Appellant placed his hand on Detective Bayes's clothed groin area. Detective Bayes then identified himself as a police officer and placed Appellant under arrest.[644]

The defendant pled guilty to the misdemeanor offense of attempted sexual misconduct in the third degree, was sentenced to two years of probation, and was placed on the sex offender registry. After *Lawrence*, he filed an action for a declaratory judgment that he not be required to remain on the sex offender registry "because attempting to engage in homosexual relations [was] no longer a criminal offense."[645] A judge denied his request on the grounds that the conduct occurred in public, but an appellate court reversed, reasoning that the underlying acts no longer constituted a criminal offense and, as such, there was "no logical existent reason to require [him] to register on the sexual offender registry."[646] The

---

642 *See generally* Eskridge, *supra* note 72, *passim*.

643 Keeney v. Fitch, 458 S.W.3d 838 (Mo. Ct. App. 2015).

644 *Id.* at 839.

645 *Id.* at 841.

646 *Id.* at 845.

court also rejected the state's attempts to bring the appellant's conduct outside of *Lawrence*'s designated parameters:

> Respondents' characterization of Detective Bayes as a "victim" of sexual contact by Appellant, and their contention that Detective Bayes did not give Appellant permission to touch his groin, are disingenuous. Detective Bayes was participating in a sting operation to rid the rest stop of homosexual behavior in 1988 and he deliberately sat in his car at that location; got into Appellant's car with him and talked for over ten minutes; and when Appellant finally made a sexual overture to Detective Bayes, Detective Bayes revealed his true identity as a police officer and placed Appellant under arrest for attempted homosexual deviate intercourse. Such a course of events would be considered a success by Detective Bayes in his undercover sting operation to rid the area of homosexual behavior that night in 1988, and to characterize himself today as a victim of unwanted sexual touching by Appellant that night is incongruous.
>
> Respondents also argue that Appellant's conduct on September 28, 1988 was committed in public, not in private, and as such does not deserve the protection of *Lawrence*. Respondents are attempting to expand upon the alleged criminality of Appellant's conduct on the night of September 28, 1988, to add a public aspect to it that was not there when charged by the State, considered by the court or pled guilty to by Appellant almost thirty years ago. . . . [T]he State chose not to charge Appellant with a crime with a public aspect to it. Rather, it chose to charge Appellant with the strict liability crime of attempted deviate sexual intercourse with a person of the same sex . . . .[647]

The court could have interpreted the underlying conduct in *Keeney v. Fitch* differently. Reasonable people might differ with regard to both questions that the court resolved in the appellant's favor. Perhaps the court was genuinely moved by the unfairness of a gay man being on the sex registry under such circumstances. When petitioners are less sympathetic, however, concerns for public safety might mask homophobia, as was arguably the case in *In re M.D.*[648]

---

647 *Id.* at 846–47.

648 757 N.W.2d 559 (N.D. 2008).

In that case, the petitioner sought his discharge from a secure facility to which he had been committed as a sexually dangerous person ten years earlier.[649] Experts disagreed about whether he was dangerous, but an appellate court upheld a lower court's determination that he was "likely to engage in further acts of sexually predatory conduct."[650] But one of the primary reasons for this conclusion was the fact that the petitioner had established a "sexual relationship with a young-looking resident in violation of the treatment program rules" during his in-patient treatment.[651] Although the justices on the Supreme Court of North Dakota signing onto the majority decision did not mention *Lawrence*, a dissenting justice noted that the sexual relationship actually involved two men who were consenting adults and, therefore, the petitioner's ongoing confinement was "based upon activity for which the State could not punish him criminally" under *Lawrence*.[652]

> While in *Lawrence* the defendant was tried criminally for his actions, and in the present case M.D. is being civilly committed for his actions, the facts of the two cases are similar. . . . Neither case involved a minor, public conduct, or prostitution. . . . [And, as in *Lawrence*, n]othing in the present case indicates coercion or consent are an issue.
>
> * * *
>
> If M.D. had engaged in an 18–month–long heterosexual relationship with a consenting adult who was not "young-looking," rather than a homosexual relationship with a "young-looking" consenting adult, the fact that such a relationship existed, albeit against treatment rules, would have been insufficient to deny M.D.'s petition for discharge. It would not have established that M.D. is likely to engage in sexually predatory conduct. Changing the sexual orientation of the consenting adults does not make the evidence more substantial.[653]

---

649 *Id.* at 560.

650 *Id.* at 561.

651 *Id.* at 562.

652 *Id.* at 563 (Kapsner, J., dissenting).

653 *Id.* at 563–64; *see also* Doe v. Sex Offender Registry Bd., 897 N.E.2d 992, 999 (Mass. 2008) (upholding, over an equal protection challenge, a sex offender classification

2. Conditions of Release Burdening Intimate Relationships

In *State v. Lee*, after the defendant was convicted of assaulting and raping a romantic partner, the trial judge sentenced him to 108 months of imprisonment followed by lifetime community supervision.[654] Two of the terms of such supervision required the defendant to inform his community corrections supervisor and his treatment providers of any dating relationships and to disclose his status as a sex offender before engaging in any sexual activity with a partner.[655] On appeal, he challenged the latter condition as violating both his right to refrain from speaking and as depriving him of sexual intimacy rights under *Lawrence*.[656] The court rebuffed him without meaningful analysis, simply saying that his arguments "disregard[ed] his status as a parolee with reduced rights" while noting that "*Lawrence* did not analyze the reduced rights of a parolee . . . [whose] constitutional rights are subject to . . . infringements."[657] Other courts have reached the same conclusion, but better explained their rationale for doing so:

> We acknowledge that the condition significantly intrudes on Allen's right to privacy and freedom of association. Intimate relationships between consenting adults are the quintessential zone of personal liberty protected from government interference under the substantive due process clause . . . . A government requirement that Allen obtain written consent obviously inhibits his freedom of association. Nevertheless, the intrusion is warranted because it is directly related to his offense and future criminality. The condition is narrowly drawn because it does not bar Allen from establishing intimate relationships or cohabitating with adult women, but merely requires disclosure to ensure that Allen's partner is vigilant as to any possible recurrence of the

system that used offenses committed by men against men more heavily in determining risk of reoffending and level of dangerousness because "the strongest deviant sexual interests have empirically been found to be more prevalent among those offenders who victimize strangers, prepubescent children, non-consenting males, [or] vulnerable persons. . . ").

654 460 P.3d 701, 705 (Wash. Ct. App.), *review denied*, 468 P.3d 622 (Wash. 2020).

655 *Id.*

656 *Id.* at 714.

657 *Id.*

crime. Also, the condition does not apply to nonintimate relationships. The condition is specifically tailored to Allen because in this case he gained the opportunity to initiate sexual contact with the victim by way of his romantic relationship with the victim's mother. When granting the clemency of probation, the court may impose conditions designed to prevent the probationer from recommitting his offense without violating constitutional limits.[658]

3. Other Restrictions on People with Sex Offense Convictions

Courts have upheld other types of restrictions beyond those involving dating or sexual activity. In *Merryfield v. Sullivan*, the Sexual Predator Treatment Program prevented its patients from seeking pen-pals for themselves.[659] Medical personnel explained that such a restriction helped to maintain "the therapeutic environment of the hospital" while simultaneously protecting the public by preventing "patients from assuming false identities and from victimizing or manipulating their correspondents, who might be children."[660] Nonetheless, one patient challenged the pen-pal restriction on First and Fourteenth Amendment grounds. The court began its analysis of the patient's substantive due

---

658 People v. Allen, No. A106272, 2005 WL 552470, at *7 (Cal. Ct. App. Mar. 9, 2005); *see also* State v. Farris, 492 P.3d 744, 750 (Or. Ct. App. 2021) ("Requiring defendant to alert his probation officer to ask permission before entering into another potentially sexual relationship is a reasonable mechanism to protect the public from defendant once again entering into an inappropriate relationship with someone he has cultivated trust. The condition serves the purposes of rehabilitation by helping to prevent defendant from reoffending through the guidance of his probation officer."); State v. Airhart-Bryon, No. 78805-1-I, 2020 WL 1853477, at *12 (Wash. Ct. App. Apr. 13, 2020), *review denied*, 474 P.3d 1052 (Wash. 2020) (noting that although *Lawrence* and *Obergefell* constitutionally protected sexual activity and romantic relations, neither case "involved convicted child molesters or restrictions that protected children" nor impacted the fact that the constitutional rights of probationers or parolees are diminished as a result of criminal convictions); State v. Staples, No. 78460-9-I, 2019 WL 7373500, at *5 (Wash. Ct. App. Dec. 30, 2019), *review denied*, 464 P.3d 199 (Wash. 2020) ("Restrictions on privacy in community custody conditions are justified when reasonably necessary to protect the community. . . . The [dating restrictions] are justified here because of [defendant's] criminal sexual conduct towards both strangers and acquaintances.").

659 No. 111204, 2015 WL 326652, at *1 (Kan. Ct. App. Jan. 16, 2015).

660 *Id.* at *2.

process claim by saying, "[n]ot every deprivation of liberty or property is subject to a substantive-due-process challenge; the right must be fundamental."[661] In support of that statement, the court cited *Washington v. Glucksberg* and Justice Scalia's dissent in *Lawrence*.[662] Those citations are suspect. First, the former case was decided six years before the latter and *Lawrence*'s central holding calls into question whether substantive due process only protects fundamental rights since *Lawrence* did not use a fundamental rights framework.[663] Second, the citation relies on the dissent in *Lawrence*, rather the majority's more expansive approach to constitutionally protected liberty interests. With these questionable citations framing the analysis, the court then applied a low level of scrutiny (despite the free speech and expression concerns raised) and upheld the restriction as being rationally related to the important governmental interest in protecting the public.[664] The court also noted that because patients were allowed to seek permissible pen-pals through their therapists, the restrictions left open alternative methods of communication.[665]

Merryfield involved a patient whose rights could be restricted for nonpunitive reasons as part of involuntary confinement for treatment purposes after a judicial determination that he should not be free because he had some "'"mental abnormality" and was dangerous.[666] But even when people are released after serving custodial sentences for sex crimes, they are often restricted from engaging in certain activities, such as visiting strip clubs, adult bookstores, and certain establishments where sexual activities might occur.[667] Courts routinely uphold such conditions over

---

661 *Id.* at *5.

662 *Id.* (citing Washington v. Glucksberg, 521 U.S. 702, 720–21 (1997); Lawrence v. Texas, 539 U.S. 558, 588 (2003) (Scalia, J., dissenting)).

663 *See supra* notes 21–29 and accompanying text.

664 *Merryfield*, 2015 WL 326652, at *6–7.

665 *Id.*

666 *See generally* Kansas v. Hendricks, 521 U.S. 346, 356–60 (1997) (holding the indefinite, involuntary commitment of sexually violent offenders does not violate due process).

667 *E.g.*, Gouldsmith v. State, No. 55A01-1605-CR-1022, 2017 WL 3165115, at *5 (Ind. Ct. App. July 26, 2017).

challenges, often distinguishing the core rights protected by *Lawrence* and other privacy cases from the behaviors that such restrictions target.

> The purpose of [such] condition[s] of [Defendant's] probation is to manage some facets of his sexual conduct, for which he has been subjected to multiple criminal convictions and required to register as a sex offender. The core rights protected by the Fourteenth Amendment, as expressed in *Lawrence*, are fundamental personal choices related to family, relationships, and childbirth . . . . [Defendant], however, does not articulate how the ability to see nude dancers or to buy pornographic videos is central to his choices concerning family relationships or personal dignity. Further, the State notes that [Defendant's] conduct in this case involved accessing and viewing videos and images of his victim, suggesting that a restriction on [Defendant's] access to and consumption of sexually-related media is related to law enforcement needs. We accordingly find no error in this [condition] that prohibits [Defendant's] patronizing of adult bookstores, strip clubs, and the like.[668]

G. Business Operations and Employment ($n = 10$, 3.3%)

Ten cases cited *Lawrence* in relation to the operation of businesses. One case was criminal in nature, while the rest were civil disputes. None of the variables in the study were significantly related to how courts interpreted and applied *Lawrence* in the business and employment law contexts, but the frequencies of those variables are presented in Table 16. Five qualitative subthemes emerged in these cases.

---

668 *Id.*

TABLE 16: VARIABLE FREQUENCIES AND RELATIONSHIPS TO TREATMENT OF *LAWRENCE* IN BUSINESS AND EMPLOYMENT LAW CASES

Category	**Treatment of *Lawrence* *n* (%)**				**Chi-Square**	**Sig.**	**Cramer's V**
Type	*Neutral*	*Narrow*	*Broad*	*Total*	4.792 (2, 10)	p > 0.050	N/A
Civil	5 (50.0%)	0 (0.0%)	3 (30.0%)	8 (80.0%)			
Criminal	1 (10.0%)	1 (10.0%)	0 (0.0%)	2 (20.0%)			
Depth	*Neutral*	*Narrow*	*Broad*	*Total*	3.651 (2, 10)	p > 0.050	N/A
Mentioned in Passing	4 (40.0%)	0 (0.0%)	3 (30.0%)	7 (70.0%)			
Key to Case	2 (20.0%)	1 (10.0%)	0 (0.0%)	3 (30.0%)			
Outcome	*Neutral*	*Narrow*	*Broad*	*Total*	10.625 (4, 10)	p > 0.050	N/A
Prosecution	0 (0.0%)	1 (10.0%)	0 (0.0%)	1 (10.0%)			
Defense	1 (10.0%)	0 (0.0%)	0 (0.0%)	1 (10.0%)			
Not Relevant (civil)	5 (50.0%)	0 (0.0%)	3 (30.0%)	8 (80.0%)			
State Politics	*Neutral*	*Narrow*	*Broad*	*Total*	2.250 (4, 10)	p > 0.050	N/A
Deep Red	3 (30.0%)	0 (0.0%)	1 (10.0%)	4 (40.0%)			
Light Red	1 (10.0%)	0 (0.0%)	0 (0.0%)	1 (10.0%)			
Purple	1 (10.0%)	0 (0.0%)	0 (0.0%)	1 (10.0%)			
Light Blue	0 (0.0%)	0 (0.0%)	0 (0.0%)	0 (0.0%)			
Deep Blue	2 (20.0%)	1 (10.0%)	2 (20.0%)	5 (50.0%)			
Region	*Neutral*	*Narrow*	*Broad*	*Total*	5.833 (6, 10)	p > 0.050	N/A
Northeast	1 (10.0%)	1 (10.0%)	0 (0.0%)	2 (20.0%)			
South	2 (20.0%)	0 (0.0%)	1 (10.0%)	3 (30.0%)			
Midwest	1 (10.0%)	0 (0.0%)	0 (0.0%)	1 (10.0%)			
West	2 (20.0%)	0 (0.0%)	2 (20.0%)	4 (40.0%)			
Judge's Sex	*Neutral*	*Narrow*	*Broad*	*Total*	2.857 (2, 10)	p > 0.050	N/A
Male	3 (30.0%)	1 (10.0%)	3 (30.0%)	7 (70.0%)			
Female	3 (30.0%)	0 (0.0%)	0 (0.0%)	3 (30.0%)			
Judge's Race/Ethnicity	*Neutral*	*Narrow*	*Broad*	*Total*	0.625 (4, 10)	p > 0.050	N/A
White	5 (50.0%)	1 (10.0%)	2 (20.0%)	8 (80.0%)			
Nonwhite	1 (10.0%)	0 (0.0%)	1 (10.0%)	2 (20.0%)			
Judge's Political Affiliation	*Neutral*	*Narrow*	*Broad*	*Total*	1.310 (4, 10)	p > 0.050	N/A
Nonpartisan	4 (40.0%)	1 (10.0%)	2 (20.0%)	7 (70.0%)			
Democrat	1 (10.0%)	0 (0.0%)	0 (0.0%)	1 (10.0%)			
Republican	1 (10.0%)	0 (0.0%)	1 (10.0%)	2 (20.0%)			

1. Business Liability

One of the business operations cases presented the question of whether an adult theater was being maintained by its owners as a public nuisance because patrons engaged in lewd conduct during movie screenings.[669] The

---

669 Commonwealth v. Can-Port Amusement Corp., No. 2005-0295, 2005 WL 937312, at *1 (Mass. Super. Ct. Mar. 31, 2005). Note that although this case arguably presented

court easily dispensed with the defendant's argument that enforcement of the state's nuisance law violated theater patrons' privacy rights since the sexual activities at issue in the case occurred in a theater open to the public, rather than anywhere private. Accordingly, a straightforward application of *Lawrence* placed the conduct in the case outside of the scope of *Lawrence*'s protections.[670] The court therefore ruled in favor of the state and against the theater.

Another business case involved whether the Board of Elders of a church had any civil liability for negligent supervision of a pastor. The pastor had been criminally convicted of using his position to sexually exploit parishioners over his defense that *Lawrence* protected his conduct.[671] The Supreme Court of Iowa held that the civil defendants could be liable for negligent supervision, but the plaintiffs' claims were time-barred by the statute of limitations.[672]

2. Disclosure of Communications by Public Employees

Another case in this category concerned an effort to limit public disclosure of emails between public employees, some of which involved sexually-explicit content.[673] Television and print media sought to obtain an unredacted report prepared by a private investigator that contained 570 email messages between a county clerk and one of that person's supervisees who claimed to have been constructively discharged and sexual harassed.[674] The Colorado Court of Appeals determined that some

---

sexual privacy claims, it is analyzed in this category because it was a civil action brought against a business.

[670] *Id.* at *10. In a related action, the court upheld the constitutionality of the public nuisance statute over the theater's claim that *Lawrence* rendered it overbroad because, although the statute did not differentiate between public and private conduct on its face, case law in Massachusetts had "invariably construed" statutes regulating sexual activity "as applying solely to public conduct." Commonwealth v. Can-Port Amusement Corp., No. 050295, 2005 WL 2009672, at *5 (Mass. Super. Ct. June 29, 2005).

[671] Bandstra v. Covenant Reformed Church, 913 N.W.2d 19, 34-35 (Iowa 2018).

[672] *Id.* at 46.

[673] *In re* Bd. of Cnty. Comm'rs of Cnty. of Arapahoe, 95 P.3d 593, 596 (Colo. App. 2003), *as modified on denial of reh'g* (Oct. 23, 2003), *aff'd in part, rev'd in part sub nom.* Denver Pub. Co. v. Bd. of Cnty. Comm'rs of Cnty. of Arapahoe, 121 P.3d 190 (Colo. 2005).

[674] *Id.* at 596.

of these emails were not appropriate for release due to the privacy rights of the two county employees. The court cited *Lawrence* in passing for the proposition that "sexual behavior is the most private human conduct."[675] Notably, the bulk of the decision concerned the application of state's public record laws and precedents interpreting it. Ultimately the court concluded that more than 100 emails could be properly disclosed, but by broadly applying *Lawrence*, it shielded disclosure of the most sexually-explicit ones, reasoning they were private and not subject to general release.[676]

3. Employee Discipline

In *Sylvester v. Director of the Arkansas Employment Security Department*, a state police officer appealed the denial of his application for unemployment benefits after he was terminated for having lied about a sexual relationship he had with a victim in one of the cases he had investigated.[677] He argued that because the relationship was consensual, it was protected by *Lawrence*.[678] But because his termination stemmed from lying about the affair—both violating policy and calling his credibility into question any time he took the witness stand in a case, the court found *Lawrence* inapplicable and upheld the denial of unemployment benefits.[679]

Unlike in cases like *Sylvester* in which dishonesty about a potentially constitutionally-protected relationship formed the basis for employee discipline, when the relationship itself triggers disciplinary action, courts recognize that employees might possess "a legally protected privacy interest in pursuing an intimate or sexual relationship," just as the court stated in *Barbee v. Household Automotive Financial Corp.*[680] Nonetheless, the court upheld the firing of a sales manager for dating one of his subordinates, reasoning that certain workplace romantic or sexual relationships present potential conflicts of interest, the likelihood of

---

675 *Id.* at 600–01.

676 *Id.* at 604.

677 No. E05-46, 2006 WL 637097, at *1 (Ark. Ct. App. Mar. 15, 2006).

678 *Id.* at *2.

679 *Id.*

680 Barbee v. Household Auto. Fin. Corp., 6 Cal. Rptr. 3d 406, 411 (Ct. App. 2003).

disparate treatment of employees due to favoritism, and possibility of claims sexual harassment.[681]

4. Wrongful Termination Claims

Several employment cases concerned wrongful termination claims by employees alleging that they had been discriminated against on the basis of their sexual orientation. Those raising religious freedom issues are presented in Section IV.I.4 of this Chapter.[682] But one such case is discussed here because it raised no First Amendment claim.

In *Tarrant County College District v. Sims*, the plaintiff alleged she had been wrongfully terminated from her job because she was gay.[683] The defense unsuccessfully moved to dismiss the case for lack of jurisdiction because the state's antidiscrimination law did not reach sexual orientation.[684] The Texas Court of Appeals affirmed, finding that the statute in question could be used as the basis for a lawsuit for employment discrimination based on sexual orientation because it prohibited "sex discrimination based on a failure to conform to gender stereotypes," mirroring the U.S. Supreme Court's logic in *Bostock v. Clayton County*.[685] In a separate opinion, a judge took issue with the majority's reasoning and argued that at the time the Texas legislature had adopted the law, the state not only prohibited same-sex marriage, but also criminalized "homosexual conduct."[686] He acknowledged that *Lawrence* had invalidated the latter statute, but nonetheless asserted that unlike the situation in *Bostock*, in which the U.S. Supreme Court "was able to draw on a plethora of federal statutes in support of its conclusion that Congress would (or should) have understood the phrase 'because of sex' to include 'sexual orientation' as a matter of federal law in 1964," the same was not true about the "statutory landscape" in Texas at the time the antidiscrimination statute was

---

681 *Id.*, 411–12 (internal citations omitted).

682 *See infra* notes 774–831 and accompanying text.

683 Tarrant Cnty. Coll. Dist. v. Sims, 621 S.W.3d 323, 325 (Tex. App. 2021) (Schneck, J., concurring in part and dissenting in part).

684 *Id.* at 326.

685 *Id.* at 326–37, 328–29 (citing Bostock v. Clayton Cnty., 140 S. Ct. 1731, 1739–40 (2020)).

686 *Id.* at 333 (Schneck, J., concurring in part and dissenting in part).

adopted.[687] Rather than engaging in a constitutional analysis about the implications of *Lawrence*, *Obergefell*, and *Bostock* for the case, the judge argued that the plaintiff's case should be dismissed because the statutory language should have been interpreted within the plain meaning of the word "sex" at the time law was adopted: "Whether any of this is good or bad policy, then as now, is a question for the legislature, not the courts. What matters, for our purposes, is what the law says and what the legislature understood it to mean at the time."[688]

5. Self-Autonomy in the Workplace

Finally, one case in this category had nothing to do with any dimension of sexual privacy, but rather a claim of self-autonomy. *American Legion Post #149 v. Washington State Dept. of Health* involved a challenge to both a statute and an ordinance banning smoking in "any place of employment."[689] The plaintiffs alleged that they possessed a constitutionally cognizable privacy interest in smoking in private facilities. In rejecting that claim, the Supreme Court of Washington noted that the constitutional right to privacy protects "autonomous decision making (including issues relating to marriage, procreation, family relationships, child rearing, and education) and . . . confidentiality, or nondisclosure[,] of personal information."[690] Because no such privacy interests were implicated by a smoking ban in a private club that had employees who would be exposed to second-hand smoke while working, the court applied the rational basis test and upheld the laws as being rationally related to the legitimate governmental interest of protecting public health.[691]

---

687 *Id.*

688 *Id.* at 334; *see also* Burns v. Ohio St. Univ. Coll. of Veterinary Med., No. 13AP–633, 2014 WL 1317499, at *4 (Ohio Ct. App. Mar. 25, 2014) (refusing to interpret discrimination on the basis of sex as including sexual orientation while noting that the case did not present either due process or equal protection claims and, therefore, cases like *Lawrence* were inapposite).

689 Am. Legion Post #149 v. Washington St. Dep't of Health, 192 P.3d 306 (Wash. 2008).

690 *Id.* at 321.

691 *Id.* at 324.

A dissenting justice would have invalidated the laws on due process grounds because the ban reached conduct in a private place.[692] He quoted *Lawrence* when he wrote,

> "[l]iberty protects the person from unwarranted government intrusions into a dwelling or *other private places*. . . . Freedom extends beyond spatial bounds. Liberty presumes an autonomy of self . . . ." This self-autonomy includes what time you go to bed at night, how much to exercise, how much fat to eat, a choice to smoke, a choice to be around smokers as well as every other myriad private decision we make to pursue happiness in our lives (even when some choices are probably not as healthy as others). Yet these choices are the very essence of personal liberty and self-autonomy.[693]

The dissent went on to question the link between second-hand smoke and cancer, heart disease, and asthma.[694] Unless such links could be established to the satisfaction of a trier-of-fact, the dissenting judge would have invalidated the anti-smoking laws as arbitrary exercises of governmental power that infringe constitutionally-protected liberty interests.

The science-denying claims in the dissenting justice's opinion in the *American Legion Post* case notwithstanding, the logic of the dissent represents a high-watermark for a libertarian view of *Lawrence*. The majority opinion in *Dobbs*) stressed that "[l]iberty is a capacious term" and, therefore, that judicial review of liberty claims that can lead to "freewheeling judicial policymaking" if its constitutional interpretation is not limited to "the teachings of history."[695] But Justice Sanders' dissent in *American Legion Post* cited *Lawrence* positively, embracing an expansive interpretation of the case that goes so far as protecting liberty vis-à-vis autonomy by questioning legislative pronouncements regarding public health.

---

692 *Id.* at 335 (Sanders, J., dissenting).

693 *Id.* at 335–36 (emphasis added by Justice Sanders in his dissent, not in the *Lawrence* decision itself).

694 *Id.* at 336–38.

695 Dobbs v. Jackson Women's Health Org., 142 S. Ct. 2228, 2248 (2022).

H. Family Law ($n = 22$, 7.2%)

Putting aside marriage equality for same-sex couples because it arguably raises significant questions of civil rights, it is clear that *Lawrence* had significant impact on more traditional questions of family law. Sometimes, this impact was tangential—largely serving as an example of changing views about LGBTQ+ rights. Other times, *Lawrence* significantly influenced either the outcome or the rationale for the decisions. But even in such cases, *Lawrence* tended to mitigate homophobia and heterosexism, rather than serving as a basis for true LGBTQ+ equality in family law.

Ten (45.5%) family law cases applied *Lawrence* neutrally, four (18.2%) construed the precedent narrowly, and the eight (36.4%) remaining cases gave *Lawrence* a broad reading. None of the variables in the study were significantly related to how courts interpreted and applied *Lawrence* in family law cases, but the frequencies of those variables are presented in Table 17. The three primary contexts of such applications cases are explored in the following subsections.

TABLE 17: VARIABLE FREQUENCIES AND RELATIONSHIPS TO TREATMENT OF *LAWRENCE* IN FAMILY LAW CASES

Category	Treatment of *Lawrence* n (%)				Chi-Square	Sig.	Cramer's V
Depth	*Neutral*	*Narrow*	*Broad*	*Total*	2.338 (2, 22)	p > 0.050	N/A
Mentioned in Passing	10 (45.5%)	3 (13.6%)	7 (31.8%)	20 (90.9%)			
Key to Case	0 (0.0%)	1 (4.5%)	1 (4.5%)	2 (9.1%)			
State Politics	*Neutral*	*Narrow*	*Broad*	*Total*	9.235 (6, 22)	p > 0.050	N/A
Deep Red	6 (27.3%)	1 (4.5%)	1 (4.5%)	8 (36.4%)			
Light Red	1 (4.5%)	0 (0.0%)	0 (0.0%)	1 (4.5%)			
Purple	1 (4.5%)	0 (0.0%)	3 (13.6%)	4 (18.2%)			
Light Blue	0 (0.0%)	0 (0.0%)	0 (0.0%)	0 (0.0%)			
Deep Blue	2 (9.1%)	3 (13.6%)	4 (18.2%)	9 (40.9%)			
Region	*Neutral*	*Narrow*	*Broad*	*Total*	6.640 (6, 22)	p > 0.050	N/A
Northeast	1 (4.5%)	1 (4.5%)	3 (13.6%)	5 (22.7%)			
South	4 (18.2%)	3 (13.6%)	4 (18.2%)	11 (50.0%)			
Midwest	2 (9.1%)	0 (0.0%)	1 (4.5%)	3 (13.6%)			
West	3 (13.6%)	0 (0.0%)	0 (0.0%)	3 (13.6%)			
Judge's Sex	*Neutral*	*Narrow*	*Broad*	*Total*	0.045 (2, 21)	p > 0.050	N/A
Male	6 (28.6%)	2 (9.5%)	5 (23.8%)	13 (61.9%)			
Female	4 (19.0%)	1 (4.8%)	3 (14.3%)	8 (38.4%)			
Judge's Race/Ethnicity	*Neutral*	*Narrow*	*Broad*	*Total*	5.408 (4, 22)	p > 0.050	N/A
White	8 (36.4%)	3 (13.6%)	7 (31.8%)	18 (81.8%)			
Nonwhite	2 (9.1%)	0 (0.0%)	1 (4.5%)	3 (13.6%)			
Not Applicable or Unknown	0 (0.0%)	1 (4.5%)	0 (0.0%)	1 (4.5%)			
Judge's Political Affiliation	*Neutral*	*Narrow*	*Broad*	*Total*	2.074 (4, 22)	p > 0.050	N/A
Nonpartisan	8 (36.4%)	3 (13.6%)	5 (22.7%)	16 (72.7%)			
Democrat	1 (4.5%)	0 (0.0%)	2 (9.1%)	3 (13.5%)			
Republican	1 (4.5%)	1 (4.5%)	1 (4.5%)	3 (13.5%)			

1. *Lawrence* as a Signpost

Under New Hampshire law, adultery qualifies as grounds for divorce.[696] But case law had previously limited the definition of adultery in this context to "extramarital, sexual intercourse between persons of the opposite sex," thereby excluding sexual activity between members of the same sex.[697] *In re Blaisdell* overruled the precedent which had established that holding.[698] The *Blaisdell* court cited *Lawrence* in passing when noting that "the law and public opinion surrounding the rights of same-sex

696 N.H. REV. STAT. § 458:7 (2020).

697 *In re* Blanchflower & Blanchflower, 834 A.2d 1010, 1011–12 (N.H. 2003).

698 261 A.3d 306, 309 (N.H. 2021).

couples to engage in intimate association" had begun to change at least eighteen years earlier.[699] But *Lawrence* was not a key precedent for the decision in *Blaisdell*. Rather, because New Hampshire embraced marriage equality for LGBTQ+ people by statute in 2009 and *Obergefell* extended that right nationwide in 2015, the court reasoned that "limiting the definition of adultery to sexual intercourse between two persons of the opposite sex would be inconsistent" with the way marriage had come to be understood.[700]

Kinnett v. Kinnett is another case in which *Lawrence* played no meaningful role in the case outcome, but nonetheless was cited in passing to illustrate that changing times might require revisiting long-standing precedents. In *Kinnett*, the Louisiana Court of Appeals grappled with the scope of biological parents' constitutionally protected liberty interests in their relationships with their children.[701] The court reversed a trial court's determination that a putative father's avowal action was preempted.[702] A judge wrote a concurring opinion to express her concerns that the statute governing the time period for paternity acknowledgments was unconstitutional.[703] In so doing, she challenged the notion of presumptive paternity for men married to a woman at the time she gives birth. In her analysis of the liberty interests at stake for both biological fathers and their children, the judge questioned a line of cases that had relied on common law presumptions of paternity and, in doing so, cited *Lawrence* and *Obergefell* for the proposition that history and tradition do not necessarily limit the constitutional protection rights:

---

699 *Id.* at 311.

700 *Id.* at 313 (citing, *inter alia*, N.H. REV. STAT. § 457:1-a (2010); *Obergefell v. Hodges*, 576 U.S. 644, 675 (2015)); *see also* Hogsett v. Neale, 478 P.3d 713, 721 (Colo. 2021) (modifying the standards for determining whether parties mutually intended to enter a common law marriage to accommodate members of the same-sex); *cf. In re* Guardianship of Dameris L., 956 N.Y.S.2d 848, 855 (Sur. Ct. 2012) (citing *Lawrence*'s use of international law as persuasive authority as a guide for examining Article 12 of the United Nations Convention on the Rights of Persons with Disabilities, as persuasive authority for interpreting constitutional protections in guardianship proceedings); *In re* Mark C.H., 906 N.Y.S.2d 419, 434 (Sur. Ct. 2010) (same).

701 302 So. 3d 157 (La Ct. App. 2020), *rev'd in part*, 332 So. 3d 1149 (La. 2021).

702 *Id.* at 187.

703 *Id.* at 187–204 (Wicker, J., concurring).

> Rigid focus upon history and tradition is inconsistent with a rich body of United States Supreme Court jurisprudence . . . and fails to consider that both history and tradition are a side effect of the passage of time and evolving social mores. . . . Supreme Court jurisprudence addressing a plethora of asserted rights affirms that history and tradition are not the sole arbiters of whether liberty interests are entitled to protection under the constitution in the face of evolving science and societal norms. *See, e.g., Lawrence v. Texas* . . . .[704]

The majority opinion in *Kennett* did not wrestle with the constitutional dimensions of the case. On appeal, the Louisiana Supreme Court reversed the appellate court's nonconstitutional ruling and remanded the action for consideration of the constitutional challenge.[705] On remand, the appellate court vacated the trial court's judgment that the statute was constitutional and remanded for a full evidentiary trial "with factual and/or expert testimony and evidence" to determine the constitutionality of the statute in question.[706] Notably, the court of appeals' decision on remand did not cite *Lawrence* or *Obergefell*, perhaps because the continued viability of these decisions was called into question by *Dobbs*, most especially by Justice Clarence Thomas' concurring opinion in which he stated the Court "should reconsider all of [its] substantive due process precedents, including *Griswold*, *Lawrence*, and *Obergefell*."[707]

Under Alabama law in effect until 2022, alimony payments were supposed to be terminated upon "proof that the spouse receiving such alimony has remarried or that such spouse is living openly or cohabiting

---

704 *Id.* at 191–92 (internal citations omitted); *see also In re* Tammy J., 270 P.3d 805, 813 (Alaska 2012) ("The United States Supreme Court has repeatedly 'confirmed that our laws and tradition afford constitutional protection to personal decisions relating to marriage, procreation, contraception, family relationships, child rearing, and education.' 'Neither the Bill of Rights nor the specific practices of States at the time of the adoption of the Fourteenth Amendment marks the outer limits of the substantive sphere of liberty which the Fourteenth Amendment protects.'" (quoting Lawrence v. Texas, 539 U.S. 558, 573–74 (2003); Planned Parenthood of S.E. Pa. v. Casey, 505 U.S. 833, 848 (1992)).

705 332 So. 3d 1149, 1157 (La. 2021).

706 Kinnett v. Kinnett, 345 So. 3d 1122, 1131 (La. App. July 7, 2022).

707 Dobbs v. Jackson Women's Health Org., 142 S. Ct. 2228, 2301 (2022) (Thomas, J., concurring).

with a member of the opposite sex."[708] In *J.L.M. v. S.A.K.*, an ex-husband moved to terminate alimony payments to his ex-wife when she began living with a female partner.[709] He claimed that his alimony payments compelled him to "'abet' his former wife's criminal conduct by subsidizing her illicit relationship with his money" in violation of the public policy of the state.[710] In support of his argument, he pointed to the state's ban on the recognition of same-sex marriages and the fact that the state's sodomy law (which was limited to acts involving members of the same-sex) remained on the books despite *Lawrence*. The court refused to modify the alimony award because the plain language of the statute applied only to cohabitation with a member of the opposite sex. Additionally, the court based its decision on the ex-wife's continued need for financial support and the fact that "[t]he former husband offered no evidence indicating that the former wife is using her alimony for anything other than the payment of her ordinary living expenses."[711] *Lawrence*, therefore, played no meaningful role in the *J.L.M. v. S.A.K.* decision. In fact, the court seemed to pay little more than lip service to the precedent by acknowledging that the Supreme Court had invalidated "a similarly-worded Texas statute" in *Lawrence*, but then went on to say that although the Alabama sodomy law could not be constitutionally applied to private sex acts between consenting adults, the state's sodomy law had "not been declared unconstitutional by any court."[712] It took until 2022 for Alabama to amend its family law to make the termination of alimony upon romantic cohabitation apply neutrally to all sexes and sexual orientations.[713]

2. Adoption by a Gay Parent

Florida was the last U.S. state to prohibit adoption by gays and lesbians. Originally enacted in 1977, the relevant statutory provision provided, "[n]o person eligible to adopt under this statute may adopt if that

---

708 ALA. CODE § 30-2-55 (1975 & 2008 Supp.).

709 18 So. 3d 384, 385–86 (Ala. Civ. App. 2008).

710 *Id.* at 389.

711 *Id.* at 390.

712 *Id.* at 388 n.4.

713 ALA. CODE § 30-2-55 (2022) (as amended by 2022 Ala. Laws 430 (H.B. 54)).

person is a homosexual."[714] That law withstood several challenges over the years before two courts in different Florida counties invalidated it on equal protection grounds (among others).[715] Both courts relied, in part, on *Lawrence*. One cited *Lawrence* to dispense with the state's claim that the adoption ban was rationally related to the promotion of public morality.[716] The other relied on *Lawrence* for the proposition that it was irrational to deny qualified parents the ability to adopt based on sexual orientation after the Supreme Court held in *Lawrence* that such status "may not be penalized."[717] Both courts gave *Lawrence* an expansive interpretation, using the case as a basis to protect the rights of LGBTQ+ people and their putative children.

3. *Lawrence* as (Mostly) Ineffective Sword or Shield in Family Law Disputes

In several cases, a spouse or former spouse attempted to use *Lawrence*

---

714 FLA. STAT. ANN. § 63.042(3) (1973 & 2008 Supp.).

715 *In re* Adoption of Doe, 2008 WL 5006172, at *29 (Fla. Cir. Ct. Nov. 25, 2008) (Miami-Dade County); *In re* Adoption of Doe, 2008 WL 5070056, at *31 (Fla. Cir. Ct. Aug. 29, 2008) (Monroe County).

716 *Doe*, 2008 WL 5006172, at *29 ("However, public morality per se, disconnected from any separate legitimate interest, is not a legitimate government interest to justify unequal treatment."). The Supreme Court of Arkansas and a court in Missouri both applied the same logic when invaliding their state bans on LGBTQ+ people serving as foster parents. Dep't of Hum. Servs. & Child Welfare Agency Rev. Bd. v. Howard, 238 S.W.3d 1, 10–11 (Ark. 2006) (declaring the ban invalid on separation of powers grounds while noting that "mere moral disapproval of sexual activity by a group does not qualify as a legitimate reason for an attack on equal protection or privacy rights"); Johnston v. Missouri Dep't of Soc. Servs., No. 0516-CV09517, 2006 WL 6903173, at *5 (Mo. Cir. Ct. Feb. 17, 2006) (holding that because *Lawrence* rendered Missouri's sodomy law unenforceable, it could not serve as the basis for state agencies to conclude gay or lesbian people lacked the moral character to serve as foster care providers).

717 *Doe*, 2008 WL 5070056, at *22 ("[The] ban on adoption by gays or lesbians discriminates against all Floridians who are gay or lesbian by arbitrarily and oppressively prejudging them as a group, *based on lawful sexual conduct alone*, as incapable of parenting a child, rather than based on each petitioner's ability or inability to parent." (emphasis in original)); *Id.* at *31 n.34 ("It is irrational to deny individualized consideration to the adoption petition of the permanent guardian of the minor whose appointment was already approved by all three branches of state government, who is otherwise qualified to adopt, whose sexual orientation the Supreme Court held in *Lawrence* may not be penalized, and whose adoption of the minor is, based on the evidence, the only way for the State to meet the outstanding psychological and emotional needs of the minor." (internal emphasis omitted)).

to support their positions in family court actions. They were almost always unsuccessful.

In *Vanderveer v. Vanderveer*, a woman challenged the award of primary child custody to her ex-husband.[718] One of the reasons a family court judge ordered that change in custody was that she had begun living with a new boyfriend—conduct, she argued, was constitutionally protected under *Lawrence*.[719] The court determined *Lawrence* was "factually inapposite" because it did not limit "the atmosphere in a parent's home" that can be considered when determining the best interest of a child.[720] Moreover, there were other reasons for the change in custody.[721]

In *Hawkins v. Grese*, an appellate court upheld the denial of custody to the former same-sex partner of the child's biological mother after the two unmarried partners ended their ten-year relationship.[722] Although the child considered both women to be his parents, the court ruled that "the term 'parent' contemplates a relationship to a child based upon either the contribution of genetic material through biological insemination or by means of legal adoption."[723] In upholding the constitutionality of that definition of parentage, the court cited *Lawrence* for the proposition that sexual orientation is not a suspect or quasi-suspect classification and, therefore, the rational basis test applied when determining the equal protection rights of LGBTQ+ people.[724] Applying that deferential standard, the court reasoned that limiting parenthood to biological or adoptive parents did not discriminate on the basis of sexual orientation. "If the couple is not married, the non-biological/non-adoptive partner is not a

---

718 No. 0122-04-2, 2004 WL 2157930, at *1 (Va. Ct. App. Sept. 28, 2004).

719 *Id.* at *4, *5.

720 *Id.* at *4.

721 *Id.* at *4, *5. *Vanderveer* involved opposite-sex partners. The same outcome occurred in a case involving same-sex partners. *See, e.g.*, Page v. Page, No. 07CA0109, 2008 WL 2469176, at *6 (Ohio Ct. App. June 20, 2008) (differentiating *Lawrence*'s due process holding as applied to criminalizing sodomy from child custody determinations which are "subject to the state's legitimate interest in insuring that the award and any subsequent modification of [child custody orders are] in the best interest of [the] children").

722 809 S.E.2d 441, 443, 452 (Va. Ct. App. 2018).

723 *Id.* at 446.

724 *Id.* at 445.

parent irrespective of gender or sexual orientation."[725]

As the facts of *Hawkins v. Grese* make clear, that case did not involve biological or adoptive parents. When a couple with biological or adoptive children split-up, courts clearly take sexual orientation into consideration when making child custody decisions. More often than not, courts awarded primary custody to the straight parent over an LGBTQ+ one.[726] Still, courts clearly have felt at least partially constrained by *Lawrence* to allow either joint custody or visitation with an LGBTQ+ parent. Consider the court's reasoning in *A.O.V. v. J.R.V.*, a case involving cross-appeals in which a mother contested a trial court decision that did not grant her sole custody of her children and the father challenged the imposition of restrictions on his visits with his children on the basis of his sexuality.[727] The court stated that although "[h]omosexuality by itself does not render a parent unfit," it may nonetheless be a factor that affects what might be in a child's best interest.[728] After discussing two cases that manifested homophobic views about the presumed negative impact on children seeing a parent in a loving same-sex relationship, the court acknowledged that those cases had been "weakened to the extent that they relied on [the state's] criminalization of certain sexual acts" that subsequently had been invalidated by *Lawrence*.[729] Still, the court emphasized that when determining custody, judges need to consider both the extent to which children are exposed to parents' romantic relationships and whether those relationships have any "adverse impact" on children.[730] The court

---

725 *Id.* at 447.

726 *E.g.*, L.A.M. v. B.M., 906 So. 2d 942, 947 (Ala. Civ. App. 2004) (upholding change in primary physical custody from mother to father after she came out, but noting additional reasons for the change).

727 No. 0219-06-4, 2007 WL 581871, at *1 (Va. Ct. App. Feb. 27, 2007).

728 *Id.* at *3–4 (citing Doe v. Doe, 284 S.E.2d 799, 805–06 (Va. 1981)); *see also* McGriff v. McGriff, 99 P.3d 111, 117 (Idaho 2004) ("But even before the *Lawrence* decision was handed down, it was established in a number of state courts across the nation that a homosexual parent may not be denied custody of a child unless there is sufficient evidence presented to show that the parent's homosexuality is having a negative effect on the child and that the parent's custody is not in the best interests of the child. Only when there is a nexus between harm to the child and a parent's homosexuality, can that parent's sexual orientation be a factor in determining custody of a child.").

729 *A.O.V.*, 2007 WL 581871, at *3–4.

730 *Id.* at *5.

concluded that because the father was a fit parent, joint custody was proper. But the court also upheld restrictions on the father when the children visited with him that prohibited him from living openly and honestly as a gay man. Specifically, the court upheld a prohibition on the father "from allowing his companion to occupy the home overnight or engaging in displays of affection while the children visit."[731]

A similar outcome occurred in *Weichman v. Weichman* when an appellate court upheld an award of child custody to a father, rather than a mother who had left her husband because she was gay.[732] But unlike the Virginia Court of Appeals' 2007 decision in *A.O.V. v. J.R.V.*, a New York City appellate court modified a custody order that had prohibited the noncustodial mother from exposing the child to any activities that violated the tenets of the child's Orthodox Jewish faith. The court found the order was overly broad and infringed on the mother's constitutionally protected liberty interest to "express oneself and live freely" since, as originally entered, the trial court's order could have prohibited her from having her child around a partner if she "became involved in a relationship with or married a woman."[733] The *Weichman* case was decided in 2021, six years after *Obergefell*'s mandate of nationwide marriage equality. Perhaps the fourteen-year timespan between *A.O.V. v. J.R.V.* and *Weichman*, along with the attendant changes in the social acceptance of LGBTQ+ people during that time, account for the difference in the two courts' willingness to control how gay parents express themselves in front of their children during visitation.

---

731 *Id.* at *6; *see also McGriff*, 99 P.3d at 120–21 (upholding similar restrictions on a gay man while his children visited).

732 158 N.Y.S.3d 154 (Sup. Ct. App. Div. 2021).

733 *Id.* at 157. Providing continuity of religious life for Orthodox Jews, especially those in the Hasidic community, was a key part of the court's rationale. That same concern manifest in other cases, as well. In *Weisberger v. Weisberger*, 60 N.Y.S.3d 265 (Sup. Ct. App. Div. 2017), the court denied a change in child custody from the biological mother to the biological father after the mother came-out as a lesbian. The court noted that children were close with their mother and that she had raised them in accordance with the tenets of their faith despite identifying as a lesbian, whereas the father had not regularly exercised his visitation rights or fulfilled his financial obligations to the children after the parties' separation. *Id.* at 274. The court emphasized that the children were to be given a Hasidic upbringing, but that did not require their mother to abandon her due process rights "to express [her]self and live freely." *Id.* at 275.

T.M.H. v. D.M.T. was the only case in which a court gave *Lawrence* an expansive reading that supported a family law claim in manner a that benefitted an LGBTQ+ litigant.[734] The case involved a lesbian couple who owned a home together and used funds in their joint bank account to have a child.[735] They had ova withdrawn from one woman (the biological mother), had them fertilized, and then had them implanted into the other woman (the birth mother). The in vitro fertilization process resulted in a successful pregnancy that yielded a child whom they named using a hyphenation of both of their last names. The women eventually separated and the biological mother sought a declaration of parentage and shared responsibility for the custody and support of the child. A trial court denied her petition because a state law provided that "other than the commissioning couple or a father who has executed a preplanned adoption agreement," people who donate ova or sperm relinquish all parental rights and obligations with respect to any resulting children.[736] The trial court considered the biological mother to be "an egg donor" within the meaning of that statute. The Florida District Court of Appeal reversed the grant of summary judgment to the birth mother, reasoning that providing ova to one's partner within the intent of coparenting any resultant children does not render someone a "donor" within the meaning of the statute because there was no intent to give one's ova away.[737] The court quoted from *Lawrence* to support its reasoning that that any contrary construction of the Florida statute would violate the biological mother's "constitutional rights to equal protection and privacy under the United States and Florida Constitutions."[738]

---

734 79 So. 3d 787, 788, 793 (Fla. Dist. Ct. App. 2011), *aff'd in part, disapproved in part*, 129 So. 3d 320 (Fla. 2013).

735 *Id.* at 788.

736 *Id.* at 790–91 (quoting FLA. STAT. ANN. § 742.14 (2016)).

737 *Id.* at 791–92 ("[T]here was no 'true egg donation' because 'K.M. did not intend to simply donate her ova to E.G., but rather provided her ova to her lesbian partner with whom she was living so that E.G. could give birth to a child that would be raised in their joint home.'" (quoting K.M. v. E.G., 117 P.3d 673, 679 (Cal. 2005))).

738 *Id.* at 793 ("[C]onstitutional protections are provided to individuals making personal decisions relating to such matters as procreation and child-rearing because the Constitution demands respect for the autonomy of the person making these decisions and that '[p]ersons in a homosexual relationship may seek autonomy for these

The birth mother appealed, and the Florida Supreme Court upheld the parental rights of the biological mother.[739] In doing so, however, the court took issue with the intermediate appellate court's determination that the biological mother was not a donor within the meaning of the statute. Nonetheless, the Florida Supreme Court declared the statute unconstitutional on due process and equal protection grounds under both the federal and state constitutions without citing *Lawrence*.

I. LGBTQ+ Civil Rights ($n = 49$, 16.0%)

Given that *Lawrence* is largely considered to be a landmark victory for LGBTQ+ rights, it is unsurprising that the category concerning LGBTQ+ civil rights contains a large number of cases citing *Lawrence*, although as Table 18 reveals, the case was far more likely to have been mentioned in passing than it was to being key to a case outcome.[740] All but three (5.9%) of the cases in this category were civil in nature. None of the other variables were significantly related to how courts applied *Lawrence* in LGBTQ+ civil rights cases. However, three findings nonetheless warrant attention. First, largely as a function of so many LGBTQ+ rights cases being litigated in highly democratic states, judges in those states applied *Lawrence* expansively by a ratio of more than six to one over narrow applications of the precedent. Second, likely also a function of forum selection for litigating LGBTQ+ rights claims, the geographical region of the country approached statistical significance ($p < 0.08$) such that courts in the Northeast and west were more likely to give *Lawrence* a broad or expansive reading when deciding such cases, as opposed to narrow or limiting constructions; the opposite pattern also occurred in South.

---

purposes, just as heterosexual persons do'" (quoting Lawrence v. Texas, 539 U.S. 558, 574 (2003))).

739 129 So. 3d 320, 328 (Fla. 2013).

740 *See infra* notes 25–29 and accompanying text.

TABLE 18: VARIABLE FREQUENCIES AND RELATIONSHIP TO TREATMENT OF *LAWRENCE* IN LGBTQ+ CIVIL RIGHTS CASES

Category	**Treatment of *Lawrence* *n* (%)**				**Chi-Square**	**Sig.**	**Cramer's V**
Type	*Neutral*	*Narrow*	*Broad*	*Total*	0.838 (2, 49)	p > 0.050	N/A
Civil	19 (38.8%)	7 (14.3%)	20 (40.8%)	46 (93.9%)			
Criminal	1 (2.0%)	0 (0.0%)	2 (4.1%)	3 (6.1%)			
Depth	*Neutral*	*Narrow*	*Broad*	*Total*	12.400 (2, 49)	Fisher's Exact p = 0.002	0.503
Mentioned in Passing	19 (38.8%)	2 (4.1%)	14 (28.6%)	35 (71.4%)			
Key to Case	1 (2.0%)	5 (10.2%)	8 (16.3%)	14 (28.6%)			
Outcome	*Neutral*	*Narrow*	*Broad*	*Total*	3.956 (4, 49)	p > 0.050	N/A
Prosecution	1 (2.0%)	0 (0.0%)	0 (0.0%)	1 (2.0%)			
Defense	0 (0.0%)	0 (0.0%)	2 (4.1%)	2 (4.1%)			
Not Relevant (civil)	19 (38.8%)	7 (14.3%)	20 (40.8%)	46 (93.9%)			
State Politics	*Neutral*	*Narrow*	*Broad*	*Total*	11.014 (8, 49)	p > 0.050	N/A
Deep Red	7 (14.3%)	2 (4.1%)	1 (2.0%)	10 (20.4%)			
Light Red	1 (2.0%)	1 (2.0%)	1 (2.0%)	3 (6.1%)			
Purple	1 (2.0%)	0 (0.0%)	0 (0.0%)	1 (2.0%)			
Light Blue	1 (2.0%)	1 (2.0%)	1 (2.0%)	3 (6.1%)			
Deep Blue	10 (20.4%)	3 (6.1%)	19 (38.8%)	32 (65.3%)			
Region	*Neutral*	*Narrow*	*Broad*	*Total*	11.378 (6, 49)	p > 0.050	N/A
Northeast	7 (14.3%)	2 (4.1%)	14 (28.6%)	23 (46.9%)			
South	5 (10.2%)	3 (6.1%)	1 (2.0%)	9 (18.4%)			
Midwest	3 (6.1%)	1 (2.0%)	0 (0.0%)	4 (8.2%)			
West	5 (10.2%)	1 (2.0%)	7 (14.3%)	13 (26.5%)			
Judge's Sex	*Neutral*	*Narrow*	*Broad*	*Total*	4.036 (2, 49)	p > 0.050	N/A
Male	13 (26.5%)	6 (12.2%)	10 (20.4%)	29 (59.6%)			
Female	7 (14.3%)	1 (2.0%)	12 (24.5%)	20 (40.8%)			
Judge's Race/Ethnicity	*Neutral*	*Narrow*	*Broad*	*Total*	3.055 (4, 49)	p > 0.050	N/A
White	15 (60.6%)	6 (12.2%)	19 (38.8%)	40 (81.6%)			
Nonwhite	5 (10.2%)	1 (2.0%)	2 (4.1%)	8 (16.3%)			
Not Applicable or Unknown	0 (0.0%)	0 (0.0%)	1 (2.0%)	1 (2.0%)			
Judge's Political Affiliation	*Neutral*	*Narrow*	*Broad*	*Total*	10.878 (6, 49)	p > 0.050	N/A
Nonpartisan	7 (14.3%)	6 (12.2%)	15 (30.6%)	28 (57.1%)			
Democrat	5 (10.2%)	0 (0.0%)	4 (8.2%)	9 (18.4%)			
Republican	8 (16.3%)	1 (2.0%)	2 (4.1%)	11 (22.4%)			
Unknown	0 (0.0%)	0 (0.0%)	1 (2.0%)	1 (2.0%)			

1. Marriage Equality[741]

The law in a handful of jurisdictions recognized transgender people's rights to marry someone of the same sex assigned to the trans-person at birth long before marriage equality for same-sex couples, presuming, however, that the transgender person had undergone gender affirmation surgery prior to the date of the marriage.[742] Other states were not so enlightened.[743] But the sex of each person in a couple became a moot point

---

[741] In light of the decision in *Obergefell* and the voluminous scholarship on marriage equality before and after that landmark decision, this section is purposefully abbreviated.

[742] *See, e.g.*, Henry F. Fradella, Megan M. Parry & Lauren E. Fradella, *Marriage, Sexuality, and Gender in* FRADELLA & SUMNER, *supra* note 5, at 330–33; Mark Strasser, *Defining Sex: On Marriage, Family, and Good Public Policy*, 17 MICH. J. GENDER & L. 57, 81 (2010) ("Current law in many states is indeterminate with respect to whether or under what conditions a trans[gender person] can marry someone of [the same sex that trans person was assigned at birth"); *see also In re* Est. of Araguz, 443 S.W.3d 233, 245 (Tex. App. 2014) (reversing a grant of summary judgment in favor of a decedent's mother because someone who underwent gender-affirmation surgery (what the court called a "sex change") would be eligible to marry a person of the opposite sex; thus, the validity of the decedent's marriage turned on genuine issues of material fact as to the sex of his former spouse); M.T. v. J.T., 355 A.2d 204, 210–11 (N.J. Super. Ct. App. Div. 1976).

> In this case the transsexual's gender and genitalia are no longer discordant; they have been harmonized through medical treatment. Plaintiff has become physically and psychologically unified and fully capable of sexual activity consistent with her reconciled sexual attributes of gender and anatomy. Consequently, plaintiff should be considered a member of the female sex for marital purposes. It follows that such an individual would have the capacity to enter into a valid marriage relationship with a person of the opposite sex and did do so here. In so ruling we do no more than give legal effect to a *fait accompli*, based upon medical judgment and action which are irreversible. Such recognition will promote the individual's quest for inner peace and personal happiness, while in no way disserving any societal interest, principle of public order or precept of morality.

Id. at 211.

[743] Kantaras v. Kantaras, 884 So. 2d 155, 161 (Fla. Dist. Ct. App. 2004) (rejecting marriage of transgender person on the grounds that the state barred same-sex marriage and a trans-male was of the same sex as his female partner because "the common meaning of male and female, as those terms are used statutorily, . . . refer to immutable traits determined at birth"); *In re* Marriage License for Nash, No. 2002–T–0149, 2003 WL 23097095, at *4–9 (Ohio Ct. App. 2003) (refusing to recognize out-of-state amended birth certificate of postoperative trans-man and prohibiting the issuance of a marriage license for him to marry a woman on public policy grounds); *In re* Est. of Gardiner, 42 P.3d 120, 136–37 (Kan. 2002) (holding that a transgender woman was not a woman

when marriage equality became the law of the land because all LGBTQ+ people can now marry their partner of choice. But it took twelve years before *Lawrence* helped to usher in that state of affairs for the whole nation.

As discussed in Chapter 1, at first, *Lawrence* had little discernable impact on LGBTQ+ rights beyond its immediate effect of decriminalization of sexual activity between members of the same sex. Judges often gave *Lawrence* a narrow reading when upholding statutory frameworks that limited marriage to people of opposite sexes.[744] These courts often cited *Lawrence* for the proposition that the rational basis test applied to review of marriage laws.[745] Applying that deferential standard to equal protection challenges, these courts upheld laws barring marriage equality on the basis that "[a]ll men and all women are equally entitled to enter the institution of marriage."[746] Of course, such a narrow framing of the issue fails to take into account the fact that lesbians and gays only had such rights to marry someone of the opposite sex, rather than the same-sex persons they loved. These courts similarly rejected due process challenges

---

within the meaning of the statutes recognizing marriage and, therefore, the marriage her and male husband was void against public policy); Littleton v. Prange, 9 S.W.3d 223, 230–31 (Tex. App. 1999), *superseded by statute as recognized in Araguz*, 443 S.W.3d at 240 (citing TEX. FAM. CODE ANN. § 2.005(b)(8) (West Supp. 2013)). For a thoughtful critique of the fundamental misunderstanding of both medical and psychological science reflected in these cases, see Lindsee A. Acton, *Overturning* In re Gardiner*: Ending Transgender Discrimination in Kansas*, 48 FAM. L.Q. 563 (2014).

744 One case even refused to grant a property tax exemption to a same-sex couple, one of whom was a disabled veteran. The couple had been lawfully married in Canada and they also entered into a legally-sanctioned civil union in Vermont. Even though a tax exemption would have been available to married, opposite-sex couple, a New Jersey court, relying on its "defense of marriage" act, reclined to recognize either out-of-state union, reasoning that the public policy exception to the usual application of comity under the Full Faith and Credit Clause of the U.S. Constitution did not require either the recognition of the marriage or the extension of equal rights commensurate with married persons. Hennefeld v. Twp. of Montclair, 22 N.J. Tax 166, 174–87 (2005).

745 *E.g.*, State *ex rel.* Alabama Pol'y Inst., 200 So. 3d 495, 532–52 (Ala. 2015), *abrogated by* Obergefell v. Hodges, 576 U.S. 644 (2015).

746 *Id.* at 533; *see also* Nat'l Pride at Work, Inc. v. Governor of Mich., 732 N.W.2d 139, 155 (Mich. Ct. App. 2007), *aff'd*, 748 N.W.2d 524 (2008) (sidestepping the majority opinion in *Lawrence*, but citing the concurring opinion to support the proposition that the state ban on marriage equality rationally served the legitimate state interest of "protecting and strengthening traditional marriages" and, therefore, public employers could lawfully be precluded from extending benefits to same-sex domestic partners).

to laws that were not inclusive of marriage equality. Even though judges recognized that marriage is a fundamental right, they limited that right to "traditional marriage" between one man and one woman.[747] Moreover, they justified this interpretation as having several rational bases, most frequently promoting procreation and child well-being within a traditional family unit.[748]

---

[747] *Alabama Pol'y Inst.*, 200 So. 3d at 534. A justice on the Supreme Court of Texas applied similar reasoning when dissenting from a decision that upheld the grant of a divorce to a same-sex couple who had been married in another state:

> Texas does not restrict access to what has traditionally been viewed as a marriage (or as a divorce, for that matter). Rather, Texas has defined the very nature of marriage (and divorce) itself, establishing it as a union (or, for divorce, as a dissolution of a union) between a man and a woman. This case is also not like cases upholding the right to certain forms of sexual conduct. *See, e.g.*, *Lawrence* . . . . The Texas laws at issue merely define marriage (and divorce).

State v. Naylor, 466 S.W.3d 783, 814 (Tex. 2015) (Divine, J., dissenting); *see also* Kern v. Taney, 11 Pa. D. & C. 5th 558, 570 (C.P. Berks Cnty. 2010) (finding lack of jurisdiction to adjudicate a divorce for a same-sex couple married out-of-state at a time before they could be legally married in Pennsylvania because such marriages were void under then-applicable state law; the court rejected full faith and credit, due process, and equal protection challenges to the state law and held that the "fundamental right to be married does not contemplate same-sex marriages"). *But see* Czekala-Chatham v. State *ex rel.* Hood, 212 So. 3d 787, 792 (Miss. 2015) (King, J., objecting to order for supplemental briefing). In that case, the Supreme Court of Mississippi ordered supplemental briefing on whether an action should be stayed pending resolution of *Obergefell* in a case in which a same-sex couple sought a divorce from an out-of-state marriage into which they could not have entered in that state. Justice Leslie D. King thought such briefing was unnecessary because, in his assessment, the ban on same-sex marriage was unconstitutional due, in part, to *Lawrence* and other cases that "found homosexuals deserving of protection against discrimination." *Id.* at 792.

[748] *Alabama Pol'y Inst.*, 200 So. 3d at 543–44. The majority decision was authored by the notoriously antigay former Alabama Supreme Court Justice Roy Moore. Moore vocally disagreed with *Lawrence* when he argued that "homosexual conduct" should be illegal. *See* Nathan McDermott & Andrew Kaczynski, *Senate Candidate Roy Moore in 2005: "Homosexual Conduct Should Be Illegal,"* CNN (Sept. 22, 2017, 7:52 PM), https://www.cnn.com/2017/09/21/politics/kfile-roy-moore-homosexuality-illegal/index.html [https://perma.cc/W4YZ-LRZ7]. For a discussion of his rocky tenure on the bench, which included being reelected after having been removed for ethics violations, see Bradley J. Watts, *Are We a Government of Laws or of Men? An Assessment of Chief Justice Roy S. Moore's Reelection and A Call for Reform in Alabama's Judicial Election Laws*, 38 J. LEGAL PROF. 313 (2014). For a broader, contextual discussion of the Alabama marriage cases, see Howard M. Wasserman, *Crazy in Alabama: Judicial Process and the Last Stand Against Marriage Equality in the Land of George Wallace*, 110 NW. U.L. REV. ONLINE 1, 17 (2015).

Other cases relied on *Lawrence*, in part, for justifying a revisiting of marriage law, as well as laws and policies affected by marital status, with an eye toward LGBTQ+ inclusion and equality.[749] Cases recognizing

For other cases refusing to recognize marriage equality using similar reasoning to that in the Alabama case (all of which were abrogated by *Obergefell*), see Conaway v. Deane, 932 A.2d 571, 633–34 (Md. 2007); Andersen v. King Cnty., 138 P.3d 963, 985–90 (Wash. 2006); *In re* Marriage of J.B. & H.B., 326 S.W.3d 654, 676–81 (Tex. App. 2010); Samuels v. New York State Dep't of Health, 811 N.Y.S.2d 136, 144 (Sup. Ct. App. Div.), *aff'd sub nom.*, Hernandez v. Robles, 855 N.E.2d 1, 7–12 (2006); Morrison v. Sadler, 821 N.E.2d 15, 29 (Ind. Ct. App. 2005); Standhardt v. Superior Ct. *ex rel.* Cnty. of Maricopa, 77 P.3d 451, 456–65 (Ariz. Ct. App. 2003); Seymour v. Holcomb, 790 N.Y.S.2d 858, 863 (Sup. Ct. 2005), *aff'd*, 811 N.Y.S.2d 134 (Sup. Ct. App. Div. 2006), *aff'd sub nom.* Hernandez v. Robles, 855 N.E.2d 1 (N.Y. 2006); Shields v. Madigan, 783 N.Y.S.2d 270, 276 (Sup. Ct. 2004), *aff'd*, 820 N.Y.S.2d 890 (Sup. Ct. App. Div. 2006); *cf.* Lockyer v. City & Cnty. of San Francisco, 95 P.3d 459, 503 (Cal. 2004) (holding that local officials exceeded the scope of their lawful authority when they issued gender-neutral marriage licenses to same-sex couples in contravention to a state law, the constitutionality of which was not properly before the court); Donaldson v. State, 292 P.3d 364, 365, 366–67 (Mont. 2012) (finding that an action for a declaratory judgment ordering the state legislature to enact a statutory scheme that honored same-sex couples rights to due process, equal protection, privacy, and dignity presented nonjusticiable claims that, if granted, would constitute an "inappropriate exercise of judicial power"). A dissenting justice in *Donaldson* argued that the court was "on the wrong side of history" and cited *Lawrence* to express his concerns that the laws of the ate served to oppress LGBTQ+ people. *Id.* at 375 (Nelson, J., dissenting).

749 *E.g.*, Mueller v. Tepler, 95 A.3d 1011, 1023–24 n.18 (Conn. 2014) (holding that same-sex couples could maintain loss of consortium claims for tortious conduct that occurred prior to the time that the law permitted them to be married); Alaska C.L. Union v. State, 122 P.3d 781, 786 (Alaska 2005) ("The Marriage Amendment effectively precludes same-sex couples from marrying in Alaska, but it does not explicitly or implicitly prohibit public employers from offering to their employees' same-sex domestic partners all benefits that they offer to their employees' spouses."); Snetsinger v. Montana Univ. Sys., 104 P.3d 445, 452 (Mont. 2004) (invalidating state university system's denial of benefits to same-sex partners on equal protection grounds when unmarried, opposite-sex partners could receive benefits simply by filing an affidavit); Godfrey v. Spano, 836 N.Y.S.2d 813, 813, 816 (Sup. Ct. 2007) (citing *Lawrence* as an example of the expanding rights of LGBTQ+ people that led to their seeking marriage equality), *aff'd*, 871 N.Y.S.2d 296 (Sup. Ct. App. Div. 2008), *aff'd* 920 N.E.2d 328 (N.Y. 2009) (upholding county executive's recognition of same-sex marriages legally performed in other jurisdictions); Golden v. Paterson, 877 N.Y.S.2d 822, 837 (Sup. Ct. 2008) (dismissing challenge to governor's executive directive recognizing same-sex marriages legally performed in other jurisdictions). *But see* Glossip v. Missouri Dep't of Transp. & Highway Patrol Emps.' Ret. Sys., 411 S.W.3d 796, 806 (Mo. 2013) (upholding limitation on survivor benefits to spouses over an equal protection claim by the surviving same-sex partner of a deceased state trooper who died prior to the era of marriage equality on the grounds that the restriction was rationally related to the legitimate state interests of providing support to spouses who were economically

marriage equality or expanding the recognition of rights attendant to marriage were usually, although not exclusively handed down by courts in "blue" states, primarily in the Northeast and Pacific coastal areas.[750] Some of these states declared sexual orientation to be a suspect or quasi-suspect classification before invalidating laws that had limited marriage to opposite-sex couples.[751]

Notably, the combination of *Lawrence* and *Obergefell* did not remedy all of the inequities of the times before marriage equality. To be sure, some courts granted LGBTQ+ people access to legal remedies that depended on giving some quasi-retroactive effect to marriage equality when a failure to do so offended equal protection, but not all courts have been willing to do so. For instance, the surviving partner of a couple in a long-term, same-sex relationship argued that he and his late partner had entered into a

---

dependent on a deceased state employee, as well as administrative efficiency and controlling costs); Langan v. St. Vincent's Hosp. of N.Y., 802 N.Y.S.2d 476, 478–80 (Sup. Ct. App. Div. 2005) (upholding the exclusion of partners in same-sex civil unions from the class of persons with standing to bring wrongful death suits over federal and state constitutional equal protection challenges); *cf.* Cote-Whitacre v. Dep't of Pub. Health, 844 N.E.2d 623, 656 (Mass. 2006) ("[I]t is neither arbitrary nor capricious for the Legislature to decide as a matter of public policy to restrict the Massachusetts marriages of out-of-state residents . . . .").

750 *See, e.g.*, Lewis v. Harris, 908 A.2d 196, 222 (N.J. 2006) (holding same-sex couples must be afforded the same rights and benefits enjoyed by married opposite-sex couples, although that need not be "marriage"); Goodridge v. Dep't of Pub. Health, 798 N.E.2d 941, 961–68 (Mass. 2003) (holding denial of civil marriage license violated state constitutional guarantee of equal protection); Garden State Equal. v. Dow, No. CIV.A. MER-L-1729-11, 2012 WL 540608, at *6 (N.J. Super. Ct. Law Div. Feb. 21, 2012) (citing *Lawrence* in a decision allowing a marriage equality case to move forward on due process and equal protection challenges); People v. Greenleaf, 780 N.Y.S.2d 899, 905 (Just. Ct. 2004) (dismissing misdemeanor charges against Unitarian ministers who officiated marriages for same-sex couples on the grounds that the law preventing the issuance of marriage licenses to such couples was unconstitutional).

751 *See, e.g.*, Griego v. Oliver, 316 P.3d 865, 881 (N.M. 2013) (recognizing sexual orientation as a "sensitive class" and applying intermediate scrutiny accordingly); Varnum v. Brien, 763 N.W.2d 862, 888 (Iowa 2009) (recognizing sexual orientation as a quasi-suspect classification and applying heightened scrutiny accordingly); *In re* Marriage Cases, 183 P.3d 384, 440–44 (Cal. 2008) (recognizing sexual orientation as a suspect classification for state equal protection clause purposes and applying strict scrutiny accordingly); Kerrigan v. Comm'r of Pub. Health, 957 A.2d 407, 432–76 (Conn. 2008) (recognizing sexual orientation as a quasi-suspect classification and applying heightened scrutiny accordingly).

common law marriage before they were abolished in their state in 2005.[752] An appellate court agreed, reasoning that because opposite-sex couples in Pennsylvania could establish the existence of a common law marriage prior to the date they were legislatively eliminated, same-sex couples needed to be able to do the same: "To deprive [them] of the opportunity to establish [their] rights as . . . common law spouse[s], simply because [they] are same-sex couple[s], would violate both the Equal Protection and Due Process Clauses of the Fourteenth Amendment."[753]

By contrast, the Supreme Court of Illinois seemed to misunderstand the implications of *Lawrence* and *Obergefell* for people in same-sex couples seeking legal remedies for which they would not have been eligible before marriage equality.[754] In *Blumenthal v. Brewer*, a woman sought to maintain an action seeking common law remedies, including restitution and unjust enrichment, against her former same-sex partner. A trial court had dismissed her claims because a 1979 case had held that public policy in the state embodied in statutory prohibition against common-law marriage precluded "unmarried cohabitants from bringing claims against one another to enforce mutual property rights where the rights asserted are rooted in a marriage-like relationship between the parties."[755] The state high court agreed and reaffirmed the nearly forty-year-old precedent over the claimant's due process and equal protection challenges:

> This court's decision in *Hewitt* only disallows unmarried cohabitants who live in a marriage-like relationship from accessing, under the guise of an implied contract, the rights and protections specified in the Marriage and Dissolution Act. In other words, individuals can enter into an intimate relationship, but the relationship itself cannot form the basis to bring common-law claims . . . . [*Hewitt*] acknowledges the legislative intent to

---

752 *In re* Est. of Carter, 159 A.3d 970, 972 (Pa. Super. Ct. 2017).

753 *Id.* at 977–78.

754 Blumenthal v. Brewer, 69 N.E.3d 834, 852 (Ill. 2016).

755 *Id.* at 839 (citing Hewitt v. Hewitt, 394 N.E.2d 1204, 1209–11 (Ill. 1979)).

> provide certain rights and benefits to those who participate in the institution of marriage.[756]

But unlike the opposite-sex couple in *Hewitt* who could have legally married, the same-sex couple in *Blumenthal v. Brewer* could not. Justice Mary Jane Theis recognized this and reasoned that *Lawrence* meant *Hewitt*'s holding was "not rationally related to a legitimate governmental interest."[757] Moreover, she agreed with the claimant that it was,

> "particularly irrational" to expand *Hewitt* from its fact context of opposite-sex domestic partners who could have married, but chose not to do so, to the fact context here of same-sex domestic partners who . . . "did not choose not to marry[, but] were barred from it" by a law, like those declared unconstitutional in *Obergefell.*[758]

She, therefore, would have overruled *Hewitt* "as an outmoded and unfair rule for all domestic partners" or alternatively would have sided with the claimant "that *Hewitt*'s rule, as applied to same-sex domestic partners . . . whose relationships ended before they were permitted to marry in Illinois, violates due process and equal protection."[759]

2. Intimate-Partner Violence Liability and Orders of Protection

For many years, the law in numerous states excluded same-sex victims of intimate-partner violence (IPV) from the scope of criminal laws targeting IPV and eligibility for a range of resources available to IPV victims in opposite-sex relationships, largely because those laws were enacted with spouses in mind.[760] Some states excluded LGBTQ+ people from eligibility for orders of protection and from victims services.[761] Prior

---

756 *Id.* at 859.

757 *Id.* at 868 (Theis, J., dissenting).

758 *Id.*

759 *Id.* at 869.

760 Sheila M. Seelau & Eric P. Seelau, *Gender-Role Stereotypes and Perceptions of Heterosexual, Gay and Lesbian Domestic Violence*, 20 J. FAM. VIOLENCE 363, 363 (2005), https://doi.org/10.1007/s10896-005-7798-4 (explaining that, at the time, only four states included people in same-sex relationships in their IPV laws).

761 *See, e.g.*, ARIZ. REV. STAT. § 13-3601 (1998); DEL. CODE ANN. tit. 10, § 1041(2)(b) (1997); MONT. CODE ANN. § 45-5-206(2)(b) (1995); N.C. GEN. STAT. §§ 50B-1(b)(1), (2), (6) (1979 & 2015 Supp). The North Carolina law remained discriminatory until

to 2003, a handful of state legislatures amended their IPV laws to become inclusive of LGBTQ+ people's relationships.[762] Other states accomplished such inclusion via judicial decisions that invalidated exclusionary statutory schemes on equal protection grounds or interpreted ambiguous IPV laws broadly so that they applied to same-sex partners.[763] *Lawrence* helped to facilitate such changes.[764]

---

declared unconstitutional in December of 2020—more than sixteen years after *Lawrence* and four and half years after *Obergefell.* M.E. v. T.J., 854 S.E.2d 74, 96–97, 100–08 (N.C. Ct. App. 2020), *aff'd as modified*, 869 S.E.2d 624, 638 (N.C. 2022). For a discussion of the impact of this state of affairs in North Carolina, see Phillip Sylvester, *Arming America's Most Dangerous Abusers: How Domestic Violence Laws Have Failed the LGBTQIA Community*, 11 DREXEL L. REV. 783 (2019) (citing H.B. 118, 19th Leg. (Haw. 1997)).

South Carolina has the dubious distinction of having amended its IPV laws specifically to exclude same-sex couples during the time in which the marriage equality movement was gaining traction. Doe v. State, 808 S.E.2d 807, 812 (S.C. 2017) (explaining that in 1994, the legislature added "a male and female who are cohabiting or formerly have cohabited" in lieu of its former gender-neutral use of "persons" who are or formerly were cohabitating (citing Act No. 519, §§ 1–3, 1994 S.C. Acts 5926, 5926–27, 5929) (codified at S.C. CODE §§ 16-25-10, 20-4-20 (1995)). Utah did the same in 1989. Utah Laws 1989, ch. 32, § 1 (codified at UTAH CODE ANN. § 30-6-1 (1990)).

762 Sylvester, *supra* note 761, at 824 (citing H.B. 118, 19th Leg. (Haw. 1997) (codified at HAW. REV. STAT. § 586-4 (1998 & 2022 Supp.))); *see also* A.B. 93, Cal. Assembly, 1993–94 1st Ex. Sess. ch. 28, § 2 (codified at CAL. PENAL CODE § 273.5 (1994)).

763 *Id.* at 799 (citing Ireland v. Davis, 957 S.W.2d 310, 312 (Ky. Ct. App. 1997)); Glater v. Fabianich, 625 N.E.2d 96, 99 (Ill. App. Ct. 1993)). For example, in *Ochoa v. State*, the Texas Court of Appeals interpreted the phrase "dating relationship" in its IPV statute to include same-sex partners over arguments from the defendant that the phrase was ambiguous and could not have been meant to apply to same-sex partners because, as the time it was adopted, the state criminalized sex acts between members of the same sex. 355 S.W.3d 48, 53 (Tex. App. 2010) (citing TEX. FAM. CODE § 71.0021 (2001)). The court reasoned that even though the state criminalized sex between members of the same sex when the IPV statute was enacted, "the Legislature could have reasonably determined that people in these relationships, whether legal at the time or not, needed special protection from an abuser." *Id.* at 54.

764 *See* Tara R. Pfeifer, Comment, *Out of the Shadows: The Positive Impact of* Lawrence v. Texas *on Victims of Same-Sex Domestic Violence*, 109 PENN ST. L. REV. 1251 (2005); *see also* M.E. v. T.J., 854 S.E.2d at 96–97, 100–08 (relying heavily on *Lawrence* and *Obergefell* in invaliding North Carolina's discriminatory IPV statutory scheme on both due process and equal protection grounds on due process and equal protection grounds).

3. Jury Selection

Batson v. Kentucky held that the use of peremptory challenges to excuse prospective jurors on the basis of their race violates the Fourteenth Amendment's guarantee of equal protection.[765] The Supreme Court extended *Batson* to peremptory challenges made on the basis of a prospective juror's sex in *J.E.B. v. Alabama ex rel. T.B.*[766] Since then, lower courts have issued decisions in which judges reasoned that *Batson* applied to select cognizable groups, such as Italians and Jews.[767] Some courts have refused to apply *Batson* to LGBTQ+ people,[768] whereas other courts have determined that "equal protection prohibits peremptory strikes based on sexual orientation."[769]

---

765 476 U.S. 79, 89 (1986); *see also* Flowers v. Mississippi, 139 S. Ct. 2228, 2241 (2019) (reaffirming *Batson* in the wake of continued discrimination on the basis of race in criminal case jury selection).

766 511 U.S. 127, 146 (1994).

767 Mark E. Wojcik, *Extending* Batson *to Peremptory Challenges of Jurors Based on Sexual Orientation and Gender Identity*, 40 N. ILL. U. L. REV. 1, 12 (2019) (citing JEFFREY T. FREDERICK , MASTERING VOIR DIRE AND JURY SELECTION 336,, 354 n.19 (4th ed. 2018); V. HALE STARR & MARK MCCORMICK , JURY SELECTION 2–35 (4th ed. 2010)).

768 *Id.* at 21; *see also* Goodman v. Lands End Homeowners Ass'n of Hilton Head, Inc., No. 91-2542, 1992 WL 91890, at *1 (4th Cir. May 6, 1992) (upholding ostensible strike on the basis of race when gender nonconformity was offered as the nonracially-discriminatory reason); Carter v. Duncan, No. C 02-0586SBA(PR), 2005 WL 2373572, at *1 (N.D. Cal. Sept. 27, 2005) (same); *cf.* United States v. Blaylock, 421 F.3d 758, 769 (8th Cir. 2005) ("[W]e doubt *Batson* and its progeny extend constitutional protection to the sexual orientations of venire persons [but even if it does], the government offered legitimate nondiscriminatory reasons for striking the panel member."); Johnson v. Campbell, 92 F.3d 951, 953 (9th Cir. 1996) ("[Appellant would have us] hold that a challenge based on sexual orientation is also subject to *Batson*, but he has not presented us with a record appropriate for such a venture."); Commonwealth v. Smith, 879 N.E.2d 87, 95 (Mass.), *cert. denied*, 555 U.S. 893 (2008) (upholding strike of prospective juror for having "some identification issues" for presenting in a gender-nonconforming manner without reaching the constitutional question for want of a sufficient factual record); State v. Weatherall, 848 S.E.2d 338, 345 (S.C. Ct. App. 2020) (referencing the trial court's determination that "sexual orientation was not a protected class and therefore not subject to a Batson analysis," but not reviewing that conclusion of law on the merits because the appellant had not established a prima facie case of discrimination).

769 Wojcik, *supra* note 767, at 21 (quoting SmithKline Beecham Corp. v. Abbott Labs., 740 F.3d 471, 474 (9th Cir. 2014)); *see also* People v. Garcia, 92 Cal. Rptr. 2d 339, 347–48 (Cal. Ct. App. 2000) (holding that LGBTQ+ people were a "cognizable group . . . [that] cannot be discriminated against in jury selection.; *cf.* Morgan v. State,

Numerous scholars, commentators, and the American Bar Association have argued that *Batson*'s logic should apply to sexual orientation during jury selection.[770] A handful of states have enacted legislation to that effect.[771] Given the U.S. Supreme Court's decision in *Bostock* holding that the Civil Rights Act's prohibition on discrimination on the basis of sex includes sexual orientation and gender identity, it seems clear that *Batson* and *J.E.B.* should prohibit discrimination in jury selection on these bases

---

416 P.3d 212, 224 (Nev. 2018) (expanding *Batson* to sexual orientation, but determining that the petitioner had not established a prima facie case for discrimination because the prosecution had offered a convincing nondiscriminatory reason for its peremptory strike of a prospective juror who indicated his approval of media criticism of the police).

770 *See, e.g.*, Wojcik, *supra* note 767, *passim*; Lauren R. Deitrich, *Transgender and the Judiciary: An Argument to Extend* Batson *Challenges to Transgender Individuals*, 50 VAL. U. L. REV. 719 (2016); Julia C. Maddera, Note, Batson *in Transition: Prohibiting Peremptory Challenges on the Basis of Gender Identity or Expression*, 116 COLUM. L. REV. 196 (2016); Giovanna Shay, *In the Box: Voir Dire on LGBT Issues in Changing Times*, 37 HARV. J.L. & GENDER 407, 413–25 (2014); *see also* ABA House of Delegates, Resolution 108D, AM. BAR ASS'N (Feb. 5, 2018), https://www.americanbar.org/content/dam/aba/directories/policy/2018-midyear/2018-mm-108d.pdf [https://perma.cc/5S74-TUL5] ("RESOLVED, That the American Bar Association urges federal, state, local, territorial and tribal courts to extend Batson v. Kentucky, 476 U.S 79 (1986), to prohibit discrimination against jurors on the basis of sexual orientation or gender identity/expression."); *cf.* Esther J. Last, *Peremptory Challenges to Jurors Based on Sexual Orientation: Preempting Discrimination by Court Rule*, 48 IND. L. REV. 313, 314 (2014) (arguing that although extending *Batson/J.E.B.* to sexual orientation "would be an appropriate application of equal protection," the existing framework "is not workable" since, in the absence of self-disclosure, it requires proof of LGBTQ+ status in ways that may invade privacy).

771 WIS. STAT. ANN. § 756.001(3) (West 2019) ("No person who is qualified and able to serve as a juror may be excluded from that service in any court of this state on the basis of sex, race, color, sexual orientation . . . , disability, religion, national origin, marital status, family status, lawful source of income, age or ancestry or because of a physical condition."). This provision does not include gender identity/expression, but those in select other states either expressly include these characteristics, *e.g.*, (state antidiscrimination provision and applicable definitions, respectively), or have defined "sex" or "sexual orientation" to include gender identity and expression. *See, e.g.*, CAL. GOV'T CODE §§ 11135(a) & 12926(r)(2) (2019) (jury provision and applicable definitions, respectively); COLO. REV. STAT. §§ 13-71-104(3)(a) & 2-4-401(13.5) (2019) (jury provision and applicable definitions, respectively); 775 ILL. COMP. STAT. 5/1-103(O-1) (2022) (antidiscrimination law that applies to a broad range of circumstances, not just jury selection); MINN. STAT. §§ 593.32 & 363A.03(44) (2018) (jury provision and applicable definitions, respectively); OR. REV. STAT. §§ 10.030 & 174.100(7) (2017) (jury provision and applicable definitions, respectively).

since they are "inextricably bound up with sex."[772] Indeed, the Supreme Judicial Court of Massachusetts relied on that logic when it held in *Commonwealth v. Carter* that sexual orientation is a protected class for jury selection purposes.[773]

4. Harassment, Discrimination, and the First Amendment

Many states have enacted anti-discrimination laws that protect LGBTQ+ people from discrimination in housing, public accommodations, employment, and public licensure.[774] But these laws have increasingly come into conflict with the First Amendment when people or organizations claim that their religious beliefs prevent them from acting in nondiscriminatory ways.

Courts appear to be willing to allow LGBTQ+ people to maintain civil rights lawsuits claiming that they were subjected to unlawful harassment by state actors. For instance, when police threatened to arrest two men for having kissed each other in a restaurant, the Texas Court of Appeals noted that the state law against "homosexual conduct" not only failed to reach kissing, but also had been declared unconstitutional in *Lawrence*.[775] It

---

772 Bostock v. Clayton Cnty. 140 S. Ct. 1731, 1742 (2020) ("[H]omosexuality and transgender status are inextricably bound up with sex.").

773 Commonwealth v. Carter, 172 N.E.3d 367, 380 (Mass. 2021). The court in *Carter* quoted *Lawrence* in support of its reasoning that LGBTQ+ people have long-face "pernicious discrimination" that is rooted in the fact that "for centuries[,] there have been powerful voices to condemn homosexual conduct as immoral." (quoting Lawrence v. Texas, 539 U.S. 558, 571 (2003)).

774 *See, e.g.*, N.Y. EXEC. LAW § 296 (2002 & 2022 Supp.); WASH REV. CODE § 49.60.040 (2006) (updating prior version to include sexual orientation protections); *see also Nondiscrimination Laws*, MOVEMENT ADVANCEMENT PROJECT (June 13, 2023), https://www.lgbtmap.org/equality-maps/non_discrimination_laws [https://perma.cc/49R4-W6QT] (noting that thirty states and the District of Columbia offer discrimination protections to LGBTQ+ people on the basis of both sexual orientation and gender identity in housing, and twenty-seven states and the District of Columbia do the same in public accommodations); *Employment Nondiscrimination*, MOVEMENT ADVANCEMENT PROJECT (June 13, 2023), https://www.lgbtmap.org/equality-maps/employment_non_discrimination_laws [https://perma.cc/KJV4-MBPW] (noting that thirty-three states and the District of Columbia offer employment discrimination protections to LGBTQ+ people on the basis of both sexual orientation and gender identity). *But see supra* note 39 and accompanying text (noting laws that facilitate anti-LGBTQ+ discrimination).

775 De Leon v. City of El Paso, 353 S.W.3d 285, 288 (Tex. App. 2011).

therefore permitted the couple's declaratory judgment action, in which they alleged police violated their equal protection rights under the state constitution, to move forward.[776] In contrast to state-sanctioned harassment, however, courts continue to struggle with how to adjudicate discrimination claims—especially when the acts giving rise to allegations of discrimination implicate the First Amendment.

a. Creativity, Compelled Speech, and Religious Beliefs

"May a wedding photographer be required to create photographs of same-sex weddings? May a freelance writer be required to write press releases for the Church of Scientology? May a calligrapher be required to create invitations for an event promoting a white supremacist organization or the Socialist Party?"[777] Law professor Eugene Volokh asked these questions and answered them by stating that there is no black letter law yet that governs the constitutionality of what he termed "compulsions to create speech."[778] Since then, the waters have gotten muddier.

The remarkably narrow decision in *Masterpiece Cakeshop, Ltd. v. Colorado Civil Rights Commission* ruled in favor of a baker who had refused to make a wedding cake for a same-sex couple.[779] But the ruling was predicated on a rather unique set of circumstances in which a state commission investigating discrimination had expressed hostility toward religion in ways that called into question the fairness and impartiality of its determination that the baker had illegally discriminated against the couple who sought the wedding cake.[780] The Court did not reach the larger

---

776 *Id.* at 290–91. The plaintiff sought a permanent injunction directing El Paso police to refrain from using the invalidated sodomy law "to threaten, harass, or arrest anyone." *Id.* at 289. This was important because sovereign immunity would have applied to claims for damages, but not for claims of equitable relief. *Id.* at 290–91.

777 Eugene Volokh, *The Law of Compelled Speech*, 97 TEX. L. REV. 355, 382–83 (2018).

778 *Id.* at 382.

779 138 S. Ct. 1719, 1732 (2018).

780 *Id.* at 1729. The Court noted that a member of the commission said the following:

> I would also like to reiterate what we said in the hearing or the last meeting. Freedom of religion and religion has been used to justify all kinds of discrimination throughout history, whether it be slavery, whether it be the holocaust, whether it be—I mean, we—we can list hundreds of situations where freedom of religion has been used to justify discrimination. And to me

constitutional question; it merely stated that such conflicts "must be resolved with tolerance, without undue disrespect to sincere religious beliefs, and without subjecting gay persons to indignities when they seek goods and services in an open market."[781] In the wake of that decision, law professor Netta Barak-Corren surveyed 1,155 wedding vendors, including bakers, photographers, and florists.[782] She found that the case "significantly reduced the willingness of businesses to serve same-sex couples: while 63.6% were willing to serve same-sex couples before *Masterpiece Cakeshop*, only 49.2% were so willing after the decision was rendered (a 14.4 percentage-point gap, or ~23 percent decrease in favorable responses)."[783]

Prior to the *Masterpiece Cakeshop* decision, several state courts sided with "creatives"—those who use their skills to create customized or unique products—when they refused to do so on First Amendment grounds involving claims of free speech or the free exercise of religion. For instance, the Kentucky Court of Appeals ruled that a print shop did not violate a Lexington antidiscrimination ordinance when it refused to print t-shirts for an LGBTQ+ pride celebration.[784] The court acknowledged that when certain conduct serves as the basis for a denial of service in places of public accommodation, intent to discriminate against some protected class of persons may be presumed.[785] The court then cited Justice O'Connor's concurring opinion in *Lawrence* as an example illustrating that point: "A shopkeeper's refusal to serve a homosexual, not because the person is homosexual, but because the shopkeeper

---

> it is one of the most despicable pieces of rhetoric that people can use to—to use their religion to hurt others.

The Court criticized this statement as disparaging religion as something "insubstantial and even insincere." *Id.*

781 *Id.* at 1732.

782 Netta Barak-Corren, *A License to Discriminate? The Market Response to* Masterpiece Cakeshop, 56 HARV. C.R.-C.L. L. REV. 315, 319 (2021).

783 *Id.*

784 Lexington Fayette Urb. Cnty. Hum. Rts. Comm'n v. Hands on Originals, Inc., No. 2015-CA-000745-MR, 2017 WL 2211381, at *1 (Ky. Ct. App. May 12, 2017), *aff'd*, 592 S.W.3d 291 (Ky. 2019).

785 *Id.* at *6 (quoting Bray v. Alexandria Women's Health Clinic, 506 U.S. 263, 270 (1993)).

disapproves of homosexual intercourse or same-sex marriage, would be the legal equivalent of sexual orientation discrimination."[786] But without citations to any authority, the court then stated:

> [T]he "service" [the shop] offers is the promotion of *messages*. The "conduct" [the shop] chose not to promote was pure speech. There is no contention that [the shop] is a public forum in addition to a public accommodation. Nothing in the fairness ordinance prohibits [the shop], a private business, from engaging in viewpoint or message censorship. Thus, although the menu of services [the shop] provides to the public is accordingly limited, and censors certain points of view, it is the same limited menu [the shop] offers to every customer and is not, therefore, prohibited by the fairness ordinance.[787]

By contrast, other courts sided with LGBTQ+ people when they have been the victims of discrimination. Most of these cases turn on the U.S. Supreme Court's decision in *Employment Division, Department of Human Resources of Oregon v. Smith*, which held that the Free Exercise Clause "does not relieve an individual of the obligation to comply with a valid and neutral law of general applicability on the ground that the law proscribes (or prescribes) conduct that his religion prescribes (or proscribes)."[788] Under *Smith*, neutral laws of general applicability are constitutional if they are rationally related to a legitimate governmental interest,[789] but those that burden a religious practice and are neutral or generally applicable, must be narrowly tailored to advance a compelling government interest.[790] Courts applying *Smith* to laws barring discrimination in places of public accommodation have repeatedly upheld such laws as serving the legitimate, indeed compelling governmental interest in eliminating discrimination.[791]

---

786 *Id.* at *6 (citing Lawrence v. Texas, 539 U.S. 558, 583 (2003) (O'Connor, J., concurring)).

787 *Id.* at *7.

788 494 U.S. 872, 879 (1990).

789 *Id.*

790 *Id.* at 883.

791 The lower court decision in *Craig v. Masterpiece Cakeshop, Inc.* serves as a good example. 370 P.3d 272, 293–94 (Colo. App. 2015), *rev'd*, 138 S. Ct. 1719 (2018); *see also* Elane Photography, LLC v. Willock, 309 P.3d 53, 73–75 (N.M. 2013); State v.

In *Gifford v. McCarthy*, for example, the owners of a farm rented portions of it for a variety of events, including both religious and secular weddings.[792] The venue was prepared to host a wedding reception for a woman until she used a feminine pronoun to refer to her fiancé. At that point, the owner indicated there was "a problem" because they did not host same-sex marriage at their venue due to their religious beliefs.[793] The New York State Division of Human Rights subsequently determined that the venue had unlawfully discriminated on the basis of sexual orientation in violation of the state's nondiscrimination law.[794] An appellate court upheld that determination, reasoning that the venue was a place of public accommodation and thus subject to the nondiscrimination law,[795] and that the law was neutral, generally applicable, and did not target religious practices.[796] The court therefore concluded that the venue operators were "free to adhere to and profess their religious beliefs that same-sex couples should not marry, but they must permit same-sex couples to marry on the premises if they choose to allow opposite-sex couples to do so."[797] The court also rejected a free speech challenge to the antidiscrimination law as applied to the facts of the case:

> [The law] does not compel the [venue operators] to endorse, espouse or promote same-sex marriages, nor does it require them to recite or display any message at all. The[y] remain free to express whatever views they may have on the issue of same-sex marriage. The determination simply requires them to abide by the

---

Arlene's Flowers, Inc., No. 13-2-00871-5, 2015 WL 720213, *21–22 (Wash. Super. Ct. Feb. 18., 2015), *aff'd*, 389 P.3d 543 (Wash. 2017), *vacated and remanded*, 138 S. Ct. 2671 (2018), *aff'd on remand*, 441 P.3d 1203 (Wash. 2019), *cert. denied*, 141 S. Ct. 2884 (2021).

792 23 N.Y.S.3d 422, 426 (Sup. Ct. App. Div. 2016).

793 *Id.*

794 *Id.* at 426–27 (citing N.Y. EXEC. LAW § 290 (McKinney 2011).

795 *Id.* at 428.

796 *Id.* at 429–31. The court cited *Lawrence* in support of its rejection of the operators' argument that they had not discriminated on the basis of sexual orientation, but rather made a decision based on their religious beliefs against marriage equality. *Id.* at 428 ("Such attempts to distinguish between a protected status and conduct closely correlated with that status have been soundly rejected. . . . Lawrence v. Texas, 539 U.S. 558, 575 . . . (2003)").

797 *Id.* at 431.

> law and offer the same goods and services to same-sex couples that they offer to other couples. Despite the[ir] assertion that their direct participation in same-sex wedding ceremonies would "broadcast to all who pass by the Farm" their support for same-sex marriage, reasonable observers would not perceive the[ir] provision of a venue and services for a same-sex wedding ceremony as an endorsement of same-sex marriage. . . . [T]here is no real likelihood that the[y] would be perceived as endorsing the values or lifestyle of the individuals renting their facilities as opposed to merely complying with anti-discrimination laws. We thus conclude that the conduct allegedly compelled is not sufficiently expressive so as to trigger First Amendment protections.[798]

Gifford v. McCarthy was decided before the U.S. Supreme Court's decision in *Masterpiece Cakeshop*. But *Klein v. Oregon Bureau of Labor and Industries* was decided after the Court vacated a prior decision and remanded the case for reconsideration in light of *Masterpiece Cakeshop*.[799] In reaffirming its prior ruling against a baker who had refused to make a cake for a same-sex couple, the Oregon Court of Appeals stated the following about how it interpreted its obligations after *Masterpiece Cakeshop*:

> [W]e discern three principles to guide our review on remand. The first is that, in evaluating on direct review a litigant's claim that an adjudication is premised, in whole or in part, on unconstitutional hostility to religious beliefs, a reviewing court must examine the entire record of the case, including each stage of the case. The second is that, where, as here, a governmental adjudicator is called upon to determine whether a person's conduct violates a generally applicable, neutral law, and that conduct was motivated by a religious belief, the adjudicator must walk a tightwire, acting scrupulously to ensure that the adjudication targets only the unlawful conduct, and is not, in any way, the product of the adjudicator's hostility toward the belief itself. Third, and finally, because even "subtle departures" from

---

[798] *Id.* at 432.

[799] 410 P.3d 1051, 1064 (Or. Ct. App. 2017), *vacated*, 139 S. Ct. 2713 (2019) (vacating for reconsideration in light of *Masterpiece Cakeshop*), *aff'd after remand*, 506 P.3d 1108, 1113–14 (Or. Ct App.), *review denied*, 509 P.3d 119 (Or. 2022).

> neutrality violate the First Amendment, even "subtle departures" require some form of corrective action from a reviewing court.[800]

The court overturned the award of damages based on a finding that the prior administrative proceedings in the case had not been neutral toward religion as mandated by *Masterpiece Cakeshop.*[801] But it affirmed its prior holding that the bakers had violated Oregon's nondiscrimination law, which the court upheld as a "generally applicable law" under *Smith.*[802]

b. Noncreative Religious Exemptions from Antidiscrimination Laws

A year after *Masterpiece Cakeshop*, the Supreme Court decided another case on narrow grounds that pitted First Amendment rights against nondiscrimination protections for LGBTQ+ people, but that case did not involve the creation of something unique or artistic. *Fulton v. City of Philadelphia* invalidated a city contract with foster care agencies that contained a provision mandating that prospective foster parents be considered regardless of sexual orientation.[803] Catholic Social Services (CSS) challenged that provision after a determination that it violated the contract by refusing the place children with same-sex couples due to the Catholic Church's opposition to marriage equality. Although the Court sided with CSS, the rationale for doing so again sidestepped the constitutional question about how to balance First Amendment liberties against statutory provisions that advance Fourteenth Amendment equal protection rights. The Court noted that the provision was not generally applicable and neutral with respect to religion as required by *Smith*,[804]

---

800 *Klein*, 506 P.3d at 1124–25.

801 *Id.* 1122–28.

802 *Id.* at 1120–22. The court in *Klein* noted that the Oregon nondiscrimination statute did not permit the types of individual exceptions that the U.S. Supreme Court found constitutionally fatal in *Fulton v. City of Philadelphia*, 141 S. Ct. 1868, 1874–75 (2021); *see infra* note 803–806 and accompanying text. The Oregon Supreme Court declined review of the case in May of 2022. 509 P.3d 119 (Or. 2022).

803 *Fulton*, 141 S. Ct. at 1874–75.

804 494 U.S. 872, 884 (1990) ("A law is not generally applicable if it invites the government to consider the particular reasons for a person's conduct by providing a mechanism for individualized exemptions." (internal quotations, citations, and alterations omitted)).

because exceptions to the nondiscrimination provision could be granted for "good cause" as determined by the commissioner of the Department of Human Services in the commissioner's "sole discretion."[805] Despite all of the city's proffered interests in preventing discrimination in the certification of foster parents, none satisfied strict scrutiny because Philadelphia could not offer "a compelling reason why it has a particular interest in denying an exception to CSS while making them available to others."[806]

When laws apply more evenly than the one at issue in *Fulton*, courts have had to engage in careful balancing acts. In *Laguerre v. Maurice*, the plaintiff filed an action for defamation per se against the pastor of a church at which he had been formerly employed.[807] He alleged that the pastor told congregants that the plaintiff was gay and had used a church computer to view gay pornography.[808] The pastor attempted to have the suit dismissed on the grounds that the courts lacked jurisdiction to adjudicate the claim because it would require the impermissible judicial inquiry "into ecclesiastical proceedings, discipline, and church doctrine."[809] An appellate court in New York disagreed, reasoning that a defamation claim could be decided "solely upon the application of neutral principles of law, without reference to any religious principle."[810] The court went on to rule in favor of the pastor, however, finding that social attitudes toward homosexuality had changed sufficiently since the time cases had first recognized that false allegations about one's sexuality can constitute defamation per se, thereby obviating the need for proof of special damages.[811] The court cited *Lawrence* and *Obergefell* in support of its

805 *Fulton*, 141 S. Ct. at 1875.

806 *Id.* at 1882.

807 138 N.Y.S.3d 123, 126 (Sup. Ct. App. Div. 2020).

808 *Id.*

809 *Id.*

810 *Id.* at 127 (quoting *In re* Congregation Yetev Lev D'Satmar, Inc. v. Kahana, 879 N.E.2d 1282, 1285 (N.Y. 2007)).

811 *Id.* at 129 (citing Matherson v. Marchello, 473 N.Y.S.2d 998, 1005 (Sup. Ct. App. Div. 1984), *abrogated by Laguerre*, 138 N.Y.S.3d at 130–31).

reasoning that public policy dictated that false imputations of homosexuality can no longer constitute defamation per se.[812]

That same court subsequently refused to extend its holding in *Laguerre v. Maurice* to a case in which a model sued for defamation per se for the unauthorized use of her photo on an HIV educational ad.[813] The court reasoned that unlike the progress on social views of sexuality, infection with HIV still carried significant social stigma.[814]

When legal questions cannot be determined without regard to religious principles, the question of whether the First Amendment can shield an actor or entity from discrimination liability is far more complicated. Consider what transpired in *Woods v. Seattle's Union Gospel Mission* (SUGM),[815] a case involving Washington's antidiscrimination law and its specific exemption of religious and nonprofit organizations from the definition of an "employer."[816] The Supreme Court of Washington explained in *Woods* that this provision in the law "created a *statutory* right for employees to be free from discrimination in the workplace while allowing employers to retain their *constitutional* right, as constrained by state and federal case law, to choose workers who reflect the employers' beliefs when hiring ministers."[817] The case arose from developments after a gay man volunteered for a legal clinic run by SUGM, an evangelical Christian organization that served Seattle's unsheltered population.[818] When a staff position arose, he applied for it, but was denied the position because he was in a same-sex relationship with a man he hoped to

---

812 *Id.* at 130–31; *see also* Yonaty v. Mincolla, 945 N.Y.S.2d 774, 777 (Sup. Ct. App. Div. 2012).

813 Nolan v. State, 69 N.Y.S.3d 277, 279, 285 (Sup. Ct. App. Div. 2018) (differentiating imputation of HIV infection as defamation per se from the *Yonaty* court's analysis of the imputation of sexuality or the same tort classification).

814 *Id.* at 284–85.

815 481 P.3d 1060 (Wash. 2021), *cert. denied*, 142 S. Ct. 1094 (2022).

816 WASH REV. CODE § 49.60.040(11) (2020) ("'Employer' includes any person acting in the interest of an employer, directly or indirectly, who employs eight or more persons, and does not include any religious or sectarian organization not organized for private profit.").

817 *Woods*, 481 P.3d at 1062.

818 *Id.* at 1063.

marry.[819] He sued, claiming that the application of the statutory exemption for religious organizations, as applied to him, was unconstitutional "because the staff attorney job duties were 'wholly unrelated to SUGM's religious practices or activities.'"[820] He argued that the religious exemption from the state's nondiscrimination law violated a provision in the Washington State Constitution which states: "No law shall be passed granting to any citizen, class of citizens, or corporation other than municipal, privileges or immunities which upon the same terms shall not equally belong to all citizens, or corporations."[821] Specifically, he argued the exemption burdened two of his constitutional rights—his right to live his life in accordance with his sexual orientation (relying on *Lawrence*) and his right to marry (relying on *Obergefell*).[822]

Because *Woods* involved an as-applied constitutional challenge, it was unnecessary for the court to analyze the facial validity of the law. Although it may be considered dicta, the court stated that the exemption was facially valid because it served to prevent "state interference with religious freedoms."[823] The court then went on to analyze the plaintiff's as-applied challenge to the exemption. It began doing so by noting that the First Amendment, vis-à-vis what has been termed the "ministerial exception," prevents government from interfering with matters of "faith and doctrine," including internal management decisions.[824] The moniker given to that exception is misleading, as it does not only apply to those who are

---

[819] *Id.*

[820] *Id.*

[821] *Id.* at 1065 (quoting WASH. CONST. art. I, § 12).

[822] *Id.*

[823] *Id.* at 1067 (citing Ockletree v. Franciscan Health Sys., 317 P.3d 1009, 1017 (Wash. 2014) ("The United States Supreme Court has recognized that exemptions for religious organizations from civil discrimination suits protect religious freedom by avoiding state interference with religious autonomy and practice. Corp. of Presiding Bishop of Church of Jesus Christ of Latter-Day Saints v. Amos, 483 U.S. 327, 336 . . . (1987)")).

[824] *Id.* at 1068 (citing Our Lady of Guadalupe Sch. v. Morrissey-Berru, 140 S. Ct. 2049, 2060 (2020) (holding that the ministerial exception barred Catholic school teachers' claims that had alleged age and disability discrimination in employment)); *see also* Hosanna-Tabor Evangelical Lutheran Church & Sch. v. E.E.O.C., 565 U.S. 171, 190–92 (2012) (holding a teacher who had to undergo religious training to qualify the position at a religiously-affiliated school was a "minister" for the purposes of the ministerial exception).

ordained or have formal titles as ministers; rather, it turns on "what the employee does."[825] For instance, the U.S. Supreme Court previously determined that the ministerial exception applied to lay teachers at religiously-affiliated schools because they "performed vital religious duties: guiding the faith lives of their students, providing instruction on subjects that included religion, praying and attending religious services with students, and preparing students for other religious activities."[826] Whether the organization in *Woods* had acted unconstitutionally turned on whether a person in a legal staff position would trigger the ministerial exception.[827] Because such a determination had not been made by lower courts, the state high court remanded the case for a factual determination of whether a staff attorney, noting that some of the in the key indicators of that the ministerial exception would apply were present in the case, while others were not:

> [A]ll [of the organization's SUGM employees are expected to evangelize, but there is no evidence that staff attorneys had titles as ministers or training in religious matters comparable to *Hosanna-Tabor*'s teacher. And while staff attorneys are expected to share their faith with clients as opportunities arise, there is no evidence that they are expected to nurture their converts' development in the Christian faith similar to the job duties performed by the teachers in *Our Lady of Guadalupe* and *Hosanna-Tabor*. Further, neither SUGM nor [its legal clinic] is a church or religious entity principally responsible for the spiritual lives of its members. SUGM employees are expected to be active members of local churches; SUGM employment alone does not appear to be sufficient religious affiliation. Employees held to be ministers in *Our Lady of Guadalupe* and *Hosanna-Tabor* led faith groups and taught religious doctrine. The record indicates that these duties occur outside SUGM, in local churches for SUGM employees. Moreover, Woods sought employment with SUGM as a lawyer specifically, not as a religious minister or teacher, and

825 *Id.* (quoting *Our Lady of Guadalupe*, 140 S. Ct. at 2064)).

826 *Id.* at 1069 (citing *Our Lady of Guadalupe*, 140 S. Ct. at 2064–65)).

827 *Id.* at 1070.

> there is no indication that religious training is necessary for the staff attorney position, unlike the teachers in *Hosanna-Tabor*.[828]

A concurring justice opined that staff attorneys at the SUGM legal clinic were not likely ministers because they "are not charged with the responsibility of elucidating or teaching the tenets of the faith. They are first and foremost charged with providing objective legal advice that may, in fact, conflict with the employing entity's religious doctrine."[829] She went on to state that religious organizations that employ attorneys "in order to provide civil legal aid cannot control the legal advice by requiring the attorney[s] to serve as minister[s] and attorney[s] at the same time."[830] The U.S. Supreme Court denied certiorari in the case and it remains pending in the Washington state court system as of this writing.[831]

J. Miscellaneous Types of Claims ($n = 24$; 7.8%)

Of the 307 relevant cases, 282 dealt with claims that fit into one of the nine categories discussed thus far in this chapter. The remaining twenty-four cases presented issues that were either unique or comparatively rare

---

828 *Id.* (internal citations omitted).

829 *Id.* at 1073 (Yu, J., concurring).

830 *Id.* ; *see also* Barrett v. Fontbonne Acad., No. NOCV2014-751, 2015 WL 9682042, at *2 (Mass. Super. Ct. Dec. 16, 2015) (granting summary judgment to a qualified food service employee who, after a Catholic school told him he had the job, was not ultimately hired after he completing hiring paperwork listing a same-sex spouse as his emergency contact). In *Barrett*, the court reasoned that the refusal to hire the plaintiff in a food service position could not be justified under the ministerial exception:

> He has no duties as an administrator or teacher of religious matters. Fontbonne bases its case on this point exclusively upon its own statement that each of its employees is a "minister of the mission" to support its claim to this exemption. Assuming that Fontbonne meant this statement literally and not metaphorically, only Justice Thomas espoused the view that the ministerial exception applies whenever the religious organization "sincerely considered [the employee] a minister. . . ." That none of the other justices agreed with a view so clearly expressed to them strongly suggests that more is required. Indeed, to apply the "ministerial" exception here would allow all religious schools to exempt all of their employees from employment discrimination laws simply by calling their employees ministers. If that were the rule, most of the discussion in *Hosanna–Tabor* would have been unnecessary.

Id. at *11 (quoting Hosanna-Tabor Evangelical Lutheran Church & Sch. v. E.E.O.C., 565 U.S. 171, 197–98 (2012) (Thomas, J., concurring)).

831 Seattle's Union Gospel Mission v. Woods, 142 S. Ct. 1094 (2022) (denying certiorari).

(i.e., only two or three such cases compared to the higher numbers in the enumerated categories). This final section of this chapter explores some of the commonalities among these cases and Table 19 summarizes the frequencies of the variables as they manifest in these cases and their relationships to how courts applied *Lawrence*.

TABLE 19: VARIABLE FREQUENCIES AND RELATIONSHIP TO TREATMENT OF *LAWRENCE* IN MISCELLANEOUS CASES

	Treatment of *Lawrence* *n* (%)				**Chi-Square**	**Sig.**	**Cramer's V**
Type	*Neutral*	*Narrow*	*Broad*	*Total*	9.267 (2, 24)	Fisher's Exact p = 0.004	0.621
Civil	4 (16.0%)	3 (12.0%)	5 (20.0%)	12 (50.0%)			
Criminal	11 (45.8%)	1 (4.0%)	0 (0.0%)	12 (50.0%)			
Depth					8.160 (2, 24)	Fisher's Exact p = 0.032	0.583
Mentioned in Passing	15 (62.5%)	2 (8.3%)	3 (12.5%)	20 (83.3%)			
Key to Case	0 (0.0%)	2 (8.3%)	2 (8.3%)	4 (16.7%)			
Outcome					16.233 (4, 24)	Fisher's Exact p = 0.001	0.582
Prosecution	11 (45.8%)	0 (0.0%)	0 (0.0%)	11 (45.8%)			
Defense	0 (0.0%)	1 (4.2%)	0 (0.0%)	1 (4.2%)			
Not Relevant (civil)	4 (16.7%)	3 (12.5%)	5 (20.8%)	12 (50.0%)			
State Politics	*Neutral*	*Narrow*	*Broad*	*Total*	8.374 (8, 24)	p > 0.050	N/A
Deep Red	5 (20.8%)	1 (4.2%)	0 (0.0%)	6 (25.0%)			
Light Red	0 (0.0%)	0 (0.0%)	1 (4.2%)	1 (4.2%)			
Purple	1 (4.2%)	0 (0.0%)	1 (4.2%)	2 (8.3%)			
Light Blue	2 (8.3%)	0 (0.0%)	0 (0.0%)	2 (8.3%)			
Deep Blue	7 (29.2%)	3 (12.5%)	3 (12.5%)	13 (54.2%)			
Region					8.516 (6, 24)	p > 0.050	N/A
Northeast	4 (16.7%)	1 (4.2%)	3 (12.5%)	8 (33.3%)			
South	6 (25.0%)	1 (4.2%)	0 (0.0%)	7 (29.2%)			
Midwest	2 (8.3%)	0 (0.0%)	2 (8.3%)	4 (16.7%)			
West	3 (12.5%)	2 (8.3%)	0 (0.0%)	5 (20.8%)			
Judge's Sex					5.867 (4, 24)	p > 0.050	N/A
Male	10 (41.7%)	4 (16.7%)	3 (12.5%)	17 (70.8%)			
Female	5 (20.8%)	0 (0.0%)	1 (4.2%)	6 (25.0%)			
Not Applicable (per curiam)	0 (0.0%)	0 (0.0%)	1 (4.2%)	1 (4.2%)			
Judge's Race/Ethnicity					5.562 (4, 24)	p > 0.050	N/A
White	14 (58.3%)	4 (16.7%)	3 (12.5%)	21 (87.5%)			
Nonwhite	1 (4.2%)	0 (0.0%)	1 (4.2%)	2 (8.3%)			
Not Applicable or Unknown	0 (0.0%)	0 (0.0%)	1 (4.2%)	1 (4.2%)			
Judge's Political Affiliation					8.526 (6, 24)	p > 0.050	N/A
Nonpartisan	7 (29.2%)	1 (4.2%)	3 (12.5%)	11 (45.8%)			
Democrat	2 (8.3%)	2 (8.3%)	1 (4.2%)	5 (20.8%)			
Republican	6 (25.0%)	1 (4.2%)	0 (0.0%)	7 (29.2%)			
Not Applicable or Unknown	0 (0.0%)	0 (0.0%)	1 (4.2%)	4 (4.2%)			

1. Bodily Autonomy

a. Abortion

In the wake of *Dobbs* overturning substantive due process protections for abortion, the nature and scope of the rights to privacy and bodily autonomy under state constitutional law will likely become even more important than they were during the period of time in which the cases in this study were decided.[832] But even when *Roe* and *Casey* were still good law, courts were still called upon to balance the central holdings of these cases against abortion restrictions.

Planned Parenthood of the Heartland v. Reynolds, illustrates this point.[833] In *Reynolds*, the Supreme Court of Iowa invalidated a statutory provision that imposed a mandatory seventy-two hour waiting period before a woman could have an abortion in the state.[834] The court gave *Lawrence* an expansive reading as evidenced by its statement that *Lawrence* had involved the "*fundamental right* of consenting adults to engage in private, consensual conduct without government intervention."[835] The court went on to say the following:

> Autonomy and dominion over one's body go to the very heart of what it means to be free. At stake in this case is the right to shape, for oneself, without unwarranted governmental intrusion, one's own identity, destiny, and place in the world. Nothing could be more fundamental to the notion of liberty. We therefore hold, under the Iowa Constitution, that implicit in the concept of ordered liberty is the ability to decide whether to continue or terminate a pregnancy.[836]

Having determined that the waiting period infringed upon a fundamental right, the court applied strict scrutiny and concluded that the waiting

---

832 Dobbs v. Jackson Women's Health Org., 142 S. Ct. 2228, 2242 (2022).

833 915 N.W.2d 206, 237 (Iowa 2018), *overruled by* Planned Parenthood of the Heartland, Inc. v. Reynolds, 975 N.W.2d 710 (Iowa 2022) (holding that the Iowa constitutional guarantees of due process and equal protection do not encompass the decision to have an abortion as a fundamental right).

834 *Id.* at 237.

835 *Id.* at 235 (citing Lawrence v. Texas, 539 U.S. 558, 578 (2003) (emphasis added)).

836 *Id.* at 237.

period did not further any compelling state interest because empirical data demonstrated that it did not cause "a measurable number of women" to change their minds and "continue a pregnancy they otherwise would have terminated without the mandatory delay."[837] Perhaps as a harbinger of *Dobbs*, the Iowa Supreme Court retreated from the holding in this case in 2022.[838] Notably, only a dissenting opinion discussed *Lawrence*; the majority decision did not even cite the case.[839]

b. Assisted Suicide

In *Morris v. Brandenburg*, the New Mexico Court of Appeals held that the state constitution conferred no due process rights to assisted suicide on individuals or their health care providers.[840] The decision drew heavily from the U.S. Supreme Court's decision in *Washington v. Glucksberg*, which held that physician-assisted suicide implicates no liberty interests protected by the Fourteenth Amendment.[841] The court narrowly construed *Lawrence* as applying to "sexual relationships" and not to supporting "the position that 'death' or 'aid in dying' . . . have either been recognized as embedded principles within our democratic society or as a modern interpretation of certain fundamental interests that have been applied to some members of society but historically denied to others."[842]

The highest court in New York similarly neglected *Lawrence* when it held that neither due process nor equal protection implicate any right to

---

[837] *Id.* at 243. The court also held that the waiting period violated women's state constitutional guarantee of equal protection. *Id.* at 245–46.

[838] *Reynolds*, 975 N.W.2d at 742.

[839] *Reynolds*, 975 N.W.2d at 776–77, 794–95 (Appel, J., dissenting) (arguing that *Lawrence* "compels" the rejection of any "fundamental rights" analysis that relies on an "18th century mentality"). At least five U.S. Supreme Court Justices seemingly disagree with that interpretation of *Lawrence* as evidenced by their embrace of such a narrow "fundamental rights" analysis using originalist jurisprudence in *Dobbs*. Dobbs v. Jackson Women's Health Org., 142 S. Ct. 2228, 2244–45 (2022) ("Constitutional analysis must begin with 'the language of the instrument,' . . . which offers a 'fixed standard' for ascertaining what our founding document means . . . ." (quoting Gibbons v. Ogden, 22 U.S. (9 Wheat.) 1, 186–89 (1824); 1 J. STORY, COMMENTARIES ON THE CONSTITUTION OF THE UNITED STATES § 399, p. 383 (1833))).

[840] 356 P.3d 564 (N.M. Ct. App. 2015).

[841] 521 U.S. 702, 728, 735 (1997).

[842] *Morris*, 356 P.3d at 578.

assisted suicide.[843] In a concurring opinion, Judge Jenny Rivera agreed with the majority that the New York State Constitution does not confer any "unrestricted state constitutional right to physician-prescribed medications that hasten death."[844] But she went on to conclude that terminally-ill people nearing death possess both due process and equal protection rights "to physician-prescribed medication that allows the patient in the last painful stage of life to achieve a peaceful death as the end draws near."[845] Judge Rivera cited *Lawrence* in support of her reasoning that people's "interests in autonomy and freedom are not less substantial when facing the choice of how to bear the suffering and physical pain of a terminal illness at the end of life" than they are when making decisions "about life's most private matters—e.g. sexuality, marriage, procreation, and child-rearing—all choices that reflect personal beliefs and desires."[846]

c. Breaches of Bodily Integrity

A prison inmate prison system filed a civil action to enjoin the state force-feeding him. He argued that the Washington Department of Correction's policy to force the administration of food and fluids via a nasogastric tube violated rights to privacy and bodily autonomy.[847] Although the Washington Supreme Court recognized these interests persisted in the correctional environment, it reasoned that the rights that normally would protect a competent person from refusing artificial nutrition and hydration were outweighed by four compelling state interests, including "the maintenance of security and orderly administration within the prison system," "the preservation of life," "the protection of innocent third parties," and "the maintenance of the ethical integrity of the medical profession."[848]

843 Myers v. Schneiderman, 85 N.E.3d 57, 62–63 (N.Y. 2017).

844 *Id.* at 66 (Rivera, J., concurring).

845 *Id.*

846 *Id.* at 71.

847 McNabb v. Dep't of Corr., 180 P.3d 1257, 1259 (Wash. 2008).

848 *Id.* at 1265 (emphasis in original).

Justice Richard B. Sanders, the lone dissenter in the case, took issue with the majority's framing of the issues in the case:

> The lead opinion incorrectly frames the privacy interest at stake as the right to suicide. This case is no more about the right to suicide than *Lawrence v. Texas* . . . was about the right to sodomy. Rather, this case is about "the most comprehensive of rights and the right most valued by civilized men," namely, "the right to be let alone . . . ." Once incorrectly framed, the lead opinion and concurrence easily strike down its "straw man" because our prior case law, based on federal precedent, limits the right to die to terminally ill patients only.
>
> Nowhere does [plaintiff] state a wish to commit suicide. His "only wish is for [his] personal decision not to eat to be respected and to be left in peace for [his] fast to take its course . . . ." In other words, he wishes "to be let alone . . . ."
>
> Furthermore, the right of terminally ill patients to refuse food and water under the federal constitution does not answer the question of whether [plaintiff] may live free from the State's invasion of his body under our state constitution. Our guarantee of privacy is not found in the unstated "penumbra" of federal rights but is explicit in our state constitution: "[n]o person shall be disturbed in his private affairs . . . without authority of law."[849]

Justice Sanders went on to opine that the right to privacy under the state constitution could not be infringed "even for a compelling reason" absent "authority of law," primarily because privacy is "antimajoritarian" and, therefore, not subject to balancing against the will or interests of a majoritarian government.[850] Notably, no other justice indicated agreed with his reasoning as evidenced by the fact that none joined his dissent.

Given Justice Sanders' expansive view of the primacy of the rights to privacy and bodily autonomy, one might wonder how he would have ruled on the constitutionality of vaccine mandates. Once vaccinations were available to ameliorate the COVID-19 pandemic, many public and private employers mandated them for all of their employees, just as the City of New York did for its teachers and public school employees and

---

[849] *Id.* at 1268–69 (citing WASH. CONST. art. I, § 7; other internal citations omitted).

[850] *Id.* at 1270.

contractors.[851] Some of those employees turned to the courts to enjoin the mandate, arguing that it violated their "substantive due process rights by threatening their personal autonomy, bodily integrity and right to reject medical treatment."[852] Specifically, these employees argued that the line of privacy cases summarized in Chapter 2, Sections C–E, including *Lawrence*, changed the landscape of due process rights since the U.S. Supreme Court had uphold mandatory smallpox vaccinations in the landmark 1905 case of *Jacobson v. Commonwealth of Massachusetts.*[853] The court dismissed this argument by saying that those cases were "not germane to the issues here" since they dealt primarily with issues of contraception, procreation, marriage, and intimate relations, whereas "the case before this Court addresses the sole issue of whether vaccination may be compelled as a condition of employment."[854] The court went on to uphold the vaccinate mandate, reasoning that although due process implicated some limited liberty rights to pursue one's chosen field, it did not create a right to any "specific job" since employment in certain fields could be constitutionally subject to reasonable governmental regulations.[855]

2. Informational Privacy

In 2009, U.S. Circuit Judge Alex Kozinski rhetorically asked, "Is there a constitutional right to informational privacy?"[856] He then noted that the U.S. Supreme Court had hinted there may be such a right in its 1977 decision in *Whalen v. Roe* when the Court alluded to "the individual interest in avoiding disclosure of personal matters," but subsequently had "never said another word about it."[857] Since Kozinski offered that

---

851 New York City Mun. Lab. Comm. v. City of New York, 156 N.Y.S.3d 681, 684 (Sup. Ct. 2021).

852 *Id.* at 685.

853 *Id.* at 686 (citing 197 U.S. 11, 27–33 (1905)).

854 *Id.*

855 *Id.* at 687.

856 Nelson v. Nat'l Aeronautics & Space Admin., 568 F.3d 1028, 1052 (9th Cir. 2009) (Kozinski, C.J., dissenting from denial of rehearing en banc), *rev'd*, 562 U.S. 134 (2011).

857 *Id.* (quoting Whalen v. Roe, 429 U.S. 589, 599 (1977)).

observation, the U.S. Supreme Court assumed that there is such a right, but it only did so for sake of argument because the Court found it unnecessary to reach the constitutional question to resolve the particular dispute.[858] Still, nearly every circuit in the federal appellate system has determined that there is such a right.[859] Most circuits require a balancing of interests that include weighing:

> [T]he type of record requested, the information it does or might contain, the potential for harm in any subsequent nonconsensual disclosure, the injury from disclosure to the relationship in which the record was generated, the adequacy of safeguards to prevent unauthorized disclosure, the degree of need for access, and whether there is an express statutory mandate, articulated public policy, or other recognizable interest militating toward access.[860]

Until the U.S. Supreme Court squarely addresses whether the constitution protects the right "to control the acquisition or dissemination of information about [oneself],"[861] courts strive to contour the scope of privacy protections under "a patchwork of common law, statutes, and constitutional protections."[862]

Planned Parenthood of Indiana v. Carter illustrates an informational privacy claim within the context of health records.[863] Indiana law requires health care providers to report child sexual abuse.[864] The state sought

---

858 Nat'l Aeronautics & Space Admin. v. Nelson, 562 U.S. 134, 151–52 (2011).

859 Helen L. Gilbert, *Minors' Constitutional Right to Informational Privacy*, 74 U. CHI. L. REV. 1375, 1378 (2007).

860 Russell T. Gorkin, Comment, *The Constitutional Right to Informational Privacy:* NASA v. Nelson, 6 DUKE J. CONST. L. & PUB. POL'Y SIDEBAR 1, 8 (2010) (quoting United States v. Westinghouse Elec. Corp., 638 F.2d 570, 578 (3d Cir. 1980)).

861 Nina A. Kohn, *Outliving Civil Rights*, 86 WASH U. L. REV. 1053, 1067–68 (2009); *see also* Larry J. Pittman, *The Elusive Constitutional Right to Informational Privacy*, 19 NEV. L.J. 135, 141 (2018) (positing that the "liberty interest component of the Fourteenth Amendment provides support for a constitutional right to informational privacy" that is "consistent with the Court's substantive due process precedent, as articulated in *Washington v. Glucksberg*, *Lawrence v. Texas*, and *Obergefell v. Hodges*" (internal citations omitted)).

862 Laura Ruppalt, *The Impact of Silver Alerts on an Older Adult's Right to Informational Privacy*, 27 GEO. MASON L. REV. 651, 666 (2020).

863 Planned Parenthood of Ind. v. Carter, 854 N.E.2d 853, 883 (Ind. Ct. App. 2006).

864 IND. CODE § 31-33-5-1 (1997).

access to minors' medical records at a reproductive services clinic as part of an investigation that the clinic had failed to report abuse pursuant to that law.[865] The clinic sought a preliminary injunction barring the state from accessing the minors' health records on the grounds that, among other theories, they are constitutionally-protected, private medical records.[866] An intermediate appellate court agreed.[867] In their opinion, the majority relied heavily on a dissenting opinion from a Tenth Circuit case, that interpreted a Kansas law, which stated "states cannot extinguish federal privacy rights simply by criminalizing certain behavior."[868] The court concluded that "a minor consulting with a health care professional in an effort to seek treatment for a reproductive health condition related to sexual activity has a legitimate expectation of privacy as to that information."[869] The court noted, however, that such a right to information privacy is not unlimited, but rather must be balanced against the interest of the state in investigating claims of child abuse, patient neglect, medical fraud, and the like. Given the possibility of unauthorized disclosure of such private information during investigations and any potential subsequent judicial proceedings, the court decided that the state needed to use less intrusive means than unlimited access to patients' medical records to investigate such claims.[870]

Claims concerning informational privacy also commonly arise with regard to employment records as illustrated by cases pitting law enforcement officers' claims of informational privacy against public policies designed to keep policing activities transparent. A comparison of two cases illustrates the factors that might be decisive in such cases.

The New Jersey State Police (NJSP) began disciplinary proceedings against seven state troopers who were involved in a group sexual

---

865 *Carter*, 854 N.E.2d at 856.

866 *Id.* at 857.

867 *Id.* at 883.

868 *Id.* at 874–78 (quoting Aid for Women v. Foulston, 441 F.3d 1101, 1123 (10th Cir. 2006) (Herrera, J., dissenting) (citing, *inter alia*, Lawrence v. Texas, 539 U.S. 558, 578 . . . (2003)).

869 *Id.* at 878.

870 *Id.* at 883.

encounter with a woman.[871] The event came to light after the woman sought treatment in a hospital following the incident. "She acknowledged that some of the activity was consensual; she equivocated whether all of it was consensual."[872] After an investigation, prosecutors declined to seek charges from a grand jury—a move an appellate court subsequently commented upon after reviewing relevant discovery documents by saying that "much of the information provided by the alleged victim about the location and circumstances of the events was roundly discredited" which, in turn, raised "very substantial doubt that any fact-finder [would] find that some or all of the activities were without the consent of the woman."[873] Given this determination, the court sided with the troopers who sought to keep their names private during the pendency of the disciplinary proceedings against them. In coming to this conclusion, the court first cited a number of the foundational privacy cases discussed in Chapter 2 to support the premise that some matters "fall within a zone of privacy which bars inquiry by the government or an employer."[874] Still, the court recognized that public employers like the NJSP have a bona-fide interest in investigating certain aspects of troopers' personal lives, especially when sexual activities might impact their job performance.[875] But something more than perceived immorality must support the investigation since moral disapproval, without more, "cannot form the basis of discipline when [sexual] activity occurs off-duty in a private place among consenting adults."[876] Thus, if evidence at the disciplinary hearing established that the events in question were consensual, "the factual predicate for the charges dissipates."[877] Yet, if their identities were publicly disclosed before such a determination, their reputations and family relationships could be irreparably damaged. Accordingly, the court ruled that the privacy interests of the individual troopers needed to prevail, at least until a fact-

---

871 *In re* Seven State Troopers, No. A-2833-09T2, 2010 WL 668718, at *1 (N.J. Super. Ct. App. Div. Feb. 25, 2010).

872 *Id.*

873 *Id.* at *5.

874 *Id.* at *3.

875 *Id.*

876 *Id.* (citing Lawrence v. Texas, 539 U.S. 558, 566 (2003)).

877 *Id.* at *5.

finder determined there was some basis for the charges "after a full evidentiary hearing."[878]

Without the arguably unique facts present in *Seven State Troopers*, law enforcement personnel likely cannot shield their identities and information about alleged misconduct from the public by arguing a right to informational privacy under the Fourteenth Amendment. Consider what occurred in *Burton v. York County Sheriff's Department*.[879] In that case, a newspaper filed Freedom of Information Act (FOIA) requests to obtain information about why four deputy sheriffs had been suspended without pay for "conduct unbecoming an officer" after a citizen tipped-off a reporter that the suspensions had been prompted by official misconduct, included "falsification of investigative reports, possession of stolen property, abuse of authority, and sexual activity in patrol cars."[880] The sheriff's department asserted that the information was exempt from FOIA disclosure because it would engender a "unreasonable invasion of personal privacy."[881] After the newspaper sued, a trial court conducted an *in camera* review of the records and determined that the FOIA requests were valid and needed to be honored, with the exception of certain allegations against a deputy involving off-duty sexual activities.[882] On appeal initiated by the sheriff's department, the court largely affirmed the trial court's determination:

> In the present case, we find the manner in which the employees of the Sheriff's Department prosecute their duties to be a large and vital public interest that outweighs their desire to remain out of the public eye. The newspaper, in fulfilling its obligation to report on and hold to account those in public service, had a legitimate need to access the records . . . requested.
>
> By raising . . . constitutional [privacy] argument[s], the Sheriff's Department urges this Court to add another category of protection to the privacy rights the Supreme Court has found under the Fourteenth Amendment: the right of an individual's performance

878 *Id.*

879 594 S.E.2d 888 (S.C. Ct. App. 2004).

880 *Id.* at 891.

881 *Id.*

882 *Id.*

> of his public duties to be free from public scrutiny. We find this would be ill-advised. Unless and until the Supreme Court rules otherwise, we will follow its precedent and not expand the "right of privacy" under the Fourteenth Amendment beyond those situations which the Court has ruled bear on the most intimate decisions affecting personal autonomy—namely reproductive rights, familial and marital relations.[883]

As the description of the *Seven State Troopers* case indicates, the troopers' attempt to shield their identities was grounded in the fact that they engaged in sexual activities that a court determined were very likely protected by *Lawrence* and, therefore, could not be used to discipline the off-duty troopers. Private information about off-duty sexual behavior was similarly shielded in *Burton*, while other aspects of official misconduct—including allegations of sexual activity in patrols cars—was not. In *Cortez v. Johnston*, however, the claim of informational privacy was well beyond the scope of any protection that a plain reading of *Lawrence* offers.

In *Cortez*, a Texas judge filed a defamation lawsuit against his former attorney.[884] He sought to avoid disclosure of certain court records which had been filed in response to discovery requests. In his efforts to have the records sealed, he argued that *Lawrence* should protect those documents—a move the Texas Court of Appeals characterized as seeking "to place the documents within the outer fringes of *Lawrence* [by] suggesting that the landmark decision will logically and necessarily extend farther than its facts into information about other types of relationships."[885] It is no surprise he tried hard to keep those records secret, as they included allegations "that he used cocaine, paid for sex, choked a woman who accused him of fathering her son, and sexually assaulted a little girl."[886] Although the court did not disclose the nature of these allegations, it

---

883 *Id.* at 895–96.

884 No. 06-13-00120-CV, 2014 WL 1513306, at *1 (Tex. App. Apr. 16, 2014).

885 *Id.* at *5.

886 *Files Detail Allegations That Dallas Judge Used Coke, Bought Sex, Raped Young Girl*, DALL. MORNING NEWS (Apr. 17, 2014, 12:01 AM), https://www.dallasnews.com/news/investigations/2014/04/17/files-detail-allegations-that-dallas-judge-used-coke-bought-sex-raped-young-girl/ [https://perma.cc/XM6J-YMGH].

acknowledged that the records were "embarrassing and offensive."[887] But because Cortez was a public figure, and because his own actions triggered the situation in which he found himself— namely that he "claimed to be defamed, filed suit, demanded proof, and then, when responsive evidence was filed, dismissed his suit and demanded that the evidence be sealed— the court ultimately refused his request to seal the records.[888]

3. *Lawrence* and Criminal Offenses Other than Sex Crimes

As explored in Section D of this Chapter, defendants sometimes tried to use *Lawrence* to escape criminal liability for their violence against intimate partners. As previously explained, such cases did not raise genuine issues about the nature and scope of consent to sexual violence, but rather presented spurious claims of consensual BDSM activities in desperate attempts to explain injuries defendants had inflicted on their intimate partners.[889] Some defendants similarly attempted to use *Lawrence* as a constitutional shield in cases involving other crimes—namely those that did not involve any sexual component, while others attempted to use *Lawrence* to challenge judicial orders or procedures in criminal cases not involving sexually-based offenses.

a. Arguments that *Lawrence* Invalidates the Constitutionality of Other Crimes or Their Punishments

The defendant in *State v. Theeler* was convicted of physically assaulting his girlfriend under a domestic violence statute that, at the time of the incident, limited its application to "persons who have been or are currently in a dating or ongoing intimate relationship with a person of the opposite sex."[890] Relying, in part, on *Lawrence* and *Obergefell*, he argued

---

887 *Cortez*, 2014 WL 1513306, at *5.

888 *Id.*

889 *See supra* notes 417–432 and accompanying text.

890 385 P.3d 551, 552 (Mont. 2016) (citing MONT. CODE ANN. § 45–5–206(2)(b) (2011)). That statute has since been twice amended such that it currently applies to "spouses, former spouses, persons who have a child in common, and persons who have been or

the statute violated the constitutional guarantee of equal protection because it treated same-sex and opposite-sex partners differently.[891] The court agreed with him, reasoning that "the statute expose[d] him to greater punishment than a same-sex abuser would face if charged with simple assault" and that it "facially discriminate[d] against similarly-situated classes without justification."[892] But the court disagreed with the defendant that his conviction had to be reversed. Rather, the Supreme Court of Montana invoked the severability clause in the statute and excised the phrase "with a person of the opposite sex," thereby leaving the crux of the statute and the defendant's conviction in-tact.[893]

Theeler, at least, involved a classification on the basis of sexual orientation that implicated *Lawrence*. It therefore stands in contrast to the defendant's attempt to escape criminal liability for fraud in *State v. Garcia*, which had nothing to do with the line of substantive process cases to which *Lawrence* belongs. In *Garcia*, a fifty-two-year-old teacher duped an eighty-four-year-old widower with Parkinson's disease "into believing that she was his loving partner and thereby gained access to his bank accounts and depleted over $50,000."[894] She challenged her conviction, arguing that "false statements regarding romantic interests and affections" could not underpin fraud charges because they concern "both the right to free speech protected by the First Amendment and the due process right to privacy relating to marriage and familial relationships under the Fourteenth Amendment."[895] Her "undeveloped" brief relied on *United States v. Alvarez* for the first of these constitutional claims and on *Lawrence* for the second.[896] The court criticized the defendant for failing

---

are currently in a dating or ongoing intimate relationship." MONT. CODE ANN. § 45–5–206(2)(b) (2017 & 2022 Supp.)).

891 *Id.* at 553.

892 *Id.*

893 *Id.* at 554.

894 State v. Garcia, No. 33,249, 2017 WL 1372808, at *1 (N.M. Ct. App. Mar. 28, 2017).

895 *Id.* at *4.

896 *Id.* at *4 n.2 (citing *Lawrence* and United States v. Alvarez, 567 U.S. 709, 724–29 (2012) (invalidating the Stolen Valor Act as a content-based restriction on free speech, thereby overturning the defendant's conviction for falsely stating he had been awarded the Congressional Medal of Honor)).

to "adequately explain how these cases [were] applicable to her case," noting "merely providing a summary that describes the rights protected under *Alvarez* and *Lawrence*" was insufficient to allow the court to determine how those cases affected the validity of the defendant's fraud conviction.[897] Given the facts of the case, it is difficult to imagine how such arguments could have been persuasively developed.[898]

Courts similarly rejected arguments that *Lawrence* should be interpreted as creating any right to the "use, possession, manufacture, or delivery of marijuana"; to drive under the influence, to serve alcohol to minors; to carry a concealed weapon; to engage in disorderly conduct; or to cause fatal injuries to a baby while trying to give birth to it via a self-delivery process.[899] And one court dismissed an argument that *Lawrence*'s

---

897 *Id.*

898 *See also* Turner v. State, No. 10-06-00055-CR, 2007 WL 475420, at *2 n.2 (Tex. App. Feb. 14, 2007) (noting that the defendant cited *Lawrence* in his attempt to escape criminal liability for theft, but not engaging in any analysis of the claim).

899 Commonwealth v. Elansari, No. 2235 MDA 2015, 2016 WL 6092949, at *2 (Pa. Super. Ct. Oct. 18, 2016).

> The substantive rights recognized under United States Supreme Court jurisprudence all bear some relation to a person's right to autonomy or the right to privacy . . . . However, the right asserted by Appellant falls outside the scope of currently recognized substantive rights. Although the use and possession of marijuana certainly is a personal decision, it is not such an "intimate choice" as to affect one's "individual dignity . . . ." At its best, marijuana's palliative qualities may ease the anguish associated with serious medical conditions. In its most common usage, it is merely a recreational activity. This is not the sort of conduct that we consider so essential to our concept of ordered liberty that "neither liberty nor justice would exist" if its use were prohibited entirely.

Id. (internal citations omitted); State v. Beecraft, No. 2006AP982–CR, 2006 WL 3842171, at *2 (Wis. Ct. App. Dec. 28, 2006) ("[Defendant] has provided no legal authority for treating, for purposes of the liberty interest protected by the Fifth and Fourteenth Amendment, marijuana use in one's home the same as adult-consenting sexual conduct in one's home."); *see also* State v. Russell, 890 A.2d 453, 463 (R.I. 2006) (stating that none of the leading privacy cases were "remotely . . . relevant" to the issue of whether one can be lawfully convicted of disorderly conduct for having thrown furniture out the window in one's home during a fit of rage); Florance v. State, No. 05-08-00707-CR, 2009 WL 1267350, at *7 (Tex. App. May 8, 2009) (rejecting claim the right to privacy as interpreted in *Lawrence* prevented the state from criminalizing a serving alcohol to a minor in the home of someone who is not the parent, guardian, or spouse of the minor); State v. Cicione, No. 1307019559, 2014 WL 4656426, at *3 (Del. Super. Ct. Sept. 16, 2014) (noting there were no protected liberty interests in a claimed right to drive or claimed right to use drugs); State v. Griffin, No.

citation to international law when invaliding sodomy laws somehow rendered the death penalty for capital murder constitutionally invalid under the Eighth Amendment because capital punishment is disfavored among other democratic nations.[900]

b. Criminal Procedure Arguments Invoking *Lawrence*

Prosecutors charged the defendant in *Ex parte Bleimeyer* with injuring a child and endangering a child for allegedly having starved her five-year-old.[901] One of the conditions of her pretrial release was that she needed to let the court know if she became pregnant. She challenged that condition, arguing that it interfered with her Fourteenth Amendment rights during the first trimester of any prospective pregnancy. The court rejected that contention because the condition required only notification to the court, but did not otherwise interfere with her rights to make decisions about such a pregnancy.[902] Additionally, the condition constituted a reasonable restriction on any privacy rights because it would place the court "in a better position to protect that child, a member of the community, from the moment of its birth."[903]

The connection to *Lawrence* was even more attenuated in *State v. Aalim*, a case in which the defendant had been charged with aggravated robbery with a firearm.[904] Because he was sixteen-years-old at the time of the offense, he was charged in juvenile court, but the case was transferred to adult criminal court where he was sentenced to four years in prison

---

1004021962, 2011 WL 2083893, at *8 n.64 (Del. Super. Ct. May 16, 2011) (concluding that, unlike the sodomy law invalidate din *Lawrence*, Delaware's prohibition of carrying a concealed weapon even in one's own home furthered a legitimate, if not "weighty," governmental interest in protecting police officer safety); Commonwealth v. Pugh, No. CR2007-1323, 2009 WL 890988, at *1 (Mass. Super. Ct. Jan. 26, 2009) ("[T]there is no claim in this case that principles of substantive due process under either state or federal law forbid the Commonwealth from prosecuting a woman for inflicting fatal injuries on a viable and near full term fetus during the birthing process."), *rev'd on other grounds*, 969 N.E.2d 672 (Mass. 2012).

900 Newton v. State, 78 So. 3d 458, 475 (Ala. Crim. App. 2009).

901 *Ex parte* Bleimeyer, No. 01-16-00838-CR, 2017 WL 586509, at *1 (Tex. App. Feb. 14, 2017).

902 *Id.* at *2.

903 *Id.*

904 83 N.E.3d 883, 887 (Ohio 2017).

pursuant to the terms of a plea agreement after the court denied his motion to dismiss in which he had challenged the constitutionality of mandatory transfers from juvenile court.[905] He appealed, arguing that the statutorily mandated transfer of juveniles charged with armed robberies violated both due process and equal protection.[906] The Ohio Supreme Court dispensed with the former claim because both the federal and state constitutional guarantees of due process had been adopted prior to the creation of the juvenile court system; those provisions, therefore, could not "have created a substantive right to a specific juvenile-court proceeding."[907] A dissenting justice, however, noted that the U.S. Supreme Court had sometimes refused to rely on history and tradition when determining the scope of substantive due process rights.[908] The majority agreed, but noted that such departures were limited to cases presenting privacy or liberty claims as they related to marriage, family, procreation, bodily integrity, and private sexual intimacy between consenting adults.[909] The court then upheld the mandatory transfer over the defendant's equal protection claim, reasoning it was "rationally related to the legitimate governmental purpose of increased punishments for serious juvenile offenders."[910]

4. Substantive Due Process in the Civil Context

Finally, a party in a handful of civil cases asserted claims largely unrelated to *Lawrence*, but nonetheless relied on the case despite its ostensible inapplicability. One of these cases tangentially involved sexual privacy,[911] while the others did not.

In *Doe v. Moe*, the plaintiff filed a personal injury case against a female sex partner because his penis was fractured when she changed

---

905 *Id.* at 888.

906 *Id.* at 888–89.

907 *Id.* at 891 ("Therefore, an amenability hearing [in juvenile court] cannot be 'deeply rooted in this Nation's history and tradition' and 'implicit in the concept of ordered liberty." (internal citations omitted)).

908 *Id.* at 916 (O'Neill, J., dissenting).

909 *Id.* at 891 ("Importantly, the [C]ourt has been far more skeptical of creating new rights based on substantive due process in criminal-procedure cases.").

910 *Id.* at 896.

911 Doe v. Moe, 827 N.E.2d 240 (Mass. App. Ct. 2005).

positions during consensual sexual activity with him.[912] A trial court granted summary judgment to the defendant on a theory that when such an injury occurred during constitutionally protected sexual activity, liability could not attach for mere civil negligence, but rather that recklessness needed to be proven.[913] On appeal, the court cited the leading substantive due process cases, including *Lawrence*, in support of the proposition that contemporary jurisprudence shied away "from governmental regulation of consensual sexual conduct."[914] It affirmed the trial court's determination, saying the following:

> While it is inappropriate and unworkable to hold consenting adults to a standard of reasonable care in the conduct of private consensual sexual behavior, we conclude that it is appropriate that they be held to a standard that requires them not to engage in wanton or reckless conduct toward each other during such consensual sexual conduct. The words "wanton" and "reckless" are not merely rhetorical or vituperative expressions used instead of negligent or grossly negligent. They express a difference in the degree of risk and in the voluntary taking of risk so marked, as compared with negligence, as to amount substantially and in the eyes of the law to a difference in kind . . . . Since the essence of wanton or reckless conduct is intentional conduct which involves a high degree of likelihood that substantial harm will result to another . . . , we believe that a fact finder is capable of recognizing such extreme conduct, impartially and without prejudice, even in the context of consensual sexual behavior.[915]

There were no sexual privacy issues in other cases that raised civil claims that did not fit well in the other categories of cases. In *City of Seattle v. Long*, a man who owned a truck and lived in it filed a lawsuit against the city for having towed the vehicle when it was illegally parked.[916] He argued that because he lived in the truck, the impoundment violated his substantive due process rights because it deprived him of shelter and

---

[912] *Id.* at 243.

[913] *Id.*

[914] *Id.* at 245 n.5.

[915] *Id.* at 245 (internal quotations and citations omitted).

[916] City of Seattle v. Long, 467 P.3d 979, 991 (Wash. Ct. App. 2020), *aff'd in part, rev'd in part*, 493 P.3d 94 (Wash. 2021).

exposed him to inclement weather.[917] Specifically, he relied on *Lawrence* and *Foucha v. Louisiana* to argue that the state-created danger doctrine should provide him with relief from civil enforcement of the parking violation.[918] That doctrine provides a narrow exception to the usual rule in 42 U.S.C. § 1983 actions that due process does not guarantee minimum levels of safety and security.[919] But when "state action creates or exposes [people] to a danger which they would not have otherwise faced," some courts allow plaintiffs to hold states liable.[920] The court rejected the plaintiffs attempt to use *Lawrence* and *Foucha* in this manner, simply saying that neither case "addresses the state-created danger doctrine or suggests that [courts] should expand a narrow exception for liability to serve as a way to pursue relief in civil enforcement actions. As a result, we determine [plaintiff] cannot raise the state-created danger doctrine to seek relief from impoundment."[921]

Perhaps no case in the study better captured judicial hostility to substantive due process than *Price v. New York City Board of Education*.[922] In that case, parents of public-school children filed a declaratory judgement action seeking to invalidate a ban on public school students possessing pagers and cell phones while in school without special permission. They argued that although the city could restrict the use of such equipment on school premises, the prohibition on the mere possession of cell phones violated due process.[923] A Manhattan judge, Lewis Bart Stone, upheld the rules, finding there were rational bases for keeping cell phones out of public schools, including burdening teachers with enforcement (rather than security personnel screening children upon

---

917 *Id.* at 991.

918 *Id.* at 991–92 (citing, *inter alia*, Lawrence v. Texas, 539 U.S. 558, 578–79 (2003); Foucha v. Louisiana, 504 U.S. 71, 80 (1992)).

919 *Id.* at 991 (citing DeShaney v. Winnebago Cnty. Dep't of Soc. Servs., 489 U.S. 189, 195 (1989)).

920 *Id.* at 992 (quoting Henry A. v. Willden, 678 F.3d 991, 1002 (9th Cir. 2012) (internal alterations omitted)).

921 *Id.*

922 837 N.Y.S.2d 507 (Sup. Ct. 2007), *abrogated by* 855 N.Y.S.2d 530 (Sup. Ct. App. Div. 2008).

923 *Id.* at 511.

entry to schools) and preventing children "whose self-control may not be perfectly formed" from being distracted by the temptation to use their phones.[924] When he addressed the plaintiffs' constitutional arguments, he expressed the same type of hostility to the notion of substantive due process that conservative U.S. Supreme Court Justices Scalia and Thomas had previously expressed:[925]

> There is nothing presently more controversial in the body politic of this country and State than attempts by competing advocates to enlist courts to address issues of sex which they are unable to resolve through the usual political process. Cases . . . which have grasped this judicial "third rail" include *Griswold v. Connecticut* . . . (contraceptives), *Roe v. Wade* . . . (abortion), *Lawrence v. Texas* . . . (sodomy), and [the N.Y. state case of] *Hernandez v. Robles* . . . (same sex marriage). The intense and *sui generis* nature of these controversies rarely commends the principles enunciated in such decisions as precedent to be expanded to unrelated matters.[926]

With that preface, Stone (who had been a real estate lawyer before being a judge and who resigned from the bench while facing an ethics complaint)[927] boldly declared that the doctrine of substantive due process "no longer exists as a principle of [f]ederal constitutional law."[928] He went

---

924 *Id.* at 519.

925 In *McDonald v. City of Chicago*, for instance, Justices Scalia and Thomas both expressed their doubts about substantive due process as a viable legal theory. 561 U.S. 742, 791 (2010) (Scalia, J., concurring) (reiterating his "misgivings" about substantive due process"); *id.* at 812 (Thomas, J., concurring in part and concurring in judgment) (stating that "any serious argument over the scope of the Due Process Clause must acknowledge that neither its text nor its history suggests that it protects the many substantive rights this Court's cases now claim it does"). Justice Thomas would go on to repeat this mantra when, in his concurring opinion in *Dobbs*, he called for the Court to "reconsider all of [its] substantive due process precedents, including *Griswold, Lawrence*, and *Obergefell*." Dobbs, v. Jackson Women's Health Org., 142 S. Ct. 2228, 2301 (2022) (Thomas, J., concurring).

926 *Price*, 837 N.Y.S.2d at 524 (internal citations omitted).

927 Kenneth Lovett, *Hevesi's Judge Retiring Amid an Investigation into His Own Conduct on the Bench*, N.Y. DAILY NEWS
(Dec. 6, 2012, 12:34 AM), https://www.nydailynews.com/new-york/hevesi-judge-retiring-probe-article-1.1215307 [https://perma.cc/6VNH-N6RZ].

928 *Price*, 837 N.Y.S.2d at 525.

on to differentiate a string of cases in which the federal courts, including the U.S. Supreme Court, had determined that parents possess a constitutionally protected liberty interest in raising their children. He dismissed the applicability of *Meyer v. Nebraska* and *Pierce v. Society of Sisters* as follows:

> In *Meyer*, the party seeking to void State law was a parochial schoolteacher and in *Pierce*, the plaintiffs were schools. In neither case was a parent a party. Although the Court in both cases used language relating to the "liberty" of parents, the actual decisions in both cases turned on the business and commercial interests of the party seeking to void the State law . . . to ply their trades without unreasonable state interference. Thus, although "parental liberty" was discussed, such issue was hardly central to the decisions which instead focused on the [F]ourteenth [A]mendment as a matter of "[s]ubstantive [d]ue [p]rocess" to enable the Court to void economic restrictions on business relationships.[929]

Stone similarly differentiated *Ingraham v. Wright* [930]and *Moore v. City of East Cleveland*.[931] He reasoned that *Ingraham*, which upheld corporal punishment in schools, was an Eighth Amendment case.[932] But that analysis ignores the fact that the majority opinion in *Ingraham* specifically rejected the notion that the Eighth Amendment had applicability in the context of discipline in schools and, therefore, that the "pertinent constitutional question" in the case was "whether the imposition is consonant with the requirements of due process."[933] The Court determined that although a constitutionally protected liberty interest was at stake, due process is satisfied so long as corporal punishment is imposed withing the common law limitations that the amount of force used is not excessive, is reasonably believed to be necessary for discipline, and not is maliciously

---

929 *Id.* at 526 (citing Meyer v. Nebraska, 262 U.S. 390 (1923); Pierce v. Soc'y of the Sisters of the Holy Names of Jesus & Mary, 268 U.S. 510 (1925)) (internal footnotes omitted). For a brief summary of these two foundational cases, see supra notes 140–144 and accompanying text.

930 Ingraham v. Wright, 430 U.S. 651, 671 (1977).

931 Moore v. City of E. Cleveland, 431 U.S. 494, 504–05 (1977).

932 *Price*, 837 N.Y.S.2d at 526 (citing *Ingraham*, 430 U.S. at 671).

933 *Ingraham*, 430 U.S. at 671.

inflicted.[934] In short, Stone's hostility toward due process protections of liberty interests either caused him to stop reading *Ingraham* halfway through the opinion or to view the entirety to the Court's due process analysis as dicta despite it being the central holding of the case.

Stone similarly distinguished *Moore*, which invalidated an ordinance that operated to prevent certain relatives from living together. His articulated reason for doing so was that only four Justices in *Moore* relied on substantive due process (which, again, Stone viewed as now defunct), whereas the decisive factor in the case outcome depended on a fifth Justice's view that the ordinance "unreasonably impinged on Ms. Moore's property rights as to the uses she could put her house."[935] This interpretation, which treats liberty and property interests as distinct, ignores the fact that the U.S. Supreme Court itself stated that "the dichotomy between personal liberties and property rights is a false one."[936] Although it is true that a plurality of four Justices in *Moore* relied on a liberty-based substantive due process analysis for invalidating the ordinance in question, the reason that the concurring opinion by Justice Stevens did not do so had nothing to do with his rejection of that theory. Indeed, Justice Stevens' opinions in many cases make it clear that he embraced the notion of substantive due process protecting liberty interests.[937] Rather, Justice Stevens felt it unnecessary to even address the

---

[934] *Id.* at 677–78.

[935] *Price*, 837 N.Y.S.2d at 526–27 (citing *Moore*, 431 U.S. at 504–05).

[936] Lynch v. Household Fin. Corp., 405 U.S. 538, 552 (1972). For discussions of how substantive due process protects property, see Ronald J. Krotoszynski, Jr., *Fundamental Property Rights*, 85 GEO. L.J. 555 (1997); *see also* Erica Chee, Comment, *Property Rights: Substantive Due Process and the "Shocks the Conscience" Standard*, 31 U. HAW. L. REV. 577 (2009).

[937] Justice Stevens "wholly approve[d]" of the shift from economic and property rights to a substantive due process jurisprudence. Douglas S. Broyles, *Have Justices Stevens and Kennedy Forged a New Doctrine of Substantive Due Process? An Examination of* McDonald v. City of Chicago *and* United States v. Windsor, 1 TEX. A&M L. REV. 129, 131–33 (2013).

> Justice Stevens's argument [in his *McDonald v. Chicago* dissent] is consistent with his longstanding contention that substantive due process is the constitutionally correct way in which to determine what rights are fundamental, and that this analysis is essentially a matter of determining what rights are comprehended under the meaning of "liberty" set forth in the Fourteenth Amendment. In so doing, Justice Stevens rejects the analysis of the

constitutionality of the ordinance because it failed to meet the minimum standards under relevant precedent for valid zoning ordinances: "The city has failed totally to explain the need for a rule which would allow a homeowner to have two grandchildren live with her if they are brothers, but not if they are cousins."[938] Moreover, it is worth noting that despite Judge Stone's eagerness to present property rights as something wholly different from due process rights, it is the Fourteenth Amendment's Due Process Clause itself that provides constitutional protection of property from governmental interference.[939]

Stone then rebuffed the plaintiffs' efforts to use *Troxel v. Granville* as a basis for their arguments.[940] *Troxel* affirmed a state court determination that allowing anyone to petition for visitation rights by asserting such visits would be in the best interest of a child violated parents' fundamental due process rights "to make decisions concerning the care, custody, and control" of their children.[941] Stone said that although "the language of the case mentions the fundamental constitutional rights of parents to make decisions as to how they raise their children, *Troxel* does not indicate that the possession of a cell phone by a child in school may fall into this category of a fundamental constitutional right."[942] Again, this glib, conclusory statement does not engage in an analysis of parental rights, but rather misstates the issue of what rights were claimed in the case. It was no more about a fundamental right to use cell phones in school than *Bowers* was about a fundamental right to engage in sodomy.

Finally, Stone conceded that the Third Circuit's decision in *Gruenke v. Seip* was relevant to the *Price* plaintiffs' claims.[943] That Section 1983

> conservative members of the Court who "incorporate" against the states those rights they find to be "fundamental to our scheme of ordered liberty and system of justice" and "deeply rooted in this Nation's history and tradition."

Id. at 131.

938 *Moore*, 431 U.S. at 520 (Stevens, J., concurring) (citing Village of Euclid v. Ambler Realty Co., 272 U.S. 365 (1926)).

939 U.S. CONST. amend XIV, § 1 ("[N]or shall any State deprive any person of life, liberty, or *property*, without due process of law." (emphasis added)).

940 *Price*, 837 N.Y.S.2d at 525 (citing 530 U.S. 57 (2000)).

941 *Id.*

942 *Id.* at 527.

943 225 F.3d 290 (3d Cir. 2000).

case centered around the potential liability of a swimming coach who asked a member of the team to take a pregnancy test. A divided panel held that the student's mother had stated a viable claim for violation of her due process rights to manage the upbringing of her child, but because that right was not "clearly established," the coach was entitled to qualified immunity.[944] From this holding, Stone concluded that "although there has been some judicial discussion of a 'fundamental parental right' or 'parental liberty to rear children'" *Gruenke* supported the proposition that "the parameters" of such rights were "hardly established."[945]

Notably, the entirety of Stone's opinion devoted to dismissing the *Price* plaintiffs' use of authority was unnecessary. He could have recognized that due process rights were implicated in the case, but then articulated why the ban on cell phones withstood constitutional challenge. Certainly, such a policy is supported by several rational bases, just as Stone opined in the portion of his decision *before* he attempted to justify the death of substantive due process.[946] That is exactly what happened when the final judgment in the case was appealed—and without any unnecessary minimization of Fourteenth Amendment jurisprudence.[947]

944 *Id.* at 307.

945 *Price*, 837 N.Y.S.2d at 528.

946 *Id.* at 519.

947 Price v. New York City Bd. of Educ., 855 N.Y.S.2d 530, 542 (Sup. Ct. App. Div. 2008). The appellate court noted "that reasonable regulations that do not directly and substantially' interfere with a fundamental right need not be strictly scrutinized." *Id.* (internal quotations and other citations omitted). The court quoted from *McCurdy v. Dodd*'s holding that "[i]n the context of parental liberty interests . . . the Due Process Clause only protects against deliberate violations of a parent's fundamental rights—that is, where the state action at issue was specifically aimed at interfering with protected aspects of the parent-child relationship." *Id.* (quoting 352 F.3d 820, 827–828 (3d Cir. 2003)). It then reasoned as follows:

Thus, much of the opinion in *Price* seems to have been less about an meaningful analysis of the relevant law than it was about presenting a judicial diatribe against substantive due process protection of liberty interests.

> The cell phone ban does not directly and substantially interfere with any of the rights alleged by the Parents. Nothing about the cell phone policy forbids or prevents parents and their children from communicating with each other before and after school. Accordingly, the only analysis that need be applied is the rational basis test. That is, the policy will stand if it is rationally related to a legitimate goal of government . . . . Here, the Chancellor reasonably determined that a ban on cell phone possession was necessary to maintain order in the schools. The goal of discipline is unquestionably a legitimate one. Accordingly, the policy withstands rational basis review and is not constitutionally infirm.

Id.

Chapter 6:
Conclusion

One of the more surprising results of this study, at least to its author, was just how few state court decisions relied on *Lawrence*. Indeed, only 441 cases—both civil and criminal, published and unpublished alike—even cited *Lawrence* between the date it was decided and the end of 2021. By contrast, Westlaw's KeyCite feature indicates that 1,124 state court cases cited *Roe v. Wade* during the first twenty years after it was decided. The relatively low number of citations to *Lawrence* in state courts adds long-term validity to the observations of those who previously noted *Lawrence*'s comparatively limited impact in the first decade after it was decided.[948]

A second finding of note is that *Lawrence* did not frequently serve as a key precedent in most civil cases other than those raising LGBTQ+ civil rights claims. Perhaps that was to be expected because *Lawrence* was a criminal case; thus, one might assume that its impact would be more significant in criminal and quasi-criminal cases. Indeed, that was the case, as Table 3 illustrates. In those criminal cases, judges are far more likely to apply *Lawrence* neutrally (n = 121, 39.4%) or narrowly (n = 66, 2.5%) than expansively (n = 26, 8.5%). As Table 9 demonstrates, *Lawrence* being broadly or expansively interpreted is associated with 78.5% lower odds in criminal and quasi-criminal cases compared to civil ones.

Another interesting finding from this study is that judicial demographic characteristics were not significantly related to how judges treated *Lawrence*. The sex of a judge approached (but just missed) statistical significance at the 0.05 alpha level such that female judges were

---

948 Black, *supra* note 25, at 330; Buchanan, *supra* note 25, at 1237; Reinheimer, *supra* note 25, at 505; Sparling, *supra* note 25, at 82.

nearly 2.5 times more likely to apply *Lawrence* expansively than their male counterparts. The only salient extralegal factor to rise to the level of statistical significance concerns the geographic region in which cases were decided. Before discussing that particular result in more detail, it is worthwhile to recap the qualitative results with an eye toward what they might portend for the future.

A. Salient Findings from Qualitative Analyses of Case Categories

1. Laws Targeting Sodomy, Fornication, Adultery, and Prostitution

Lawrence provided constitutional protection to noncommercial sexual activity that occurs in private between consenting adults. A handful of courts extended *Lawrence*'s holding to invalidate criminal laws against fornication and adultery, although the scant number of decisions doing so over the past twenty years suggests that authorities have largely abandoned prosecution of these offenses.[949]

Lawrence specifically limited its holding with the following language: "The present case does not involve minors. It does not involve persons who might be injured or coerced or who are situated in relationships where consent might not easily be refused. It does not involve public conduct or prostitution."[950] It should come as no surprise, then, that judges have overwhelmingly refused to extend *Lawrence* in cases with facts that fall within the ambit of one of these specific exclusions. In fact, sodomy laws that remain "on the books" continue to be criminally enforced when applied to acts of bestiality,[951] prostitution,[952] and those that occur in public, as well as to related inchoate offenses, such as solicitation to commit sodomy under circumstances implicating one of *Lawrence*'s exclusions.[953] Notably, the definition of what constitutes "in public" is broad, reaching consensual activity that occurs outdoors in remote areas

---

[949] *See supra* notes 336–344 and accompanying text.

[950] Lawrence v. Texas, 539 U.S. 558, 578 (2003).

[951] *See supra* notes 325–326 and accompanying text.

[952] *See supra* notes 356–363 and accompanying text.

[953] *See supra* notes 327–330 and accompanying text.

where discovery by third-parties is theoretically possible, albeit unlikely, as well as sex that occurs in inmates' cells in correctional institutions.[954]

2. Obscenity, Pornography, and the Sale of Adult-Oriented Materials

Defendants who attempted to extend *Lawrence* to the protection of child pornography possession universally failed in convincing judges to do so. And although the possession of pornography involving adults is constitutionally protected, appellate courts give trial court judges some latitude in considering what is depicted in such pornography when imposing sentences for other offenses.[955]

Courts are divided, however, on whether *Lawrence* should invalidate laws banning the sale of sex toys and related adult materials. Some courts interpreted the case as offering protection for such sales reasoning that the government cannot constitutionally intrude into the privacy of sexual behaviors during which such materials might be used; other courts hold that because *Lawrence* offers no protection to any commercial activities, its holding does not reach the sale of adult-related goods.[956] But because such devices can be used in private, the former interpretation better aligns with *Lawrence*'s central holding.

3. Sexual Assault and Statutory Rape

Courts unanimously agreed that *Lawrence* does not shield criminal liability for any sexual acts to which all participants did not willingly consent. That, however, did not stop those accused of sexual assaults from trying to make such arguments in vain. Still, some courts found that *Lawrence* limits the types of arguments that prosecutors can make during sexual assault trials. Specifically, testimony about the particular proclivities of a criminal defendant may be improper if it reveals details about constitutionally protected sexual activities.[957]

---

954 *See id.*

955 *See supra* notes 364–377 and accompanying text.

956 *See supra* notes 378–392 and accompanying text.

957 *See supra* notes 394–432 and accompanying text.

Judges similarly enforced sex offenses whenever the activities involved minors under the age of consent.[958] Indeed, no court overturned a statutory rape law or conviction on the basis that *Lawrence* somehow protected the activity in question. Importantly, although *Kansas v. Limon* is cited as an example of the ways in which enforcement of statutory rape laws disproportionately burdens LGBTQ+ youth, *Limon* appears to have been an anomaly, as no other cases revealed such a blatantly discriminatory, narrow application of *Lawrence* to sodomy or statutory rape cases involving minors.[959]

Finally, most courts uphold laws that criminalize private sexual activity between adults when it occurs under circumstances in which a power imbalance calls into question whether consent was truly voluntarily granted. Thus, most defendants fail when asserting that *Lawrence* invalidates statutory factors vitiating consent, including unconsciousness, intoxication, cognitive deficits, and certain relationships such as between teachers and their students, health care providers and their patients, and spiritual leaders and their congregants. Still, in a handful of isolated cases, judges curiously extended *Lawrence*'s scope to encompass private, sexual activity between persons over the applicable age of consent even when the nature of some relationship called into question whether consent was granted as a function of coercion or undue influence.[960] Court doing so, however, render anomalous decisions that not only deviate from the overwhelming majority of cases in other jurisdictions, but also from precedents withing the same state.[961]

4. Privacy and Other Sex Crimes

Contrary to some bloviated prognostications that *Lawrence* would usher an end to a range of sex crimes that have strong, long-standing, moral foundations, no courts have relied on *Lawrence* since it was decided

---

958 *See supra* notes 331–334, 433–473 and accompanying text.

959 *See supra* notes 470–473 and accompanying text.

960 *See supra* notes 474–500 and accompanying text.

961 *Compare* Paschal v. State, 388 S.W.3d 429, 434 (Ark. 2012) (setting aside teacher's conviction for sex with a student over the age of consent), *with* Talbert v. State, 239 S.W.3d 504, 511 (Ark. 2006) (upholding a pastor's conviction for sex with a congregant over the age of consent).

to invalidate laws against bigamy,[962] incest,[963] or lewdness and other forms of public sexual indecency.[964] That being said, some statutes criminalizing lewd or lascivious conduct give rise to vagueness concerns that can be addressed through careful legislative drafting.

By contrast, *Lawrence*'s vision of privacy in the sexual sphere caused numerous courts to offer protection to those who are the victims of nonconsensual voyeurism or the knowing distribution of revenge porn over constitutional challenges to laws criminalizing such conduct. That being said, third parties who receive intimate media and forward them to others without knowing the disclosure did not have the consent of the person depicted likely falls outside the scope of permissible criminal regulation.[965]

Similarly, laws criminalizing the knowing exposure to STIs have routinely withstood constitutional challenges, presuming they had a scienter requirement. Courts repeatedly found that *Lawrence* offers no protection for sexual conduct under circumstances in which consent may have been tainted by nondisclosure of a STI, primarily because the case specifically excluded situations where persons might be injured.[966]

5. Post-Conviction Claims Filed by Sex Offenders

For the most part, *Lawrence* has not had any palpable impact on either the custodial sentences to which sex offenders were sentenced or the regulations under which they must live after being released from incarceration. Indeed, courts seemed loathe to vacate the convictions of people who were convicted of sodomy for any actions that do not fit squarely within the confines of *Lawrence*. Thus, the overwhelming majority of people seeking to be removed from sex offender registries, for instance, were unsuccessful if their conduct involved violence, nonconsent, minors, or public acts that were not a product of police stings that targeted closeted gay men. Courts similarly upheld most probation or

---

962 *See supra* notes 507–517 and accompanying text.

963 *See supra* notes 518–538 and accompanying text.

964 *See supra* notes 539–596 and accompanying text.

965 *See supra* notes 597–610 and accompanying text.

966 *See supra* notes 611–634 and accompanying text.

parole restrictions placed on sex offenders—even those that restricted dating and sexual activity that would normally be constitutionally protected, provided they were rationally related to legitimate law enforcement efforts designed to prevent reoffending.[967]

6. Business Operations and Employment Law

Most of the cases in this study applying *Lawrence* in lawsuits concerning business operations did so neutrally. When courts needed to interpret the precedent, though, they tended to do so in an expansive manner, especially when it protected the privacy of employees from public disclosure of intimate details about their sex lives or to protect LGBTQ+ people from employment discrimination.[968] Given the U.S. Supreme Court's decision in *Bostock v. Clayton County*, one hopes that judicial decisions in the business context will, at minimum, apply that precedent neutrally and, in doing so, protect LGBTQ+ people from employment discrimination.[969]

7. The Future of Fourteenth Amendment Liberty Interests in Family Law Cases

Family law has been resistant to significant changes in the wake of LGBTQ+ equality. As the family law cases in this study illustrate, at first, judges routinely construed *Lawrence* narrowly in the family law context. Over time, family law decisions relying on *Lawrence* became at least more tolerant of LGBTQ+ people.[970] But family law's slow evolution to LGBTQ+ inclusion is not limited to the way that judges apply *Lawrence*, as evidenced by a 2020 Nebraska decision that declined to follow *Obergefell*'s central holding. In *Tyler F. v. Sara P.*, a trial court had awarded joint custody to the biological mother, biological father, and nonbiological, but legal father of a child.[971] When the Supreme Court of Nebraska reversed that determination, it acknowledged an incongruity in

---

967 *See supra* notes 635–653 and accompanying text.

968 *See supra* notes 669–695 and accompanying text.

969 Bostock v. Clayton Cnty., 140 S. Ct. 1731 (2020).

970 *See supra* notes 696–739 and accompanying text.

971 945 N.W.2d 502 (Neb. 2020).

the state's statutory framework for family law in the age of marriage equality:

> We are mindful that following the U.S. Supreme Court's decision in *Obergefell v. Hodges*, our courts are now hearing cases involving two legal mothers or two legal fathers. But our current parentage statutes have not changed, and these statutes are still gender based . . . . In other words, Nebraska's statutory scheme on parentage accommodates only two parents and primarily refers to one mother and one father. Here, the trial judge recognized three legal parents (one mother and two fathers), and that is simply not supported by Nebraska law.[972]

Assuming that *Lawrence* and *Obergefell* remain good law in spite of Justice Thomas' articulated desires to the contrary,[973] states need to undertake comprehensive revisions of their family law statutes to align them with the Fourteenth Amendment's guarantees of due process and equal protections for all persons regardless of sex, sexual orientation, or gender identity.

8. The Future of LGBTQ+ Civil Rights in the Shadow of the First Amendment

Given that neither *Masterpiece Cakeshop*[974] nor *Fulton*[975] involved nondiscrimination protections that were both generally applicable and neutral with respect to religion as required by *Smith*,[976] it remains to be seen whether laws barring discrimination on the basis of sexual orientation that meet the *Smith* standard can withstand First Amendment challenges. It is noteworthy, however, that several current U.S. Supreme Court Justices have indicated their willingness—if not outright desire—to overrule *Smith* and replace it with a constitutional framework that might

---

972 *Id.* at 513 (internal citation omitted).

973 Dobbs v. Jackson Women's Health Org., 142 S. Ct. 2228, 2301 (2022) (Thomas, J., concurring).

974 Masterpiece Cakeshop, Ltd. v. Colorado Civ. Rts. Comm'n, 138 S. Ct. 1719, 1720 (2018).

975 Fulton v. City of Philadelphia, 141 S. Ct. 1868, 1874–75 (2021).

976 Emp. Div., Dep't of Hum. Res. of Or. v. Smith, 494 U.S. 872, 884 (1990).

insulate anti-LGBTQ+ discrimination in the name of religious freedom.[977] In short, the current composition of the Court suggests bleak times lie ahead for LGBTQ+ people who, despite precedents stating that "gay persons and gay couples cannot be treated as social outcasts or as inferior in dignity and worth," may find themselves subjected to purportedly religious-based discrimination without legal remedy.

9. Other Type of Substantive Due Process Claims

The miscellaneous cases in the study raised a diverse series of questions about privacy and autonomy rights. Among others, the cases grappled with issues ranging from restrictions on abortion and assisted suicide, to the scope of informational privacy and parental rights.

a. Autonomy and Bodily Integrity

In the wake of *Dobbs* overturning substantive due process protections for abortion, the nature and scope of the rights to privacy and bodily autonomy under state constitutional law will likely become even more important than they were during the period of time in which the cases in this study were decided. As with the geographical divide with regard to LGBTQ+ civil rights, similar divisions have emerged with regard to women's control over their own reproductive choices. To wit, in the wake of *Dobbs*, roughly fourteen states—most of which are "red" states in the South and Midwest—have enacted law either completely banning abortions or severely curtailing their availability.[978] By contrast, there are few restrictions on abortion during the first half of pregnancy in the Northeast and Pacific coastal states.[979]

---

[977] *Fulton*, 141 S. Ct. at 882–83 (2021) (Barrett and Kavanaugh, J.J., concurring); *id.* at 1883–1926 (Alito, Thomas, and Gorsuch, J.J., concurring).

[978] Julia Haines, Kaia Hubbard & Christopher Wolf, *Where State Abortion Laws Stand Without* Roe, U.S NEWS & WORLD REP. (June 6, 2022, 2:45 PM), https://www.usnews.com/news/best-states/articles/a-guide-to-abortion-laws-by-state [https://perma.cc/2AWZ-YR37] (noting abortion bans in Alabama, Arkansas, Idaho, Kentucky, Louisiana, Mississippi, Missouri, North Dakota, Oklahoma, South Dakota, Tennessee, Texas, and West Virginia; significant restrictions on abortions in Arizona, Florida, Georgia, Nebraska, Ohio, and Utah; and an effect bans in Wisconsin).

[979] *Id.*

Dobbs represents a significant retreat from *Lawrence*'s approach to looking beyond history and tradition to protect liberty interests without resorting to a fundamental rights analysis.[980] Indeed, *Dobbs* cited *Washington v. Glucksberg* to support its analysis that substantive due process only protects rights "'deeply rooted in this Nation's history and tradition' and 'implicit in the concept of ordered liberty.'"[981] It is therefore highly unlikely that state or federal courts would depart from *Glucksberg*'s holding that the Fourteenth Amendment does not protect any rights attendant to assisted suicide.[982] Of course, state courts might find that their state constitutions provide some limited right in this regard.[983] Alternatively, state legislative actions or statewide ballot initiatives might cause more jurisdictions to join the District of Columbia and the ten states that currently permit mentally competent, terminally ill people to elect medical aid in active euthanasia.[984] But *Dobbs* strongly signals that *Lawrence* will not be judicially interpreted to provide such rights as a matter of federal constitutional law.

State courts have not been receptive to arguments that substantive due process cases, including *Lawrence*, provide people with the right to refuse forced feeding in correctional institutions, to opt out of public employer vaccine mandates, or for parents to override school determinations about contraband.[985] Nor have courts accepted the often "undeveloped"

---

980 Dobbs v. Jackson Women's Health Org., 142 S. Ct. 2228, 2242 (2022).

981 *Id.* ("The Constitution makes no reference to abortion, and no such right is implicitly protected by any constitutional provision, including the one on which the defenders of *Roe* and *Casey* now chiefly rely—the Due Process Clause of the Fourteenth Amendment. That provision has been held to guarantee some rights that are not mentioned in the Constitution, but any such right must be 'deeply rooted in this Nation's history and tradition' and 'implicit in the concept of ordered liberty.'" (quoting Washington v. Glucksberg, 521 U.S. 702, 721 (1997))).

982 *Glucksberg*, 521 U.S. at 728.

983 *See supra* notes 841–842 and accompanying text; *cf.* Baxter v. Montana, 224 P.3d 1211, 1214–15 (Mont. 2009) (allowing physician-assisted on statutory grounds because state law provided that consent could be a defense to homicide under certain circumstances).

984 *See Physician-Assisted Suicide Fast Facts*, CNN (May 26, 2022, 11:40 AM), https://www.cnn.com/2014/11/26/us/physician-assisted-suicide-fast-facts [https://perma.cc/9RDS-5M9V].

985 *See supra* notes 847–855, 922–947 and accompanying text.

assertions that *Lawrence* shields defendants from criminal liability for non-sex crimes,[986] including those in which they argued that their autonomy rights should allow them to possess and use controlled substances.[987]

b. Informational Privacy

In 2011, the U.S. Supreme Court avoided determining whether there is a constitutional right to information privacy in a case in which it assumed, for the sake of argument, that such a right existed, but nonetheless would not bar disclosure of the information at issue in the case (which concerned asking potential NASA employees about their treatment or counseling for recent illegal-drug use).[988] Until the Court squarely addresses whether the constitution protects the right "to control the acquisition or dissemination of information about [oneself],"[989] courts strive to contour the scope of privacy protections under "a patchwork of common law, statutes, and constitutional protections."[990] The cases in the present study suggest that courts are, on the whole, quite amendable to claims of informational privacy. They appear to be particularly willing to protect intimate personal information for public disclosure, especially when the information touches on statutorily recognized or constitutionally protected liberty interests.[991]

B. *Lawrence*'s Geographic Divide

Across all types of civil and criminal cases, state courts in the South, Midwest, and West applied *Lawrence* more narrowly than state courts in the Northeast. The differences in the ways that courts in the Northeast and

986 State v. Garcia, No. 33,249, 2017 WL 1372808, at *4 (N.M. Ct. App. Mar. 28, 2017).

987 *See supra* notes 894–910 and accompanying text.

988 Nat'l Aeronautics & Space Admin. v. Nelson, 562 U.S. 134, 151–52 (2011).

989 Kohn, *supra* note 861, at 1067–68; *see also* Pittman, *supra* note 861, at 141 (positing that the "liberty interest component of the Fourteenth Amendment provides support for a constitutional right to informational privacy" that is "consistent with the Court's substantive due process precedents . . . ." (internal citations omitted)).

990 Ruppalt, *supra* note 862, at 666.

991 *See supra* notes 856–888 and accompanying text.

the South treated the precedent were particularly pronounced as Tables 5 and 9 both illustrate.

On the fifteenth anniversary of *Lawrence v. Texas*, journalists Emma Platoff and Sydney Greene published a newspaper story in which they referred to *Lawrence* as a "watershed moment" for LGBTQ+ people—one that opened doors to "new jobs, new opportunities, and new freedom in their skin."[992] But they also reported that despite U.S. Supreme Court wins in *Lawrence* and *Obergefell*, many LGBTQ+ Texans were "still reckoning with the legal and political landscape in a state where they have few protections against discrimination and their rights as couples [were] again being questioned in court."[993] The story went on to quote law professor Dale Carpenter, who opined that the "almost casual dismissal of the rights of gay people" which had been "characteristic of Texas courts before *Lawrence*" continued in the courts at that time. The Texas Supreme Court's decision in *Pidgeon v. Turner* undergirded that conclusion.[994]

Pidgeon v. Turner arose before *Obergefell* when the mayor of Houston extended benefits to the same-sex spouses of city employees who got legally married in other states, thereby treating them the same way the city handled benefits for opposite-sex spouses.[995] A group of antiequality taxpayers challenged that action in court, claiming that it expended "significant public funds on an illegal activity."[996] A trial court granted the plaintiffs' requested injunction prohibiting Houston from furnishing the benefits in question and the mayor appealed.[997] While the case was pending, the *Obergefell* decision brought marriage equality to all U.S. states and, as a result, the plaintiffs in *Pidgeon* filed a supplemental brief arguing that *Obergefell* did not require "states to pay taxpayer-funded benefits to same-sex relationships . . . because federal courts cannot

---

992 Emma Platoff & Sydney Greene, *Fifteen Years After Landmark Gay Rights Case, Same-Sex Couples in Texas Still Face Challenges in Court*, TEX. TRIB. (June 26, 2018, 1:00 PM), https://www.texastribune.org/2018/06/26/fifteen-years-after-landmark-gay-rights-win-same-sex-couples-face-anot/ [https://perma.cc/V469-YD7S].

993 *Id.*

994 538 S.W.3d 73 (Tex.), *cert denied*, 138 S. Ct. 505 (2017).

995 *Id.* at 78.

996 *Id.*

997 *Id.* at 79–80.

'commandeer state spending decisions.'"[998] Relying on *Obergefell*, the appeals court lifted the injunction.[999] The taxpayers appealed and the Supreme Court of Texas sided with them and remanded the case for a full evidentiary hearing to "fully explor[e] *Obergefell*'s reach and ramifications."[1000]

It took until late April of 2021 before a decision on the merits was issued on remand. The court did not cite *Lawrence*, but instead relied on *Obergefell* and *Pavan v. Smith*.[1001] In *Pavan*, the U.S. Supreme Court summarily reversed a decision of the Arkansas Supreme Court which had upheld the validity of a law that prevented a birth mother's same-sex spouse from being listed on their child's birth certificate.[1002] The Court reasoned that under the law in question, "same-sex parents in Arkansas lack[ed] the same right as opposite-sex parents to be listed on a child's birth certificate," a disparate treatment under law that *Obergefell* proscribes.[1003] Applying these key precedents to the *Pidgeon* plaintiffs' cause of action, the Texas Court of Appeals ruled in favor of the City of Houston:

> [A]ppellants urge us to enforce a law providing for marriage on separate terms and conditions as applied to employment benefits: one for different-sex couples that includes benefits and one for same-sex couples that excludes them. Because appellants' attempt to prevent the City from offering employment benefits to married same-sex couples on the same terms and conditions as married different-sex couples cannot be reconciled with the requirements of the U.S. Constitution; we reject it.[1004]

Pavan and *Pidgeon* illustrate that *Obergefell* was not given full and immediate effect by the high courts of Arkansas and Texas, respectively.

---

[998] *Id.* at 80.

[999] *Id.* at 80..

[1000] *Id.* at 89.

[1001] 137 S. Ct. 2075, 2078 (2017) (per curiam).

[1002] State v. Pavan, 505 S.W.3d 169, 177 (Ark. 2016), *rev'd* 137 S. Ct. 2075 (2017) (upholding ARK. CODE § 20–18–401 (1989)).

[1003] *Pavan*, 137 S. Ct. at 2078.

[1004] Pidgeon v. Turner, 625 S.W.3d 583, 603 (Tex. App. 2021), *review denied*, No. 21-0510, 2022 WL 1696441 (Tex. May 27, 2022).

But they are just two examples of the ways in which state courts in certain geographic regions narrowly construe key precedents to avoid granting full equality to LGBTQ+ people.

The findings from the present study demonstrate that courts in the South are less likely to interpret *Lawrence v. Texas* in expansive ways that benefit the due process and equal protection rights of LGBTQ+ people than their counterparts are in the Northeast or West. These empirically derived results are not surprising, especially with regard to courts in the South. That region "has the most hostile policy landscape in the country for LGBTQ issues, as Southern states are far less likely to have LGBTQ-inclusive laws and protections, and instead are far more likely to have harmful, discriminatory laws."[1005] As journalist and social commentor Frank Bruni previously noted,

> There's no such thing as [LGBTQ+] life in America, a country even more divided on this front than on others. There's [LGBTQ+] life in a group of essentially progressive places like New York, Maryland, Oregon and California, which bans government-funded travel to states it deems unduly discriminatory. Then there is [LGBTQ+] life on that blacklist, which includes Texas, Kansas, Mississippi and South Dakota.[1006]

That, of course, does not mean that anti-LGBTQ+ animus does not exist everywhere; it does. As Judge Stone's bizarre opinion in *Price v. New York City Board of Education* demonstrates,[1007] even judges in supposedly liberal New York City can be hostile to substantive due process and, therefore, bend over backward to avoid application of key precedents applying the constitutional doctrine. But there is little doubt that legal backlash to substantive due process cases recognizing LGBTQ+ rights, in particular, appears to be more geographically concentrated in some areas

---

1005 MOVEMENT ADVANCEMENT PROJECT & CAMPAIGN FOR SOUTHERN EQUALITY, TELLING A NEW SOUTHERN STORY: LGBTQ RESILIENCE, RESISTANCE, AND LEADERSHIP, at ii (2020), https://www.lgbtmap.org/file/2020-report-southern_broad.pdf [https://perma.cc/D8GA-TP8B].

1006 Frank Bruni, Opinion, *The Worst (and Best) Places to Be Gay in America*, N.Y. TIMES (Aug. 25, 2017), https://www.nytimes.com/interactive/2017/08/25/opinion/sunday/worst-and-best-places-to-be-gay.html [https://perma.cc/V7Y8-KT7V].

1007 837 N.Y.S.2d 507 (Sup. Ct. 2007).

than others. Consider, for example, that the states enacting "Don't Say Gay" bills, "bathroom bills," and the like are concentrated in the states where courts narrowly construed *Lawrence* to limit due process and equal protection rights far more frequently than they broadly interpreted the precedent to expand such rights.[1008]

Jon Davidson, the former legal director for Lambda Legal—one of the leading LGBTQ+ rights organizations in the United States, is quoted as saying that the "southeastern quarter, from Texas to South Carolina . . . may well generate more than half of the lawsuits that Lambda becomes involved in."[1009] This study's results call into question the wisdom of resorting to the courts in those states. Since the cases in this study were decided before *Dobbs* curtailed substantive due process rights, lawyers litigating LGBTQ+ rights cases in jurisdictions that are less accepting of those rights may be well advised to ground their federal constitutional claims in equal protection and First Amendment arguments, and in state constitutional due process guarantees since *Lawrence*'s approach to substantive due process under the Fourteenth Amendment is now in question.

C. Some Final Thoughts

In 2011, Professor Strader concluded his thoughtful analysis of *Lawrence*'s limited impact on criminal law by distilling its holding to one that prohibits the criminalization of acts on the basis of majoritarian morality in the absence of additional harms.[1010] The data from the present study support his view insofar as courts have used *Lawrence* to invalidate

---

[1008] States enacting such laws include Alabama, Arizona, Arkansas, Florida, Georgia, Indiana, Iowa, Indiana, Kentucky, Louisiana, Mississippi, Missouri, Oklahoma, Tennessee, and Texas. *LGBTQ Curricular Laws*, *supra* note 46. Other states are considering such bans. *See* Dustin Jones & Jonathan Franklin, *Not Just Florida. More Than a Dozen States Propose So-Called 'Don't Say Gay' Bills*, NPR (Apr. 10, 2022, 7:01 AM), https://www.npr.org/2022/04/10/1091543359/15-states-dont-say-gay-anti-transgender-bills [https://perma.cc/V6QB-VQ5X]; Orion Rummler, *10 Anti-LGBTQ+ Bills Impacting Students Go into Effect Across Six States*, THE 19TH (July 1, 2022, 1:58 PM), https://19thnews.org/2022/07/florida-dont-say-gay-other-anti-lgbtq-bills-take-effect/ [https://perma.cc/AUT5-4CJ7].

[1009] Bruni, *supra* note 1006.

[1010] Strader, *supra* note 10, at 106 (noting that "majoritarian morality will no longer justify the decision to send a person to jail").

very few criminal laws or convictions other than those targeting fornication and adultery.[1011] Often, criminal courts simply find *Lawrence* inapplicable without engaging in any analysis of the purported harmfulness of defendant's actions. Indeed, some judges went out of their way to give *Lawrence* such a narrow interpretation that they refused to invalidate sodomy laws or convictions if there were any bases to avoid doing so, such as when inmates masturbated or engaged in consensual sexual activities inside their prison cells.[1012] By contrast, judges routinely interpreted *Lawrence* as requiring nothing more than any rational basis beyond the alleged immorality of the conduct in question in order to uphold criminal laws and convictions which, in turn, led to few, if any, changes in the ways that sex crimes—including prostitution, incest, bigamy, lewdness, public sexual indecency, sexual assault, statutory rape, voyeurism, revenge porn, and the knowing transmission of sexually transmitted diseases—and other criminal offenses are prosecuted, or the ways that sex offenders are treated.[1013]

In 2011, law professor Carlos Ball wrote eloquently on the striking disparity between judicial hesitancy to make constitutional rulings on liberty grounds and judicial confidence in making constitutional rulings rooted in equality principles.[1014] He attributed some that disparity to how *Brown v. Board of Education* became one of the most celebrated U.S. Supreme Court decisions of all time,[1015] whereas several due process precedents—especially *Lochner v. New York* and *Roe v. Wade*—were among the Court's more controversial decisions.[1016] Ball also noted that equality review is often perceived as reinforcing democratic ideals,

---

[1011] *See supra* notes 322–335 and accompanying text.

[1012] *See supra* note 330 and accompanying text.

[1013] *See supra* notes 356–668 and accompanying text.

[1014] Carlos A. Ball, *Why Liberty Judicial Review Is As Legitimate As Equality Review: The Case of Gay Rights Jurisprudence*, 14 U. PA. J. CONST. L. 1 (2011).

[1015] *Id.* at 2–4 (citing Brown v. Bd. of Educ. of Topeka, 347 U.S. 483 (1954)).

[1016] *Id.* (citing Lochner v. New York, 198 U.S. 45, 57 (1905) (invalidating a law that prohibited bakers from working more than sixty-hours per week on due process grounds); Roe v. Wade, 410 U.S. 113 (1973) (holding due process protects a woman's right to choose to have an abortion during the first trimester of pregnancy)).

whereas liberty review is viewed as antidemocratic.[1017] Although he went on to spend the rest of his article explaining why liberty review was just as constitutionally valid as equality review, the Court's retreat in *Dobbs* from *Lawrence*'s approach to liberty suggests that a majority of the Justices who currently sit on the Court consider liberty review to be highly suspect. In fact, the majority told us so in no uncertain terms:

> "Liberty" is a capacious term. As Lincoln once said: "We all declare for Liberty; but in using the same word we do not all mean the same thing . . . ."
>
> In interpreting what is meant by the Fourteenth Amendment's reference to "liberty," we must guard against the natural human tendency to confuse what that Amendment protects with our own ardent views about the liberty that Americans should enjoy. That is why the Court has long been "reluctant" to recognize rights that are not mentioned in the Constitution.[1018]

To be sure, the Court in *Dobbs* did not declare substantive due process protections of liberty to be dead (unlike Judge Stone did in his *Pierce* diatribe). But it clearly resituated such interests back into the realm of history and tradition in ways that *Lawrence* and *Obergefell* had largely eschewed. In light of this recoiling, it seems likely that judges will be more hesitant to give *Lawrence* an expansive substantive due process reading beyond its clear implications for limiting the criminalization of private sexual intimacy between consenting adults.[1019] If that trend materializes, the results of this study suggest that it will have little impact on either criminal law or business and employment law. But narrow interpretations of liberty portend that, at least in the more conservative areas of the United States, LGBTQ+ civil rights litigation may face a renewed uphill battle.

[1017] *Id.* at 4–5.

[1018] Dobbs v. Jackson Women's Health Org., 142 S. Ct. 2228, 2247 (2022) (internal citations omitted).

[1019] For instance, *Dobbs* presages that courts will not embrace Kevin Kennedy's suggestion that substantive due process should protect a right to "a life-sustaining climate" because that is "fundamental to a free and ordered society." Kevin Kennedy, *Watching the World Burn: Substantive Due Process and the Right to A Sustainable Climate*, 93 TEMP. L. REV. ONLINE 61, 62 (2021) (quoting Juliana v. United States, 217 F. Supp. 3d 1224, 1248–50 (D. Or. 2016), *rev'd*, 947 F.3d 1159 (9th Cir. 2020)).

Bibliography

<u>Cases</u>

1568 Montgomery Highway, Inc. v. City of Hoover, 45 So. 3d 319 (Ala. 2010). 108, 109, 110

A.O.V. v. J.R.V., No. 0219-06-4, 2007 WL 581871 (Va. Ct. App. Feb. 27, 2007). 196, 197

Aid for Women v. Foulston, 441 F.3d 1101 (10th Cir. 2006). 231

Akers v. State, 464 S.W.3d 483 (Ark. Ct. App. 2015). 138

Alaska C.L. Union v. State, 122 P.3d 781 (Alaska 2005). 204

Am. Civ. Liberties Union of N.M. v. City of Albuquerque, 137 P.3d 1215 (N.M. 2006) 172

Am. Legion Post #149 v. Washington St. Dep't of Health, 192 P.3d 306 (Wash. 2008). 187, 188

Andersen v. King Cnty., 138 P.3d 963 (Wash. 2006), *abrogated by* Obergefell v. Hodges, 576 U.S. 644 (2015). 8, 58, 204

Andersen v. King Cnty., No. 04–2–04964–4–SEA, 2004 WL 1738447 (Wash. Super. Ct. Aug. 4, 2004), *rev'd*, 138 P.3d 963 (Wash. 2006). 58

Aptheker v. Secretary of State, 378 U.S. 500 (1964). 40

Arias v. State, 503 S.W.3d 523 (Tex. App. 2016). 126, 127

Askew v. Commonwealth, No. 0235-03-1, 2004 WL 234810 (Va. Ct. App. Feb. 10, 2004). 94

Baird v. State, 379 S.W.3d 353 (Tex. App. 2012), *aff'd*, 398 S.W.3d 220 (Tex. Crim. App. 2013) 107

Bandstra v. Covenant Reformed Church, 913 N.W.2d 19 (Iowa 2018). 135, 184

Brush & Nib Studio, LC v. City of Phoenix, 448 P.3d 890 (Ariz. 2019). 12

Buck v. Bell, 274 U.S. 200 (1927). 51

Buckner v. Fam. Servs. of Cent. Fla., Inc., 876 So. 2d 1285 (Fla. Dist. Ct. App. 2004). 64

Burns v. Ohio St. Univ. Coll. of Veterinary Med., No. 13AP–633, 2014 WL 1317499 (Ohio Ct. App. Mar. 25, 2014).......... 187

Burton v. York Cnty. Sheriff's Dep't, 594 S.E.2d 888 (S.C. Ct. App. 2004). 233, 234

Bush v. State, 428 S.W.3d 1 (Tenn. 2014). 62

Campos v. State, No. 03-18-00788-CR, 2020 WL 6834216 (Tex. App. Nov. 20, 2020). 123

Cardoso-Reyna v. State, No. 03-19-00050-CR, 2021 WL 219303 (Tex. App. Jan. 22, 2021). 102

Carl J. Battaglia, M.D., P.A. v. Alexander, 177 S.W.3d 893 (Tex. 2005). 67

Carter v. Duncan, No. C 02-0586SBA(PR), 2005 WL 2373572 (N.D. Cal. Sept. 27, 2005).......... 209

Castle v. State, No. 04-2-00614-4, 2004 WL 1985215 (Wash. Super. Ct. Sept. 7, 2004),
rev'd sub nom. Andersen v. King Cnty., 138 P.3d 963 (Wash. 2006). 58

Cendant Corp. v. Dep't of Revenue, 226 P.3d 1102 (Colo. App. 2009). 64

Chelsey Nelson Photography LLC v. Louisville/Jefferson Cnty. Metro Gov't, No. 3:19-CV-851-JRW,
2020 WL 4745771 (W.D. Ky. Aug. 14, 2020) 12

City of Seattle v. Long, 467 P.3d 979 (Wash. Ct. App. 2020), *aff'd in part, rev'd in part*, 493 P.3d 94 (Wash. 2021). 240, 241

City of Tucson v. Wolfe, 917 P.2d 706 (Ariz. Ct. App. 1995).......... 159

Cochran v. State, 111 So. 3d 148 (Ala. Crim. App. 2012). 106

Colleps v. State, No. 02-12-00396-CR, 2014 WL 1324422 (Tex. App. Apr. 3, 2014). 134

Collins v. State, 479 S.W.3d 533 (Tex. App. 2015). 134

Commonwealth v. Wasson, 842 S.W.2d 487 (1992). 34, 52

Commonwealth v. Wilbur W., 95 N.E.3d 259 (Mass. 2018). 130

Conaway v. Deane, 932 A.2d 571 (Md. 2007), *abrogated by* Obergefell v. Hodges, 576 U.S. 644 (2015).. 7, 204

Corp. of Presiding Bishop of Church of Jesus Christ of Latter-Day Saints v. Amos, 483 U.S. 327 (1987). 220

Cortez v. Johnston, No. 06-13-00120-CV, 2014 WL 1513306 (Tex. App. Apr. 16, 2014). 234, 235

Cote-Whitacre v. Dep't of Pub. Health, 844 N.E.2d 623 (Mass. 2006). 205

Courtemanche v. State, 507 S.W.2d 545 (Tex. Crim. App. 1974). 156

Craft v. Hodel, 683 F. Supp. 289 (D. Mass. 1988). 159

Craig v. Masterpiece Cakeshop, Inc., 370 P.3d 272 (Colo. App. 2015), *rev'd*, 138 S. Ct. 1719 (2018)... 214

Crooks v. State, No. 93,759, 2006 WL 90104 (Kan. Ct. App. Jan. 13, 2006). 122

Czekala-Chatham v. State *ex rel.* Hood, 212 So. 3d 787 (Miss. 2015). 203

D.C. v. City of St. Louis, 795 F.2d 652 (8th Cir. 1986). 156

De Leon v. City of El Paso, 353 S.W.3d 285 (Tex. App. 2011). . 211, 212

Deane v. Conaway, No. 24-C-04-005390, 2006 WL 148145 (Md. Cir. Ct. Jan. 20, 2006), *rev'd*, 932 A.2d 571 (2007), *opinion extended after remand*, (Md. Cir. Ct. 2008). 58

Dep't of Hum. Servs. & Child Welfare Agency Rev. Bd. v. Howard, 238 S.W.3d 1 (Ark. 2006)... 194

DeShaney v. Winnebago Cnty. Dep't of Soc. Servs., 489 U.S. 189 (1989). 241

District of Columbia v. Walters, 319 A.2d 332 (D.C. 1974)............... 156

Dobbs v. Jackson Women's Health Org., 142 S. Ct. 2228 (2022). . 16, 44, 188, 192, 225, 226, 242, 255, 257, 264

Doe v. Commonwealth's Att'y, 403 F. Supp. 1199 (E.D. Va. 1975), *summarily aff'd*, 425 U.S. 901 (1976).. 46

Doe v. Moe, 827 N.E.2d 240 (Mass. App. Ct. 2005). 239, 240

Ex parte Jones, No. PD-0552-18, 2021 WL 2126172 (Tex. Crim. App. May 26, 2021). 165

Ex parte Masonheimer, 220 S.W.3d 494 (Tex. Crim. App. 2007). 61

Ex parte Metzger, 610 S.W.3d 86 (Tex. App. 2020). 162

Ex parte Morales, 212 S.W.3d 483 (Tex. App. 2006). 134

Faber v. State, 521 P.2d 671 (Ariz. 1944). 35

Ferdon *ex rel.* Petrucelli v. Wisconsin Patients Comp. Fund, 701 N.W.2d 440 (Wis. 2005), *overruled by* Mayo v. Wisconsin Injured Patients & Fams. Comp. Fund, 914 N.W.2d 678 (Wis. 2018). 63

Fergusson v. Commonwealth, 838 S.E.2d 75 (Va. Ct. App. 2020). 146, 147

Fisk v. State, 538 S.W.3d 763 (Tex. App. 2017), *rev'd*, 574 S.W.3d 917 (Tex. Crim. App. 2019). 95

Fleming v. State, 323 S.W.3d 540 (Tex. App. 2010), *vacated and remanded*, 341 S.W.3d 415 (Tex. Ct. Crim. App. 2011). 58

Fleming v. State, 376 S.W.3d 854 (Tex. App. 2012), *aff'd*, 455 S.W.3d 577 (Tex. Ct. Crim. App. 2014). 57

Fleming v. State, 455 S.W.3d 577 (Tex. Crim. App. 2014). 123

Florance v. State, No. 05-08-00707-CR, 2009 WL 1267350 (Tex. App. May 8, 2009). 237

Flowers v. Mississippi, 139 S. Ct. 2228 (2019). 209

Foucha v. Louisiana, 504 U.S. 71 (1992). 241

Fulton v. City of Philadelphia, 141 S. Ct. 1868 (2021). 217, 218, 255, 256

Garden State Equal. v. Dow, No. CIV.A. MER-L-1729-11, 2012 WL 540608 (N.J. Super. Ct. Law Div. Feb. 21, 2012). 205

Gibbons v. Ogden, 22 U.S. (9 Wheat.) 1 (1824). 226

Gifford v. McCarthy, 23 N.Y.S.3d 422 (Sup. Ct. App. Div. 2016). 215, 216

Gilbert v. State, 220 So. 3d 1099 (Ala. Crim. App. 2016). 113

Gilliam v. McGrady, 673 S.E.2d 474 (Va. Ct. App. 2009), *aff'd in part, rev'd in part*, 691 S.E.2d 797 (Va. 2010). 61

Harrison v. Vanderkooi, No. 330537, 2017 WL 2262889 (Mich. Ct. App. May 23, 2017), *rev'd in part sub nom.* Johnson v. Vanderkooi, 918 N.W.2d 785 (Mich. 2018). 64

Harvey v. City of Newark, No. CIV. A. 5023-VCS, 2010 WL 4240625 (Del. Ch. Oct. 20, 2010). 65

Hawkins v. Grese, 809 S.E.2d 441 (Va. Ct. App. 2018) 63, 195, 196

Haynes v. State, No. W201500919CCAR3PC, 2016 WL 750233 (Tenn. Crim. App. Feb. 26, 2016). 135, 136

Helvering v. Hallock, 309 U.S. 106 (1940). 65

Hennefeld v. Twp. of Montclair, 22 N.J. Tax 166 (2005). 202

Henry A. v. Willden, 678 F.3d 991 (9th Cir. 2012). 241

Hernandez v. Banks, 65 A.3d 59 (D.C. 2013). 65

Hernandez v. Robles, 794 N.Y.S.2d 579 (Sup. Ct.), *rev'd and vacated*, 805 N.Y.S.2d 354 (App. Div., 2005), *aff'd*, 855 N.E.2d 1 (N.Y. 2006), *abrogated by* Obergefell v. Hodges, 576 U.S. 644 (2015). 58

Hernandez v. Robles, 805 N.Y.S.2d 354 (Sup. Ct. App. Div. 2005), *aff'd*, 855 N.E.2d 1 (N.Y. 2006), *abrogated by* Obergefell v. Hodges, 576 U.S. 644 (2015). 58

Hernandez v. Robles, 855 N.E.2d 1 (N.Y. 2006), *abrogated by* Obergefell v. Hodges, 576 U.S. 644 (2015). 7, 58, 204

Herrington v. United States, 6 A.3d 1237 (D.C. 2010). 61

Hewitt v. Hewitt, 394 N.E.2d 1204 (Ill. 1979). 206

Hilburn v. Enerpipe Ltd., 442 P.3d 509 (Kan. 2019). 65

Hobbs v. Smith, No. 05 CVS 267, 2006 WL 3103008, at *1 (N.C. Super. Ct. Aug. 25, 2006). 72, 98

Hogan v. State, 441 P.2d 620 (Nev. 1968). 31

Hogsett v. Neale, 478 P.3d 713 (Colo. 2021). 191

Home Paramount Pest Control Companies, Inc. v. Shaffer, 718 S.E.2d 762 (Va. 2011). 65

Hopkins v. State, 615 S.W.3d 530 (Tex. App. 2020). 132

In re Congregation Yetev Lev D'Satmar, Inc. v. Kahana, 879 N.E.2d 1282 (N.Y. 2007). 218

In re Coordination Proceeding, Special Title Rule 1550(c), No. 4365, 2005 WL 583129 (Cal. Super. Ct. Mar. 14, 2005), *aff'd in part, rev'd in part sub nom. In re* Marriage Cases, 49 Cal. Rptr. 3d 675 (Ct. App. 2006), *superseded by* 149 P.3d 737 (Cal. 2006), *rev'd*, 183 P.3d 384 (2008). 58

In re Detention of Cubbage, 671 N.W.2d 442 (Iowa 2003). 63

In re Est. of Araguz, 443 S.W.3d 233 (Tex. App. 2014). 201, 202

In re Est. of Carter, 159 A.3d 970 (Pa. Super. Ct. 2017). 206

In re Est. of Gardiner, 42 P.3d 120 (Kan. 2002). 201

In re Guardianship of Dameris L., 956 N.Y.S.2d 848 (Sur. Ct. 2012). 191

In re J.F., 766 S.E.2d 341 (N.C. Ct. App. 2014). 113

In re J.R., 171 S.W.3d 558 (Tex. App. 2005). 64

In re M.D., 757 N.W.2d 559 (N.D. 2008). 177, 178

In re Mark C.H., 906 N.Y.S.2d 419 (Sur. Ct. 2010). 191

In re Marriage Cases, 183 P.3d 384 (Cal. 2008). 205

In re Marriage Cases, 49 Cal. Rptr. 3d 675 (Cal. Ct. App. 2006), *rev'd*, 183 P.3d 384 (Cal. 2008). 7, 58

In re Marriage License for Nash, No. 2002–T–0149, 2003 WL 23097095 (Ohio Ct. App. 2003). 201

In re Marriage of J.B. & H.B., 326 S.W.3d 654 (Tex. App. 2010), *abrogated by* Obergefell v. Hodges, 576 U.S. 644 (2015). 204

In re N.G., 115 N.E.3d 102 (Ill. 2018). 61, 62

In re R.L.C., 635 S.E.2d 1 (N.C. Ct. App. 2006), *aff'd*, 643 S.E.2d 920 (N.C.), *cert. denied*, 552 U.S. 1024 (2007). 58

In re R.L.C., 643 S.E.2d 920 (N.C. 2007). 127

In re Seven State Troopers, No. A-2833-09T2, 2010 WL 668718 (N.J. Super. Ct. App. Div. Feb. 25, 2010). 232, 233

In re Tammy J., 270 P.3d 805 (Alaska 2012). 192

In re V.R., No. NN 5616-04, 2004 WL 3029874 (N.Y. Fam. Ct. 2004).64

Kemmer v. State, No. A04-1913, 2005 WL 2277253 (Minn. Ct. App. Sept. 20, 2005). 62

Kent v. Dulles, 357 U.S. 116 (1958). 40

Kern v. Taney, 11 Pa. D. & C. 5th 558 (C.P. Berks Cnty. 2010). 203

Kerrigan v. Comm'r of Pub. Health, 957 A.2d 407 (Conn. 2008). 205

Kerrigan v. State, 909 A.2d 89 (Conn. Super. Ct. 2006), *rev'd*, 957 A.2d 407 (Conn. 2008). 7

King v. Wiseman, 92 Eng. Rep. 774 (K.B. 1718). 22

Kinnett v. Kinnett, 302 So. 3d 157 (La Ct. App. 2020), *rev'd in part*, 332 So. 3d 1149 (La. 2021) 191, 192

Kinnett v. Kinnett, 332 So. 3d 1149 (La. 2021). 192

Kinnett v. Kinnett, 345 So. 3d 1122 (La. App. July 7, 2022) 192

Klein v. Oregon Bureau of Lab. & Indus. 410 P.3d 1051, 1064 (Or. Ct. App. 2017), *vacated & remanded*,
139 S. Ct. 2713 (2019), *aff'd after remand*, 506 P.3d 1108 (Or. Ct App.), *review denied*, 509 P.3d 119 (Or. 2022). 216

Klein v.Oregon Bureau of Lab. & Indus., 506 P.3d 1108 (Or. Ct. App.), *review denied*, 509 P.3d 119 (Or. 2022). 217

Korematsu v. United States, 323 U.S. 214 (1944), *abrogation recognized by* 584 F. Supp. 1406 (N.D. Cal. 1984) 52

Kupper v. State, No. 05-03-00486-CR, 2004 WL 60768 (Tex. App. Jan. 14, 2004). 139, 140

L.A.M. v. B.M., 906 So. 2d 942 (Ala. Civ. App. 2004). 196

Laguerre v. Maurice, 138 N.Y.S.3d 123 (Sup. Ct. App. Div. 2020)... 218, 219

Langan v. St. Vincent's Hosp. of N.Y., 802 N.Y.S.2d 476 (Sup. Ct. App. Div. 2005). 205

Lansing Sch. Educ. Ass'n v. Lansing Bd. of Educ., 792 N.W.2d 686 (Mich. 2010). 65

Lawrence v. State, 41 S.W.3d 349 (Tex. App. 2001), *rev'd*, 539 U.S. 558 (2003), *dismissed on remand*,
No. 14-99-00109-CR, 2003 WL 22453791 (Tex. App. Oct. 30, 2003). 53

M.T. v. J.T., 355 A.2d 204 (N.J. Super. Ct. App. Div. 1976). 201

MacDonald v. Moose, 710 F.3d 154 (4th Cir. 2013). 95

Malecek v. Williams, 804 S.E.2d 592 (N.C. Ct. App. 2017). 100

Martin v. Ziherl, 607 S.E.2d 367 (Va. 2005)................................... 97, 98

Masterpiece Cakeshop, Ltd. v. Colorado Civ. Rts. Comm'n, 138 S. Ct. 1719 (2018)... 212, 213, 214, 255

Matheney v. Commonwealth, 191 S.W.3d 599 (Ky. 2006). 65

Matherson v. Marchello, 473 N.Y.S.2d 998 (Sup. Ct. App. Div. 1984), *abrogated by Laguerre v. Maurice*, 138 N.Y.S.3d 123 (Sup. Ct. App. Div. 2020). 218

Mays v. Governor of Mich., 954 N.W.2d 139 (Mich. 2020).................. 66

McClary v. Commonwealth, No. 0240-13-4, 2014 WL 1707377 (Va. Ct. App. Apr. 29, 2014), *aff'd*, No. 140785, 2015 WL 10945036 (Va. Feb. 26, 2015). 94, 95

McCormick v. Carrier, 795 N.W.2d 517 (Mich. 2010)......................... 65

McCoy v. People, 442 P.3d 379 (Colo. 2019).................................... 134

McCurdy v. Dodd, 352 F.3d 820 (3d Cir. 2003). 246

McDonald v. City of Chicago, 561 U.S. 742 (2010)........................... 242

McDonald v. Commonwealth, 630 S.E.2d 754 (Va. Ct. App. 2006), *aff'd*, 645 S.E.2d 918 (Va. 2007). 58

McDonald v. Commonwealth, 645 S.E.2d 918 (Va. 2007)........... 95, 128

McGriff v. McGriff, 99 P.3d 111 (Idaho 2004)........................... 196, 197

McLaughlin v. Becerra, No. B280529, 2018 WL 654556 (Cal. Ct. App. Feb. 1, 2018). 93

McNabb v. Dep't of Corr., 180 P.3d 1257 (Wash. 2008). 227, 228

Merryfield v. Sullivan, No. 111204, 2015 WL 326652 (Kan. Ct. App. Jan. 16, 2015).. 180, 181

Meyer v. Nebraska, 262 U.S. 390 (1923)...................................... 38, 243

Miller v. California, 413 U.S. 15 (1973). 103

Miller v. Johnson, 289 P.3d 1098 (Kan. 2012), *abrogated by* Hilburn v. Enerpipe Ltd., 442 P.3d 509 (Kan. 2019). 65

On Lee v. United States, 343 U.S. 747 (1952). 39

Osborne v. Ohio, 495 U.S. 103 (1990). 104

Our Lady of Guadalupe Sch. v. Morrissey-Berru, 140 S. Ct. 2049 (2020). 220, 221

Page v. Page, No. 07CA0109, 2008 WL 2469176 (Ohio Ct. App. June 20, 2008). 195

Painter v. State, No. 11-15-00318-CR, 2017 WL 6559653 (Tex. App. Dec. 21, 2017). 135

Palko v. Connecticut, 302 U.S. 319 (1937). 47

Palmer v. Atl. Coast Pipeline, LLC, 801 S.E.2d 414 (Va. 2017). 66

Paschal v. State, 388 S.W.3d 429 (Ark. 2012). 134, 137, 138, 252

Pavan v. Smith, 137 S. Ct. 2075 (2017). 260

Payne v. Tennessee, 501 U.S. 808 (1991). 54, 65

People v. Allen, No. A106272, 2005 WL 552470 (Cal. Ct. App. Mar. 9, 2005). 180

People v. Boston, No. C086940, 2021 WL 5027416 (Cal. Ct. App. Oct. 29, 2021), *review granted* (Jan. 26, 2022). 172

People v. Calderon, No. H030215, 2007 WL 1683576 (Cal. Ct. App. June 12, 2007). 64

People v. Cassala, 15 N.Y.S.3d 479 (Sup. Ct. App. Div. 2015)........... 115

People v. Castellanos, No. H032865, 2009 WL 2438434 (Cal. Ct. App. Aug. 11, 2009). 64

People v. Conroy, 145 N.E.3d 537 (2019). 101

People v. Dancy, 124 Cal. Rptr. 2d 898 (2002).................................. 133

People v. Davidson, No. D064880, 2015 WL 4751166 (Cal. Ct. App. Aug. 12, 2015). 119

People v. Delacy, 122 Cal. Rptr. 3d 216 (Ct. App. 2011). 64

People v. Downin, 828 N.E.2d 341 (Ill. Ct. App. 2005). 125

People v. Febrissy, No. C049033, 2006 WL 2006161 (Cal. Ct. App. July 19, 2006). 119, 120

People v. Feezel, 783 N.W.2d 67 (Mich. 2010). 65

People v. Krause, No. C050840, 2007 WL 1152688 (Cal. Ct. App. Apr. 19, 2007). 157

People v. Lemons, No. D050763, 2008 WL 4335684 (Cal. Ct. App. Sept. 24, 2008). 135

People v. Manicap, 260 P.2d 137 (Cal. 1953). 35

People v. Martinez, No. H033918, 2009 WL 3777413 (Cal. Ct. App. Nov. 12, 2009). 64

People v. McCullon, No. B231429, 2012 WL 1548062 (Cal. Ct. App. May 3, 2012). 172

People v. McDermitt, No. C047482, 2005 WL 995520 (Cal. Ct. App. Apr. 29, 2005). 175

People v. McEvoy, 154 Cal. Rptr. 3d 914 (Ct. App. 2013). 147

People v. McPhee, No. 258285, 2007 WL 912116 (Mich. Ct. App. Mar. 27, 2007). 150

People v. Miller, No. B267728, 2016 WL 6835497 (Cal. Ct. App. Nov. 21, 2016). 102

People v. Moi, No. 1114–87, 2005 WL 1618124 (N.Y. Co. Ct. June 3, 2005). 172

People v. Novie, 976 N.Y.S.2d 636 (Sup. Ct. App. Term 2013). 64

People v. Noyan, 181 Cal. Rptr. 3d 601 (Ct. App. 2014). 64

People v. Perez, 961 N.Y.S.2d 51 (Sup. Ct. App. Div. 2013). 72, 175

People v. Petrenko, 931 N.E.2d 1198 (Ill. 2010). 65

People v. Randall, 203 N.Y.S.2d 372 (1960), *aff'd*, 9 N.Y.2d 413, 174 N.E.2d 507 (1961). 31

People v. Rotroff, 100 Cal. Rptr. 3d 558 (Ct. App. 2009), *review granted and opinion superseded*, 223 P.3d 1 (Cal. 2010). 64

People v. Sanches, No. G032738, 2004 WL 2757435 (Cal. Ct. App. Dec. 2, 2004). 113

People v. Schneider, No. A145308, 2016 WL 4183943 (Cal. Ct. App. Aug. 8, 2016). 119

People v. Scott, 54 Cal. Rptr. 3d 674 (Cal. Ct. App.), *vacated and remanded*, 169 P.3d 95 (Cal. 2007) 58, 59

Prather v. Commonwealth, No. 2012-CA-001725-MR, 2014 WL 2536866 (Ky. Ct. App. June 6, 2014). 147

Price v. New York City Bd. of Educ., 837 N.Y.S.2d 507 (Sup. Ct. 2007), *abrogated by* 855 N.Y.S.2d 530 (Sup. Ct. App. Div. 2008). 241, 242, 243, 244, 245, 246, 261

Price v. New York City Bd. of Educ., 855 N.Y.S.2d 530 (Sup. Ct. App. Div. 2008). 246, 247

Proceeding for the Appointment of a Guardian for Leon, No. 2016–XXXX, 2016 WL 5724234 (N.Y. Sur. Ct. 2016). 64

Pruitt v. State, 272 So. 3d 732 (Ala. Crim. App. 2018). 134

Pryor v. Municipal Ct., 599 P.2d 636 (Cal. 1979). 156

Pub. Utils. Comm'n v. Pollak, 343 U.S. 451 (1952). 39

Quinn v. Quinn, 137 A.3d 423 (N.J. 2016). 65

R.H. v. State, 849 N.E.2d 1165 (Ind. Ct. App. 2006). 133

Ramirez v. Bank of America, N.A., 627 S.W.3d 486 (Tex. App. 2021).65

Ramirez v. State, 557 S.W.3d 717 (Tex. App. 2018). 134

Ray v. Swager, 903 N.W.2d 366 (Mich. 2017). 65

Raynor v. State, 99 A.3d 753 (Md. 2014). 63

Regents of Univ. of Mich. v. Titan Ins. Co., 791 N.W.2d 897 (Mich. 2010), *overruled by* Joseph v. Auto Club Ins. Ass'n, 815 N.W.2d 412 (Mich. 2012). 65

Reliable Consultants, Inc. v. Earle, 517 F.3d 738 (5th Cir. 2008). 109, 110

Reno v. Flores, 507 U.S. 292 (1993). 63

Rex v. Jacobs, 168 Eng. Rep. 830 (1817). 22

Riddle v. State, No. 39A04-1712-CR-2975, 2018 WL 5274027 (Ind. Ct. App. Oct. 24, 2018). 152, 153

Robles v. State, 585 S.W.3d 591 (Tex. App. 2019). 101

Roe v. Wade, 410 U.S. 113 (1973). 16, 37, 44, 263

Romer v. Evans, 517 U.S. 620 (1996). 8, 143

Stanley v. Georgia, 394 U.S. 557 (1969)................................ 42, 43, 104

State *ex rel.* Alabama Pol'y Inst., 200 So. 3d 495 (Ala. 2015), *abrogated by* Obergefell v. Hodges, 576 U.S. 644 (2015)...................... 202, 203

State *ex rel.* Branson v. Fabian, No. A09-0814, 2009 WL 2447531 (Minn. Ct. App. Aug. 11, 2009)... 64

State Route 4 Bypass Auth. v. Superior Ct., 64 Cal. Rptr. 3d 286 (Ct. App. 2007). 64

State v. Aalim, 83 N.E.3d 883 (Ohio 2017). 238, 239

State v. Acosta, No. 08-04-00312-CR, 2005 WL 2095290 (Tex. App. Aug. 31, 2005). 109

State v. Airhart-Bryon, No. 78805-1-I, 2020 WL 1853477 (Wash. Ct. App. Apr. 13, 2020),
review denied, 474 P.3d 1052 (Wash. 2020). 180

State v. Arlene's Flowers, Inc., 389 P.3d 543 (Wash. 2017), *vacated*, 138 S. Ct. 2671 (2018)... 57, 59, 215

State v. Arlene's Flowers, Inc., 441 P.3d 1203 (Wash. 2019), *cert. denied*, 141 S. Ct. 2884 (2021). 59, 215

State v. Arlene's Flowers, Inc., No. 13-2-00871-5, 2015 WL 720213 (Wash. Super. Ct. Feb. 18., 2015),
aff'd, 389 P.3d 543 (Wash. 2017), *vacated and remanded*, 138 S. Ct. 2671 (2018), *aff'd on remand*,
441 P.3d 1203 (Wash. 2019), *cert. denied*, 141 S. Ct. 2884 (2021). 214

State v. Baldon, 829 N.W.2d 785 (Iowa 2013). 67

State v. Bateman, No. 1 CA-CR 07-0043, 2008 WL 4516447 (Ariz. Ct. App. Oct. 2, 2008)... 146

State v. Beecraft, No. 2006AP982–CR, 2006 WL 3842171 (Wis. Ct. App. Dec. 28, 2006)... 237

State v. Bodyke, 933 N.E.2d 753 (Ohio 2010)...................................... 65

State v. Brown, 156 S.W.3d 722 (2004)... 65

State v. Brown, 919 A.2d 107 (N.J. 2007). 65

State v. Brown, 945 N.W.2d 584 (Wis.), *cert. denied*, 141 S. Ct. 881 (2020)... 66

State v. Browning, 629 S.E.2d 299 (N.C. Ct. App. 2006).................. 123

State v. Gentle, 817 S.E.2d 833 (N.C. Ct. App. 2018), *aff'd*, 822 S.E.2d 616 (N.C. 2019). 94

State v. Goewey, 135 A.3d 1220 (Vt. 2015). 113

State v. Gomez-Alas, 477 P.3d 911 (Idaho 2020). 132

State v. Green, 706 S.E.2d 720 (Ga. Ct. App. 2011). 175

State v. Green, 989 N.E.2d 1088 (Ohio Ct. App. 2013). 102

State v. Griffin, No. 1004021962, 2011 WL 2083893 (Del. Super. Ct. May 16, 2011). 238

State v. Hamlin, 324 P.3d 1006 (Idaho Ct. App. 2014) 135

State v. Hollenbeck, 53 A.3d 591 (N.H. 2012). 134

State v. Holm, 137 P.3d 726 (Utah 2006). 144, 145

State v. Holmes, 920 A.2d 632 (N.H. 2007). 123

State v. Horn, No. 91,692, 2005 WL 823896 (Kan. Ct. App. Apr. 8, 2005). 106

State v. Hunt, 710 S.E.2d 339, 347 (N.C. Ct. App. 2011), *rev'd*, 722 S.E.2d 484 (2012). 58

State v. Hunt, 728 S.E.2d 409 (N.C. App. 2012), *aff'd in part*, 766 S.E.2d 288 (N.C. 2014). 114

State v. Irby, No. 95,349, 2007 WL 219971 (Kan. Ct. App. Jan. 26, 2007). 113

State v. J.P., 907 So. 2d 1101 (Fla. 2004). 65

State v. Jenkins, No. C–040111, 2004 WL 3015091 (Ohio Ct. App. Dec. 30, 2004). 109

State v. Jensen, 118 P.3d 762 (N.M. Ct. App. 2005) 118, 119

State v. John M., 894 A.2d 376 (Conn. Ct. App. 2006), *rev'd*, 940 A.2d 755 (Conn. 2008). 147, 148, 149

State v. John M., 940 A.2d 755 (Conn. 2008). 149

State v. Johnson, 425 S.W.3d 542 (Tex. App. 2014), *aff'd*, 475 S.W.3d 860 (Tex. Crim. App. 2015) 67

State v. Jones, No. 95,558, 2007 WL 656367 (Kan. Ct. App. Mar. 2, 2007). 72, 125

State v. Music, No. 33285–3–III, 2016 WL 1704687, (Wash. Ct. App. Apr. 28, 2016). 113

State v. Musser, 721 N.W.2d 734 (Iowa 2006). 170

State v. Naylor, 466 S.W.3d 783 (Tex. 2015). 203

State v. Nelson, 271 N.W. 114 (Minn. 1937). 36

State v. Oakley, 605 S.E.2d 215 (N.C. Ct. App. 2004). 116, 117

State v. Odell, No. 105,311, 2013 WL 310335 (Kan. Ct. App. Jan. 18, 2013). 64

State v. Pavan, 505 S.W.3d 169 (Ark. 2016), *rev'd*, 137 S. Ct. 2075 (2017). 260

State v. Peeler, 140 A.3d 811 (Conn. 2016). 65, 73

State v. Pena-Flores, 965 A.2d 114 (N.J. 2009), *abrogated by* State v. Witt, 126 A.3d 850 (N.J. 2015). 65

State v. Pope, 608 S.E.2d 114 (N.C. Ct. App. 2005). 94

State v. Pryes, No. 2009AP2–CR, 2009 WL 1606746 (Wis. Ct. App. June 10, 2009). 125

State v. Reine, No. 19157, 2003 WL 77174 (Ohio Ct. App., Jan. 10, 2003), *dismissed* 795 N.E.2d 686 (Ohio 2003). 172

State v. Richardson, 209 P.3d 696 (Kan. 2009). 168, 169

State v. Roberson, 935 N.W.2d 813 (Wis. 2009). 66

State v. Robinson, 873 So. 2d 1205 (Fla. 2004). 172

State v. Romano, 155 P.3d 1102 (2007). 101, 103

State v. Rung, 774 N.W.2d 621 (Neb. 2009). 122

State v. Russell, 890 A.2d 453 (R.I. 2006). 237

State v. S.F., 483 S.W.3d 385 (Mo. 2016). 169, 170

State v. Schrader, No. 97,206, 2007 WL 4577915 (Kan. Ct. App. Dec. 21, 2007). 113

State v. Seering, 701 N.W.2d 655 (Iowa 2005). 63

State v. Senters, 699 N.W.2d 810 (2005). 106

State v. Solomon, 274 So. 3d 1017 (Ala. Crim. App. 2018). 134

T.M.H. v. D.M.T., 79 So. 3d 787 (Fla. Dist. Ct. App. 2011), *aff'd in part, disapproved in part*, 129 So. 3d 320 (Fla. 2013). 198

Tagami v. City of Chicago, 875 F.3d 375 (7th Cir. 2017), *cert. denied*, 138 S. Ct. 1577 (2018). 159

Talbert v. State, 239 S.W.3d 504 (Ark. 2006)..................... 134, 138, 252

Tarrant Cnty. Coll. Dist. v. Sims, 621 S.W.3d 323 (Tex. App. 2021). 186, 187

Teague v. Lane, 489 U.S. 288 (1989).. 61

Territory v. Bell, 43 Haw. 23 (1958).. 31

Texas Dep't of Fam. & Prot. Servs. v. Grassroots Leadership, Inc., NO. 03-18-00261-CV,
2019 WL 6608700 (Tex. App. Dec. 5, 2019). 66

Tjan v. Commonwealth, 621 S.E.2d 669 (Va. Ct. App. 2005).............. 94

Toghill v. Commonwealth, 768 S.E.2d 674 (2015)........................ 95, 122

Toghill v. Commonwealth, No. 2230–12–2, 2014 WL 545728 (Va. Ct. App. Feb.11, 2014), *aff'd* 768 S.E.2d 674 (Va. 2015). 57

Toledo v. State, 519 S.W.3d 273 (Tex. App. 2017). 134

Troxel v. Granville, 530 U.S. 57 (2000)... 245

Turner v. State, No. 10-06-00055-CR, 2007 WL 475420 (Tex. App. Feb. 14, 2007). 237

Tyler F. v. Sara P., 945 N.W.2d 502 (Neb. 2020)....................... 254, 255

Union Pacific Railway Co. v. Botsford, 141 U.S. 250 (1891). 36, 37

United States v. Alvarez, 567 U.S. 709 (2012). 236

United States v. Blaylock, 421 F.3d 758 (8th Cir. 2005). 209

United States v. Westinghouse Elec. Corp., 638 F.2d 570 (3d Cir. 1980). 230

United States v. Windsor, 570 U.S. 744 (2013). 8

Vanderveer v. Vanderveer, No. 0122-04-2, 2004 WL 2157930 (Va. Ct. App. Sept. 28, 2004). 195

Vann v. Pixley, No. CL13000066–00, 2013 WL 9564167 (Va. Ct. App. 2013). 95

Statutes and Constitutional Provisions

CONN. GEN. STAT. ANN. § 46b-21 (1978). 149

CONN. GEN. STAT. ANN. § 53a-72a (2002). 149

DEL. CODE ANN. tit. 10, § 1041(2)(b) (1997). 207

Edw. 1, c. 13 (1275). 122

Employment Non-Discrimination Act (ENDA) of 2013, S. 815, 113th Cong. (as passed by Senate, Nov. 7, 2013). 11

Employment Non-Discrimination Act of 1994, H.R. 4636, 103rd Cong. (1994). 11

Equality Act of 1974, H.R. 14752, 93rd Congress (1974). 11

FLA. STAT. ANN. § 384.24 (1986 & 2022 Supp.). 166

FLA. STAT. ANN. § 63.042(3) (1973 & 2008 Supp.). 194

FLA. STAT. ANN. § 742.14 (2016). 198

FLA. STAT. ANN. § 800.02 (1993 & 2022 Supp.) 151

GA. CODE ANN. § 16-6-3(c) (2022). 126

H.B. 118, 19th Leg. (Haw. 1997). 208

IDAHO CODE § 39-608(3)(a) (1988 & 2022 Supp.). 166

Immigration Act of 1990, Pub. L. No. 101-649, 104 Stat. 4978 (1990). 27

IND. CODE § 31-33-5-1 (1997). 230

IND. CODE § 35-42-4-5(c)(3) (2014). 152

IND. CODE § 35-45-4-1 (2014). 152

KAN. STAT. ANN. § 21-3435(a)(1) (1999) (recodified as amended at KAN. STAT. ANN. § 21-5424 (2011 & 2022 Supp.)). 168

KAN. STAT. ANN. § 21-3505 (1969). 34

KAN. STAT. ANN. § 21-3522 (2000), *repealed by* Laws 2010, ch. 136, § 307, eff. July 1, 2011, *recodified as amended at* KAN. STAT. ANN. § 21-5507 (2011). 131

KAN. STAT. ANN. § 21-5506 (2011). 129

KAN. STAT. ANN. § 21-5507 (2011). 128, 131

KAN. STAT. ANN. § 21-5513(a)(2) (2011 & 2022 Supp.) 156

N.J. STAT. ANN. § 2C:14-4 (c) (1992 & 2022 Supp.). 156

N.Y. EXEC. LAW § 290 (McKinney 2011). 215

N.Y. EXEC. LAW § 296 (2002 & 2022 Supp.) 211

N.Y. PENAL LAW § 690 (1909). 31

N.Y. PENAL LAW 245.00 (2015 & 2022 Supp.). 156

NEB. REV. STAT. § 28-934 (2011 & 2022 Supp.) 166

NEV. REV. LAWS § 6459 (1911). 31

NEV. REV. STAT. § 201.210 (2017 & 2022 Supp.). 151

OHIO REV. CODE § 2907.03(A)(2)–(3) (2019). 121, 133, 135, 136

OR. REV. STAT. § 10.030 (2017). 210

OR. REV. STAT. § 174.100(7) (2017). 210

Pub. L. No. 615-428, 62 Stat. 346, 347 (1948). 33

REV. CODE WASH. § 9A.88.010(1) (2004 & 2022 Supp.) 156

Ryan White Comprehensive AIDS Resources Emergency Act, Pub. L. No. 101-381, 104 Stat. 576 (1990) (codified as amended at 42 U.S.C. §§ 300ff (2022)). 165

TENN. CODE ANN. § 39-13-109 (1994 & 2022 Supp.). 166

TEX. FAM. CODE § 71.0021 (2001). 208

TEX. FAM. CODE ANN. § 2.005(b)(8) (Supp. 2013). 202

TEX. PENAL CODE § 21.12 (2021). 133, 135

TEX. PENAL CODE § 21.15(b) (2015). 161

TEX. PENAL CODE § 43.21 (1994). 110

TEX. PENAL CODE ANN. § 21.06 (1973). 34

TEX. PENAL CODE ANN. § 21.06 (a) (West 2003). 53

TEX. PENAL CODE ANN. § 22.011 (2009). 95, 125

The Stopping Harmful Image Exploitation and Limiting Distribution Act of 2022 (SHIELD Act), S.3777, 117th Cong. (2022). 163

Other Authorities

AGRESTI, ALAN, AN INTRODUCTION TO CATEGORICAL DATA ANALYSIS (3d ed. 2019). 75, 77

Akoglu, Haldun, *User's Guide to Correlation Coefficients*, 18 TURK. J. EMERGENCY MED. 91 (2018). 76

ALLYN, DAVID, MAKE LOVE, NOT WAR – THE SEXUAL REVOLUTION: AN UNFETTERED HISTORY (2016). 34

ALTHEIDE, DAVID L., & CHRISTOPHER J. SCHNEIDER, QUALITATIVE MEDIA ANALYSIS (2d ed. 2013). 59, 60, 77

Amgott, Jonathan E., *Post-*Windsor *Prospects for Morals Legislation: The Case of Polygamous Immigrants*, 26 STAN. L. & POL'Y REV. 513 (2015). 55

Anderson, Ellen Ann, *The Stages of Sodomy Reform*, 23 T. MARSHALL L. REV. 283 (1998). 24, 29

Antisodomy Laws Targeted for Repeal After High Court Ruling, WASH. POST, Feb. 4, 1987, at A16. 52

Apasu-Gbotsu, Yao, et al., *Survey on the Constitutional Right to Privacy in the Context of Homosexual Activity*, 40 U. MIAMI L. REV. 521, 526 (1986). 28, 46, 52

Baia, Elizabeth J., Note, *Akin to Madmen: A Queer Critique of the Gay Rights Cases*, 104 VA. L. REV. 1021 (2018). 6

Ball, Carlos A., *Why Liberty Judicial Review Is As Legitimate As Equality Review: The Case of Gay Rights Jurisprudence*, 14 U. PA. J. CONST. L. 1 (2011). 263

Bans on Transgender Youth Participation in Sport, MOVEMENT ADVANCEMENT PROJECT (June 14, 2023), https://www.lgbtmap.org/equality-maps/sports_participation_bans [https://perma.cc/VF5J-W6W5]. 13

Barak-Corren, Netta, *A License to Discriminate? The Market Response to* Masterpiece Cakeshop, 56 HARV. C.R.-C.L. L. REV. 315, (2021) 213

Barnett, Randy E., *Justice Kennedy's Libertarian Revolution:* Lawrence v. Texas, 2003 CATO SUP. CT. REV. 21 .... 4, 5

Barnett, Randy E., *The Ninth Amendment: It Means What It Says*, 85 TEX. L. REV. 1 (2006). 42

BARNETT, WILLIAM, SEXUAL FREEDOM AND THE CONSTITUTION (1973). 29

Baume, Matt, *51 Years After Stonewall, Police Raided Two Gay Bars Aiding Protestors*, Them (June 5, 2020), https://www.them.us/story/police-raided-two-gay-bars-aiding-george-floyd-protestors [https://perma.cc/34PR-RDGL] 30

Bedi, Sonu, *Repudiating Morals Legislation: Rendering the Constitutional Right to Privacy Obsolete*, 53 CLEV. ST. L. REV. 447 (2005). 3

Bensing, Robert C., *Comparative Study of American Sex Statutes*, 42 J. CRIM. L. 57 (1951) 29

Bishin, Benjamin G., Thomas J. Hayes, Matthew B. Incantalupo & Charles Anthony Smith, *Elite Mobilization: A Theory Explaining Opposition to Gay Rights*, 54 LAW& SOC'Y REV. 233 (2020). 10

Bishin, Benjamin G., Thomas J. Hayes, Matthew B. Incantalupo & Charles Anthony Smith, *Opinion Backlash and Public Attitudes: Are Political Advances in Gay Rights Counterproductive?*, 60 AM. J. POL. SCI. 625 (2016). 10

Black, Jonathan M., *Sexual Privacy After* Lawrence v. Texas, 10 GEO. J. GENDER & L. 297 (2009) 7, 17, 249

BLACK'S LAW DICTIONARY (11th ed. 2019) 41, 161

BLACKSTONE, WILLIAM, COMMENTARIES ON THE LAWS OF ENGLAND (1765–1769) 23

BOSWELL, JOHN, CHRISTIANITY, SOCIAL TOLERANCE & HOMOSEXUALITY (1980). 21

Boswell, John, *On the History of Social Attitudes Toward Homosexuality from Ancient Greece to the Present*, *in* GAYS AND THE MILITARY: THE UNITED STATES VERSUS JOSEPH STEFFAN 40–48 (Marc Wolinsky & Kenneth Sherrill eds., 1993) 21

Brinster, Jeremy W., Note, *Taking Congruence and Proportionality Seriously*, 95 N.Y.U. L. REV. 580 (2020). 11

Brooks, Arthur E., Note, Doe *and* Dronenburg*: Sodomy Statutes Are Constitutional*, 26 WM. & MARY L. REV. 645 (1985). 21, 22

Broughton, J. Richard, *The Criminalization of Consensual Adult Sex After* Lawrence, 28 NOTRE DAME J.L. ETHICS & PUB. POL'Y 125 (2014)................... 55

Broyles, Douglas S., *Have Justices Stevens and Kennedy Forged a New Doctrine of Substantive Due Process? An Examination of* McDonald v. City of Chicago *and* United States v. Windsor, 1 TEX. A&M L. REV. 129 (2013)... 244, 245

Bruni, Frank, Opinion, *The Worst (and Best) Places to Be Gay in America*, N.Y. TIMES (Aug. 25, 2017), https://www.nytimes.com/interactive/2017/08/25/opinion/sunday/worst-and-best-places-to-be-gay.html [https://perma.cc/V7Y8-KT7V].. 261, 262

Bruton, H. Hunter, *The Questionable Constitutionality of Curtailing Cuckolding: Alienation-of-Affection and Criminal-Conversation Torts*, 65 DUKE L.J. 755 (2016)... 55

Buchanan, G. Sidney, *The Right of Privacy: Past, Present, and Future*, 16 OHIO N.U. L. REV. 403 (1989)... 40, 42

Buchanan, Kim Shayo, Lawrence v. Geduldig: *Regulating Women's Sexuality*, 56 EMORY L.J. 1235 (2007). 7, 17, 249

Bush, Joshua, *The Difference Between Bivariate & Multivariate Analyses*, SCIENCING (June 4, 2018), https://sciencing.com/difference-between-bivariate-multivariate-analyses-8667797.html [https://perma.cc/7BKR-LFZ8]... 76

BUTLER, JUDITH, GENDER TROUBLE: FEMINISM AND THE SUBVERSION OF IDENTITY (1990)... 2

BYRNE, R.S. FONE, HOMOPHOBIA: A HISTORY (2000).......................... 22

Caplan, Russell L., *The History and Meaning of the Ninth Amendment*, 69 VA. L. REV. 223 (1983)... 42

Caraveo-Parra, Diana, Henry F. Fradella, Jessica Salerno & Cody W. Telep, *Does Homophobia Affect Prosecutorial Discretion in Ambiguous Statutory Rape Cases?*, 3 WILLAMETTE SOC. JUST. & EQUITY L.J. 1 (2019)............... 131, 132

Carpenter, Catherine L., *On Statutory Rape, Strict Liability, and the Public Welfare Offense Model*, 53 AM. U. L. REV. 313 (2003)... 122

Carpenter, Dale, *Is* Lawrence *Libertarian?*, 88 MINN. L. REV. 1140 (2004).. 5, 98

Carpenter, Dale, *The Unknown Past of* Lawrence v. Texas, 102 MICH. L. REV. 1464 (2004).. 53

Census Regions and Divisions of the United States, U.S. CENSUS BUREAU, https://www2.census.gov/geo/pdfs/maps-data/maps/reference/us_regdiv.pdf [https://perma.cc/LT7J-EUE8]... 69, 71

Chee, Erica, Comment, *Property Rights: Substantive Due Process and the "Shocks the Conscience" Standard*, 31 U. HAW. L. REV. 577 (2009).. 244

Citron, Danielle Keats, *Sexual Privacy*, 128 YALE L.J. 1870 (2019)... 162

Conkle, Daniel O., *The Second Death of Substantive Due Process*, 62 IND. L.J. 215 (1987)... 48

CONRON, KERITH J., KATHRYN K. O'NEILL, LUIS A. VASQUEZ & CHRISTY MALLORY, WILLIAMS INST. PROHIBITING GENDER-AFFIRMING MEDICAL CARE FOR YOUTH (2022), https://williamsinstitute.law.ucla.edu/wp-content/uploads/Trans-Youth-Health-Bans-Mar-2022.pdf [https://perma.cc/KTF2-95JB]............... 13

COOLEY, THOMAS M., A TREATISE ON THE LAW OF TORTS, OR THE WRONGS WHICH ARISE INDEPENDENT OF CONTRACT (2d ed. 1888)... 36, 37

Courts and Judges by State, BALLOTPEDIA, https://ballotpedia.org/Courts_and_judges_by_state [https://perma.cc/C4GJ-YFAK]... 74

Crompton, Louis, *Homosexuals and the Death Penalty in Colonial America*, 1 J. HOMOSEXUALITY 278 (1976). 23

Ctrs. for Disease Control & Prevention, *HIV and AIDS–United States, 1981–2000*, 50 MORBIDITY & MORTALITY WEEKLY REPT. 430 (June 1, 2001), http://www.cdc.gov/mmwr/preview/mmwrhtml/mm5021a2.htm [https://perma.cc/LHV9-S89P]. 166

D'EMILIO, JOHN, SEXUAL POLITICS, SEXUAL COMMUNITIES: THE MAKING OF A HOMOSEXUAL MINORITY IN THE UNITED STATES, 1940–1970 (2d ed. 1998). 33, 34

DAVENPORT-HINES, RICHARD, SEX, DEATH AND PUNISHMENT: ATTITUDES TO SEX AND SEXUALITY IN BRITAIN SINCE THE RENAISSANCE (1990). 22

Day, John A., *A New Arrow in the Quiver to Fight Revenge Porn*, TENN. B.J., May/June 2022, at 38. 163

Deitrich, Lauren R., *Transgender and the Judiciary: An Argument to Extend* Batson *Challenges to Transgender Individuals*, 50 VAL. U. L. REV. 719 (2016). 210

Döring, Matthias, *Testing Independence: Chi-Squared vs Fisher's Exact Test*, DATA SCI. BLOG (Oct. 17, 2018), https://www.datascienceblog.net/post/statistical_test/contingency_table_tests/ [https://perma.cc/C36Q-4WG8]. 76

DOVER, KENNETH J. GREEK HOMOSEXUALITY (1978). 22

Dunlap, Mary C., *Gay Men and Lesbians Down by Law in the 1990's USA: The Continuing Toll of* Bowers v. Hardwick, 24 GOLDEN GATE U. L. REV. 1 (1994). 35

Dunski, Sara L., *Make Way for the New Kid on the Block: The Possible Zoning Implications of* Lawrence v. Texas, 2005 U. ILL. L. REV. 847 55

ELLIS, HAVELOCK, THE PSYCHOLOGY OF SEX: A MANUAL FOR STUDENTS (1933). 22

Ellis, Havelock, *The Study of Sexual Inversion*, 12 MED.-LEGAL J. 148 (1894–1895). 25

Employment Nondiscrimination, MOVEMENT ADVANCEMENT PROJECT (June 13, 2023), https://www.lgbtmap.org/equality-maps/employment_non_discrimination_laws [https://perma.cc/KJV4-MBPW]. 211

Englert, Patrick, & Elizabeth G. Dinkins, *An Overview of Sex, Gender, and Sexuality*, *in* SEX, SEXUALITY, LAW & (IN)JUSTICE 7 (Henry F. Fradella & Jennifer Sumner eds., 2016). 2

Entrikin, J. Lyn, *Disrespectful Dissent: Justice Scalia's Regrettable Legacy of Incivility*, 18 J. APP. PRAC. & PROCESS 201 (2017). 143

Escoffier, Jeffrey, *The Sexual Revolution, 1960–1980*, THE GLBTQ ENCYCLOPEDIA PROJECT ARCHIVES (Claude Summers ed., 2004), http://www.glbtqarchive.com/ssh/sexual_revolution_S.pdf [https://perma.cc/6XV4-GCBQ]. 34

ESKRIDGE, JR., WILLIAM N., DISHONORABLE PASSIONS (2008). 29, 98

Eskridge, Jr., William N., Hardwick *and Historiography*, 1999 U. ILL. L. REV. 631 (1999). 33

Eskridge, Jr., William N., *Law and the Construction of the Closet: American Regulation of Same-Sex Intimacy, 1880–1946*, 82 IOWA L. REV. 1007 (1997).....22, 23, 24, 25, 26, 27, 28, 29, 50, 176

Files Detail Allegations That Dallas Judge Used Coke, Bought Sex, Raped Young Girl, DALL. MORNING NEWS (Apr. 17, 2014, 12:01 AM), https://www.dallasnews.com/news/investigations/2014/04/17/files-detail-allegations-that-dallas-judge-used-coke-bought-sex-raped-young-girl/ [https://perma.cc/XM6J-YMGH]. 234

Fischer, Ryan G., Henry F. Fradella & Connie E. Ireland, *Sex, Violence, and the Boundaries of the Defense of Consent*, 45 CRIM. L. BULL. 1137 (2009). 117

Fleming, James E., *Constructing the Substantive Constitution*, 72 TEX. L. REV. 211 (1993). 51

Flores, Andrew R., & Scott Barclay, *Backlash, Consensus, Legitimacy, or Polarization: The Effect of Same-Sex Marriage Policy on Mass Attitudes*, 69 POL. RES. Q. 43 (2016)........ 10

Fradella, Henry F., *In Search of Meritorious Claims: A Study of the Processing of Prisoner Civil Rights Cases in a Federal District Court*, 21 JUST. SYS. J. 23 (1999). 18

Fradella, Henry F., & Alexis Rowland, *Baseless Anti-Trans Claims Fuel Adoption of Harmful Laws – Two Criminologists Explain*, THE CONVERSATION (June 5, 2023), https://theconversation.com/baseless-anti-trans-claims-fuel-adoption-of-harmful-laws-two-criminologists-explain-206570 [https://perma.cc/P9RX-HWFA]. 13, 14

Fradella, Henry F., & Kenneth Grundy, *The Criminal Regulation of Sex: The Limits of Morality and Consent*, *in* SEX, LAW, AND (IN)JUSTICE 183 (Henry F. Fradella & Jennifer Sumner eds., 2016). 21, 121

Fradella, Henry F., Adam Fogarty & Lauren O'Neill, *The Impact of ion the Admissibility of Behavioral Science Testimony*, 30 PEPP. L. REV. 403 (2002). 18

FRADELLA, HENRY F., CRIMINAL LAW: AN INTRODUCTION TO KEY CASES AND COMMENTS (2022)........................ 121, 122, 126, 166, 167

Fradella, Henry F., Lawrence v. Texas: *Genuine or Illusory Progress for Gay Rights in America*, 39 CRIM. L. BULL. 597 (2003). 1, 2, 3, 4, 34, 52, 53, 55, 56

Fradella, Henry F., *Legal, Moral, and Social Reasons for Decriminalizing Sodomy*, 18 J. CONTEMP. CRIM. JUST. 279 (2002). 14, 21, 48, 49, 52

Fradella, Henry F., Megan M. Parry & Lauren E. Fradella, *Marriage, Sexuality, and Gender in* SEX, LAW, AND (IN)JUSTICE 294 (Henry F. Fradella & Jennifer Sumner eds., 2016). 201

Frank, Barney, *Justice Scalia Is a Homophobe*, POLITICO (June 26, 2015), https://www.politico.com/magazine/story/2015/06/justice-scalia-gay-marriage-ruling-119480/ [https://perma.cc/NB38-9298]. 143

Franke, Katherine M., *The Domesticated Liberty of* Lawrence v. Texas, 104 COLUM. L. REV. 1399 (2004)... 6

Franklin, Kris, *Homophobia and the "Matthew Shepard Effect" in* Lawrence v. Texas, 48 N.Y.L. SCH. L. REV. 657 (2004).................. 34

FREDERICK, JEFFREY T., MASTERING VOIR DIRE AND JURY SELECTION (4th ed. 2018). 209

Freedman, Estelle B., "*Uncontrolled Desires": The Response to the Sexual Psychopath, 1920-1960*, J. AM. HIST., June 1987, at 83. 27

FREUD, SIGMUND, THREE ESSAYS ON SEXUALITY (A.A. Brill trans., Global Grey e-book ed. 2021) (1905). 27

Galletly, Carol L. et al., *New Jersey's HIV Exposure Law and HIV-Related Attitudes, Beliefs, and Sexual and Seropositive Status Disclosure Behaviors of Persons Living with HIV*, 102 AM. J. PUB. HEALTH 2135 (2012). 167

Glover, Richard, *Can't Buy A Thrill: Substantive Due Process, Equal Protection, and Criminalizing Sex Toys*, 100 J. CRIM. L. & CRIMINOLOGY 555 (2010). 55

Gnuse, Robert K., *Seven Gay Texts: Biblical Passages Used to Condemn Homosexuality*, 45 BIBLICAL THEOLOGY BULL. 68 (2015). 21

Goldstein, Anne B., *History, Homosexuality, and Political Values: Searching for the Hidden Determinants of* Bowers v. Hardwick, 97 YALE L.J. 1073 (1988). 49

Gong, LiJia, & Rachel Shapiro, *Sexual Privacy After* Lawrence v. Texas, 13 GEO. J. GENDER & L. 487 (2012). 55

Goodwin, Michele, & Erwin Chemerinsky, *The Transgender Military Ban: Preservation of Discrimination Through Transformation*, 114 NW. U. L. REV. 751 (2019). 15

Gordon, Daniel, *Symptoms for Scalia and Texas: Gay Rights and American Nationalism*, 35 GOLDEN GATE U. L. REV. 111 (2005). 143

Gorkin, Russell T., Comment, *The Constitutional Right to Informational Privacy:* NASA v. Nelson, 6 DUKE J. CONST. L. & PUB. POL'Y SIDEBAR 1 (2010). 230

Governor Newsom Swears in Justice Patricia Guerrero to California Supreme Court, the First Latina to Serve on State's Highest Court, CAL. OFF. OF GOVERNOR (Mar. 28, 2022), https://www.gov.ca.gov/2022/03/28/governor-newsom-swears-in-justice-patricia-guerrero-to-california-supreme-court-the-first-latina-to-serve-on-states-highest-court/ [https://perma.cc/E3UD-D2Z9]. 74

Grant, Isabel, *Rethinking Risk: The Relevance of Condoms and Viral Load in HIV Nondisclosure Prosecutions*, 54 MCGILL L.J. 389 (2009). 167

Green, Jr., Matthew W., Lawrence*: An Unlikely Catalyst for Massive Disruption in the Sphere of Government Employee Privacy and Intimate Association Claims,* 29 BERKELEY J. EMP. & LAB. L. 311 (2008). 55

Greene, Jamal, *The Anticanon*, 125 HARV. L. REV. 379 (2011). 51

GRUBERG, SHARITA, LINDSAY MAHOWALD & JOHN HALPIN, CTR. AM. PROGRESS, THE STATE OF THE LGBTQ COMMUNITY IN 2020: A NATIONAL PUBLIC OPINION STUDY (2020), https://americanprogress.org/wp-content/uploads/2020/10/LGBTQpoll-report.pdf [https://perma.cc/KL8B-AK42]....................... 9

Haines, Julia, Kaia Hubbard & Christopher Wolf, *Where State Abortion Laws Stand Without* Roe, U.S NEWS & WORLD REP. (June 6, 2022, 2:45 PM), https://www.usnews.com/news/best-states/articles/a-guide-to-abortion-laws-by-state [https://perma.cc/2AWZ-YR37]. 256

Hall, Mark A., & Ronald F. Wright, *Systematic Content Analysis of Judicial Opinions*, 96 CALIF. L. REV. 63 (2008)................................ 17

Halley, Janet E., *Reasoning About Sodomy: Acts and Identity in and After* Bowers v. Hardwick, 79 VA. L. REV. 1721 (1993).................. 35

Hampton, James, *Homosexuality: An Aggravating Factor*, 28 TUL. J.L. & SEXUALITY 25 (2019). 23

Hanna, Cheryl, *Sex is Not a Sport: Consent and Violence in Criminal Law*, 42 B.C. L. REV. 239 (2001).. 118

Harcourt, Bernard E., *Foreword: "You are Entering a Gay and Lesbian Free Zone": On the Radical Dissents of Justice Scalia and Other (Post-) Queers [Raising Questions About* Lawrence, *Sex Wars, and the Criminal Law]*, 94 J. CRIM. L. & CRIMINOLOGY 503 (2004). 1, 2, 3, 4, 6

Harrison, Karen, *Sentencing High-Risk Sex Offenders: Policy and Legislation*, *in* THE OXFORD HANDBOOK OF SEX OFFENCES AND SEX OFFENDERS 327–43 (Teela Sanders ed., 2017)............................... 171

Hassel, Diana, *Sex and Death:* Lawrence*'s Liberty and Physician-Assisted Suicide*, 9 U. PA. J. CONST. L. 1003 (2007). 55

Hauck, Grace, *Anti-LGBT Hate Crimes Are Rising, the FBI Says. But It Gets Worse*, USA TODAY (June 28, 2019), https://www.usatoday.com/story/news/2019/06/28/anti-gay-hate-crimes-rise-fbi-says-and-they-likely-undercount/1582614001/ [https://perma.cc/D8SM-2BRK]. 9

Hefner, Hugh, *The Legal Enforcement of Morality*, 40 U. COLO. L. REV. 199 (1968)... 29

Herr, Jeet, *Antonin Scalia Does Not Understand the Difference Between Gay People and Child Abusers*, NEW REPUBLIC (Nov. 17, 2005), https://newrepublic.com/article/124002/antonin-scalia-not-understand-difference-gay-people-child-abusers [https://perma.cc/LMC5-ZH4Z]. 143

Higdon, Michael J., *Queer Teens and Legislative Bullies: The Cruel and Invidious Discrimination Behind Heterosexist Statutory Rape Laws*, 42 U.C. DAVIS L. REV. 195 (2008). 131

HIV and STD Criminalization Laws, CTRS. FOR DISEASE CONTROL & PREVENTION (n.d.), https://www.cdc.gov/hiv/policies/law/states/exposure.html [https://perma.cc/DF3H-NL9G]. 166

Horvath, Keith J., Richard Weinmeyer & Simon Rosser, *Should It Be Illegal for HIV-Positive Persons to Have Unprotected Sex Without Disclosure? An Examination of Attitudes Among US Men Who Have Sex with Men and the Impact of State Law*, 22 AIDS CARE 1221 (2010). 167

Huff, Leslye M., *Deconstructing Sodomy*, 5 AM. U. J. GENDER & L. 553 (1997). 45, 46

Hughes, C.H., *Postscript to a Paper on Érotopathia*, 14 ALIENIST & NEUROLOGIST 731 (1895). 25

Hunt, Jerome, *A History of the Employment Non-Discrimination Act*, CTR. FOR AM. PROGRESS (July 19, 2011), https://www.americanprogress.org/article/a-history-of-the-employment-non-discrimination-act/ [https://perma.cc/HWE9-GVQW] 1, 11

Hunter, Nan D., *Living with* Lawrence, 88 MINN. L. REV. 1103 (2004).. 5

Hunter, Nan D., *Sexual Orientation and the Paradox of Heightened Scrutiny*, 102 MICH. L. REV. 1528 (2004). 10

Hutchinson, Darren Lenard, *The Majoritarian Difficulty: Affirmative Action, Sodomy, and Supreme Court Politics*, 23 LAW & INEQ. 1 (2005). 35

Inter-rater Reliability IRR: Definition, Calculation, STAT. HOW TO (July 17, 2016), https://www.statisticshowto.com/inter-rater-reliability/ [https://perma.cc/RG46-XFSH]. 78

Irons, Peter, *Interview with Michael Hardwick*, *in* LESBIANS, GAY MEN AND THE LAW 125 (William Rubenstein ed., 1993). 45, 46

James, Steve, Comment, *Romeo and Juliet Were Sex Offenders: An Analysis of the Age of Consent and A Call for Reform*, 78 UMKC L. REV. 241 (2009)... 126

JOHNSON, DAVID K., THE LAVENDER SCARE: THE COLD WAR PERSECUTION OF GAYS AND LESBIANS IN THE FEDERAL GOVERNMENT (2004)... 33, 34

JOHNSON, JOHN W., *GRISWOLD V. CONNECTICUT*: BIRTH CONTROL AND THE CONSTITUTIONAL RIGHT OF PRIVACY (2005). 41

Jones, Dustin, & Jonathan Franklin, *Not Just Florida. More Than a Dozen States Propose So-Called 'Don't Say Gay' Bills*, NPR (Apr. 10, 2022, 7:01 AM), https://www.npr.org/2022/04/10/1091543359/15-states-dont-say-gay-anti-transgender-bills [https://perma.cc/V6QB-VQ5X].................. 262

Kane, Melinda D., *Social Movement Policy Success: Decriminalizing State Sodomy Laws, 1969-1998*, 8 MOBILIZATION 313 (2003). 52

Kaplan, Margo, *Sex-Positive Law*, 89 N.Y.U. L. REV. 89 (2014). 6

Katyal, Sonia K., *Sexuality and Sovereignty: The Global Limits and Possibilities of* Lawrence, 14 WM. & MARY BILL RTS. J. 1429 (2006)... 5

KATZ, JONATHAN NED, GAY/LESBIAN ALMANAC (1983). 23

Kelsey Butler, *Anti-LGBTQ Proposals Are Flooding U.S. State Legislatures at a Record Pace*, BLOOMBERG (Apr. 8, 2022, 5:00 AM), https://www.bloomberg.com/news/articles/2022-04-08/mapping-the-anti-lgbtq-proposals-flooding-u-s-state-legislatures [https://perma.cc/65QN-EJ4A]. 14

Kennedy, Kevin, *Watching the World Burn: Substantive Due Process and the Right to A Sustainable Climate*, 93 TEMP. L. REV. ONLINE 61 (2021). 264

KINSEY, ALFRED C., WARDELL B. POMEROY & CLYDE E. MARTIN, SEXUAL BEHAVIOR IN THE HUMAN MALE (1948)............................ 30

KINSEY, ALFRED C., WARDELL B. POMEROY, CLYDE E. MARTIN & PAUL H. GEBHARD, SEXUAL BEHAVIOR IN THE HUMAN FEMALE (1953)... 30

Knauer, Nancy J., *Historical Contingency and the Limits of Identity: Implications for Law and Policy*, 28 S. CAL. INTERDISC. L.J. 387 (2019). 15

Knauer, Nancy J., Lawrence v. Texas: *When "Profound and Deep Convictions" Collide with Liberty Interests*, 10 CARDOZO WOMEN'S L.J. 325 (2004).......... 143

Kohn, Nina A., *Outliving Civil Rights*, 86 WASH U. L. REV. 1053 (2009). 230, 258

Kort, Fred, *Predicting Supreme Court Decisions Mathematically: A Quantitative Analysis of the "Right to Counsel" Cases*, 51 AM. POL. SCI. REV. 1 (1957).......... 18

Kras, Kimberly R., *Informal Social Control of Sex Offenders: The Family and Other Forms of Support*, *in* THE OXFORD HANDBOOK OF SEX OFFENCES AND SEX OFFENDERS 415–36 (Teela Sanders ed., 2017).......... 171

KRIPPENDORFF, KLAUS, CONTENT ANALYSIS: AN INTRODUCTION TO ITS METHODOLOGY (1980).......... 59

Krotoszynski, Jr., Ronald J., *Fundamental Property Rights*, 85 GEO. L.J. 555 (1997).......... 244

Last, Esther J., *Peremptory Challenges to Jurors Based on Sexual Orientation: Preempting Discrimination by Court Rule*, 48 IND. L. REV. 313 (2014). 210

LAWS, D. RICHARD, SOCIAL CONTROL OF SEX OFFENDERS: A CULTURAL HISTORY (2016).......... 170, 171

Lehman, J. Stan et al., *Prevalence and Public Health Implications of State Laws that Criminalize Potential HIV Exposure in the United States*, 18 AIDS BEHAV. 997 (2014).......... 167

Leslie, Christopher R., *Creating Criminals: The Injuries Inflicted by "Unenforced" Sodomy Laws*, 35 HARV. C.R.-C.L. L. REV. 103 (2000).......... 28

Leviticus 18:22 21

LGBTQ Curricular Laws, MOVEMENT ADVANCEMENT PROJECT (June 13, 2023). https://www.lgbtmap.org/equality-maps/curricular_laws [https://perma.cc/SZL2-JT5J]. 14, 262

Lösel, Friedrich, & Martin Schmucker, *Treatment of Sex Offenders: Concepts and Empirical Evaluations*, *in* THE OXFORD HANDBOOK OF SEX OFFENCES AND SEX OFFENDERS 392–414 (Teela Sanders ed., 2017).. 171

Louis D. Brandeis, 1916–1939, SUP. CT. HIST. SOC'Y, https://supremecourthistory.org/associate-justices/louis-d-brandeis-1916-1939/ [https://perma.cc/EGS6-9WJ2]. 37

Lovett, Kenneth, *Hevesi's Judge Retiring Amid an Investigation into His Own Conduct on the Bench*, N.Y. DAILY NEWS (Dec. 6, 2012, 12:34 AM), https://www.nydailynews.com/new-york/hevesi-judge-retiring-probe-article-1.1215307 [https://perma.cc/6VNH-N6RZ]............... 242

Lutes, Erin, James A. Purdon, & Henry F. Fradella, *When Music Takes the Stand: A Content Analysis of How Courts Use and Misuse Rap Lyrics in Criminal Cases*, 46 AM. J. CRIM. L. 77 (2019). 18

Lydston, G. Frank, Clinical Lecture: *Sexual Perversion, Satyriasis and Nymphomania*, 61 MED. & SURGICAL REP. 253 (1889). 25

LYDSTON, G. FRANK, THE DISEASES OF SOCIETY (THE VICE AND CRIME PROBLEM) (1905). 25

Maddera, Julia C., Note, Batson *in Transition: Prohibiting Peremptory Challenges on the Basis of Gender Identity or Expression*, 116 COLUM. L. REV. 196 (2016).. 210

Malhiot, Emily, *Chapter 86: Nevada Finally Outlaws Bestiality*, 49 U. PAC. L. REV. 555 (2018). 93

Manuel, Victoria D., *Trump's Transgender Military Ban: Policy, Law, and Litigation*, 29 TUL. J.L. & SEXUALITY 75 (2020). 13, 26

Manuel, Victoria D., *The Future of LGBTQ+ Equality After* Obergefell *and* Bostock, 49 RUTGERS L. REC. 60 (2021)................................... 11

McCarthy, Eugene, *In Defense of* Griswold v. Connecticut: *Privacy, Originalism, and the Iceberg Theory of Omission*, 54 WILLAMETTE L. REV. 335 (2018)........................ 36, 37, 39, 41, 42

McDermott, Nathan, & Andrew Kaczynski, *Senate Candidate Roy Moore in 2005: "Homosexual Conduct Should Be Illegal,"* CNN (Sept. 22, 2017, 7:52 PM), https://www.cnn.com/2017/09/21/politics/kfile-roy-moore-homosexuality-illegal/index.html [https://perma.cc/W4YZ-LRZ7]. 203

McGowan, Miranda Oshige, *From Outlaws to Ingroup:* Romer, Lawrence*, and the Inevitable Normativity of Group Recognition*, 88 MINN. L. REV. 1312, 1313 (2004)... 3

MCWHIRTER, DARIEN A., & JON D. BIBLE, PRIVACY AS A CONSTITUTIONAL RIGHT (1992)... 39

MILL, JOHN STUART, ON LIBERTY (David Bromwich & George Kateb eds., 2003) (1859). 3

Minter, Shannon, *Sodomy and Public Morality Offenses Under U.S. Immigration Law: Penalizing Lesbian and Gay Identity*, 26 CORNELL INT'L L.J. 771 (1993). 27

Mohr, Richard D., *Mr. Justice Douglas at Sodom: Gays and Privacy*, 18 COLUM. HUM. RTS. L. REV. 43 (1986–1987). 48, 51

MOVEMENT ADVANCEMENT PROJECT & CAMPAIGN FOR SOUTHERN EQUALITY, TELLING A NEW SOUTHERN STORY: LGBTQ RESILIENCE, RESISTANCE, AND LEADERSHIP, at ii (2020), https://www.lgbtmap.org/file/2020-report-southern_broad.pdf [https://perma.cc/D8GA-TP8B]. 261

Navarro, John C., *Sex Offenders, Policies, and Social Control*, *in* POLITICAL AUTHORITY, SOCIAL CONTROL AND PUBLIC POLICY 155 (Cara E. Rabe-Hemp & Nancy S. Lind eds., 2019). 171

Neira, Paula M., & An Na Lee, *Under Attack: Transgender Health in 2020*, 24 J. HEALTH CARE L. & POL'Y 109 (2021)............................. 9

NEUENDORF, KIMBERLY A., THE CONTENT ANALYSIS GUIDEBOOK (2d ed. 2017). 59, 60

Nominal Variable Association, STAT. SOLUTIONS, https://www.statisticssolutions.com/free-resources/directory-of-statistical-analyses/nominal-variable-association/ [https://perma.cc/9R2Y-C5J6] (last visited Aug. 19, 2022)............... 76

Nondiscrimination Laws, MOVEMENT ADVANCEMENT PROJECT (June 13, 2023), https://www.lgbtmap.org/equality-maps/non_discrimination_laws [https://perma.cc/49R4-W6QT]. ... 211

Not in Our Town, THE ADVOCATE, Mar.–Apr. 2022, at 9. 14

Note, *Post-Kinsey: Voluntary Sex Relations as Criminal Offenses*, 17 U. CHI. L. REV. 162 (1949–50). 30, 31

Note, *Right to Privacy and Consensual Sodomy:* Bowers v. Hardwick, 100 HARV. L. REV. 210 (1986). 49

Oberman, Michelle, *Turning Girls into Women: Re-Evaluating Modern Statutory Rape Law*, 8 DEPAUL J. HEALTH CARE L. 109 (2004–2005). 122

Ogles, Jacob, *30 Infamous Police Raids of Gay Bars and Bathhouses*, THE ADVOCATE (Mar. 1, 2017), https://www.advocate.com/politics/2017/3/01/30-infamous-police-raids-gay-bars-and-bathhouses#media-gallery-media-29 [https://perma.cc/3EGW-68HN]. 30

OSHINSKY, DAVID M., A CONSPIRACY SO IMMENSE: THE WORLD OF JOE MCCARTHY (1983). 33

Packer, Herbert L., *The Model Penal Code and Beyond*, 63 COLUM. L. REV. 594 (1963). 32

Patricia Guerrero, Associate Justice, CAL. CTS., https://www.courts.ca.gov/38044.htm [https://perma.cc/5F85-LA89]. 74

Patricia Guerrero, BALLOTPEDIA, https://ballotpedia.org/Patricia_Guerrero [https://perma.cc/Z7ZD-D32J]. 74

PAUL E. BOWERS, A SURVEY OF TWENTY-FIVE HUNDRED PRISONERS IN THE PSYCHOPATHIC LABORATORY AT THE INDIANA STATE PRISON (n.d.). 28

Pearl, Mitchell Lloyd, Note, *Chipping Away at* Bowers v. Hardwick: *Making the Best of an Unfortunate Decision*, 63 N.Y.U. L. REV. 154 (1988). 52

Pfeifer, Tara R., Comment, *Out of the Shadows: The Positive Impact of* Lawrence v. Texas *on Victims of Same-Sex Domestic Violence*, 109 PENN ST. L. REV. 1251 (2005). 208

Physician-Assisted Suicide Fast Facts, CNN (May 26, 2022, 11:40 AM), https://www.cnn.com/2014/11/26/us/physician-assisted-suicide-fast-facts [https://perma.cc/9RDS-5M9V]. 257

Pittman, Larry J., *The Elusive Constitutional Right to Informational Privacy*, 19 NEV. L.J. 135 (2018)... 230, 258

Platoff, Emma, & Sydney Greene, *Fifteen Years After Landmark Gay Rights Case, Same-Sex Couples in Texas Still Face Challenges in Court*, TEX. TRIB. (June 26, 2018, 1:00 PM), https://www.texastribune.org/2018/06/26/fifteen-years-after-landmark-gay-rights-win-same-sex-couples-face-anot/ [https://perma.cc/V469-YD7S]. 259

POSNER, RICHARD A., SEX AND REASON (1994). 30

Posner, Richard A., *The Anti-Hero*, NEW REPUBLIC, Feb. 24, 2003, at 27.. 39

Potok, Mark, & Janet Smith, S. POVERTY L. CTR., *Anti-Gay Hate Crimes: Doing the Math*, INTELLIGENCE REP. (Feb. 27, 2011), https://www.splcenter.org/fighting-hate/intelligence-report/2011/anti-gay-hate-crimes-doing-math [https://perma.cc/TB3N-2NWQ]. 9

Rains, Robert E., *The Future of Justice Scalia's Predictions of Family Law Doom*, 29 BYU J. PUB. L. 353 (2015).. 98

Reed, Alex, *Beyond* Bostock: *Employment Protections for LGBTQ Workers Not Covered by Title VII*, 23 N.Y.U. J. LEGIS. & PUB. POL'Y 537 (2021)............................. 9, 14

Reinheimer, Justin, Note, *What* Lawrence *Should Have Said: Reconstructing an Equality Approach*, 96 CAL. L. REV. 505 (2008)... 7, 17, 249

Religious Exemption Laws, MOVEMENT ADVANCEMENT PROJECT (June 13, 2023), https://www.lgbtmap.org/equality-maps/religious_exemption_laws [https://perma.cc/6JUD-NN85]. ... 12, 13

Richards, David A.J., *Constitutional Legitimacy and Constitutional Privacy*, 61 N.Y.U. REV. 800 (1986). 48, 49

Rizzo, James J., Note, *The Constitutionality of Sodomy Statutes*, 45 FORDHAM L. REV. 553 (1977). 28, 29

Robert Post & Reva Siegel, Roe *Rage: Democratic Constitutionalism and Backlash*, 42 HARV. C.R.-C.L. L. REV. 373 (2007). 10

Robertson, Stephen, *Shifting the Scene of the Crime: Sodomy and the American History of Sexual Violence*, 19 J. HIST. SEXUALITY 240 (2010). 29

Robinson, Paul H., & Markus D. Dubber, *The American Model Penal Code: A Brief Overview*, 10 NEW CRIM. L. REV. 319 (2007)........... 32

Romero, Victor C., *Reading (into)* Windsor*: Presidential Leadership, Marriage Equality, and Immigration Policy*, 23 S. CAL. REV. L. & SOC. JUST. 1 (2013)....................................... 27

Ronner, Amy D., *Homophobia: In the Closet and in the Coffin*, 21 LAW & INEQ. 65 (2003). 45

Rosenbury, Laura A., & Jennifer E. Rothman, *Sex in and Out of Intimacy*, 59 EMORY L.J. 809 (2010). 6

Rosse, Irving C., *Sexual Hypochondriasis and Perversion of the Genetic Instinct*, 17 J. NERVOUS & MENTAL DISEASE 795 (1892)................ 25

Rowland, Alexis, & Henry F. Fradella, *A Surge in Anti-Trans Laws Ignore Criminology*, CRIME REP. (May 16, 2023), https://thecrimereport.org/2023/05/16/a-surge-of-anti-trans-laws-ignore-criminology/ [https://perma.cc/BKF4-N5KS]. 13

Rummler, Orion, *10 Anti-LGBTQ+ Bills Impacting Students Go into Effect Across Six States*, THE 19TH (July 1, 2022, 1:58 PM), https://19thnews.org/2022/07/florida-dont-say-gay-other-anti-lgbtq-bills-take-effect/ [https://perma.cc/AUT5-4CJ7]. 262

Ruppalt, Laura, *The Impact of Silver Alerts on an Older Adult's Right to Informational Privacy*, 27 GEO. MASON L. REV. 651 (2020). 230, 258

Ruskola, Teemu, *Gay Rights Versus Queer Theory: What is Left of Sodomy After* Lawrence v. Texas?, 23 SOC. TEXT 235 (2005)........... 6

Sachs, Andrea, *The Worst Supreme Court Decisions Since 1960*, TIME (Oct. 6, 2015, 11:36 AM), https://time.com/4056051/worst-supreme-court-decisions/ [https://perma.cc/6QLY-C26L]. 51

Sacks, Deana Pollard, *Elements of Liberty*, 61 SMU L. REV. 1557 (2008)... 1

Sanders, Steve, *Dignity and Social Meaning:* Obergefell*,* Windsor*, and* Lawrence *as Constitutional Dialogue*, 87 FORDHAM L. REV. 2069 (2019). 9

Saperstein, Aliya, *Double-Checking the Race Box: Examining Inconsistency Between Survey Measures of Observed and Self-Reported Race*, 85 SOC. FORCES 57 (2006), https://doi.org/10.1353/sof.2006.0141. 75

Schwartz, Louis B., *Morals Offenses and the Model Penal Code*, 63 COLUM. L. REV. 669 (1963).......... 32

Seelau, Sheila M., & Eric P. Seelau, *Gender-Role Stereotypes and Perceptions of Heterosexual, Gay and Lesbian Domestic Violence*, 20 J. FAM. VIOLENCE 363 (2005), https://doi.org/10.1007/s10896-005-7798-4. 207

Self, Janet, Bowers v. Hardwick*: A Study of Aggression*, 10 HUM. RTS. Q. 395 (1988). 51

Shay, Giovanna, *In the Box: Voir Dire on LGBT Issues in Changing Times*, 37 HARV. J.L. & GENDER 407 (2014). 210

Sherry, Suzanna, *The Founders' Unwritten Constitution*, 54 U. CHI. L. REV. 1127 (1987). 41

Shvartsman, Shulamit H., *"Romeo and Romeo": An Examination of* Limon v. Kansas *in Light of* Lawrence v. Texas, 35 SETON HALL L. REV. 359 (2004). 131

Silhan, Caitlyn, Comment, *The Present Case Does Involve Minors: An Overview of the Discriminatory Effects of Romeo and Juliet Provisions and Sentencing Practices on Lesbian, Gay, Bisexual, and Transgender Youth*, 20 LAW & SEXUALITY 97 (2011).......... 131

Slakoff, Danielle, & Pauline K. Brennan, *White, Black, and Latina Female Victims in U.S. News: A Multivariate and Intersectional Analysis of Story Differences*, 13 RACE & JUST. 155 (2023), https://doi.org/10.1177/2153368720961837. 74

SMITH-ROSENBERG, CARROLL, DISORDERLY CONDUCT: VISIONS OF GENDER IN VICTORIAN AMERICA (1985). 24

Sobel, Stacey L., The Backlash Boomerang: Using Reverse Animus and Hostility to Limit LGBTQ Equality, 22 U. PA. J. CONST. L. 1155 (2020). 12, 14

Sosin, Kate, & Orion Rummler, *What Happens If* Roe v. Wade *Is Overturned? LGBTQ+ Legal Experts Are Worried about*

Sullivan, Casey C., *13 Worst Supreme Court Decisions of All Time*, FINDLAW (Oct. 14, 2015 12:51 PM), https://www.findlaw.com/legalblogs/supreme-court/13-worst-supreme-court-decisions-of-all-time/ [https://perma.cc/B8ZE-X9QD].. 51

Sunstein, Cass R., *What Did* Lawrence *Hold? Of Autonomy, Desuetude, Sexuality, and Marriage*, 2003 SUP. CT. REV. 27................................ 3

Supreme Court, Current Supreme Court Justices, N.M. CTS., https://supremecourt.nmcourts.gov/supreme-court/supreme-court-justices/current-supreme-court-justices/ [https://perma.cc/BV8W-X259].. 74

Sussmane, Alexa, *The Far-Right Push to Outlaw Gender-Affirming Treatment for Minors*, 30 TUL. J.L. & SEXUALITY 91 (2021)... 13

Sweeny, Joanne, *Undead Statutes: The Rise, Fall, and Continuing Uses of Adultery and Fornication Criminal Laws*, 46 LOY. U. CHI. L.J. 127 (2014). 98

Swendemana, Dallas, Barbara L. Ingramb & Mary Jane Rotheram-Borus, *Common Elements in Self-Management of HIV and Other Chronic Illnesses: An Integrative Framework*, 21 AIDS CARE 1321 (2009). 167

Sylvester, Phillip, *Arming America's Most Dangerous Abusers: How Domestic Violence Laws Have Failed the LGBTQIA Community*, 11 DREXEL L. REV. 783 (2019).. 208

Teleky, Seth, *You Know It When You See It: Punishments for and Regulation Against Revenge Porn*, 1 GEO. L. TECH. REV. 175 (2016).. 163

Thomas, Kendall, *The Eclipse of Reason: A Rhetorical Reading of* Bowers v. Hardwick, 79 VA. L. REV. 1805 (1993)........................... 51

Tribe, Laurence H., Lawrence v. Texas: *The "Fundamental Right" That Dare Not Speak Its Name*, 117 HARV. L. REV. 1893 (2004). 4

TRUMAN, JENNIFER L., & RACHEL E. MORGAN, BUREAU OF JUST. STAT., VIOLENT VICTIMIZATION BY SEXUAL ORIENTATION AND GENDER IDENTITY, 2017–2020 (2022), https://bjs.ojp.gov/content/pub/pdf/vvsogi1720.pdf [https://perma.cc/F7VC-SGC3]. 9

TRUMBULL, J. HAMMOND, THE TRUE-BLUE LAWS OF CONNECTICUT AND NEW HAVEN (1879). 23

UNITED STATES, MANUAL FOR COURTS-MARTIAL (1917).......... 26

UNITED STATES, MANUAL FOR COURTS-MARTIAL (1982).......... 96

Using Chi-Square Statistic in Research, STAT. SOLS., https://www.statisticssolutions.com/using-chi-square-statistic-in-research/ [https://perma.cc/9Q3Q-8WEK].......... 75

Valcore, Jace, Henry F. Fradella, Xavier Guadalupe-Diaz, Matthew J. Ball, Angela Dwyer, Christina DeJong, Allyn Walker, Aimee Wodda & Meredith G. F. Worthen, *Building an Intersectional and Trans-Inclusive Criminology: Responding to the Emergence of "Gender Critical" Perspectives in Feminist Criminology*, 29 CRITICAL CRIMINOLOGY 687 (2021). 11

Valdes, Francisco, *Anomalies, Warts and All: Four Score of Liberty, Privacy and Equality*, 65 OHIO ST. L.J. 1341 (2004).......... 4, 51

Valdes, Francisco, *Culture by Law: Backlash as Jurisprudence*, 50 VILL. L. REV. 1135 (2005).......... 4

Vella, Lauren, *How* Roe v. Wade*'s Reversal Could Affect the LGBT Community*, THE HILL (May 8, 2022, 8:00 AM), https://thehill.com/news/state-watch/3479755-how-roe-v-wades-reversal-could-effect-the-lgbt-community/ [https://perma.cc/6MF6-Q9HU]. 16

Velte, Kyle C., *The Precarity of Justice Kennedy's Queer Canon*, 13 CONLAWNOW 75 (2022),.......... 10

Vickovic, Samuel G., Marie L. Griffin & Henry F. Fradella, *Depictions of Correctional Officers in Newspaper Media: An Ethnographic Content Analysis*, 26 CRIM. JUST. STUD. 455 (2013). 18

Volokh, Eugene, *The Law of Compelled Speech*, 97 TEX. L. REV. 355 (2018).......... 212

VON KRAFFT-EBING, RICHARD, PSYCHOPATHIA SEXUALIS, WITH SPECIAL REFERENCE TO ANTIPATHIC SEXUAL INSTINCT: A MEDICO-FORENSIC STUDY (F.J. Rebman ed., Physicians & Surgeons Book Co. 1931) (1899).......... 25

Voyeurism, MERRIAM-WEBSTER DICTIONARY, https://www.merriam-webster.com/dictionary/voyeurism [https://perma.cc/FL56-TWR2]. 161

Waldman, Ari Ezra, *Exceptions: The Criminal Law's Illogical Approach to HIV-Related Aggravated Assaults*, 18 VA. J. SOC. POL'Y & L. 550 (2011).. 167

Warren, Samuel D., & Louis D. Brandeis, *The Right to Privacy*, 4 HARV. L. REV. 193 (1890). 36

Wasserman, Howard M., *Crazy in Alabama: Judicial Process and the Last Stand Against Marriage Equality in the Land of George Wallace*, 110 NW. U.L. REV. ONLINE 1 (2015)... 203

Watts, Bradley J., *Are We a Government of Laws or of Men? An Assessment of Chief Justice Roy S. Moore's Reelection and A Call for Reform in Alabama's Judicial Election Laws*, 38 J. LEGAL PROF. 313 (2014). 203

Wechsler, Herbert, *Codification of Criminal Law in the United States: The Model Penal Code*, 68 COLUM. L. REV. 1425 (1968)................. 32

Wechsler, Herbert, *The Challenge of A Model Penal Code*, 65 HARV. L. REV. 1097 (1952). 32

WESTLAW, GUIDE TO LAW REVIEW RESEARCH (2007), http://lscontent.westlaw.com/images/banner/documentation/LawReviewResearchGuide.pdf [https://perma.cc/5LSH-95AX]. 72

What Is Linear Regression?, STAT. SOLUTIONS, https://www.statisticssolutions.com/free-resources/directory-of-statistical-analyses/what-is-linear-regression/ [https://perma.cc/3FYP-NK2K]. 76, 77

What Is Logistic Regression?, STAT. SOLUTIONS, https://www.statisticssolutions.com/free-resources/directory-of-statistical-analyses/what-is-logistic-regression/ [https://perma.cc/UC6Z-FEJ2]... 77

Whitehurst, Lindsay, & Zeke Miller, *LGBTQ Advocates Worry Other Rights at Risk If Court Overturns* Roe v. Wade, PBS NEWS (May 4, 2022, 7:44 PM), https://www.pbs.org/newshour/politics/lgbtq-advocates-worry-other-rights-at-risk-if-court-overturns-roe-v-wade [https://perma.cc/UEK2-ZN3M]. 17

Briefs

Index

www.ingramcontent.com/pod-product-compliance
Lightning Source LLC
LaVergne TN
LVHW010718210926
848485LV00008B/1439/J